THE ENGLISH LIBRARY

THE WORKS OF
SIR THOMAS BROWNE

VOLUME I

F. H. Van Houe sculp

Effigies Viri Doc- tissimi Tho: Browne
Equ: Aur: et Med: Doctoris.

THE WORKS OF
SIR THOMAS BROWNE

EDITED BY
CHARLES SAYLE

VOLUME I

EDINBURGH: JOHN GRANT
31 GEORGE IV. BRIDGE
1927

PRINTED IN GREAT BRITAIN BY
OLIVER AND BOYD, EDINBURGH

15 835

PREFATORY NOTE

THIS edition is an endeavour to arrive at a more satisfactory text of the work of Sir Thomas Browne, and to reproduce the principal part of it, as faithfully as seems advisable, in the form in which it was presented to the public at the time of his death. For this purpose, in the first volume, the text of the *Religio Medici* follows more particularly the issue of 1682. The *Pseudodoxia Epidemica* here given is based upon the sixth edition of ten years earlier, with careful revision. In every case in which a spelling or punctuation was dubious, a comparison was made of nearly all the issues printed during the lifetime of the writer, and their merits weighed. By this means it is hoped that the true flavour of the period has been preserved.

The Annotations upon the *Religio Medici*, which were always reprinted with the text during the seventeenth century, are here restored. They will appeal to a certain class of readers which has a right to be considered. It is to be regretted that every quotation given in these pages has not been verified. Several have been corrected; but to have worked through

v

them all, in these busy days, would have been a labour
of some years, which it is not possible to devote to the
purpose. It has been thought best to leave these
passages therefore, in the main, as they stand.[1]

The portrait of Sir Thomas Browne here prefixed
is reproduced from the engraving published in 1672
with the edition of the *Religio Medici* and *Pseudodoxia
Epidemica.*

C. S.

August, 1903.

---

[1] The quotation, now corrected, from Montaigne, on p. xxii,
is a typical example of the pitfall into which one is liable to
stumble. The passage there cited is in chapter xl. of the French
author's later arrangement: a clear indication of the edition of
the *Essais* used by the author of the Annotations. What is one
to make of the readings in Lucretius on p. xxv? No light
is thrown upon these difficulties by the edition of Browne's
works published in 1686. Wilkin did not reprint the Annotations, except in selection.

CONTENTS

CONTENTS

ANNOTATIONS UPON
RELIGIO MEDICI

Nec satis est vulgasse fidem. ——
Pet. Arbit. fragment.

a

THE ANNOTATOR TO THE READER

A. GELLIUS (noct. Attic. l. 20. cap. *ult.*) *notes some Books that had strange Titles*; Pliny (Prefat. Nat. Hist.) *speaking of some such, could not pass them over without a jeer: So strange (saith he) are the Titles of some Books,* Ut multos ad vadimonium deferendum compellant. *And* Seneca *saith, some such there are,* Qui patri obstetricem parturienti filiæ accersenti moram injicere possint. *Of the same fate this present Tract* Religio Medici *hath partaken: Exception by some hath been taken to it in respect of its Inscription, which say they, seems to imply that* Physicians *have a Religion by themselves, which is more than* Theologie *doth warrant: but it is their Inference, and not the Title that is to blame; for no more is meant by that, or endeavoured to be prov'd in the* Book *then that (contrary to the opinion of the unlearned)* Physitians *have Religion as well as other men.*

For the Work it self, the present Age hath produced none that has had better Reception amongst the learned; it has been received and fostered by almost all, there having been but one that I knew of (to verifie that Books *have their Fate from the Capacity of the* Reader*) that has had the face to appear against it; that is Mr.* Alexander[1] Rosse; *but he is dead, and it is uncomely to skirmish with his shadow. It shall be sufficient to remember to the* Reader, *that the noble and most learned* Knight, *Sir* Kenelm Digby, *has delivered his opinion of it in another sort, who though in some things he differ from the* Authors *sense, yet hath he most candidly and ingeniously allow'd it to be a very learned and excellent* Piece; *and I think no* Scholar *will say there can be an approbation more authentique. Since the time he Published his Observations upon it, one Mr.* Jo. Merryweather, *a* Master *of* Arts *of the* University *of* Cambridge, *hath deem'd it worthy to be put into the universal Language, which about the year* 1644 *he performed; and that hath carried the* Authors *name not only into the* Low-Countries *and* France *(in both which places the* Book *in Latin hath since been printed) but into* Italy *and* Germany; *and in* Germany *it hath since fallen into the hands of a Gentleman of that* Nation[2] *(of his name he hath given us no more than* L.N.M.E.N.) *who hath written learned* Annotations *upon it in Latin, which were Printed together with the* Book *at Strasbourg* 1652. *And for the general good*

[1] In his *Medicus Medicatus.*

[2] That he was a *German* appears by his notes *page 35,* where he useth these words, *Dulcissima nostra Germania,* etc

xi

opinion the World had entertained both of the Work and Author, *this Stranger tells you* [1] : Inter alios Auctores incidi in librum cui Titulus *Religio Medici,* jam ante mihi innotuerat lectionem istius libri multos præclaros viros delectasse, imo occupasse. Non ignorabam librum in *Anglia, Gallia, Italia, Belgio, Germania,* cupidissime legi ; constabat mihi eum non solum in *Anglia ac Batavia,* sed et *Parisiis* cum præfatione, in qua Auctor magnis laudibus fertur, esse typis mandatum. Compertum mihi erat multos magnos atq; eruditos viros sensere Auctorem (quantum ex hoc scripto perspici potest) sanctitate vitæ ac pietare elucere, *etc. But for the worth of the Book it is so well known to every* English-man *that is fit to read it, that this attestation of a* Forrainer *may seem superfluous.*

The German, *to do him right, hath in his Annotations given a fair specimen of his learning, shewing his skill in the Languages, as well antient as modern ; as also his acquaintance with all manner of Authors, both sacred and profane, out of which he has amass'd a world of Quotations : but yet, not to mention that he hath not observed some Errors of the Press, and one or two main ones of the Latin Translation, whereby the Author is much injured ; it cannot be denyed but he hath pass'd over many hard places untoucht, that might deserve a Note ; that he hath made Annotations on some, where no need was ; in the explication of others hath gone besides the true sense.*

And were he free from all these, yet one great Fault there is he may be justly charg'd with, that is, that he cannot manum de Tabula *even in matters the most obvious : which is an affectation ill-becoming a* Scholar ; *witness the most learned Annotator,* Claud. Minos. Divion. in præfat. commentar. Alciat. Emblemat. præfix. Præstat *(saith he)* brevius omnia persequi, et leviter attingere quæ nemini esse ignota suspicari possint, quam quasi ῥαψωδεῖν, perq; locos communes identidem expatiari.

I go not about by finding fault with his, obliquely to commend my own ; I am as far from that, as 'tis possible others will be : All I seek, by this Preface, next to acquainting the Reader with the various entertainment of the Book, is, that he would be advertized that these Notes were collected ten [2] *years since, long before the* German's *were written ; so that I am no Plagiary (as who peruseth his Notes and mine, will easily perceive): And in the second place, that I made this Recueil meerly for mine own entertainment, and not with any intention to evulge it ; Truth is my witness, the publication proceeds meerly from the importunity of the Book-seller (my special friend) who being acquainted with what I had done, and about to set out another Edition of the Book, would not be denied these notes to attex to it ; 'tis he (not I) that divulgeth it, and whatever the success be, he alone is concern'd in it ; I only say for my self what my Annotations bear in the Frontispiece—*

Nec satis est vulgasse fidem——

[1] In *Præfat.* Annotat.

[2] Excepting two or three particulars in which reference is made to some Books that came over since that time.

That is, that it was not enough to all persons (though pretenders to Learning) that our Physitian *had publish'd his Creed, because it wanted an exposition. I say further, that the* German's *is not full; and that (—— Quicquid sum Ego quamvis infra Lucilli censum ingeniumq;——) my explications do in many things illustrate the Text of my Author.*

24 *Martii,*
1654.

ANNOTATIONS UPON RELIGIO MEDICI

The Epistle to the *READER*

CERTAINLY *that man were greedy of life, who should desire to live when all the World were at an end ;*] This Mr. *Merryweather* hath rendred thus ; *Cupidum esse vitæ oportet, qui universo jam expirante mundo vivere cuperet*; and well enough : but it is not amiss to remember, that we have this saying in *Seneca* the *Tragœdian*, who gives it us thus, *Vitæ est avidus quisquis non vult mundo secum pereunte mori.*

There are many things delivered Rhetorically.] The Author herein imitates the ingenuity of St. *Austin*, who in his *Retract.* corrects himself for having delivered some things more like a young Rhetorician than a sound Divine ; but though St. *Aug.* doth deservedly acknowledge it a fault in himself, in that he voluntarily published such things, yet cannot it be so in this Author, in that he intended no publication of it, as he professeth in this Epistle, and in that other to Sir *Kenelm Digby.*

THE FIRST PART

Sect. 1.
Pag. 1.

THE *general scandal of my Profession.*] Physitians (of the number whereof it appears by several passages in this Book the Author is one) do commonly hear ill in this behalf. It is a common speech (but only amongst the unlearn'd sort) *Ubi tres Medici, duo Athei.* The reasons why those of that Profession (I declare my self that I am none, but *Causarum Actor Mediocris,* to use *Horace* his Phrase) may be thought to deserve that censure, the Author rendreth *Sect.* 19.

The natural course of my studies.] The vulgar lay not the imputation of Atheism only upon Physitians, but upon Philosophers in general, who for that they give themselves to understand the operations of *Nature*, they calumniate them, as though they rested in the second causes without any respect to the

xiv

first. Hereupon it was, that in the tenth Age Pope *Silvester* the second pass'd for a Magician, because he understood Geometry and natural Philosophy. *Baron. Annal.* 990. And *Apuleius* long before him laboured of the same suspicion, upon no better ground ; he was accus'd, and made a learned Apology for himself, and in that hath laid down what the ground is of such accusations, in these words : *Hæc fermè communi quodam errore imperitorum Philosophis objectantur, ut partem eorum qui corporum causas mærus et simplices rimantur, irreligiosos putant, eosque aiunt Deos abnuere, ut Anaxagoram, et Lucippum, et Democritum, et Epicurum, cœterosq; rerum naturæ Patronos.* Apul. in Apolog. And it is possible that those that look upon the second Causes scattered, may rest in them and go no further, as my Lord *Bacon* in one of his *Essayes* observeth ; but our Author tells us there is a true Philosophy, from which no man becomes an Atheist, *Sect.* 46.

The indifferency of my behaviour and Discourse in matters of Religion.] Bigots are so oversway'd by a preposterous Zeal, that they hate all moderation in discourse of Religion ; they are the men forsooth—*qui solos credant habendos esse Deos quos ipsi colunt.* *Erasmus* upon this accompt makes a great complaint to Sir *Tho. More* in an Epistle of his, touching one *Dorpius* a Divine of *Lovain,* who because, upon occasion of discourse betwixt them, *Erasmus* would not promise him to write against *Luther,* told *Erasmus* that he was a *Lutheran,* and afterwards published him for such ; and yet as *Erasmus* was reputed no very good Catholick, so for certain he was no Protestant.

Not that I meerly owe this Title to the Font] as most do, taking up their Religion according to the way of their Ancestors ; this is to be blamed among all persons : It was practised as well amongst Heathens as Christians.

Per caput hoc juro per quod Pater antè solebat, saith *Ascanius* in *Virgil* : and *Apuleius* notes it for an absurdity. *Utrum Philosopho, putas turpe scire ista, an nescire ? negligere, an curare ? nosse quanta sit etiam in istis providentiæ ratio, an de diis immortalibus Matri et Patri cedere ?* saith he in *Apolog.* and so doth *Minutius. Unusquisq; vestrum non cogitat prius se debere deum nosse quàm colere, dum inconsulte gestiuntur parentibus obedire, dum fieri malunt alieni erroris accessio, quam sibi credere.* Minut. in Octav.

But having in my ripers examined, etc.] according to the Apostolical Precept, *Omnia probate, quod bonum est tenete.*

There being a Geography of Religion] i.e. of Christian Religion, which you may see described in Mr. *Brerewood's* Enquiries : he means not of the Protestant Religion ; for though there be a difference in Discipline, yet the *Anglican, Scotic, Belgic, Gallican,* and *Helvetic* Churches differ not in any essential matter of the Doctrine, as by the *Harmony* of *Confessions* appears.   5. Epist. *Theod. Bezæ Edmundo Grindallo Ep. Lon-dinens.*

Wherein I dislike nothing but the Name] that is *Lutheran, Calvinist, Zuinglian,* etc.

Now the accidental occasion wherein, etc.] This is graphically described by *Thuanus* in his History: but because his words are too large for this purpose, I shall give it you somewhat more briefly, according to the relation of the Author of the History of the Council of *Trent.* The occasion was the necessity of Pope *Leo* the Tenth, who by his profusion had so exhausted the Treasure of the *Church,* that he was constrained to have recourse to the publishing of Indulgencies to raise monies: some of which he had destined to his own Treasury, and other part to his Allyes, and particularly to his Sister he gave all the money that should be raised in *Saxony* ; and she, that she might make the best profit of the donation, commits it to one *Aremboldus,* a Bishop to appoint Treasurers for these Indulgences. Now the custome was, that whensoever these Indulgences were sent into *Saxony,* they were to be divulged by the Fryars *Eremites* (of which Order *Luther* then was), but *Aremboldus* his Agents thinking with themselves, that the Fryars *Eremites* were so well acquainted with the trade, that if the business should be left to them, they should neither be able to give so good an account of their Negotiation, nor yet get so much themselves by it as they might do in case the business were committed to another Order ; they thereupon recommend it to (and the business is undertaken by) the *Dominican* Fryars, who performed it so ill, that the scandal arising both from thence, and from the ill lives of those that set them on work, stirred up *Luther* to write against the abuses of these Indulgences ; which was all he did at first ; but then, not long after, being provoked by some Sermons and small Discourses that had been published against what he had written, he rips up the *business* from the beginning, and publishes xcv *Theses* against it at *Wittenberg.* Against these *Tekel* a *Dominican* writes ; then *Luther* adds an explication to his. *Eckius* and *Prierius* Dominicans, thereupon take the controversie against him : and now *Luther* begins to be hot ; and because his adversaries could not found the matter of Indulgences upon other Foundations then the *Popes* power and infallibility, that begets a disputation betwixt them concerning the Popes power, which *Luther* insists upon as inferiour to that of a *general Council* ; and so by degrees he came on to oppose the Popish Doctrine of *Remission of sins, Penances,* and *Purgatory* ; and by reason of Cardinal *Cajetans* imprudent management of the conference he had with him, it came to pass that he rejected the whole body of Popish doctrine. So that by this we may see what was the accidental occasion wherein, the slender means whereby, and the abject condition of the person by whom, the work of Reformation of Religion was set on PART I. foot.

Yet I have not so shaken hands with those desperate Resolutions, Sect. 3. *(Resolvers it should be, without doubt) who had rather venture at* Pag. 8. *large their decayed Bottom, than bring her in to be new trimm'd in the Dock; who had rather promiscuously retain all, than abridge any; and obstinately be what they are, than what they have been; as to stand in a diameter and at swords point with them: we have reformed from them, not against them, etc.]* These words by Mr. Merryweather are thus rendred, sc. *Nec tamen in vecordem illum pertinacium hominum gregem memet adjungo, qui labefactatum navigium malunt fortunæ committere quàm in navale de integro resarciendum deducere, qui malunt omnia promiscuè retinere quam quicquam inde diminuere, et pertinaciter esse qui sunt quam qui olim fuerunt, ita ut iisdem ex diametro repugnent: ab illis, non contra illos, reformationem instituimus,* etc. And the Latine Annotator sits down very well satisfied with it, and hath bestowed some notes upon it; but under the favour both of him and the Translator, this Translation is so far different from the sense of the Author, that it hath no sense in it; or if there be any construction of sense in it, it is quite besides the Author's meaning; which will appear if we consider the context: by that we shall find that the Author in giving an account of his Religion, tells us first, that he is a Christian, and farther, that he is of the reform'd Religion; but yet he saith, in this place, he is not so rigid a Protestant, nor at defiance with Papists so far, but that in many things he can comply with them, (the particulars he afterwards mentions in this Section) for, saith he, we have reform'd from them, not against them, that is, as the *Archbishop* of *Canterbury* against the *Jesuit* discourseth well. We have made no new Religion nor Schism from the old; but in calling for the old, and desiring that which was novel and crept in might be rejected, and the Church of *Rome* refusing it, we have reform'd from those upstart novel Doctrines, but against none of the old: and other sense the place cannot bear; therefore how the *Latine Annotator* can apply it as though in this place the Author intended to note the *Anabaptists,* I see not, unless it were in respect of the expression *Vecordem pertinacium hominum gregem,* which truly is a description well befitting them, though not intended to them in this place: howsoever, I see not any ground from hence to conclude the Author to be any whit inclining to the *Bulk* of Popery (but have great reason from many passages in this Book to believe the contrary,) as he that prefix'd a Preface to the Parisian Edition of this Book hath unwarrantably done.

But for the mistake of the Translator, it is very obvious from whence that arose. I doubt not but it was from mistake of the sense of the English Phrase *Shaken hands,* which he hath

b

PART I. rendered by these words, *Memet adjungo*, wherein he hath too
Sect. 3. much play'd the Scholar, and show'd himself to be more skilful
in forraign and antient customs, then in the vernacular practise
and usage of the language of his own Country; for although
amongst the Latines protension of the Hand were a Symbole
and sign of Peace and Concord (as *Alex. ab Alexandro*; *Manum
verò protendere, pacem peti significabant* (saith he) *Gen. Dier. lib.*
4. *cap. ult.* which also is confirmed by *Cicero pro Dejotaro*; and
Cæsar. l. 2. *de Bellico Gallico*) and was used in their first meet-
ings, as appears by the Phrase, *Jungere hospitio Dextras*; and by
that of *Virgil*,

> *Oremus pacem, et Dextras tendamus inermes,*

And many like passages that occur in the Poets, to which I
believe the Translator had respect; yet in modern practise,
especially with us in *England*, that ceremony is used as much
in our *Adieu's* as in the *first Congress*; and so the Author
meant in this place, by saying he had not *shaken hands*; that
is, that he had not so deserted, or bid farewel to the *Romanists*,
as to stand at swords point with them: and then he gives his
reasons at those words, *For omitting those improperations*, etc.
So that instead of *memet adjungo*, the Translator should have
used some word or Phrase of a clean contrary signification; and
instead of *ex diametro repugnent*, it should be *repugnem*.

Sect. 5. *Henry* the Eighth, who, though he rejected the Pope, refused
Pag. 11. not the faith of *Rome*.] So much *Buchanan* in his own life
written by himself testifieth, who speaking of his coming into
England about the latter end of that King's time, saith, *Sed ibi
tum omnia adeo erant incerta, ut eodem die, ac eodem igne* (very
strange!) *utriusque factionis homines cremarentur, Henrico* 8,
jam seniore suæ magnis securitati quam Religionis puritati intento.
And for the confirmation of this assertion of the Author, *vide
Stat.* 31. *H.* 8, *cap.* 14.

And was conceived the state of Venice *would have attempted in
our dayes*.] This expectation was in the time of Pope *Paul* the
Fifth, who by excommunicating that Republique, gave occasion
to the Senate to banish all such of the Clergy as would not by
reason of the Popes command administer the Sacraments; and
upon that account the *Jesuits* were cast out, and never since
receiv'd into that State.

Sect. 6. *Or be angry with his judgement for not agreeing with me in
Pag.* 12. *that, from which perhaps within a few days I should dissent my
self.*] I cannot think but in this expression the Author had
respect to that of that excellent French Writer *Monsieur
Mountaign* (in whom I often trace him). *Combien diversement
jugeons nous de choses? Combien de fois changeons nous nos
fantasies? Ce que je tien aujourdhuy, ce que je croy, je le tien et
le croy de toute ma Creance, mais ne m'est il pas advenu non une*

fois mais cent, mais mille et tous les jours d'avoir embrasse quelque autre chose? Mountaign lib. 2. *Des Essais.* Chap. 12.

Every man is not a proper Champion for truth, etc.] A good cause is never betray'd more than when it is prosecuted with much eagerness, and but little sufficiency ; and therefore *Zuinglius,* though he were of *Carolostadius* his opinion in the point of the Sacrament of the *Eucharist* against *Luther,* yet he blamed him for undertaking the defence of that cause against *Luther,* not judging him able enough for the encounter : *Non satis habet humerorum,* saith he of *Carolostad ,* alluding to that of *Horace, Sumite materiam vestris qui scribitis æquam Viribus, et versate diu quid ferre recusent Quid valeant humeri.* —— So *Minutius Fœlix ; Plerumq; pro disserentium viribus, et eloquentiæ potestate, etiam perspicuæ veritatis conditio mutetur.* Minut. in Octav. And *Lactantius* saith, this truth is verified in *Minutius* himself : for *Him, Tertullian* and *Cyprian,* he spares not to blame (all of them) as if they had not with dexterity enough defended the Christian cause against the *Ethniques. Lactant. de justitia,* cap. 1. I could wish that those that succeeded him had not as much cause of complaint against him : surely he is noted to have many errors *contra fidem.*

In Philosophy —— *there is no man more Paradoxical then my self, but in Divinity I love to keep the Road,* etc.] Appositely to the mind of the Author, saith the Publisher of Mr. *Pembel's* Book *de origine formarum, Certe* (saith he) *in locis Theologicis ne quid detrimenti capiat vel Pax, vel Veritas Christi* —— *à novarum opinionum pruritu prorsus abstinendum puto, usq; adeo ut ad certam regulam etiam loqui debeamus, quod pie et prudenter monet Augustinus (de Civ. Dei.* l. 10, cap. 23.) [*ne verborum licentia impia vi gignat opinionem,*] *at in pulvere Scholastico ubi in nullius verba juramus, et in utramvis partem sine dispendio vel pacis, vel salutis ire liceat, major conceditur cum sentiendi tum loquendi libertas,* etc. Capel. *in Ep. Dedicat. Pembel. de origine form. præfix.*

Heresies perish not with their Authors, but like the River Arethusa, *though they lose their Currents in one place, they rise again in another.*] Who would not think that this expression were taken from Mr. *Mountaigne, l. 2, des Ess. cap.* 12. Where he hath these words, *Nature enserre dans les termes de son progress ordinaire comme toutes autres choses aussi les creances les judgements et opinions des hommes elles ont leur revolutions ;* and that *Mountaigne* took his from *Tully. Non enim hominum interitu sententiæ quoque occidunt, Tull. de nat. deorum l.* 1, etc. Of the River *Arethusa* thus *Seneca. Videbis celebratissimum carminibus fontem Arethusam limpidissimi ac perludicissimi ad imum stagni gelidissimas aquas profundentem, sive illas primum nascentes invenit, sive flumen integrum subter tot maria, et à confusione pejoris undæ servatum reddidit.* Senec. *de consolat. ad Martiam.*

Pag. 13.

PART I.

Sect. 7.
Pag. 14.

Now the first of mine was that of the Arabians.] For this Heresie, the Author here sheweth what it was; they are called *Arabians* from the place where it was fostered; and because the *Heresiarch* was not known, *Euseb.* St. *Aug.* and *Nicephorus* do all write of it: the reason of this Heresie was so specious, that it drew Pope *John* 22. to be of the same perswasion. Where then was his infallibility? Why, *Bellarmine* tells you he was nevertheless infallible for that: for, saith he, he maintained this opinion when he might do it without peril of Heresie, for that no definition of the Church whereby 'twas made Heresie, had preceded when he held that opinion. *Bellar. l.* 4, *de Pontif. Roman. cap.* 4. Now this definition was first made ('tis true) by Pope *Benedict* in the 14 Age: but then I would ask another question, that is, If 'till that time there were nothing defined in the Church touching the beatitude of Saints, what certainty was there touching the sanctity of any man? and upon what ground were those canonizations of Saints had, that were before the 14 Age?

The second was that of Origen.] Besides St. *Augustine*, *Epiphanius*, and also S. *Hierom*, do relate that *Origen* held, that not only the souls of men, but the *Devils* themselves should be discharged from torture after a certain time: but *Genebrard* endeavours to clear him of this. *Vid. Coquæum, in* 21. *lib. Aug. de Civ. Dei. cap.* 17.

These opinions though condemned by lawful Councils, were not Heresie in me, etc.] For to make an Heretique, there must be not only *Error in intellectu,* but *pertinacia in voluntate.* So St. *Aug. Qui sententiam suam quamvis falsam atque perversam nulla pertinaci animositate defendunt, quærunt autem cauta solicitudine veritatem, corrigi parati cum invenerint, nequaquam sunt inter Hæreticos deputandi.* Aug. cont. Manich. 24, qu. 3.

Sect. 9.
Pag. 16.

The deepest mysteries ours contains have not only been illustrated, but maintained by Syllogism and the Rule of Reason,] and since this Book was written, by Mr. *White* in his *Institutiones Sacræ.*

And when they have seen the Red Sea, doubt not of the Miracle.] Those that have seen it, have been better informed then Sir *Henry Blount* was, for he tells us that he desired to view the passage of *Moses* into the Red Sea (not being above three days journey off) but the *Jews* told him the precise place was not known within less than the space of a days journey along the shore; wherefore (saith he) I left that as too uncertain for any Observation. *In his Voyage into the Levant.*

Sect. 10.
Pag. 18.

I had as lieve you tell me that *Anima est Angelus hominis, est corpus Dei,* as *Entelechia ; Lux est umbra Dei,* as *actus perspicui.*] Great variety of opinion there hath been amongst the Ancient Philosophers touching the definition of the Soul. *Thales,* his was, that it is a *Nature without Repose. Asclepiades,* that it is *an Exercitation of Sense. Hesiod,* that it is a *thing composed of*

Earth and Water; Parmenides holds, *of Earth and Fire; Galen*
that it is *Heat*; *Hippocrates,* that it is *a spirit diffused through
the body.* Some others have held it to be *Light; Plato* saith,
'tis *a Substance moving itself*; after cometh *Aristotle* (whom
the Author here reproveth) and goeth a degree farther, and
saith it is *Entelechia,* that is, that which naturally makes the
body to move. But this definition is as rigid as any of the
other; for this tells us not what the *essence, origine* or *nature* of
the *soul* is, but only marks an *effect* of it, and therefore signifieth
no more than if he had said (as the Author's Phrase is) that it
is *Angelus hominis,* or an *Intelligence* that moveth man, as he
supposed those other to do the Heavens.

Now to come to the definition of Light, in which the Author
is also unsatisfied with the School of *Aristotle,* he saith, It satis-
fieth him no more to tell him that *Lux est actus perspicui,* than
if you should tell him that it is *umbra Dei.* The ground of this
definition given by the *Peripateticks,* is taken from a passage in
Aristot. de anima l. 2, *cap.* 7, where *Aristotle* saith, That the
colour of the thing seen, doth move that which is *perspicuum
actu* (i.e. *illustratam naturam quæ sit in aere aliove corpore trans-
parente*) and that that, in regard of its continuation to the eye,
moveth the eye, and by its help the internal *sensorium*; and
that so vision is perform'd. Now as it is true that the Sectators
of *Aristotle* are to blame, by fastening upon him by occasion of this
passage, that he meant that those things that made this impress
upon the Organs are meer accidents, and have nothing of substance; which is more than ever he meant, and cannot be maintained without violence to Reason, and his own Principles; so
for *Aristotle* himself, no man is beholding to him for any Science
acquir'd by this definition : for what is any man the near for his
telling him that Colour (admitting it to be a body, as indeed it
is, and in that place he doth not deny) doth move *actu perspicuum,* when as the perspicuity is in relation to the *eye*; and
he doth not say how it comes to be perspicuous, which is the
thing enquired after, but gives it that donation before the eye
hath perform'd its office; so that if he had said it had been
umbra Dei, it would have been as intelligible, as what he hath
said. He that would be satisfied how Vision is perform'd, let
him see Mr. *Hobbs* in *Tract. de nat. human.* cap. 2.

For God hath not caused it to rain upon the Earth.] St. *Aug.
de Genes. ad literam,* cap. 5, 6, salves that expression from any
inconvenience; but the Author in *Pseudodox. Epidemic.* l. 7,
cap. 1, shews that we have no reason to be confident that this
Fruit was an *Apple.*

I believe that the Serpent (*if we shall literally understand it*)
*from his proper form and figure made his motion on his belly before
the curse.*] Yet the Author himself sheweth in *Pseudodox.
Epidemic.* lib. 7, cap. 1, that the form or kind of the *Serpent* is

PART I.
Sect. 10.

not agreed on : yet *Comestor* affirm'd it was a *Dragon*, *Eugubinus* a *Basilisk*, *Delrio* a *Viper*, and others a common *Snake* : but of what kind soever it was, he sheweth in the same Volume, *lib.* 5, c. 4, that there was no inconvenience, that the temptation should be perform'd in this proper shape.

I find the tryal of Pucelage and the Virginity of Women which God ordained the Jews, *is very fallible.*] *Locus extat*, Deut. c. 22, the same is affirm'd by *Laurentius* in his *Anatom.*

Whole Nations have escaped the curse of Child-birth, which God seems to pronounce upon the whole sex.] This is attested by M. *Mountaigne. Les doleurs de l'enfantiment par les medicins, et par Dieu mesme estimees grandes, et que nous passons avec tant de Ceremonies, il y a des nations entieres qui ne'n fuit nul conte. l. 1, des Ess. c.* 14.

Sct. 11.
Page 19.

Who can speak of Eternity *without a Solœcism, or think thereof without an Extasie?* Time *we may comprehend, etc.*] Touching the difference betwixt *Eternity* and *Time*, there have been great disputes amongst Philosophers ; some affirming it to be no more than *duration perpetual consisting of parts* ; and others (to which opinion, it appears by what follows in this Section, the Author adheres) affirmed (to use the Authors Phrase) that it hath no distinction of Tenses, but is according to *Boetius* (lib. 5, *consol. pros.* 6), his definition, *interminabilis vitæ tota simul et perfecta possessio.* For me, *non nostrum est tantas componere lites.* I shall only observe what each of them hath to say against the other. Say those of the first opinion against those that follow *Boetius* his definition, That definition was taken by *Boetius* out of *Plato's Timæus*, and is otherwise applyed, though not by *Boetius*, yet by those that follow him, than ever *Plato* intended it ; for he did not take it in the Abstract, but in the Concrete, for an *eternal thing, a Divine substance,* by which he meant *God*, or his *Anima mundi* : and this he did, to the intent to establish this truth, That no mutation can befal the Divine Majesty, as it doth to things subject to generation and corruption ; and that *Plato* there intended not to define or describe any *species* of duration : and they say that it is impossible to understand any such *species* of duration that is (according to the Authors expression) but one *permanent point.*

Now that which those that follow *Boetius* urge against the other definition is, they say, it doth not at all difference *Eternity* from the nature of *Time* ; for they say if it be composed of many *Nunc's*, or many instants, by the addition of one more it is still encreased ; and by that means *Infinity* or *Eternity* is not included, nor ought more than *Time*. For this, see Mr. *White, de dial. mundo, Dial.* 3. *Nod.* 4.

Indeed he only is, etc.] This the Author infers from the words of God to *Moses, I am that I am* ; and this to distinguish him from all others, who (he saith) have and shall be : but

those that are learned in the *Hebrew*, do affirm that the words **PART I.**
in that place (*Exod.* 3) do not signifie, *Ego sum qui sum, et
qui est*, etc. but *Ero qui ero, et qui erit*, etc. *vid Gassend. in
animad. Epicur. Physiolog.*

   I wonder how Aristotle *could conceive the World Eternal, or how* *Sect.* 12.
he could make two Eternities :] (that is, that God, and the World *Pag.* 20.
both were eternal.) I wonder more at either the ignorance or
incogitancy of the *Conimbricenses*, who in their Comment upon
the eighth book of *Aristotle's Physicks*, treating of the matter of
Creation, when they had first said that it was possible to know
it; and that actually it was known (for *Aristotle* knew it) yet for
all this they afterwards affirm, That considering onely the light
of Nature, there is nothing can be brought to demonstrate
Creation: and yet farther, when they had defined Creation to
be the production of a thing *ex nihilo*, and had proved that the
World was so created in time, and refused the arguments of the
Philosophers to the contrary, they added this, That the World
might be created *ab æterno*: for having propos'd this question
[*Num aliquid à Deo ex Æternitate procreari potuit?*] they defend
the affirmative, and assert that not onely incorporeal substances,
as Angels ; or permanent, as the celestial Bodies ; or corruptible
as Men, etc. might be produced and made *ab æterno*, and be
conserved by an infinite time, *ex utraq*; *parte* ; and that this is
neither repugnant to God the Creator, the things created, nor
to the nature of Creation: for proof whereof, they bring
instances of the *Sun* which if it had been eternal, had illumin-
ated eternally, (and the virtue of God is not less than the virtue
of the Sun.) Another instance they bring of the *divine Word*,
which was produced *ab æterno* : in which discourse, and in the
instances brought to maintain it, it is hard to say whether the
madness or impiety be greater ; and certainly if Christians thus
argue, we have the more reason to pardon the poor heathen
Aristotle.

   There is in us not three, but a Trinity of Souls.] The *Peripatetiques*
held that men had three distinct Souls ; whom the Heretiques,
the *Anomæi*, and the *Jacobites*, followed. There arose a great
dispute about this matter in *Oxford*, in the year 1276, and it
was then determined against *Aristotle. Daneus Christ. Eth.* l. 1.
c. 4. and *Suarez* in his Treatise *de causa formali, Quest. An
dentur plures formæ in uno composito*, affirmeth there was a Synod
that did *anathematize* all that held with *Aristotle* in this point.

   There is but one first, and four second causes in all things.] In *Sect.* 14.
that he saith there is but one first cause, he speaketh in opposi- *Pag.* 23.
tion to the *Manichees*, who held there were *Duo principia* ; one
from whom came all good, and the other from whom came all
evil : the reason of *Protagoras* did it seems impose upon their
understandings ; he was wont to say, *Si Deus non est, unde
igitur bona? Si autem est, unde mala?* In that he saith there

are but four second Causes, he opposeth *Plato,* who to the four causes, *material, efficient, formal,* and *final,* adds for a fifth *exemplar* or *Idæa,* sc. *Id ad quod respiciens artifex, id quod destinabat efficit*; according to whose mind *Boetius* speaks, *lib.* 3. *met.* 9. *de cons. Philosoph.*

> *O qui perpetua mundum ratione gubernas,*
> *Terrarum Cœliq; sator qui tempus ab ævo*
> *Ire jubes, stabilisq; manens das cuncta moveri:*
> *Quem non externæ pepulerunt fingere causæ*
> *Materiæ fluitantis opus, verum insita summi*
> *Forma boni livore carens: tu cuncta superno*
> *Ducis ab exemplo, pulchrum pulcherrimus ipse*
> *Mundum mente gerens, similique in imagine formans,*
> *Perfectasq; jubens perfectum absolvere partes.*

And St. *Augustine l.* 83. *quest.* 46. where (amongst other) he hath these words, *Restat ergo ut omnia Ratione sint condita, nec eadem ratione homo qua equus; hoc enim absurdum est existimare: singula autem propriis sunt creata rationibus.* But these *ideæ Plato's* Scholar *Aristotle* would not allow to make or constitute a different sort of cause from the *formal* or *efficient*, to which purpose he disputes, *l.* 7. *Metaphysic.* but he and his Sectators, and the *Ramists* also, agree (as the Author) that there are but the four remembred Causes: so that the Author, in affirming there are but four, hath no Adversary but the *Platonists*; but yet in asserting there are four (as his words imply) there are that oppose him, and the *Schools* of *Aristot.* and *Ramus.* I shall bring for instance Mr. *Nat Carpenter,* who in his *Philosophia Libera* affirmeth, there is no such cause as that which they call the *Final cause*: he argueth thus; Every cause hath an influence upon its effect: but so has not the End, therefore it is not a Cause. The *major* proposition (he saith) is evident, because the influence of a cause upon its effect, is either the causality it self, or something that is necessarily conjoyned to it: and the *minor* as plain, for either the End hath an influence upon the effect immediately, or mediately, by stirring up the Efficient to operate; not immediately, because so it should enter either the *constitution* or *production*, or *conservation* of the things; but the constitution it cannot enter, because the constitution is only of *matter* and *form*; nor the Production, for so it should concur to the production, either as it is *simply the end,* or as *an exciter of the Efficient*; but not simply as the end, because the end *as end* doth not go before, but followeth the thing produced, and therefore doth not concur to its production: if they say it doth so far concur, as it is desired of the agent or efficient cause, it should not so have an immediate influence upon the effect, but should onely first move the efficient. Lastly, saith he, it doth not enter the conservation PART I. of a thing, because a thing is often conserved, when it is Sect. 14. frustrate of its due end, as when it's converted to a new use and end. Divers other Arguments he hath to prove there is no such cause as the final cause. *Nat. Carpenter Philosoph. liber Decad. 3. Exercitat. 5.* But for all this, the Author and he differ not in substance : for 'tis not the Author's intention to assert that the end is in nature præexistent to the effect, but only that whatsoever God has made, he hath made to some end or other ; which he doth to oppose the Sectators of *Epicurus*, who maintain the contrary, as is to be seen by this of *Lucretius* which follows.

> *Illud in his rebus vitium vehementer et istum,*
> *Effugere errorem vitareque premeditabor*
> *Lumina ne facias oculorum clara creata*
> *Prospicere ut possimus ; et, ut proferre viai*
> *Proceros passus, ideo fastigia posse*
> *Surarum ac feminum pedibus fundata plicari :*
> *Brachia tum porro validis ex apta lacertis*
> *Esse, manusq; datas utraq; ex parte ministras,*
> *Vt facere ad vitam possimus, quæ foret usus :*
> *Cætera de genere hoc, inter quæcunq; precantur*
> *Omnia perversa præpostera sunt ratione :*
> *Nil ideo quoniam natum'st in corpore, ut uti*
> *Possemus ; sed quod natum'st, id procreat usum,*
> *Nec fuit ante videre oculorum lumina nata,*
> *Nec dictis orare prius, quàm lingua creata'st,*
> *Sed potius longe linguæ præcessit origo*
> *Sermonem ; multoq; creatæ sunt prius aures*
> *Quàm sonus est auditus, et omnia deniq; membra*
> *Ante fuere, ut opinor, eorum quàm foret usus :*
> *Haud igitur potuere utendi crescere causa.*
>
> Lucret. lib. 4. [822-841.]

There are no Grotesques in nature, etc.] So *Monsr. Montaign.* Sect. 15. *Il n'ya rien d'inutil en nature, non pas l'inutilité mesmes, Rien ne* Pag. 24. *s'est ingeré en cet Univers qui n'y tienne place opportun.* Ess. l. 3. c. 1.

Who admires not Regio-montanus *his Fly beyond his Eagle ?*] Of these *Du Bartas.*

> *Que diray je de l'aigle,*
> *D'ont un doct Aleman honore nostre siecle*
> *Aigle qui deslogeant de la maistresse main,*
> *Aila loin au devant d'un Empereur Germain ;*
> *Et l'ayant recontré suddain d'une aisle accorte,*
> *Se tournant le suit au seuil de la porte*
> *Du fort Norembergois, que lis piliers dorez,*
> *Les tapissez chemins, les arcs elabourez,*

PART I.
Sect. 15.

Les fourdroyans Canons, in la jeusnesse isnelle,
In le chena Senat, n'honnoroit tant come elle.
Vn jour, que cetominer plus des esbats, que de mets,
En privé fasteyoit ses seignieurs plus amees,
Vne mousche de fer, dans sa main recelee,
Prit sans ayde d'autroy, sa gallard evolee :
Fit une entiere Ronde, et puis d'un cerveau las
Come ayant jugement, se purcha sur son bras.

Thus Englished by *Silvester.*

Why should not I that wooden Eagle mention ?
(A learned German's *late admir'd invention)*
Which mounting from his Fist that framed her,
Flew far to meet an Almain *Emperour :*
And having met him, with her nimble Train,
And weary Wings turning about again,
Followed him close unto the Castle Gate
Of Noremberg ; *whom all the shews of state,*
Streets hang'd with Arras, arches curious built,
Loud thundring Canons, Columns richly guilt,
Grey-headed Senate, and youth's gallantise,
Grac'd not so much as onely this device.
Once as this Artist more with mirth than meat,
Feasted some friends that he esteemed great ;
From under's hand an Iron Fly flew out,
Which having flown a perfect round about,
With weary wings, return'd unto her Master,
And (as judicious) on his arm she plac'd her.

Or wonder not more at the operation of two souls in those little
bodies, than but one in the Trunk of a Cedar ?] That is, the
vegetative, which according to the common opinion, is supposed
to be in *Trees,* though the *Epicures* and *Stoiques* would not allow
any Soul in Plants ; but *Empedocles* and *Plato* allowed them not
only a *vegetative* Soul, but affirm'd them to be *Animals.* The
Manichees went farther, and attributed so much of the rational
Soul to them, that they accounted it *Homicide* to gather either
the flowers or fruit, as St. *Aug.* reports.

We carry with us the wonders we seek without us.] So St. *Aug.*
l. 10. de civ. c. 3. *Omni miraculo quod fit per hominem majus*
miraculum est homo.

Sect. 16.
Pag. 25.

Another of his servant Nature, that publique and universal
Manuscript that lies expansed, etc.] So is the description of *Du*
Bartas 7. *jour de la sepm.*

Oyes ce Docteur muet estudie en ce livre
Qui nuict et jour ouvert t' apprendra de bien vivre.

All things are artificial, for Nature is the Art of God.] So Mr.
Hobbes in his *Leviathan* (*in initio*) Nature is the Art whereby
God governs the world.

Directing the operations of single and individual Essences, etc.]
Things singular or individuals, are in the opinion of Philosophers not to be known, but by the way of sense, or by that
which knows by its Essence, and that is onely God. The Devils
have no such knowledge, because whatsoever knows so, is either
the cause or effect of the thing known; whereupon *Averroes*
concluded that God was the cause of all things, because he
understands all things by his Essence; and *Albertus Magnus*
concluded, That the inferiour intelligence understands the
superiour, because it is an effect of the superiour: but neither
of these can be said of the *Devil*; for it appears he is not the
effect of any of these inferiour things, much less is he the
cause, for the power of Creation onely belongs to God.

*All cannot be happy at once, because the Glory of one State
depends upon the ruine of another.*] This Theme is ingeniously
handled by Mr. *Montaigne livr.* 1. *des Ess.* cap. 22. the title
whereof is, *Le profit de l'un est dommage de l'autre.*

'Tis the common fate of men of singular gifts of mind, to be
destitute of those of Fortune.] So *Petron. Arbiter. Amor ingenii*
neminem unquam divitem fecit, in *Satyric.* And *Apuleius* in
Apolog. *Idem mihi etiam* (saith he) *paupertatem opprobravit
acceptum Philosopho crimen et ultro profitendum;* and then a
little afterwards, he sheweth that it was the common fate of
those that had singular gifts of mind : *Eadem enim est paupertas
apud Græcos in Aristide justa, in Phocyone benigna, in Epaminonde
strenua, in Socrate sapiens, in Homero diserta.*

We need not labour with so many arguments to confute judicial
Astrology.] There is nothing in judicial *Astrology* that may
render it impious; but the exception against it is, that it is vain
and fallible; of which any man will be convinced, that has read
Tully de Divinat. and St. *Aug.* book 5. *de Civ. dei.*

There is in our soul a kind of Triumvirate ―― that distracts
the peace of our Commonwealth, not less than did that other the
State of Rome.] There were two *Triumvirates,* by which the
peace of *Rome* was distracted; that of *Crassus, Cæsar* and
Pompey, of which *Lucan, l.* 1.

―――*Tu causam aliorum*―――
*Facta tribus Dominis communis Roma, nec unquam
In turbam missi feralia fœdera Regni.*

And that other of *Augustus, Antonius* and *Lepidus,* by whom,
saith *Florus, Respublica convulsa est lacerataque,* which comes
somewhat near the Author's words, and therefore I take it that
he means this last Triumvirate.

PART I.   *Would disswade my belief from the miracle of the brazen*
Sect. 19.   *Serpent.*]   Vid. *Coqueum in, l.* 10.   Aug. *de Civ. Dei, c.* 8.
Pag. 32.   *And bid me mistrust a miracle in* Elias, etc.]   The History is
18. 1 *Reg.*   It should be *Elijah.*   The Author in 15. *cap. lib.* 7.
Pseudodox. sheweth it was not perform'd naturally ; he was (as
he saith) a perfect miracle.
    To think the combustion of Sodom *might be natural.*]   Of that
opinion was *Strabo*, whereupon he is reprehended by *Genebrard*
in these words : *Strabo falsus est —— dum eversionem addicit*
sulphuri et bitumini e terra erumpentibus, quæ erat assignanda
Cœlo, i.e. *Deo irato.   Tacitus* reports it according to the Bible,
fulminis ictu arsisse.

Sect. 20.   *Those that held Religion was the difference of man from Beasts,*
Pag. 33.   etc.]   *Lactantius* was one of those : *Religioni ergo serviendum est,*
quam qui non suspicit, ipse se prosternit in terram, et vitam
pecudum secutus humanitate se abdicat.   Lactant *de fals.*
Sapientia, cap. 10.
    The Doctrine of Epicurus *that denied the providence of God,*
was no Atheism, but, etc.]   I doubt not but he means that delivered
in his Epistle to *Menæceus*, and recorded by *Diogenes Laertius*,
lib. 10.   *Quod beatum æternumque est, id nec habet ipsum*
negotii quicquam, nec exhibet alteri, itaque neque ira, neque gratia
tenetur, quod quæ talia sunt imbecillia sunt omnia ; which the
Epicurean Poet hath delivered almost in the same words.

> *Omnis enim per se divum natura necesse 'st*
> *Immortali ævo summa cum pace fruatur,*
> *Semota à nostris rebus sejunctaq; longè :*
> *Nam privata dolore omni, privata periclis*
> *Ipsa suis pollens opibus nihil indiga nostri*
> *Nec bene pro meritis capitur, nec tangitur ira.*
>
> Lucret. *lib.* 2.

    That Villaine and Secretary of Hell, that composed that miscreant
piece of the three Impostors.]   It was *Ochinus* that composed this
piece ; but there was no less a man than the Emperour *Frederick*
the Second, that was as lavish of his tongue as the other of his
pen ; *Cui sæpe in ore, Tres fuisse insignes Impostores, qui genus*
humanum seduxerunt : Moysem, Christum, Mahumetem.   Lips.
monit. et exempl. Politic. cap. 4.   And a greater than he, Pope
Leo the Tenth, was as little favourable to our Saviour, when he
us'd that speech which is reported of him, *Quantas nobis divitias*
comparavit ista de Christo fabula.

Sect. 21.   *There are in Scripture stories that do exceed the fables of Poets.*]
Pag. 34.   So the Author of *Relig. Laici. Certè mira admodum* in S.S. *plus*
quam in reliquis omnibus Historiis traduntur ; (and then he con-
cludes with the Author) *sed quæ non retundunt intellectum, sed*
exercent.
    Yet raise no question who shall rise with that Rib *at the Resur-*

rection.] The Author *cap. 2 l. 7. Pseudodox.* sheweth that it PART I. appeares in Anatomy, that the Ribs of Man and Woman are *Sect.* 21. equal.

Whether the world were created in Autumn, Summer, or the Spring, etc.] In this matter there is a consent between two learned Poets, *Lucretius* and *Virgil*, that it begins in *Spring*.

> *At novitas mundi nec frigora dura ciebat,*
> *Nec nimios æstus, nec magnis viribus auras.*   Lucretius.

Which he would have to be understood of *Autumn*, because that resembles old age rather than Infancy. He speaks expresly of the Fowls.

> *Principio genus alituum variæq; volucres*
> *Ova relinquebant exclusæ tempore verno.*   Lucret.

Then for *Virgil*.

> *Non alios prima nascentis origine mundi*
> *Illuxisse dies aliumve habuisse tenorem*
> *Crediderim, ver illud erat, ver magnus agebat*
> *Orbis, et hibernis parcebant flatibus Euri.*
> Virgil 2. Georgic.

But there is a great difference about it betwixt Church-Doctors; some agreeing with these Poets and others affirming the time to be in Autumn : but truly, in strict speaking, it was not created in any one, but all of the seasons, as the Author saith here, and hath shewed at large. *Pseudodox. Epidemic.* lib. 6. cap. 2.

'Tis ridiculous to put off or down the general floud of Noah *in* *Sect.* 22. *that particular inundation of* Deucalion,] as the Heathens some *Pag.* 35. of them sometimes did : *Confuderunt igitur sæpe Ethnici particularia illa diluvia, quæ longe post secuta sunt, cum illo universali quod præcessit, ut ex fabulis in Diluvio Deucalionæo sparsis colligere licet ; non tamen semper nec ubique. Author. Observat. in Mytholog. Nat. Com.* Then amongst those that confound them, he reckons *Ovid* and *Plutarch*.

How all the kinds of Creatures, not onely in their own bulks, but with a competency of food and sustenance, might be preserved in one Ark, and within the extent of 300 Cubits, to a reason that rightly examines it will appear very feasible.] Yet *Apelles* the Disciple of *Mercion*, took upon him to deride the History of *Moses* in this particular, alledging that it must needs be a fable, for that it was impossible so many creatures should be contain'd in so small a space. *Origen* and St. *Aug.* to answer this pretended difficulty, alleadge that *Moses* in this place speakes of Geometrical (and not vulgar) cubits, of which every one was as much as six vulgar ones ; and so no difficulty. But *Perer. l.* 10. *com. in*

PART I.
Sect. 22.

Genes. quest. 5. *de arca,* rejects this opinion of *Origen,* as being both against reason and Scripture.

1. Because that sort of Cubit was never in use amongst any people, and therefore absurd to think *Moses* should intend it in this place.

2. If *Moses* should not speak of the same Cubits here, that he mentions in others places, there would be great æquivocation in Scripture : now in another place, *i.e. Exod.* 27. he saith, God commanded him to make an Altar three Cubits high ; which if it shall be meant of Geometrical Cubits it will contain 18 vulgar Cubits ; which would not only render it useless, but would be contrary to the command which he saith God gave him, *Exod.* 20. *Thou shalt not go up by steps to my Altar.* For without steps what man could reach it. It must therefore be meant of ordinary Cubits ; but that being so it was very feasible. I can more easily believe than understand it.

And put the honest Father to the Refuge of a Miracle.] This honest father was St. *Aug.* who delivers his opinion, that it might be miraculously done, *lib.* 16. *de Civ. Dei, cap.* 7. where having propos'd the question how it might be done, he answers, *Quod si homines eas captas secum adduxerunt, et eo modo ubi habitabant earum genera instituerunt, venandi studio fieri potuisse incredibile non est, quamvis jussu Dei sive permissu etiam opera Angelorum negandum non sit potuisse transferri ;* but St. *Aug.* saith not that it could not be done without a miracle.

And 1500 years to people the World, as full a time, etc.]

Pag. 36

That Methusalem *was the longest liv'd of all the children of* Adam, etc.] See both these Points cleared by the Author, in *Pseudodox. Epidemic.* the first *lib.* 6. *cap.* 6. the other *lib.* 7. *cap.* 3.

That Judas *perished by hanging himself, there is no certainty in Scripture, though in one place it seems to affirm it, and by a doubtful word hath given occasion to translate it ; yet in another place, in a more punctual description it makes it improbable, and seems to overthrow it.*] These two places that seem to contradict one another are *Math.* 27. 5. and *Acts* 1. 8. The doubtful word he speaks of is in the place of *Matthew* ; it is ἀπήγξατο, which signifieth suffocation as well as hanging, (ἀπελθὼν ἀπήγξατο, which may signifie literally, after he went out he was choak'd) but *Erasmus* translates it, *abiens laqueo se suspendit:* the words in the *Acts* are, *When he had thrown down himself headlong, he burst in the midst, and all his bowels gushed out* ; which seems to differ much from the expression of *Matthew* ; yet the Ancient Writers and Fathers of the Church do unanimously agree that he was hanged. Some I shall cite. *Anastas. Sinaita, l.* 7. *Anagog. Contempl. Unus latro ingratus cum esset typus Diaboli, et Serpentis, et Judæ, qui se in ligno suffocavit. Gaudentius Brixiens. tract.* 13. *de natal. Dom. Mortem debitam laqueo sibimet*

intulit præparato, etc. *Droggotoshen. de sacram. dominic. pass.*
Jamdiu erat quidem quod Christo recesserat, et avaritiæ laqueo se
suspenderat, sed quod fecerat in occulto, palam omnibus innotuit.
S. Martialis in Ep. ad Tholosanos. Non sustinuit pœnitentiam,
donec laqueo mortis seipsum consumpsit. Ignat. ad Philippens.
Diabolus laqueum ei ostendit, et suspendium docuit. Leo Serm. 3.
de passion.—— *Ut quia facinus omnem mensuram ultionis*
excesserat, te haberet impietas tua judicem te pateretur sua pæna
Carnificem. Theodoret. lib. 1. hæretic. fabul. Ille protinus
strangulatus est, quæ fuit merces ejus proditionis. Chrysostom.
Hom. 3. de proditore. Pependit Cœlum Terramque intermedius
vago funere suffocatus, et cum flagitio suo tumefacta, viscera
crepuerunt, etc. *Bernard. Serm. 8. in Psal. 9. Judas in Aere*
crepuit medius.

1. There are those that are so particular, that they acquaint
us with the manner, as *that it was done with a Cord. Antiochus*
Laurensis, Spem omnem a se cum abjecisset, insiliente in eum
inimico (sc. Diabolo) funiculo sibi præfocavit gulam. Oecumen.
in Act. Fracto funiculo quo erat suffocatus decidit in terram
præcipitio. 2. That it was done on a Fig-Tree, *Beda. Portam*
David egredientibus fons occurrit in Austrum per vallem directus,
ad cujus medietatem ab occasu Judas se suspendisse narratur :
Nam et ficus magna ibi et vetustissima stat.

> *Juvenc. lib. 4. Hist. Evangelic.*
>
> *Exorsusq; suas laqueo sibi sumere pænas,*
> *Informem rapuit ficus de vertice mortem.*

3. Some acquaint us with the time when it was done, *viz. the*
next day after he had given the kiss. So *Chrysostom. Homil. 1. de*
proditor. et Mysterio Cœn. Dominic. Guttur prophanum quod
hodie Christo extendis ad osculum, crastino es illud extensurus ad
laqueum. But there are two, that is *Euthymius* and *Oecumenius,*
that tell us, *that the hanging did not kill him,* but that either the
Rope broke, or that he was cut down, and afterwards cast himself down headlong, as it is related in the before mentioned
place of the *Acts: Agnitus à quibusdam depositus est ne præfo-*
caretur, denique postquam in secreto quodam loco modico vixisset
tempore præceps factus sive præcipitatus, inflatus diruptus, ac
diffisus est medius, et effusa sunt omnia viscera ejus; ut in Actis.
Euthym. cap. 67. in Math. Judas suspendio è vita non decessit, sed
supervixit, dejectus est enim prius quam præfocaretur, idque
Apostolorum Acta indicant, quod pronus crepuit medius. Oecumen.
in Act. And this may serve to reconcile these two seemingly
disagreeing Scriptures.

That our Fathers after the Flood erected the Tower of Babel.]
For this see what the Author saith in his *Pseudodox. Epidemic.*
l. 7. cap. 6.

PART I.
Sect. 23.
Pag. 37.

And cannot but commend the judgment of Ptolemy.] He means of *Ptolemæus Philadelphus*, who founded the Library of *Alexandria*, which he speaks of in the next Section. He was King of *Egypt*; and having built and furnish'd that Library with all the choicest Books he could get from any part of the world, and having good correspondence with *Eleazer* the high Priest of the *Jews*, by reason that he had released the *Jews* from Captivity, who were taken by his Predecessor *Ptolemæus Lagi*; he did by the advice of *Demetrius Phalereus* the *Athenian*, whom he had made his Library-Keeper, write to *Eleazer*, desiring him that he would cause the Books of the *Jews*, which contained their Laws, to be translated for him into Greek, that he might have them to put into his Library: to which the Priest consents; and for the King's better satisfaction, sends to him Copies of the Books, and with the same 72 Interpreters skilled both in the Greek and Hebrew Language, to translate them for him into Greek; which afterwards they performed. This is for certain; but whether they translated only the *Pentateuch*, as St. *Jerome* would have it, or together with the Books of the Prophets also, as *Leo de Castro* and *Baronius* contend, I undertake not to determine: but as to that part of the story, that these Interpreters were put into so many several Cells, whilst they were about the work of translation; and notwithstanding they were thus severed, that they all translated it *totidem verbis*; it is but reason to think with St. *Jerome* (notwithstanding the great current of Authority against him) that it is no better than a fable.

The Alcoran of the Turks (I speak without prejudice) is an ill-composed piece, containing in it vain and ridiculous errors in Philosophy, etc.] It is now in every mans hand, having been lately translated into English; I shall therefore observe but these few particulars in it, in regard the book it self is so common; and indeed they are not mine own, but *Lipsius* his observations. He begins, *O nugas, O deliria! primum* (saith he) *commentus est, Deum unum solidumq; (ὀλόσφυρον Græci ¦exprimunt) eundemq; incorporeum esse. Christum non Deum, sed magnum vatem et prophetam; se tamen majorem, et proxime à Deo missum, præmia qui ipsum audient Paradisum, qui post aliquot annorum millia reserabitur, ibi quatuor flumina lacte, vino, melle, aqua fluere, ibi palatia et ædificia gemmata atque aurata esse, carnes avium suavissimarum, fructus omne genus quos sparsi jacentesque sub umbra arborum edent: sed caput fælicitatis, viros fœminasque, majores solito magnis Genitalibus assidua libidine, et ejus usu sine tædio aut fatigatione.* These and some others that are in the Alcoran he reckons up. *Sed et Physica quoq; miranda* (saith he) *nam facit Solem et Lunam in equis vehi, illum autem in aquam calidam vespere mergi, et bene lotum ascendere atque oriri, Stellas in aere è catenis aureis pendere: terram in bovini cornus cuspide stabilitum, et agitante se bove ac succutiente fieri terræ*

motum; hominem autem ex hirundine aut sanguisuga nasci, etc. PART I.
Just. Lips. *Monit. et exempl. Politic.* cap. 3.

Sect. 23.
Pag. 38.

*I believe besides Zoroaster there were divers others that wrote
before Moses.*] *Zoroaster* was long before *Moses,* and of great
name; he was the father of *Ninus, Justin. lib.* 1. *Si quamlibet
modicum emolumentum probaveritis, ego ille sim Carinondas vel
Damigeron, vel is Moses, vel Joannes, vel Apollonius, vel ipse
Dardanus, vel quicunq; alius* post Zoroastrem *et Hostanem, inter
Magos celebratus est.* Apuleius *in* Apol.

Others with as many groans deplore the combustion of the Library Sect. 24.
at Alexandria.] This was that Library before spoken of, set up Pag. 38.
by *Ptolemæus Philadelphus*; in which 'tis reported by *Ammianus
Marcellinus* there were 700,000 volumes; it was burnt by *Jul.
Cæsar's* means, whose Navy being environed before *Alexandria,*
he had no means to keep off the Enemy, but by flinging of fire,
which at length caught the Library and consumed it, as
Plutarch hath it in *Vita Cæsaris*: but notwithstanding we have
no reason to believe it was quite consumed, because *Sueton.* in
Claudius, tells us, that that Emperour added another to it; and
there must be somewhat before, if it were an addition; but
true it is, too many of the Books perished; to repair which loss,
care was taken by *Domitian* the Emperour, as the same *Sueton.*
and *Aurel. Victor.* do relate.

I would not omit a Copy of Enoch's *Pillars, had they many
nearer Authors than* Josephus, *etc.*] For this the Story is, that
Enoch, or his father *Seth,* having been inform'd by *Adam,* that
the world was to perish once by water, and a second time by
fire, did cause two Pillars to be erected, the one of Stone
against the water, and another of Brick against the fire; and
that upon those Pillars was engraven all such Learning as had
been delivered to, or invented by mankind; and that thence it
came that all knowledge and learning was not lost by means of
the Floud, by reason that one of the Pillars (though the other
perished) did remain after the Floud, and *Josephus* witnesseth,
till his time, *lib.* 1. *Antiq. Judaic.* cap. 3.

Of those three great inventions of Germany, *there are two which
are not without their incommodities.*] Those two he means are
Printing and *Gunpowder,* which are commonly taken to be
German Inventions; but Artillery was in *China* above 1500
years since, and Printing long before it was in *Germany,* if we
may believe *Juan Concales Mendosa* in his *Hist.* of *China, lib.* 3.
cap. 15, 16. The incommodities of these two inventions, are
well described by *Sam. Daniel,* lib. 6. of the Civil Wars.

> *Fierce* Nemesis, *mother of fate and change,*
> *Sword-bearer of th' eternal providence,*
> *Turns her stern look at last into the West,*
> *As griev'd to see on Earth such happy rest;*

PART I.

Sect. 24.
Pag. 38.

And for Pandora *calleth presently,*
Pandora Jove's *fair gift that first deceived*
Poor Epimetheus *in his imbecility.*
That though he had a wondrous boon received,
By means whereof curious mortality
Was of all former quiet quite bereaved.
To whom being come deckt with all qualities,
The wrathful goddess breaks out in this wise :
Dost thou not see in what secure estate,
Those flourishing fair Western parts remain ?
As if they had made covenant with fate,
To be exempted free from others pain,
At one with their desires, friends with debate,
In peace with Pride, content with their own gain.
Their bounds contain their mindes, their mindes applyed
To have their bonds with plenty beautified.
Devotion (Mother of Obedience)
Bears such a hand on their credulity,
That it abates the spirit of eminence,
And busies them with humble piety :
For see what works, what infinite expence,
What Monuments of zeal they edifie,
As if they would, so that no stop were found,
Fill all with Temples, make all holy ground.
But we must cool this all-believing zeal,
That hath enjoy'd so fair a turn so long, etc.
Dislike of this first by degrees shall steal,
As upon souls of men perswaded wrong ;
And that the sacred power which thus hath wrought,
Shall give her self the sword to cut her throat.
Go therefore thou with all thy stirring train
Of swelling Sciences (the gifts of grief)
Go loose the links of that soul-binding chain,
Enlarge this uninquisitive Belief :
Call up mens spirits, that simpleness retain,
Enter their hearts, and knowledge make the Thief
To open all the Doors to let in Light,
That all may all things see but what is right.
Opinion arm against opinion (grown)
Make new-born contradictions still arise,
As if Thebes Founder (Cadmus) tongues had sown
Instead of teeth, for greater mutinies :
Bring new defended faith against faith known,
Weary the soul with contrarieties,
Till all Religion become Retrograde,
And that fair tye the mask of sin be made :
And better to effect a speedy end,
Let there be found two fatal Instruments,

The one to publish, th' other to defend
Impious contention, and proud discontents :
Make that instamped characters may send
Abroad to thousands, thousand mens intents ;
And in a moment may dispatch much more,
Than could a world of pens perform before ;
   Whereby all quarrels, titles, secrecies,
May unto all be presently made known,
Factions prepar'd, parties allur'd to rise,
Seditions under fair pretences sown ;
Whereby the vulgar may become so wise
That with a self-presumption overgrown,
They may of deepest mysteries debate,
Controul their betters, censure acts of State.

   And then when this dispersed mischief shall
Have brought confusion in each mystery,
Call'd up contempts of State in general,
And ripen'd the humour of impiety,
Then take the other engine wherewithal
They may torment their self-wrought misery ;
And scourge each other in so strange a wise,
As time or tyrants never could devise, etc.

PART I.

Sect. 24.
Pag. 39.
Printing.

Guns.

    See *Bellermontan.* in his *Dissertat. politic. dissert.*
29. and 30.

For the other Invention, the Latine Annotator doubts
whether the Author means Church-Organs, or Clocks? I
suppose he means Clocks, because I find that Invention reckon'd
by a *German*, with the other two, as a remarkable one. It is
by *Busbequius*, speaking of the Turks, who hath these words :
Testes majores minoresque bombardæ, multaque alia quæ ex nostris
excogitata ipsi ad se avertunt ; ut libros tamen typis excuderent,
horologia in publico haberent, nondum adduci potuerunt. *Epist.*
Legat. Turcic. I suppose if he had known any Invention which
next to the other two had been greater than this, he would not
have named this, and this being the next considerable, we have
no cause to doubt but the Author meant it.

    To maintain the Trade and Mystery of Typographers.] Of this
Cunæus in his *Satyre Sardi vœnales.* *Qui bis in anno nomen*
suum ad Germanorum nundinas non transmittit, eruditionem suam
in ordinem coactam credit, itaq; nunquam tot fungi una pluvia
nascuntur, quot nunc libri uno die.

    The Turk in the bulk that he now stands, is beyond all hope of *Sect.* 25.
conversion.] That is, in respect of his great strength, against *Pag.* 40.
which it is not probable the Christians will prevail, as it is
observed by *Monsieur de Silhon.* *La Race des Ottomans* (saith he)
quæ oste a Dieu la Religion qu'il a revelee, et aux hommes la
liberte que le droit des Gens leur laisse a fait tant de progres depuis

PART I.
Sect. 25.

trois Cens et quelques annees qu'il semble qu'elle n'ait plus rien a craindre de dehorse, et que son empire ne puisse perir que par la corruption de dedans, et par la dissolution des parties qui composent un corps si vaste. Mr. *de Silhon en son Minist. D'Estat. l.* 1. *c.* .

Pag. 40.

None can more justly boast of persecutions, and glory in the number and valour of martyrs.] Of the fortitude of the Christians in this particular, *Minutius Felix,* in the person of the Ethnique, hath these words, *Per mira stultitia et incredibili audacia spernunt tormenta præsentia, dum incerta metuunt et futura ; et dum mori post mortem timent, interim mori non timent.* And afterwards, when he speaks in the person of the Christian, he saith, that Christian women and children have in this surpassed *Scævola* and *Regulus* : *Viros* (saith he) *cum Mutio vel cum Atilio Regulo comparo : pueri et mulierculæ nostræ cruces et Tormenta, feros et omnes suppliciorum terriculas inspirata patientia doloris illudunt.* Minut. *in* Octav. *vide Aug. de Civit. Dei, lib.* 1. *c.* 23, 24.

If we shall strictly examine the circumstances and requisites which Aristotle *requires to true and perfect valour, we shall find the name onely in his Master* Alexander, (*that is, no more than the name) and as little in that Roman worthy* Julius Cæsar.] *Aristot.* 3. *Ethic. cap.* 6. amongst other requisites, requires to valour, that it keep a mediocrity betwixt audacity and fear ; that we thrust not our selves into danger when we need not ; that we spare not to shew our valour when occasion requires : he requires for its proper object, Death ; and to any death, he prefers death in War, because thereby a man profits his Country and Friends ; and that he calls *mors honesta,* an honest or honourable death : and thereupon he defines a valiant man to be, *Is qui morte honesta proposita, iisq; omnibus quæ cum sint repentina mortem adfuerunt metu vacat.* So that by the Author's saying, there was onely the Name in *Alexander,* he means only that which is rendred in the two last words, *metu vacans,* and not the rest that goes to make up the definition of a valiant man, which is very truly affirmed of *Alexander,* who exposed himself to hazzard many times when there was no cause for it : As you may read in *Curtius,* he did, in the siege of *Tyrus,* and many other ways. *Cettuy-cy semble rechercher et courir à force les dangiers comme un impetueux torrent, qui choque et attaque sans discretion, et sans chois tout ce qu'il rencontre,* saith *Montaign,* speaking of *Alexander,* l. 2. *des Ess.* cap. 34. And for *Cæsar,* it cannot be denied, but in his Wars he was many times (though not so generally as *Alexander*) more adventrous than reason military could warrant to him ; and therefore *Lucan* gives him no better Character than

Acer et indomitus quo spes quoq; ira vocasset
Ferre manum, etc.

Lucan. lib. 1.

To instance in some Particulars : with what an inconsiderable
strength did he enterprize the conquest of *Egypt*, and afterwards went to attaque the forces of *Scipio* and *Juba*, which were
ten times more than his own? after the Battle of *Pharsalia*,
having sent his Army before into *Asia*, and crossing the
Hellespont with one single Vessel, he there meets *Lucius Cassius*
with ten men of War, he makes up to him, summons him to
render, and he does it. In the famous and furious siege of
Alexia, where he had 80,000 men to make defence against him,
and an Army of one hundred and nine thousand Horse, and
two hundred and forty thousand foot, all marching towards
him, to raise his siege ; yet for all that he would not quit the
siege, but first fought with those without, and obtain'd a great
Victory over them, and soon afterwards brought the besieged to
his mercy.

The Council of Constance *condemns* John Husse *for an*
Heretick, the Stories of his own Party style him a Martyr.] John
Husse did agree with the Papists against us in the Point of
Invocation of Saints, Prayers and Sacrifice for the Dead, free
Will, Good Works, confession of Sins, seven Sacraments, etc.
Gordon. Hunt. l. contr. 3. de Sacr. Euch. cap. 17. Yet was he
condemned for maintaining certain Articles said by that Council
to be heretical and seditious, and was burnt for Heresie. Now
as I will not say he was an Heretick, so can I not maintain that
he was a Martyr, if it be but for this one Article, which in the
15. Sess. of that Council was objected against him, which he did
acknowledge, but would not recal, *i.e. Nullus est Dominus civilis,
dum est in peccato mortali.* If that Doctrine should be believed,
we shall have little obedience to Civil Magistrates ; and without
that, how miserable is humane condition? That which begat
compassion towards *Husse* in those of his own Party was, that
he had a safe conduct from the Emperour *Sigismund* ; and therefore it was, say they, a violation of publick faith in the *Council*
and *Emperour* in putting him to death.

That wise heathen Socrates *that suffered on a fundamental point
of Religion, the Unity of God.*] That *Socrates* suffered on this
Point, divers Christian Writers do object to the Ethniques, as
Justin Martyr, Apol. 2. *Euseb. l.* 5. *de præparat. Evangelic. c.* 14.
Tertul. in *Apolog.* cap. 14. and *Lactant. de justitia,* cap. 15.
whose words are these : *Plato quidem multa de uno Deo locutus est,
à quo ait constitutum esse mundum, sed nihil de Religione ; somni-
averat enim Deum, non cognoverat. Quod si justitiæ defensionem
vel ipse vel quilibet alius implere voluisset, imprimis Deorum
Religiones evertere debuit, quia contrariæ pietati. Quod quidem
Socrates quia facere tentavit in carcerem conjectus est, ut jam tunc
appareret quid esset futurum iis hominibus qui justitiam veram
defendere Deoque singulari servire cœpissent.*

I have often pitied the miserable Bishop that suffered in the

PART I.
Sect. 26.

cause of Antipodes.] The suffering was, that he lost his Bishoprick for denying the *Antipodes*. Vid. *Aventin. in Hist. Boio.* Besides him, there were other Church-men of great note, that denyed *Antipodes*, as *Lactantius, Augustin,* and *Bede.*

Sect. 27.
Pag. 43.

I hold that God can do all things: How he should work contradictions, I do not understand, yet dare not therefore deny.] Who would not think the Author had taken this from Mr. *Montaign*, whose words are, *Il m'a tousjours semble qu'a un homme Christien, cette sorte de parler est plein d' indiscretion et d' irreverence [Dieu ne se peut disdire,] [Dieu ne peut faire cecy ou cela]. Je ne trouve pas bon d'enfermer ainsi la puissance divine sous les loix de nostre parole. Et l'apparence qui s' offre à nous en ses propositions, il la faudroit representer plus reverement, et plus Religieusement.* Liv. 2. des Ess. c. 12.

I cannot see why the Angel of God should question Esdras *to recal the time past, if it were beyond his own power, or that God should pose mortality in that which he was not able to perform himself.*] Sir *K. Digby* in his Notes upon this place saith, There is no contradiction in this, because he saith it was but putting all things that had motion into the same state they were in at that moment, unto which time was to be reduced back, and from thence letting it travel on again by the same motions, *etc.* which God could do. But under favour, the contradiction remains, if this were done that he mentions; for Time depends not at all upon motion, but has a being altogether independent of it, and therefore the same revolution would not bring back the same time, for that was efflux'd before ; as in the time of *Joshua*, when the Sun stood still, we cannot but conceive, though there were no motion of the Sun, but that there was an efflux of Time, otherwise, how could the Text have it, *That there was not any day, before or after, that was so long as that?* for the length of it must be understood in respect of the flux of time. The reasoning of Sir *Kenelme* is founded upon the opinion of *Aristot.* who will needs have it, that Time cannot be without mutation ; he gives this for a reason, because when we have slept, and cannot perceive any mutation to have been, we do therefore use to connect the time of our sleeping and of our awaking together, and make but one of it : to which it may be answered, although some mutation be necessary, that we may mark the flux of time, it doth not therefore follow that the mutation is necessary to the flux it self.

Sect. 28.
Pag. 43.

I excuse not Constantine *from a fall off his Horse, or a mischief from his enemies, upon the wearing those nails,* etc.] *Hac de re videatur P. Diac. hist. miscell.*

Sect. 29.
Pag. 44.

I wonder how the curiosity of wiser heads could pass that great and indisputable miracle, the cessation of Oracles.] There are three opinions touching the manner how the predictions of these Oracles were perform'd : Some say by vapour, some by the intelligences, or influences of the Heavens, and others say by the assistance of the Devils. Now the indisputable miracle the Author speaks of, is, that they ceas'd upon the coming of Christ; and it is generally so believed; and the Oracle of *Delphos* delivered to *Augustus*, mentioned by the Author in this Section, is brought to prove it, which is this :

> *Me puer Hebræus divos Deus ipse gubernans*
> *Cedere sede jubet, tristemq; redire sub orcum.*
> *Aris ergo dehinc tacitus discedito nostris.*

But yet it is so far from being true that their cessation was miraculous, that the truth is, there never were any predictions given by those Oracles at all.

That their cessation was not upon the coming of Christ, we have luculent testimony out of *Tully*, in his 2. *lib. de Divinat.* which he writ many years before Christ was born; who tells us that they were silent (and indeed he never thought they were otherwise) long before that time, insomuch that they were come into contempt : *Cur isto modo jam oracula Delphis non eduntur, non modo nostra ætate, sed jamdiu jam ut nihil possit esse contemptius.* So that for that of *Delphos*, which was the most famous of them all, we see we have no reason to impute the cessation of it to Christ; Why therefore should we do so for any of the rest?

For their predictions, let us consider the three several ways before mentioned, whereby they are supposed to operate ; and from thence see whether it be probable that any such Oracles ever were.

The first Opinion is, that it was by exhalation or vapour drawn up from the earth; and gives this for a reason of their being, that they were for a time nourished by those exhalations ; and when those ceased, and were exhausted, the Oracles famish'd and died for want of their accustom'd sustenance : this is the far-fetcht reason given by *Plutarch* for their defect; but 'twas not devised by him, but long before, as appears, in that *Tully* scoffs at it, *lib. de divinat. De vino aut salsamento putes loqui* (saith he) *quæ evanescunt vetustate.* This seem'd absurd to others, who do therefore say this was not to be attributed to any power of the Earth, but to the power of the Heavens, or *Intelligences Cœlestial* ; to certain aspects whereof, they say, the Statua's of those Oracles were so adapted, that they might divine and foretel future events. But yet to others, this way seemeth as absurd as the others ; for, say they, admitting that there were an efficacy in the Heavens, more than in the Earth ; yet how can it be that men should come by the skill to fit the Statua's to the Aspects or influences of the Heavens? or if at any time they had such skill, why should not the same continue the rather, because men are more skilled in the motions of the Heavens, of later than in the former time? Again, they do not see how it should be that the cause should be of less excellency than the effect; for if a man (say they) can by his industry make such Oracles, why can he not produce the same effect in another man? for if you affirm that the Heavens influence is requisite, they will tell you that Influence may happen as well to a man, as to a Statue of wood or stone. Therefore the third sort being unsatisfied, which either of the former ways conclude, that this was perform'd by the Devil; but for that it will appear as contrary to Reason and Philosophy, as either of the former; for Philosophy teacheth that things singular, or individual, are to be known only by sense, or by such an Intellect, as doth know by its Essence; and Theology teacheth that God only knoweth the heart, and that the Devil doth not know by sense, nor by essence; and since 'tis admitted by all, that most of the answers that were pretended to be given by those Oracles, were *de rebus singularibus*, or *individuis*; it is evident that these predictions were not perform'd by Devils. How then? why those predictions which the ignorant Heathen took to come from Heaven, and some Christians (not less ignorant) from the Devil, was nothing but the jugling and impostures of the Priests, who from within the Statua's gave the answers; which Princes connived at, that they might upon occasion serve their turns upon the ignorance of the people; and the learned men, for fear of their Princes, durst not speak against it. *Lucian* hath noted it, and so a more Authentick Author, *Minut. Felix*, in *Octav. Authoritatem quasi præsentis numinis consequuntur dum inspirantur interim vatibus.* But in process of time, the people grew less credulous of their Priests, and so the Oracles became to be silent: *Cum jam* (saith he) *Apollo versus facere desisset, cujus tunc cautum illud et ambiguum defecit oraculum: Cum et politiores homines et minus creduli esse cœperunt.* Sir *H. Blount* in his *Levantine* voyage, saith he saw the Statua of *Memnon* so famous of old; he saith it was hollow at top, and that he was told by the *Egyptians* and Jews there with him, that they had seen some enter there, and come out at the Pyramid, two Bows-shoot off; then (saith he) I soon believ'd the Oracle, and believe all the rest to have been such; which indeed, is much easier to imagine than that it was perform'd by any of the three wayes before mentioned. St. *Aug.* hath composed a Book, where he handleth this point at large, and concludeth that the Devils can no more foretel things to come, than they are able to discern the thoughts that are within us. *Aug. lib. de Scientia Dæmon.*

Till I laughed my self out of it with a piece of Justin, *where he delivers that the Children of* Israel *for being scabbed were banished out of* Egypt.] These words of *Justin* are, *Sed cum scabiem*

Ægyptii et pruriginem paterentur, responso moniti, eum (sc. Moysen) PART I.
cum ægris, ne pestis ad plures serperet, terminis Ægypti pellunt. Sect. 29.
l. 36. But he is not singular in this, for *Tacitus* tells us, *Hist.* Pag. 44.
lib. 5. *Plurimi authores consentiunt orta per Ægyptum tabe quæ
corpora fædaret, Regem* (*Ochirum*) (he means *Pharaoh*) *adito Ham-
monis oraculo remedium petentem purgare Regnum et id genus
hominum——alias in terras avertere jussum.* Et paulo inferius,
Quod ipsos scabies quondam turpaverat.

I have ever believed, and do now know that there are Witches.] Sect. 30.
What sort of Witches they were that the Author knew to be Pag. 45.
such, I cannot tell; for those which he mentions in the next
Section, which proceed upon the principles of Nature, none
have denyed that such there are; against such it was, that the
Lex Julia de veneficiis was made, that is, those, *Qui noxio poculo
aut impuris medicaminibus aliquem fuerint insectati.* *Al. ab Alex.
Gen. Dier.* l. 5. c. 1. But for the opinion that there are
Witches which co-operate with the Devil, there are Divines of
great note, and far from any suspition of being irreligious, that
do oppose it. Certainly there is no ground to maintain their
being from the story of Oracles, as may be seen from what hath
been said on the precedent Section.

Nor have the power to be so much as Witches.] *Pliny* saith, so
it fared with *Nero*, who was so hot in pursuit of the Magick
Arts, that he did dedicate himself wholly to it, and yet could
never satisfie himself in that kind, though he got all the
cunning men he could from the East, for that purpose. *Plin.*
l. 3. *Nat. Hist.* c. 1.

By conjunction with the Devil.] Though, as the Author saith, Pag. 46.
it be without a possibility of Generation, yet there are great
men that hold, that such carnality is performed; as *August. in
Levit. Aquin.* l. 2. *de qu.* 73. *art. ad* 2. and *Justin Martyr,
Apol.* 1.

It is no new opinion of the Church of Rome, *but an old one* Sect. 33.
of Pythagoras *and* Plato.] This appears by *Apuleius* a Platonist, Pag. 48.
in his Book *de Deo Socratis,* and elsewhere. See *Mede's Apostasie
of the latter times,* where out of this and other Authors, you
shall see collected all the learning *de Geniis.*

I cannot with those in that great Father securely interpret the Pag. 50.
work of the first day, Fiat lux, *to the creation of Angels.*] This
great Father is S. *Chrysost. Homil. in Genes.* But yet 'tis his
opinion, as also of *Athanasius* and *Theodoret,* that there is
express mention of the creation of Angels, so that they need
not rest upon this place, which they admit to be somewhat
obscure. The place which they take to be express, is that of
the 130 *Psalm,* where *David* begins to speak of the Majesty of
God, in this manner: *Confessionem sive majestatem et decorem
induisti, amictus lumine sicut vestimento:* Next he speaks of the
Heavens, saying, *Thou hast stretched them out over us like a Tent.*

PART I.

Sect. 33.
Pag. 50.

Then he speaks of the Angels, *Qui facis Angelos tuos spiritus.* Now if it shall be objected, that this expression is onely of the time present, and without relation to the Creation : Answer is given by Divines, that the *Hebrews* have but three Tenses in their Verbs, the Preterperfect, Present, and Future Tense ; and have not the use of the Preterimperfect, and Preterpluperfect, as the *Greeks* and *Latines* have ; whence it ariseth, that the Present Tense with the *Hebrews*, may, as the sentence will bear it, be translated by the Preterimperfect, as also by the Preterperfect and Preterpluperfect Tense ; and this (they say) is practised in this very passage, where the Phrase, as it is in Hebrew, may be rendered as well *qui faciebas*, as *qui facis Angelos*, etc. Vid. *Hieronym. in Ep. ad Titum, et Thom. Aqu.* 1. *p. qu.* 61. *art.* 3. The Latine Annotator saith, the Father meant by the Author, is St. *Aug.* and quotes him, *l.* 11. *de Civ. Dei*, cap. 9. which place I have perused, and find the expression there used by St. *Aug.* is but hypothetical ; for these are his words : *Cum enim dixit Fiat lux, et facta est lux, si rectè in hac luce creatio intelligitur Angelorum*, etc. Where you see 'tis but with a *Si*, and therefore I conceive the Author intends not him, but *Chrysostom.*

Where it subsists alone, 'tis a Spiritual Substance, and may be an Angel.] Epicurus was of this opinion, and St. *Aug. in Enchirid. ad Laurentium.*

Sect. 35.
Pag. 52.

Moses decided that Question, and all is salved with the new term of Creation.] That is it which *Aristotle* could not understand ; he had learned that *ex nihilo nihil fit*, and therefore when he found those that disputed that the World had a beginning, did maintain that it was generated, and he could not understand any generation, but out of matter præ-existent *in infinitum*, therefore he took their opinion to be absurd, and upon that ground principally, concluded the World to be eternal : whereas, if he had understood that there may be such a thing as Creation, he had not done it, for that solves his *processus in infinitum.* Take from *Plato*, that the World had a beginning, and from *Aristot.* that it was not generated, and you have the (true) Christian opinion.

Sect. 36.
Pag. 54.

In our study of Anatomy, there is a mass of mysterious Philosophy, and such as reduced the very Heathens to Divinity.] So it did *Galen*, who considering the order, use, and disposition of the parts of the body, brake forth into these words : *Compono hic profecto Canticum in creatoris nostri laudem, quod ultra res suas ornare voluit melius quam ulla arte possent.* Galen, 3. *de usu partium.*

Sect. 37.
Pag. 55.

I cannot believe the wisdom of Pythagoras *did ever positively, and in a literal sense, affirm his* Metempsychosis.] In this the opinion of *Grotius* is contrary to the Author, who saith this opinion was begotten by occasion of the opinion of other Philosophers, who in their discourses of the life that is to be after

this, brought such arguments, *Quæ non magis de homine quam* **PART I.**
de bestiis procedunt. And therefore, saith he, *mirandum non est,* *Sect.* 37.
si transitum animarum de hominibus in bestias, de bestiis in *Pag.* 55.
homines alii commenti sunt. *Lib. 2. de ver. Relig. Christ. (vide
etiam Annotat. ejusd.*). But yet there is a shrewd objection
against the opinion of *Pythagoras,* if he did mean it literally,
which is cast in by the Sectators of *Democritus* and *Epicurus,*
which *Lucretius* remembers in these Verses :

> *Præterea si immortalis natura animaï
> Constat, et in corpus nascentibus insinuatur,
> Cur super anteactam ætatem meminisse nequimus?
> Nec vestigia gestarum rerum ulla tenemus?
> Namsi tantopere 'st animi mutata potestas,
> Omnis ut actarum excideret retinentia rerum,
> Non ut opinor ea ab læto jam longiter errat.*
>
> [Lib. 3.]

This Argument, 'tis true, is *pro falso contra falsum*, but yet
holds *ad hominem* so far, that it is not likely (as the Author
saith) but *Pythagoras* would observe an absurdity in the consequence of his Metempsychosis ; and therefore did not mean it
literally, but desired only to express the Soul to be immortal,
which he, and the other Philosophers that were of that opinion,
who had not heard of Creation, could not conceive, unless it
must be taken for truth, that the soul were before the body ; so
saith *Lactantius* of them. *Non putaverunt aliter fieri posse ut
supersint animæ post corpora, nisi videntur fuisse ante corpora.
De fals. Sap. c.* 18.

I do not envy the temper of Crows or Daws.] As *Theophrastus* *Sect.* 41.
did, who dying, accused Nature for giving them, to whom it *Pag.* 59.
could not be of any concernment, so large a life ; and to man,
whom it much concern'd, so short a one. *Cic. Tusc. quæst. l. 3.*
How long Daws live, see in *Not. ad Sect.* 41.

Not upon Cicero's ground, because I have liv'd them well.] I *Sect.* 42.
suppose he alludes to an expression in an Epistle of *Cicero,* *Pag.* 61.
written in his Exile, to his wife and children, where he hath
these words to his wife : *Quod reliquum est, te sustenta mea
Terentia ut potes, honestissime viximus, floruimus.* *Non vitium
nostrum sed virtus nos afflixit, peccatum est nullum nisi quod non
unà animum cum ornamentis amisimus,* l. 24, Ep. 4.

And stand in need of Eson's *bath before threescore.*] *Eson* was
the Father of *Jason,* and, at his request, was by *Medea,* by the
means of this Bath, restored to his youth. Ingredients that
went into it, and the description of *Medea's* performance, *Ovid*
gives you, *l.* 7. *Metam.*

> *Interea calido positum medicamen aheno
> Fervet et exultat, spumisq; tumentibus albet.*

PART I.

Sect. 42.
Pag. 61.

Illic Æmonia radices valle resectas,
Seminaq; et flores, et succos incoquit atros
Adjicet extremo lapides Oriente petitos,
Et quas Oceani refluum mare lavit arenas:
Addidit exceptas lunæ de nocte pruinas,
Et Strigis infames ipsis cum carnibus alas,
Inq; virum soliti vultus mutare ferinos
Ambigui prosecta lupi, nec defuit illi
Squamea Cinyphei tenuis membrana Chelidri,
Vivacisq; jecur cervi; quibus insuper addit
Ora caputq; novem cornicis secula passæ.
His et mille aliis, postquam sine nomine rebus
Propositum instruxit mortali barbara munus
Arenti ramo jampridem mitis olivæ
Omnia confudit, summisq; immiscuit ima.
Ecce vetus calido versatus stipes aheno
Fit viridis primo, nec longo tempore frondes
Induit, et subito gravidis oneratur olivis.
At quacunq; cavo spumas ejecit aheno
Ignis, et in terram guttæ cecidere calentes,
Vernat humus, floresq; et mollia pabula surgunt.
Quæ simulac vidit, stricto Medea recludit
Ense senis jugulum, veteremq; extare cruorem
Passa replet succis, quos postquam combibit Æson,
Aut ore acceptas, aut vulnere, barba comæq;
Canitie posita, nigrum rapuere colorem.
Pulsa fugit macies: abeunt pallorq; situsque:
Adjectoq; cavæ supplentur corpore rugæ;
Membraq; luxuriant. Æson miratur, et olim
Ante quater denos hunc se reminiscitur annos,
Dissimilemq; animum subiit, ætate relicta.

[262-293.]

Sect. 44.
Pag. 62.

Extol the Suicide of Cato.] As doth *Seneca* in several places; but *Lactantius* saith, he cast away his life, to get the reputation of a *Platonick* Philosopher, and not for fear of *Cæsar*; and 'tis very probable, he was in no great fear of death, when he slept so securely the night before his death, as the story reports of him.

Pag. 63.

Emori nolo, sed me esse mortuum, nihil curo. Were I of Cæsar's *Religion.*] I doubt not, but here is a fault of the Press, and that instead of *Cæsar* it should be *Cicero.* I meet not with any such saying imputed to *Cæsar*, nor any thing like it, but that he preferr'd a sudden death (in which he had his option) to any other; but I meet with such a saying in *Cicero* quoted out of *Epicharmus* [*Emori nolo, sed me esse mortuum nihili æstimo.*] Where *Cicero* sustaineth the part of the *Epicure* that there is no hurt in being dead, since there remaineth nothing after it. *Cic. 1. Thusc. qu. non procul ab initio.*

Or whence *Lucan* learn'd to say, *Communis mundo superest*
rogus, etc.] Why, *Lucan* was a Stoique, and 'twas an opinion
among them almost generally, that the world should perish by
fire ; therefore without doubt from them he learned it. *Cœlum
quoque cum omnibus quæ in cælo continentur, ita ut cœpisset
desinere, fontium dulci aqua marisve nutriri, in vim ignis abiturum.
Stoicis constans opinio est, quod consumpto humore mundus hie
omnis ignescat. Minutius in Octav.* But *Minutius* should have
excepted *Boetius, Possidonius, Diogenes Babylonius,* and *Zeno
Sidonius,* who were *Stoiques,* and yet did not think the world
should be destroyed by fire, nor yet by any other means.

How shall we interpret Elias 6000 years, etc. ?] *Lactant.* is
very positive that the world should last but 6000 years ; but his
reason for it is somewhat strange ; thus it is, *Quoniam sex diebus
cuncta Dei opera perfecta sunt, per secula sex,* i.e. *annorum sex
millia manere in hoc statu mundum necesse est. De Divino præmio,*
cap. 14.

Ipsa sui pretium virtus sibi, is but a cold principle.] It is a
Stoical principle. *Quæris enim aliquid supra summum, interrogas*
*quid petam extra virtutem ipsam. Nihil enim habet melius.
Pretium sui est.* Senec. *de vit. beat.* c. 19.

That honest artifice of Seneca.] What that article was, is to
be seen in *Senec. l.* 1. *ep.* 11. *Aliquis vir bonus nobis eligendus
est, et semper ante oculos habendus, ut sic tanquam illo spectante
vivamus, et omnia tanquam illo vidente faciamus.* Et paulo post ;
*Elige itaq; Catonem ; si hic videtur tibi nimis rigidus, elige remis-
sioris animi virum Lælium,* etc., which though, as the Author
saith, it be an honest Artifice, yet cannot I but commend the
party, and prefer the direction of him (whoever he were) who in
the Margin of my *Seneca,* over against those words, wrote these :
*Quin Deo potius qui semper omnibus omnia agentibus non tanquam
sed reipsa adest, et videt ; ac etiam ut Testis, vindex et punitor est
male agentis.*

*I have tried, if I could reach that great Resolution of his (that is
of* Seneca) *to be honest without a thought of Heaven or Hell.*]
Seneca[1] brags he could do this, in these words : *Si scirem deos*
peccata ignoscituros, et homines ignoraturos, adhuc propter vili-
tatem peccati peccare erubescerem. Credat Judæus Appella: non
ego.——

And Atheists have been the onely Philosophers.] That is, if
nothing remain after this life. St. *Aug.* was of this opinion.
Disputabam—— *Epicurum accepturum fuisse palmam in animo
meo, nisi ego credidissem post mortem restare animæ vitam,* etc.
Aug. *l.* 6. *conf. cap.* 16.

God by a powerful voice shall command them back into their
proper shapes.] So *Minutius. Cæterum quis tam stultus est aut*
*brutus, ut audeat repugnare hominem à Deo ut primum potuit fingi,
ita posse denuo reformari, nihil esse post obitum, et ante ortum*

PART I.   *nihil fuisse ; sicut de nihilo nasci licuit, ita de nihilo licere reparari.*
Sect. 48.   *Porro difficilius est id quod sit incipere, quod quam id quod fuerit*
Pag. 68.   *iterare.   Tu perire Deo credis, si quid nostris oculis hebetibus sub-*
              trahitur.   Corpus omne sive arescit in pulverem sive in humorem
              solvitur, vel in cinerem comprimitur vel in nidorem tenuatur,
              subducitur nobis, sed Deo elementorum custodi inseruntur.   In
              Octav. Vide Grot. *de veritate Relig. Christian. ubi (lib.* 2.) *solvit*
              objectionem, quod dissoluta corpora restitui nequeunt.

Sect. 50.   *Or conceive a flame that can either prey upon, or purifie the*
Pag. 71.   *substance of a soul.*] Upon this ground *Psellus lib.* 1. *de Energia*
              Dæmonum, c. 7. holds, That Angels have bodies, (though
              he grants them to be as pure, or more pure than Air is)
              otherwise he could not apprehend how they should be
              tormented in Hell ; and it may be upon this ground it was,
              that the Author fell into the error of the *Arabians,* mentioned
              by him, *Sect.* 7.

Sect. 51.   *There are as many Hells as* Anaxagoras *conceived worlds.*] I
Pag. 73.   assure my self that this is false printed, and that instead of
              Anaxagoras it should be *Anaxarchus*; for *Anaxagoras* is
              reckon'd amongst those Philosophers that maintain'd a Unity
              of the world, but *Anaxarchus* (according to the opinion of
              Epicurus) held there were infinite Worlds.   That is he that
              caus'd *Alexander* to weep by telling him that there were infinite
              worlds, whereby *Alexander* it seems was brought out of opinion
              of his Geography, who before that time thought there remained
              nothing, or not much beyond his Conquests.

Sect. 54.   *It is hard to place those souls in Hell.*] *Lactantius* is alike
Pag. 75.   charitably disposed towards those.   *Non sum equidem tam iniquus*
              ut eos putem divinare debuisse, ut veritatem per seipsos invenirent
              (quod fieri ego non posse confiteor) sed hoc ab eis exigo, quod
              ratione ipsa præstare potuerunt. Lactant. *de orig. error.* c. 3.
              which is the very same with Sir *K. Digbie's* expression in his
              Observations on this place.   I make no doubt at all (saith
              he) but if any follow'd in the whole tenour of their lives,
              the dictamens of right reason, but that their journey was secure
              to Heaven.

Sect. 55.   Aristotle *transgress'd the rule of his own Ethicks.*] And so they
Pag. 77.   did all, as *Lactantius* hath observed at large.   *Aristot.* is said to
              have been guilty of great vanity in his Clothes, of Incontinency,
              of Unfaithfulness to his Master *Alexander,* etc.   But 'tis no
              wonder in him, if our great *Seneca* be also guilty, whom truely
              notwithstanding St. *Jerome* would have him inserted in the
              Catalogue of Saints, yet I think he as little deserv'd it, as many
              of the Heathens who did not say so well as he did, for I do not
              think any of them liv'd worse : to trace him a little.   In the
              time of the Emperour *Claudius* we find he was banish'd for sus-
              pition of incontinency with *Julia* the daughter of *Germanicus.*
              If it be said that this proceeded meerly from the spight of

PART I.
Sect. 55.
Pag. 77.

Messalina, (and that *Lipsius* did not complement with him in that kind *Apostrophe, Non expetit in te hæc culpa, O Romani nominis et Sapientiæ magne. Sol. Not. in Tacit.*) why then did she not cause him to be put to death, as well as she did the other, who was her Husbands Niece? This for certain, whatever his life were, he had *paginam lascivam,* as may appear by what he hath written, *de Speculorum usu, l. 1. Nat. Qu. cap.* 16. Which (admitting it may in a Poet, yet) how it should be excus'd in a Philosopher I know not. To look upon him in his exile, we find that then he wrote his Epistle *De Consolat.* to *Polybius, Claudius* his creature (as honest a man as *Pallas* or *Narcissus*) and therein he extols him and the Emperour to the Skies; in which he did grosly prevaricate, and lost much of his reputation, by seeking a discharge of his exile by so sordid a means. Upon *Claudius* his marriage with *Agrippina,* he was recall'd from Banishment by her means, and made *Prætor,* then he forgets the Emperour, having no need of him, labours all he can to depress him and the hopeful *Brittanicus,* and procured his Pupil *Nero* to be adopted and design'd Successor, and the Emperours own Son to be disinherited; and against the Emperour whom he so much praised when he had need of him, after his death he writes a scurrilous Libel. In *Nero's* Court, how ungratefully doth he behave himself towards *Agrippina!* who although she were a wicked woman, yet she deserv'd well of him, and of her Son too, who yet never was at rest till he had taken away her life, and upon suspition cast in against her by this man. Afterwards not to mention that he made great haste to grow rich, which should not be the business of a Philosopher, towards *Nero* himself, how well did it become his Philosophy to play the Traitor against him, and to become a complice in the conspiracy of *Piso?* And then as good a Tragedian as he was, me thinks he doth in *extremo actu deficere,* when he must needs perswade *Paulina,* that excellent Lady his wife, to die with him: what should move him to desire it? it could in his opinion be no advantage to her, for he believ'd nothing of the immortality of the soul; I am not satisfied with the reason of *Tacitus, Ne sibi unice dilectam ad injurias relinqueret,* because he discredits it himself, in almost the next words, where he saith, *Nero* bore her no ill will at all, (and would not suffer her to die) it must surely be then, because he thought he had not liv'd long enough (being not above 114 years old, so much he was) and had not the fortitude to die, unless he might receive some confirmation in it by her example. Now let any man judge what a precious Legacy it is that he bequeaths by his nuncupative will to his friends in *Tacitus. Conversus ad amicos* (saith he) *quando meritis eorum referre gratiam prohiberetur, quod unum jam tamen et pulcherrimum habebat, imaginem vitæ suæ relinquere testatur.* It cannot be denied of him, that he hath said very

PART I.

Sect. 55.
Pag. 77.

well; but yet it must as well be affirmed, that his Practice hath run counter to his Theory, to use the Author's phrase.

The Scepticks *that affirmed they knew nothing.*] The ancient Philosophers are divided into three sorts, *Dogmatici, Academici, Sceptici*; the first were those that delivered their opinions positively; the second left a liberty of disputing *pro et contra*; the third declared that there was no knowledge of any thing, no not of this very proposition, that there is no knowledge, according to that,

——*Nihil sciri siquis putat, id quoq; nescit*
An sciri possit, quod se nil scire fatetur.

The Duke of Venice *that weds himself to the Sea by a Ring of Gold,* etc.] The Duke and Senate yearly on *Ascension-day* use to go in their best attire to the Haven of *Lido*, and there by throwing a Ring into the water, do take the Sea as their spouse. *Vid. Hist. Ital.* by *Will Thomas Cambrobrit. Busbequius* reports that there is a custom amongst the Turks, which they took from the Greek Priests, not much unlike unto this. *Cum Græcorum sacerdotibus mos sit certo veris tempore aquas consecrando mare clausum veluti reserare, ante quod tempus non facile se committunt fluctibus; ab ea Ceremonia nec Turcæ absunt. Busb. Ep. 3. legat. Tursic.*

But the Philosopher that threw his money into the Sea, to avoid avarice, etc.] This was *Apollonius Thyaneus*, who threw a great quantity of Gold into the Sea with these words, *Pessundo divitias, ne pessundarem ab illis. Polycrates* the Tyrant of *Samos* cast the best Jewel he had into the Sea, that thereby he might learn to compose himself against the vicissitude of Fortune.

There go so many circumstances to piece up one good action.] To make an action to be good, all the causes that concur must be good; but one bad amongst many good ones, is enough to make it vitious, according to the rule, *Bonum ex causa integra, malum ex partiali.*

Sect. 56.
Pag. 78.

The vulgarity of those judgements that wrap the Church of God in Strabo's *Cloak, and restrain it unto* Europe.] 'Tis *Strabonis tunica* in the translation, but *Chlamydi* would do better, which is the proper expression of the word that *Strabo* useth: it is not *Europe*, but the known part of the world that *Strabo* resembleth to a Cloak, and that is it the Author here alludeth to; but we have no reason to think that the resemblance of *Strabo* is very proper. *Vid.* Sir *Hen. Savil. in not. ad Tac. in vita Agricolæ.*

Sect. 57.
Pag. 79.

Those who upon a rigid Application of the Law, sentence Solomon *unto damnation,* etc.] St. *Aug.* upon *Psal.* 126. and in many other places, holds that *Solomon* is damned. Of the same opinion is *Lyra*, in 2 *Reg.* c. 7. and *Bellarm.* 1 *Tom. lib.* 1. *Controv.* c. 5.

THE SECOND PART

I WONDER *not at the* French *for their Frogs, Snails and Toad-* PART II.
stools.] Toad-stools are not peculiar to the *French;* they *Sect.* 1.
were a great delicacy among the *Romans*, as appears every *Pag.* 83.
where in *Martial.* It was conceived the Emperor *Claudius*
received his death by Poyson, which he took in Mushroom.
Suet. and *Tac.*

How among so many millions of faces, there should be none alike.] *Sect.* 2.
It is reported there have been some so much alike, that they *Pag.* 87.
could not be distinguished; as King *Antiochus*, and one
Antemon, a Plebeian of *Syria*, were so much alike, that *Laodice*,
the Kings widow, by pretending this man was the King,
dissembled the death of the King so long, till according to her
own mind, a Successor was chosen. *Cn. Pompeius*, and one
Vibius the Orator; *C. Plancus*, and *Rubrius* the Stage-player;
Cassius Severus the Orator, and one *Mirmello*; *M. Messala
Censorius*, and one *Menogenes*, were so much alike, that unless
it were by their habit, they could not be distinguished: but
this you must take upon the Faith of *Pliny* (*lib.* 7. *e.* 12.) and
Solinus, (*cap.* 6.) who as this Author tells elsewhere, are
Authors not very infallible.

What a βατροχομυομαχία *and hot skirmish is betwixt* S. *and* T. *Sect.* 3.
in Lucian.] In his *Dialog. judicium vocalium*, where there is *Pag.* 89.
a large Oration made to the Vowels, being Judges, by *Sigma*
against *Tau*, complaining that *Tau* has bereaved him of many
words, which should begin with *Sigma*.

Their Tongues are sharper than Actius *his razor.*] *Actius
Navius* was chief Augur, who (as the story saith) admonishing
Tarqu. Priscus that he should not undertake any action of
moment, without first consulting the Augur, the King (shewing
that he had little faith in his skill) demanded of him, whether
by the rules of his skill, what he had conceived in his mind
might be done: to whom when *Actius* had answered it might be
done, he bid him take a Whetstone which he had in his hand,
and cut it in two with a Razor; which accordingly the Augur
did. *Livy.* And therefore we must conceive it was very sharp.
Here the Adage was cross'd, ξυρὸς εἰς ἀκόνην, i.e. *novacula in
cotem. Vid. Erasm. Chiliad.*

It is not meer Zeal to Learning, or devotion to the Muses, that *Pag.* 90.
wiser Princes Patronize the Arts, etc. *but a desire to have their
names eterniz'd by the memory of their Writings.*] There is
a great Scholar, who took the boldness to tell a Prince so much.
*Est enim bonorum principum cum viris eruditis tacita quædam
naturalisque Societas, ut alteri ab alteris illustrentur, ac dum sibi
mutuo suffragantur, et gloria principibus, et doctis authoritas*

d

PART II. *concilietur.* Politian. *Ep. Ludovic. Sfort. quæ extat, lib.* 11. *Ep.*
Sect. 3. *ep.* 1. And to this Opinion astipulates a Country man of our
Pag. 90. own, whose words are these: *Ignotus esset Lucilius, nisi eum
Epistolæ Senecæ illustrarent. Laudibus Cæsareis plus Virgilius et
Varus Lucanusq; adjecerunt, quam immensum illud ærarium quo
urbem et orbem spoliavit. Nemo prudentiam Ithaci aut Pelidæ
vires agnosceret, nisi eas Homerus divino publicasset ingenio: unde
nihil mihi videtur consultius viro ad gloriam properanti fidelium
favore scriptorum.* Joan. Sarisb. *Polycrat. l.* 8. *c.* 14. And that
Princes are as much beholding to the Poets Pens as their own
Swords, *Horace* tells *Censorinus* with great confidence. *Od.* 8.
l. 4. *Non incisa notis,* etc.

Sect. 4.   *St.* Paul *that calls the* Cretians *Lyars, doth it but indirectly, and
Pag. 90. upon quotation of one of their own Poets.*] That is, *Epimenides ;* the
place is *Tit.* 1. *v.* 12. where *Paul* useth this verse, taken out of
Epimenides.

Κρῆτες ἀεὶ ψεῦσται, κακὰ θηρία, γαστέρες ἀργαί.

It is as bloody a thought in one way, as Nero's *was in another.
For by a word we wound a thousand.*] I suppose he alludes to
that passage in *Sueton.* in the life of *Nero,* where he relates that
a certain person upon a time, spoke in his hearing these words,

Ἐμοῦ θανόντος γαῖα μιχθήτω πυρί.

i.e. When I am dead let Earth be mingled with Fire. Whereupon the Emperour uttered these words, Ἐμοῦ ζῶντος, *i.e.* Yea
whilst 1 live: there by one word, he express'd a cruel thought,
which I think is the thing he meant ; this is more cruel than
the wish of *Caligula,* that the people of *Rome* had but one Neck,
that he might destroy them all at a blow.

Sect. 6.   *I cannot believe the story of the* Italian, *etc.*] It is reported
Pag. 95. that a certain *Italian* having met with one that had highly provoked him, put a Ponyard to his breast, and unless he would
blaspheme God, told him he would kill him, which the other
doing to save his life, the *Italian* presently kill'd him, to the
intent he might be damned, having no time of Repentance.

Sect. 7.   *I have no sins that want a Name.*] The Author in *cap. ult. lib.*
Pag. 97. *ult. Pseudodox.* speaking of the Act of carnality exercised by
the *Egyptian* Pollinctors with the dead carcasses, saith we want
a name for this, wherein neither *Petronius* nor *Martial* can
relieve us ; therefore I conceive the Author here means a
venereal sin.

This was the Temper of that Leacher that carnal'd with a Statua.]
The Latine Annotator upon this hath these words: *Romæ
refertur de Hispano quodam.* But certainly the Author means
the Statue of *Venus Gnidia* made by *Praxiteles,* of which a certain young man became so enamoured, that *Pliny* relates, *Ferunt*

amore captum cum delituisset noctu simulachro cohæsisse, ejusq; PART II.
cupiditatis esse indicem maculum. Lucian also has the story in Sect. 7.
his *Dialog.* [*Amores.*] Pag. 97.

And the constitution of Nero *in his Spintrian recreations.*] The
Author doth not mean the last *Nero*, but *Tiberius* the Emperour,
whose name was *Nero* too ; of whom *Sueton.* *Secessu vero Capreensi
etiam sellariam excogitavit sedem arcanarum libidinum, in quam
undique conquisiti puellarum et exoletorum greges monstrosiq; con-
cubitus repertores, quos spintrias appellabat, triplici serie connexi
invicem incestarent se coram ipso, ut adspectu deficientes libidines
excitaret.* Suet. *in Tib.* 43.

I have seen a Grammarian toure and plume himself over a single Sect. 8.
line in Horace, *and shew more pride,* etc.] *Movent mihi stomachum* Pag. 98.
*Grammatistæ quidam, qui cum duas tenuerint vocabulorum origines
ita se ostentant, ita venditant, ita circumferunt jactabundi, ut præ
ipsis pro nihilo habendos Philosophos arbitrentur.* Picus Mirand.
in Ep. ad Hermol. Barb. quæ extat lib. nono Epist. Politian.

> *Garsio quisq; duas postquam scit jungere partes,*
> *Sic stat, sic loquitur, velut omnes noverit artes.*

I cannot think that Homer *pin'd away upon the Riddle of the* Pag. 99.
Fishermen.] The History out of *Plutarch* is thus : Sailing from
Thebes to the Island *Ion*, being landed and set down upon the
shore, there happen'd certain Fishermen to pass by him, and he
asking them what they had taken, they made him this Enig-
matical answer, That what they had taken, they had left behind
them ; and what they had not taken, they had with them :
meaning, that because they could take no Fish, they went to
loose themselves ; and that all which they had taken, they had
killed, and left behind them, and all which they had not taken,
they had with them in their clothes : and that *Homer* being
struck with a deep sadness because he could not interpret this,
pin'd away, and at last dyed. *Pliny* alludes to this Riddle, in
his *Ep.* to his Friend *Fuscus*, where giving an account of spend-
ing his time in the Country, he tells him, *Venor aliquando, sed
non sine pugillaribus, ut quamvis nihil ceperim, non nihil referam.*
Plin. *Ep. lib. 9, Ep.* 36.

Or that Aristot.——*did ever drown himself upon the flux or
reflux of* Euripus.] *Laertius* reports that *Aristotle* dyed of a
disease at 63 years of age. For this and the last, see the Author
in *Pseudodox.*

Aristotle *doth but instruct us as* Plato *did him, to confute himself.*] In the matter of *Idea's*, Eternity of the world, etc.

I could be content that we might procreate like trees without con- Sect. 9.
junction, or that there were any way to perpetuate the world without Pag. 100.
*this trivial and vulgar way of Coition : It is the foolishest act a wise
man commits in all his life.*] There was a Physitian long before

PART II.

Sect. 9.
Pag. 100.

the Author, that was of the same opinion, *Hippocrates*; for which *vide A. Gel. l.* 19. *Noct. Attic. c.* 2. And so of late time was *Paracelsus*, who did undertake to prescribe a way for the generation of a man without coition. *Vide Campanel. de sensu rerum, in Append. ad* cap. 19. *l.* 4. *Monsieur Montaignes* words on this subject, are worth the reading; these they are: *Je trouve apres tout, que l'amour n'est autre chose que la fame de cette jouyssance, et considerant maintes fois la ridicule titillation de ce plaiser par ou il nous tient, les absurdes movements escervelez et estourdis dequoy il agite Zenon et Cratippus, ceste rage indiscrete, ce visage inflamme de fureur et de cruaute au plus doux effect de l'amour, et puis cette morgue grave severe et extatique en une action si folle, et que la supreme volupte aye du trainsy et du plaintiff commer la douleur, je croye qu'on se joue de nous, et que c'est par industrie que nature nous a laisse la plus trouble de nos actions les plus communes pour nous esgaller par la et apparier les fols et les sages, et nous et les bestes. Le plus contemplatif et prudent homme quand je l'imagin en cette assiette je le tien pour un affronteur, de faire le prudent et le contemplatif: ce sont les pieds du paon qui abbatent son orgueil. Nous mangeons bien et beuvons comme les bestes, mais ce ne sont pas actions, qui empeschent les operations de nostre ame, en celles-la nous gardons nostre advantage sur elles: cettecy met tout autre pensee sous le joug, abrutist et abesiit par son imperieuse authorite toute la Theology et Philosophy, qui est en Platon et si il ne s'en plaint pas. Par tout ailleurs vous pouvez garder quelque decence; toutes autres operations souffrent des Regles d'honestete: cettecy ne se peut seulement imaginer que vitieuse ou ridicule; trouvez y pour voir un proceder sage et discret. Alexander disoit qu'il se cognossoit principalement mortel par cette action et par le dormir: le sommeil suffoque et supprime les facultez de nostre ame, la besoigne les absorbe et dissipe de mesme. Certes c'est une marque non seulement de nostre corruption originelle, mais aussi de nostre vanite et disformite. D'un coste nature nous y pousse ayant attaché à ce desire la plus noble, utile et plaisante de toutes ses operations, et la nous laisse d'autre part accuser et fuyr comme insolent et dishoneste, en rougir et recommander l'abstinence,* etc. Montaign *liv.* 3. *chapit.* 5.

Sect. 10.
Pag. 103.

And may be inverted on the worst.] That is, that there are none so abandoned to vice, but they have some sprinklings of vertue. There are scarce any so vitious, but commend virtue in those that are endued with it, and do some things laudable themselves, as *Plin.* saith in *Panegyric. Machiavel* upon *Livy, lib.* 1. *cap.* 27. sets down the ensuing relation as a notable confirmation of this truth. *Julius Pontifex, ejus nominis secundus, anno salutis* 1505. *Bononiam exercitus duxit, ut Bentivolorum familiam, quæ ejus urbis imperium centum jam annos tenuerat, loco moveret. Eademque in expeditione etiam Johannem Pagolum, Bagloneum tyrannum Perusinum sua sede expellere decreverat, ut*

cæteros item, qui urbes Ecclesiæ per vim tenerent.   Ejus rei causa
cum ad Perusinam urbem accessisset, et notum jam omnibus esset
quid in animo haberet: tamen impatiens moræ, noluit exercitus
expectare, sed inermis quasi urbem ingressus est, in quam Johannes Pagolus defendendi sui causa, non exiguas copias contraxerat. Is autem eodem furore, quo res suas administrare solebat, una cum milite, cui custodiam sui corporis demandarat, sese in pontificis potestatem dedidit; à quo abductus est relictusque alius, qui Ecclesiæ nomine urbem gubernaret. Hac ipsa in re magnopere admirati sunt viri sapientes, qui Pontificem comitabantur, cum Pontificis ipsius temeritatem, cum abjectum vilemq; Johannis Pagoli animum: nec causam intelligebant, ob quam permotus idem Pagolus, hostem suum inermem (quod illi cum perpetua nominis sui memoria facere licebat) non subitò oppresserit, et tam pretiosa spolia diripuerit; cum Pontifex urbem ingressus fuisset, Cardinalibus tantum suis stipatus, qui pretiosissimas quasq; suarum rerum secum habebant. Neque enim credebatur Pagolus a tanto facinore vel sua bonitate, vel animi conscientia abstinuisse: quod in hominem sceleratum, qui et propria sorore utebatur, et consobrinos nepotesque dominandi causa e medio sustulerat hujusmodi pii affectus cadere non viderentur.   Cum igitur hac de re variæ essent sapientum virorum sententiæ; concluserunt tandem id ei accidisse, quod ita comparatum sit, ut homines neque plane pravi esse queant, neque perfecte boni.   Pravi perfecte esse nequeant, propterea quod, ubi tale quoddam scelus est, in quo aliquid magnifici ac generosi insit, id patrare non audeant.   Nam cum Pagolus neq; incestum prius horruisset, neque patricidio abstinuisset: tamen cum oblata esset occasio, pravi quidem sed memorabilis, atque æternæ memoriæ facinoris patrandi, id attentare non ausus fuit, cum id sine infamia prestare licuisset, quod rei magnitudo omnia priora scelera obtegere potuisset, et a periculo conservare.   Quibus accedit, quod illi gratulati fuissent etiam quam plurimi, si primus ausus esset Pontificibus monstrare rationem dominandi; totiusque humanæ vitæ usum ab illis nimis parvi pendi.

Poysons contain within themselves their own Antidote.] The Poyson of a Scorpion is not Poyson to it self, nor the Poyson of a Toad is not Poyson to it self; so that the sucking out of Poyson from persons infected by Psylls, (who are continually nourished with venomous aliment) without any prejudice to themselves, is the less to be wondred at.

The man without a Navil yet lives in me.] The Latine Annotator hath explicated this by *Homo non perfectus,* by which it seems he did not comprehend the Author's meaning; for the Author means *Adam,* and by a Metonymie original sin; for the Navil being onely of use to attract the aliment *in utero materno,* and *Adam* having no mother, he had no use of a Navil, and therefore it is not to be conceived he had any; and upon that ground the Author calls him the man without a Navil.

PART II.

Sect. 11.
Pag. 106.

Our grosser memories have then so little hold of our abstracted understandings, that they forget the story, and can onely relate to our awaked senses a confused and broken tale of that that hath pass'd.] For the most part it is so. In regard of the Author's expression of forgetting the story, though otherwise it be not very pertinent to this place, I shall set down a relation given by an English Gentleman, of two dreams that he had, wherein he did not forget the story, but (what is more strange) found his dreams verified. This it is.

Whilst I lived at *Prague*, and one night had sit up very late drinking at a feast, early in the morning the Sun beams glancing on my face, as I lay in my bed, I dreamed that a shadow passing by told me that my Father was dead ; at which awaking all in a sweat, and affected with this dream, I rose and wrote the day and hour, and all circumstances thereof in a Paperbook, which book with many other things I put into a Barrel, and sent it from *Prague* to *Stode,* thence to be conveyed into *England.* And now being at *Nurenburgh,* a Merchant of a noble Family well acquainted with me and my friends, arrived there, who told me my Father dyed some two months ago. I list not to write any lyes, but that which I write, is as true as strange. When I returned into *England* some four years after, I would not open the Barrel I sent from *Prague,* nor look into the Paper-book in which I had written this dream, till I had called my Sisters and some friends to be witnesses, where my self and they were astonished to see my written dream answer the very day of my Father's death.

I may lawfully swear that which my Kinsman hath heard witnessed by my brother *Henry* whilst he lived, that in my youth at *Cambridge,* I had the like dream of my Mother's death, where my brother *Henry* living with me, early in the morning I dreamed that my Mother passed by with a sad countenance, and told me that she could not come to my Commencement : I being within five months to proceed Master of Arts, and she having promised at that time to come to *Cambridge.* And when I related this dream to my brother, both of us awaking together in a sweat, he protested to me that he had dreamed the very same ; and when we had not the least knowledge of our Mother's sickness, neither in our youthful affections were any whit affected with the strangeness of this dream, yet the next Carrier brought us word of our Mother's death. Mr. *Fiennes Morison* in his Itinerary. I am not over-credulous of such relations, but methinks the circumstance of publishing it at such a time, when there were those living that might have disprov'd it, if it had been false, is a great argument of the truth of it.

Sect. 12.
Pag. 107.

I wonder the fancy of Lucan *and* Seneca *did not discover it.*] For they had both power from *Nero* to chuse their deaths.

To conceive our selves Urinals is not so ridiculous.] *Reperti sunt* PART II.
Galeno et Avicenna testibus qui se vasa fictilia crederent, et idcirco Sect. 13.
hominum attactum ne confringerentur solicite fugerent. Pontan. Pag. 108.
in Attic. bellar. (*Hist.* 22.) Which proceeds from extremity of
Melancholy.

    Aristot. *is too severe, that will not allow us to be truely liberal* Pag. 109.
without wealth.] *Aristot. l.* 1. *Ethic. c.* 8.

    Thy will be done though in mine own undoing.] This should be Sect. 15.
the wish of every man, and is of the most wise and knowing, Pag. 112.
Le Christien plus humble et plus sage et mieux recognoissant que c'est
que de luy se rapporte a son createur de choisir et ordonner ce qu' il
luy faut. Il ne le supplie dautre chose que sa volunte soit faite.
Montaign.

A Letter sent upon the information of Anim-adversions *to come forth, upon the imperfect and surreptitious copy of* Religio Medici, *whilst this true one was going to Press.*

HONOURED SIR, Give your Servant, who hath ever honour'd you, leave to take notice of a Book at present in the Press, intituled (as I am informed) *Animadversions* upon a Treatise lately printed under the name of *Religio Medici*; hereof, I am advertised, you have descended to be the Author. Worthy Sir, permit your Servant to affirm there is contain'd therein nothing that can deserve the Reason of your Contradictions, much less the Candor of your *Animadversions*: and to certifie the truth thereof, That Book (whereof I do acknowledge myself the Author) was penn'd many years past, and (what cannot escape your apprehension) with no intention for the Press, or the least desire to oblige the Faith of any man to its assertions. But what hath more especially emboldened my Pen unto you at present, is, That the same Piece, contrived in my private study, and as an Exercise unto my self, rather than Exercitation for any other, having past from my hand under a broken and imperfect Copy, by frequent transcription it still run forward into corruption, and

A

after the addition of some things, omission of others, & transposition of many, without my assent or privacy, the liberty of these times committed it unto the Press; whence it issued so disguised, the Author without distinction could not acknowledge it. Having thus miscarried, within a few weeks I shall, God willing, deliver unto the Press the true and intended Original (whereof in the mean time your worthy Self may command a view); otherwise when ever that Copy shall be extant, it will most clearly appear how far the Text hath been mistaken, and all Observations, Glosses, or Exercitations thereon, will in a great part impugn the Printer or Transcriber, rather than the Author. If after that, you shall esteem it worth your vacant hours to discourse thereon, you shall but take that liberty which I assume my self, that is, freely to abound in your sense, as I have done in my own. However you shall determine, you shall sufficiently honour me in the Vouchsafe of your Refute, and I oblige the whole World in the occasion of your Pen.

Your Servant.

T. B.

Norwich, *March* 3, 1642.

TO THE READER

CERTAINLY that man were greedy of Life, who
should desire to live when all the world were at
an end; and he must needs be very impatient,
who would repine at death in the society of all things
that suffer under it. Had not almost every man suffered
by the Press or were not the tyranny thereof become
universal, I had not wanted reason for complaint: but in
times wherein I have lived to behold the highest perversion of that excellent invention, the name of his Majesty
defamed, the Honour of Parliament depraved, the Writings of both depravedly, anticipatively, counterfeitly
imprinted; complaints may seem ridiculous in private
persons; and men of my condition may be as incapable
of affronts, as hopeless of their reparations. And truely
had not the duty I owe unto the importunity of friends,
and the allegiance I must ever acknowledge unto truth,
prevailed with me; the inactivity of my disposition
might have made these sufferings continual, and time that
brings other things to light, should have satisfied me in
the remedy of its oblivion. But because things evidently
false are not onely printed, but many things of truth
most falsely set forth, in this latter I could not but think
my self engaged. For though we have no power to
redress the former, yet in the other, reparation being
within our selves, I have at present represented unto the

3

world a full and intended Copy of that Piece, which was most imperfectly and surreptitiously published before.

This, I confess, about seven years past, with some others of affinity thereto, for my private exercise and satisfaction, I had at leisurable hours composed, which being communicated unto one, it became common unto many, and was by Transcription successively corrupted, untill it arrived in a most depraved Copy at the Press. He that shall peruse that Work, and shall take notice of sundry particularities and personal expressions therein, will easily discern the intention was not publick: and being a private Exercise directed to my self, what is delivered therein, was rather a memorial unto me, than an Example or Rule unto any other: and therefore if there be any singularity therein correspondent unto the private conceptions of any man, it doth not advantage them: or if dissentaneous thereunto, it no way over-throws them. It was penned in such a place, and with such disadvantage, that (I protest) from the first setting of pen unto paper, I had not the assistance of any good Book, whereby to promote my invention, or relieve my memory; and therefore there might be many real lapses therein, which others might take notice of, and more that I suspected my self. It was set down many years past, and was the sense of my conception at that time, not an immutable Law unto my advancing judgement at all times; and therefore there might be many things therein plausible unto my passed apprehension, which are not agreeable unto my present self. There are many things delivered Rhetorically, many expressions therein meerly Tropical, and as they best illustrate my intention; and therefore also there are many things to be taken in a soft and flexible sense, and not to be called unto the rigid test of Reason. Lastly, all that is contained therein is in submission unto maturer discernments; and, as I have declared, shall no further father them than the best and learned judgments shall authorize them: under favour of which considerations I have made its secrecy publick, and committed the truth thereof to every Ingenuous Reader.

THO. BROWNE.

RELIGIO MEDICI

FOR my Religion, though there be several
Circumstances that might perswade the
World I have none at all, as the general
scandal of my Profession, the natural course of
my Studies, the indifferency of my Behaviour and
Discourse in matters of Religion, neither violently
Defending one, nor with that common ardour and
contention Opposing another; yet, in despight hereof,
I dare, without usurpation, assume the honourable
Stile of a Christian. Not that I meerly owe this Title
to the Font, my Education, or Clime wherein I was
born, as being bred up either to confirm those Principles my parents instilled into my Understanding, or
by a general consent proceed in the Religion of my
Country: But having in my riper years and confirmed
Judgment, seen and examined all, I find my self
obliged by the Principles of Grace, and the Law of
mine own Reason, to embrace no other name but this:
Neither doth herein my zeal so far make me forget the
general Charity I owe unto Humanity, as rather to
hate than pity *Turks*, *Infidels*, and (what is worse)
Jews; rather contenting my self to enjoy that happy
Stile, than maligning those who refuse so glorious a
Title.

7

BUT because the Name of a Christian is become too general to express our Faith, there being a Geography of Religion as well as Lands, and every Clime distinguished not only by their Laws and Limits, but circumscribed by their Doctrines and Rules of Faith; to be particular, I am of that Reformed new-cast Religion, wherein I dislike nothing but the Name; of the same belief our Saviour taught, the Apostles disseminated, the Fathers authorized, and the Martyrs confirmed, but by the sinister ends of Princes, the ambition and avarice of Prelates, and the fatal corruption of times, so decayed, impaired, and fallen from its native Beauty, that it required the careful and charitable hands of these times to restore it to its primitive Integrity. Now the accidental occasion whereupon, the slender means whereby the low and abject condition of the Person by whom so good a work was set on foot, which in our Adversaries beget contempt and scorn, fills me with wonder, and is the very same Objection the insolent Pagans first cast at Christ and his Disciples.

YET have I not so shaken hands with those desperate Resolutions, who had rather venture at large their decayed bottom, than bring her in to be new trimm'd in the Dock; who had rather promiscuously retain all, than abridge any, and obstinately be what they are, than what they have been, as to stand in Diameter and Swords point with them: We have reformed from them, not against them; for omitting those Improperations and Terms of Scurrility betwixt us, which only difference our Affections, and not our Cause, there is between us one common Name and Appellation, one Faith and necessary body of Principles common to us both; and therefore I am not scrupulous to converse and live with them, to enter their Churches in defect of ours, and either pray with them, or for them. I could never perceive any rational Consequence from those many Texts which prohibit the Children of *Israel* to pollute themselves with the Temples of the Heathens; we being all Christians, and not divided by such detested impieties as might prophane our Prayers, or the place wherein we make them; or that a resolved Conscience may not adore her Creator any where, especially in places devoted to his Service; where, if their Devotions offend him, mine may please him; if theirs prophane it, mine may hallow it. Holy-water and Crucifix (dangerous to the common people) deceive not my judgment, nor abuse my devotion at all: I am, I confess, naturally inclined to that which misguided Zeal terms Superstition: my common conversation I do acknowledge austere, my behaviour full of rigour, sometimes not without morosity; yet at my Devotion I love to use the civility of my knee, my hat, and hand, with all those outward and sensible motions which may express or promote my invisible Devotion. I should violate my own arm rather than a Church; nor willingly deface the name of Saint or Martyr. At the sight of a Cross or Crucifix I can dispense with my hat, but scarce with the thought or memory of my Saviour: I cannot laugh at, but rather pity, the fruitless journeys of Pilgrims, or contemn the miserable condition of Fryars; for though misplaced in Circumstances there is something in it of Devotion. I could never hear the *Ave-Mary* Bell[1] without an elevation, or think it a sufficient warrant, because they erred in one circumstance, for me to err in all, that is, in

[1] *A Church Bell that tolls every day at six and twelve of the clock; at the hearing whereof, every one in what place soever, either of House or Street, betakes himself to his prayer which is commonly directed to the Virgin.*

silence and dumb contempt; whilst therefore they
directed their Devotions to Her, I offered mine to
God, and rectifie the Errors of their Prayers by
rightly ordering mine own: At a solemn Procession I
have wept abundantly, while my consorts blind with
opposition and prejudice, have fallen into an excess of
scorn and laughter: There are questionless both in
Greek, *Roman*, and *African* Churches, Solemnities
and Ceremonies, whereof the wiser Zeals do make a
Christian use, and stand condemned by us, not as
evil in themselves, but as allurements and baits of
superstition to those vulgar heads that look asquint
on the face of Truth, and those unstable Judgments
that cannot resist in the narrow point and centre
of Virtue without a reel or stagger to the Circumference.

SECT.
4

AS there were many Reformers, so likewise
many Reformations; every Country proceeding in a particular way and method,
according as their national Interest, together with
their Constitution and Clime, inclined them; some
angrily, and with extremity; others calmly, and with
mediocrity; not rending, but easily dividing the
community, and leaving an honest possibility of a reconciliation; which though peaceable Spirits do desire,
and may conceive that revolution of time and the
mercies of God may effect, yet that judgment that
shall continue the present antipathies between the two
extreams, their contrarieties in condition, affection,
and opinion, may with the same hopes expect an
union in the Poles of Heaven.

BUT to difference my self nearer, and draw into a lesser Circle, There is no Church, whose every part so squares unto my Conscience; whose Articles, Constitutions, and Customs, seem so consonant unto reason, and as it were framed to my particular Devotion, as this whereof I hold my Belief, the Church of *England*, to whose Faith I am a sworn Subject; and therefore in a double Obligation subscribe unto her Articles, and endeavour to observe her Constitutions; whatsoever is beyond, as points indifferent, I observe according to the rules of my private reason, or the humour and fashion of my Devotion; neither believing this, because *Luther* affirmed it, or disproving that, because *Calvin* hath disavouched it. I condemn not all things in the Council of *Trent*, nor approve all in the Synod of *Dort*. In brief, where the Scripture is silent, the Church is my Text; where that speaks, 'tis but my comment: where there is a joynt silence of both, I borrow not the rules of my Religion from *Rome* or *Geneva*, but the dictates of my own reason. It is an unjust scandal of our adversaries, and a gross errour in our selves, to compute the Nativity of our Religion from *Henry* the Eighth, who, though he rejected the Pope, refus'd not the faith of *Rome*, and effected no more than what his own Predecessors desired and assayed in Ages past, and was conceived the State of *Venice* would have attempted in our days. It is as uncharitable a point in us to fall upon those popular scurrilities and opprobrious scoffs of the Bishop of *Rome*, to whom as a temporal Prince, we owe the duty of good language: I confess there is cause of passion between us; by his sentence I stand excommunicated, Heretick is the best language he affords me; yet can no ear witness I ever returned him the

name of Antichrist, Man of Sin, or Whore of *Babylon*.
It is the method of Charity to suffer without reaction:
Those usual Satyrs and invectives of the Pulpit may
perchance produce a good effect on the vulgar, whose
ears are opener to Rhetorick than Logick; yet do they
in no wise confirm the faith of wiser Believers, who
know that a good cause needs not to be pardon'd by
passion, but can sustain it self upon a temperate
dispute.

SECT.
6

I COULD never divide my self from any man upon
the difference of an opinion, or be angry with
his judgment for not agreeing with me in that
from which perhaps within a few days I should dissent
my self. I have no Genius to disputes in Religion,
and have often thought it wisdom to decline them,
especially upon a disadvantage, or when the cause of
truth might suffer in the weakness of my patronage:
Where we desire to be informed, 'tis good to contest
with men above our selves; but to confirm and establish our opinions, 'tis best to argue with judgments
below our own, that the frequent spoils and Victories
over their reasons may settle in ourselves an esteem
and confirmed Opinion of our own. Every man is not
a proper Champion for Truth, nor fit to take up the
Gauntlet in the cause of Verity: Many, from the
ignorance of these Maximes, and an inconsiderate Zeal
unto Truth, have too rashly charged the Troops of
Error, and remain as Trophies unto the enemies of
Truth: A man may be in as just possession of Truth
as of a City, and yet be forced to surrender; 'tis therefore far better to enjoy her with peace, than to hazzard
her on a battle: if therefore there rise any doubts in
my way, I do forget them, or at least defer them till

my better setled judgement and more manly reason be able to resolve them; for I perceive every man's own reason is his best *Œdipus*, and will upon a reasonable truce, find a way to loose those bonds wherewith the subtleties of error have enchained our more flexible and tender judgements. In Philosophy, where Truth seems double-fac'd, there is no man more Paradoxical than my self: but in Divinity I love to keep the Road; and, though not in an implicite, yet an humble faith, follow the great wheel of the Church, by which I move, not reserving any proper Poles or motion from the Epicycle of my own brain; by this means I leave no gap for Heresie, Schismes, or Errors, of which at present I hope I shall not injure Truth to say I have no taint or tincture: I must confess my greener studies have been polluted with two or three, not any begotten in the latter Centuries, but old and obsolete, such as could never have been revived, but by such extravagant and irregular heads as mine: for indeed Heresies perish not with their Authors, but, like the river *Arethusa*, though they lose their currents in one place, they rise up again in another: One General Council is not able to extirpate one single Heresie; it may be cancell'd for the present; but revolution of time, and the like aspects from Heaven, will restore it, when it will flourish till it be condemned again. For as though there were a *Metempsuchosis*, and the soul of one man passed into another; Opinions do find, after certain Revolutions, men and minds like those that first begat them. To see ourselves again, we need not look for Plato's year:[1] every man is not only himself; there hath been many *Diogenes*, and as many *Timons*, though but few of that name; men are liv'd over again, the world is now as it was in Ages past; there

[1] *A revolution of certain thousand years, when all things should return unto their former estate, and he be teaching again in his School as when he delivered this Opinion.*

was none then, but there hath been some one since that
Parallels him, and is, as it were, his revived self.

NOW the first of mine was that of the
Arabians, That the Souls of men perished with their Bodies, but should yet
be raised again at the last day: not that I did
absolutely conceive a mortality of the Soul; but if
that were, which Faith, not Philosophy hath yet
thoroughly disproved, and that both entred the grave
together, yet I held the same conceit thereof that we
all do of the body, that it should rise again. Surely
it is but the merits of our unworthy Natures, if we
sleep in darkness until the last Alarm. A serious
reflex upon my own unworthiness did make me backward from challenging this prerogative of my Soul;
so that I might enjoy my Saviour at the last, I could
with patience be nothing almost unto Eternity. The
second was that of *Origen*, That God would not persist in his vengeance for ever, but after a definite time
of his wrath, he would release the damned Souls from
torture: which error I fell into upon a serious contemplation of the great Attribute of God, his Mercy;
and did a little cherish it in my self, because I found
therein no malice, and a ready weight to sway me from
the other extream of despair, whereunto Melancholy
and Contemplative Natures are too easily disposed. A
third there is which I did never positively maintain or
practise, but have often wished it had been consonant
to Truth, and not offensive to my Religion, and that is
the Prayer for the dead; whereunto I was inclin'd
from some charitable inducements, whereby I could
scarce contain my Prayers for a friend at the ringing
of a Bell, or behold his Corps without an Orison for

his Soul : 'Twas a good way, methought, to be remembred by posterity, and far more noble than an History. These opinions I never maintained with pertinacy, or endeavoured to inveagle any mans belief unto mine, nor so much as ever revealed or disputed them with my dearest friends; by which means I neither propagated them in others, nor confirmed them in my self; but suffering them to flame upon their own substance, without addition of new fuel, they went out insensibly of themselves: therefore these Opinions, though condemned by lawful Councels, were not Heresies in me, but bare Errors, and single Lapses of my understanding, without a joynt depravity of my will : Those have not onely depraved understandings, but diseased affections, which cannot enjoy a singularity without an Heresie, or be the Author of an Opinion without they be of a Sect also; this was the villany of the first Schism of *Lucifer*, who was not content to err alone, but drew into his Faction many Legions; and upon this experience he tempted only *Eve*, as well understanding the Communicable nature of Sin, and that to deceive but one, was tacitely and upon consequence to delude them both.

THAT Heresies should arise, we have the Prophesie of Christ; but that old ones should be abolished, we hold no prediction. That there must be Heresies, is true, not only in our Church, but also in any other : even in doctrines heretical, there will be super-heresies; and Arians not only divided from their Church, but also among themselves : for heads that are disposed unto Schism and complexionally propense to innovation, are naturally disposed for a community ; nor will be ever confined unto

SECT.
8

the order or œconomy of one body; and therefore
when they separate from others, they knit but loosely
among themselves, nor contented with a general breach
or dichotomy with their Church, do subdivide and mince
themselves almost into Atoms. 'Tis true, that men of
singular parts and humours have not been free from
singular opinions and conceits in all Ages; retaining
something, not only beside the opinion of his own
Church or any other, but also any particular Author;
which notwithstanding a sober Judgment may do
without offence or heresie; for there is yet, after all
the Decrees of Councils and the niceties of Schools,
many things untouch'd, unimagin'd, wherein the
liberty of an honest reason may play and expa-
tiate with security, and far without the circle of an
Heresie.

SECT.
9

AS for those wingy Mysteries in Divinity, and
airy subtleties in Religion, which have
unhing'd the brains of better heads, they
never stretched the *Pia Mater* of mine. Methinks
there be not impossibilities enough in Religion for an
active faith; the deepest Mysteries ours contains have
not only been illustrated, but maintained, by Syllogism
and the rule of Reason. I love to lose my self in a
mystery, to pursue my Reason to an *O altitudo!* 'Tis
my solitary recreation to pose my apprehension with
those involved Ænigma's and riddles of the Trinity,
with Incarnation, and Resurrection. I can answer all
the Objections of Satan and my rebellious reason with
that odd resolution I learned of *Tertullian, Certum est
quia impossibile est.* I desire to exercise my faith in
the difficultest point; for to credit ordinary and visible
objects is not faith, but perswasion. Some believe the

better for seeing Christ's Sepulchre; and when they
have seen the Red Sea, doubt not of the Miracle.
Now contrarily, I bless my self and am thankful that
I lived not in the days of Miracles, that I never saw
Christ nor His Disciples; I would not have been one
of those *Israelites* that pass'd the Red Sea, nor one of
Christ's patients on whom he wrought his wonders;
then had my faith been thrust upon me, nor should I
enjoy that greater blessing pronounced to all that
believe and saw not. 'Tis an easie and necessary
belief, to credit what our eye and sense hath examined :
I believe he was dead, and buried, and rose again;
and desire to see him in his glory, rather than to contemplate him in his Cenotaphe or Sepulchre. Nor is
this much to believe; as we have reason, we owe this
faith unto History : they only had the advantage of a
bold and noble Faith, who lived before his coming,
who upon obscure prophesies and mystical Types
could raise a belief, and expect apparent impossibilities.

'TIS true, there is an edge in all firm belief, and   SECT.
with an easie Metaphor we may say, the   10
Sword of Faith; but in these obscurities I
rather use it in the adjunct the Apostle gives it, a
Buckler; under which I conceive a wary combatant
may lye invulnerable. Since I was of understanding
to know we knew nothing, my reason hath been more
pliable to the will of Faith; I am now content to
understand a mystery without a rigid definition, in an
easie and Platonick description. That [1] allegorical [1] *Sphæra*
description of *Hermes*, pleaseth me beyond all the *cujus cen-*
trum ubique,
Metaphysical definitions of Divines : where I cannot *circumfer-*
entia nullibi.
satisfie my reason, I love to humour my fancy : I had

B

as live you tell me that *anima est angelus hominis, est
Corpus Dei*, as *Entelechia* ; *Lux est umbra Dei*, as *actus
perspicui* ; where there is an obscurity too deep for our
Reason, 'tis good to sit down with a description, peri-
phrasis, or adumbration ; for by acquainting our Reason
how unable it is to display the visible and obvious
effects of nature, it becomes more humble and sub-
missive unto the subtleties of Faith ; and thus I teach
my haggard and unreclaimed reason to stoop unto the
lure of Faith. I believe there was already a tree whose
fruit our unhappy Parents tasted, though, in the same
Chapter when God forbids it, 'tis positively said, the
plants of the field were not yet grown, for God had not
caus'd it to rain upon the earth. I believe that the
Serpent (if we shall literally understand it) from his
proper form and figure, made his motion on his belly
before the curse. I find the tryal of the Pucellage and
virginity of Women, which God ordained the *Jews*, is
very fallible. Experience and History informs me, that
not onely many particular Women, but likewise whole
Nations have escaped the curse of Childbirth, which
God seems to pronounce upon the whole Sex ; yet do
I believe that all this is true, which indeed my Reason
would perswade me to be false ; and this I think is no
vulgar part of Faith, to believe a thing not only above,
but contrary to Reason, and against the Arguments of
our proper Senses.

SECT.
11
IN my solitary and retired imagination (*Neque
enim cum porticus, aut me lectulus accepit, desum
mihi*) I remember I am not alone, and therefore
forget not to contemplate him and his Attributes who
is ever with me, especially those two mighty ones, his
Wisdom and Eternity ; with the one I recreate, with

the other I confound my understanding: for who can
speak of Eternity without a solœcism, or think thereof
without an Extasie? Time we may comprehend; 'tis
but five days elder than our selves, and hath the same
Horoscope with the World; but to retire so far back
as to apprehend a beginning, to give such an infinite
start forwards as to conceive an end in an essence that
we affirm hath neither the one nor the other, it puts
my Reason to *St. Paul's* Sanctuary: my Philosophy
dares not say the Angels can do it; God hath not
made a Creature that can comprehend him; 'tis a
privilege of His own nature. *I am that I am,* was his
own definition unto *Moses*; and 'twas a short one, to
confound mortality, that durst question God, or ask
him what he was; indeed he only is; all others have
and shall be; but in Eternity there is no distinction
of Tenses; and therefore that terrible term *Predestina-
tion,* which hath troubled so many weak heads to
conceive, and the wisest to explain, is in respect to
God no prescious determination of our Estates to come,
but a definitive blast of his Will already fulfilled, and
at the instant that he first decreed it; for to his
Eternity which is indivisible and all together, the last
Trump is already sounded, the reprobates in the flame,
and the blessed in *Abraham's* bosome. *St. Peter* speaks
modestly, when he saith, a thousand years to God are
but as one day: for to speak like a Philosopher, those
continued instances of time which flow into a thousand
years, make not to Him one moment; what to us is to
come, to his Eternity is present, his whole duration
being but one permanent point, without Succession,
Parts, Flux, or Division.

THERE is no Attribute that adds more difficulty to the mystery of the Trinity, where, though in a relative way of Father and Son, we must deny a priority. I wonder how *Aristotle* could conceive the World eternal, or how he could make good two Eternities: his similitude of a Triangle, comprehended in a square, doth somewhat illustrate the Trinity of our Souls, and that the Triple Unity of God; for there is in us not three, but a Trinity of Souls, because there is in us, if not three distinct Souls, yet differing faculties, that can and do subsist apart in different Subjects, and yet in us are thus united as to make but one Soul and substance: if one Soul were so perfect as to inform three distinct Bodies, that were a pretty Trinity: conceive, the distinct number of three, not divided nor separated by the Intellect, but actually comprehended in its Unity, and that is a perfect Trinity. I have often admired the mystical way of *Pythagoras*, and the secret Magick of numbers. Beware of Philosophy, is a precept not to be received in too large a sense; for in this Mass of Nature there is a set of things that carry in their Front, though not in Capital Letters, yet in Stenography and short Characters, something of Divinity, which to wiser Reasons serve as Luminaries in the Abyss of Knowledge, and to judicious beliefs as Scales and Roundles to mount the Pinacles and highest pieces of Divinity. The severe Schools shall never laugh me out of the Philosophy of *Hermes*, that this visible World is but a Picture of the invisible, wherein as in a Pourtraict, things are not truely, but in equivocal shapes, and as they counterfeit some more real substance in that invisible Fabrick.

THAT other Attribute wherewith I recreate my devotion, is his Wisdom, in which I am happy; and for the contemplation of this only, do not repent me that I was bred in the way of Study: The advantage I have of the vulgar, with the content and happiness I conceive therein, is an ample recompence for all my endeavours, in what part of knowledge soever. Wisdom is his most beauteous Attribute, no man can attain unto it, yet *Solomon* pleased God when he desired it. He is wise, because he knows all things; and he knoweth all things, because he made them all: but his greatest knowledge is in comprehending that he made not, that is, himself. And this is also the greatest knowledge in man. For this do I honour my own profession, and embrace the Counsel even of the Devil himself: had he read such a Lecture in Paradise as he did at *Delphos*,[1] we had better known our selves; nor had we stood in fear to know him. I know he is wise in all, wonderful in what we conceive, but far more in what we comprehend not; for we behold him but asquint, upon reflex or shadow; our understanding is dimmer than *Moses* Eye; we are ignorant of the back-parts or lower side of his Divinity, therefore to prie into the maze of his Counsels is not only folly in man, but presumption even in Angels; like us, they are his Servants, not his Senators; he holds no Counsel, but that mystical one of the Trinity, wherein though there be three Persons, there is but one mind that decrees without Contradiction: nor needs he any; his actions are not begot with deliberation, his Wisdom naturally knows what's best; his intellect stands ready fraught with the superlative and purest *Idea's* of goodness; consultation and election, which are two motions in us, make but one in him; his

[1] Γνῶθι σεαυτὸν, *Nosce teip-sum.*

actions springing from his power at the first touch of
his will.   These are Contemplations Metaphysical: my
humble speculations have another Method, and are
content to trace and discover those expressions he hath
left in his Creatures, and the obvious effects of Nature;
there is no danger to profound these mysteries, no
sanctum sanctorum in Philosophy: the World was
made to be inhabited by Beasts, but studied and con-
templated by Man: 'tis the Debt of our Reason we
owe unto God, and the homage we pay for not being
Beasts; without this, the World is still as though it
had not been, or as it was before the sixth day, when
as yet there was not a Creature that could conceive, or
say there was a World.   The wisdom of God receives
small honour from those vulgar Heads that rudely
stare about, and with a gross rusticity admire his
works; those highly magnifie him, whose judicious
inquiry into His Acts, and deliberate research into
His Creatures, return the duty of a devout and learned
admiration.   Therefore,

> Search while thou wilt, and let thy reason go,
> To ransome truth, even to th' Abyss below;
> Rally the scattered Causes; and that line
> Which Nature twists, be able to untwine:
> It is thy Makers will, for unto none,
> But unto reason can he e'er be known.
> The Devils do know Thee, but those damn'd Meteors
> Build not thy Glory, but confound thy Creatures,
> Teach my indeavours so thy works to read,
> That learning them in thee, I may proceed.
> Give thou my reason that instructive flight,
> Whose weary wings may on thy hands still light.
> Teach me to soar aloft, yet ever so,
> When neer the Sun, to stoop again below.
> Thus shall my humble Feathers safely hover,
> And, though near Earth, more than the Heavens discover.

And then at last, when homeward I shall drive,
Rich with the Spoils of nature to my hive,
There will I sit like that industrious Flie,
Buzzing thy praises, which shall never die,
Till death abrupts them, and succeeding Glory
Bid me go on in a more lasting story.

And this is almost all wherein an humble Creature may endeavour to requite and some way to retribute unto his Creator: for if not he that saith, *Lord, Lord,* but *he that doth the will of his Father, shall be saved*; certainly our wills must be our performances, and our intents make out our Actions; otherwise our pious labours shall find anxiety in our Graves, and our best endeavours not hope, but fear a resurrection.

THERE is but one first cause, and four second causes of all things; some are without efficient, as God; others without matter, as Angels; some without form, as the first matter: but every Essence created or uncreated, hath its final cause, and some positive end both of its Essence and Operation; this is the cause I grope after in the works of Nature; on this hangs the providence of God: to raise so beauteous a structure as the World and the Creatures thereof, was but his Art; but their sundry and divided operations, with their predestinated ends, are from the Treasure of his wisdom. In the causes, nature, and affections of the Eclipses of the Sun and Moon, there is most excellent speculation; but to profound farther, and to contemplate a reason why his providence hath so disposed and ordered their motions in that vast circle as to conjoyn and obscure each other, is a sweeter piece of Reason, and a diviner point of Philosophy; therefore sometimes, and in some

SECT.
14

things, there appears to me as much Divinity in *Galen* his books *De Usu Partium*, as in *Suarez* Metaphysicks: Had *Aristotle* been as curious in the enquiry of this cause as he was of the other, he had not left behind him an imperfect piece of Philosophy, but an absolute tract of Divinity.

SECT.
15 *NATURA nihil aget frustra*, is the only indisputed Axiome in Philosophy; there are no *Grotesques* in nature; not any thing framed to fill up empty Cantons, and unnecessary spaces: in the most imperfect Creatures, and such as were not preserved in the Ark, but having their Seeds and Principles in the womb of Nature, are every where, where the power of the Sun is; in these is the Wisdom of his hand discovered. Out of this rank *Solomon* chose the object of his admiration; indeed what reason may not go to School to the wisdom of Bees, Ants, and Spiders? what wise hand teacheth them to do what reason cannot teach us? ruder heads stand amazed at those prodigious pieces of Nature, Whales, Elephants, Dromidaries and Camels; these, I confess, are the Colossus and Majestick pieces of her hand: but in these narrow Engines there is more curious Mathematicks; and the civility of these little Citizens, more neatly sets forth the Wisdom of their Maker. Who admires not *Regio-Montanus* his Fly beyond his Eagle, or wonders not more at the operation of two Souls in those little Bodies, than but one in the Trunk of a Cedar? I could never content my contemplation with those general pieces of wonder, the Flux and Reflux of the Sea, the increase of *Nile*, the conversion of the Needle to the North; and have studied to match and parallel those in the more obvious and neglected pieces of Nature, which without further trouble I can do in the Cosmography of my self; we carry with us the wonders we seek without us: There is all *Africa* and her prodigies in us; we are that bold and adventurous piece of nature, which he that studies wisely learns in a *compendium* what others labour at in a divided piece and endless volume.

THUS there are two Books from which I collect my Divinity; besides that written one of God, another of his servant Nature, that universal and publick Manuscript, that lies expans'd unto the Eyes of all, those that never saw him in the one, have discovered him in the other: this was the Scripture and Theology of the Heathens: the natural motion of the Sun made them more admire him, than its supernatural station did the Children of *Israel*; the ordinary effects of nature wrought more admiration in them than in the other all his Miracles; surely the Heathens knew better how to joyn and read these mystical Letters than we Christians, who cast a more careless Eye on these common Hieroglyphicks, and disdain to suck Divinity from the flowers of Nature. Nor do I so forget God as to adore the name of Nature; which I define not with the Schools, to be the principle of motion and rest, but that streight and regular line, that settled and constant course the Wisdom of God hath ordained the actions of His creatures, according to their several kinds. To make a revolution every day, is the Nature of the Sun, because of that necessary course which God hath ordained it, from which it cannot swerve but by a faculty from that voice which first did give it motion. Now this course of Nature God seldome alters or

SECT.
16

perverts, but like an excellent Artist hath so contrived his work, that with the self same instrument, without a new creation, he may effect his obscurest designs. Thus he sweetneth the Water with a Word, preserveth the Creatures in the Ark, which the blast of his mouth might have as easily created; for God is like a skilful Geometrician, who when more easily and with one stroak of his Compass he might describe or divide a right line, had yet rather do this in a circle or longer way; according to the constituted and fore-laid principles of his Art: yet this rule of his he doth sometimes pervert, to acquaint the World with his Prerogative, lest the arrogancy of our reason should question his power, and conclude he could not; and thus I call the effects of Nature the works of God, whose hand and instrument she only is; and therefore to ascribe his actions unto her, is to devolve the honour of the principal agent upon the instrument; which if with reason we may do, then let our hammers rise up and boast they have built our houses, and our pens receive the honour of our writings. I hold there is a general beauty in the works of God, and therefore no deformity in any kind or species of creature whatsoever: I cannot tell by what Logick we call a *Toad,* a *Bear,* or an *Elephant* ugly, they being created in those outward shapes and figures which best express the actions of their inward forms. And having past that general Visitation of God, who saw that all that he had made was good, that is, conformable to his Will, which abhors deformity, that is the rule of order and beauty; there is no deformity but in Monstrosity; wherein, notwithstanding, there is a kind of Beauty. Nature so ingeniously contriving the irregular parts, as they become sometimes more remarkable than the

principal Fabrick. To speak yet more narrowly, there
was never any thing ugly or mis-shapen, but the Chaos;
wherein, notwithstanding, to speak strictly, there was
no deformity, because no form; nor was it yet impreg-
nant by the voice of God; now Nature was not at
variance with Art, nor Art with Nature, they being
both servants of his providence: Art is the perfection
of Nature: were the World now as it was the sixth
day, there were yet a Chaos: Nature hath made one
World, and Art another. In brief, all things are
artificial; for Nature is the Art of God.

THIS is the ordinary and open way of his
providence, which Art and Industry have
in a good part discovered, whose effects we
may foretel without an Oracle: to foreshew these, is
not Prophesie, but Prognostication. There is another
way, full of Meanders and Labyrinths, whereof the
Devil and Spirits have no exact Ephemerides, and that
is a more particular and obscure method of his providence, directing the operations of individuals and single
Essences: this we call Fortune, that serpentine and
crooked line, whereby he draws those actions his
wisdom intends, in a more unknown and secret way:
This cryptick and involved method of his providence
have I ever admired, nor can I relate the History of
my life, the occurrences of my days, the escapes of
dangers, and hits of chance, with a *Bezo las Manos*
to Fortune, or a bare Gramercy to my good Stars:
Abraham might have thought the *Ram* in the thicket
came thither by accident; humane reason would have
said, that meer chance conveyed *Moses* in the Ark to
the sight of *Pharoh's* daughter: what a Labyrinth is
there in the story of *Joseph*, able to convert a Stoick?

SECT.
17

Surely there are in every man's Life certain rubs, doub-
lings, and wrenches, which pass a while under the effects
of chance, but at the last well examined, prove the
meer hand of God. 'Twas not dumb chance, that to
discover the Fougade or Powder-plot, contrived a mis-
carriage in the Letter. I like the victory of 88. the
better for that one occurrence, which our enemies
imputed to our dishonour and the partiality of
Fortune, to wit, the tempests and contrariety of
Winds. King *Philip* did not detract from the Nation,
when he said, he sent his Armado to fight with men,
and not to combate with the Winds. Where there is
a manifest disproportion between the powers and forces
of two several agents, upon a Maxime of reason we may
promise the Victory to the Superiour; but when unexpected accidents slip in, and unthought of occur-
ences intervene, these must proceed from a power that
owes no obedience to those Axioms; where, as in the
writing upon the wall, we may behold the hand, but
see not the spring that moves it. The success of that
petty province of *Holland* (of which the Grand *Seignour*
proudly said, if they should trouble him as they did
the *Spaniard*, he would send his men with shovels and
pick-axes, and throw it into the Sea,) I cannot altogether ascribe to the ingenuity and industry of the
people, but the mercy of God, that hath disposed them
to such a thriving Genius; and to the will of his Providence, that disposeth her favour to each Country in
their pre-ordinate season. All cannot be happy at
once ; for, because the glory of one State depends upon
the ruine of another, there is a revolution and vicissitude of their greatness, and must obey the swing of
that wheel, not moved by Intelligences, but by the
hand of God, whereby all Estates arise to their *Zenith*

and Vertical points according to their predestinated
periods. For the lives, not only of men, but of
Commonwealths, and the whole World, run not upon
an Helix that still enlargeth; but on a Circle, where
arriving to their Meridian, they decline in obscurity,
and fall under the Horizon again.

THESE must not therefore be named the effects
of Fortune, but in a relative way, and as we
term the works of Nature: it was the ignorance of mans reason that begat this very name, and by
a careless term miscalled the Providence of God: for
there is no liberty for causes to operate in a loose and
stragling way; nor any effect whatsoever, but hath its
warrant from some universal or superiour Cause. 'Tis
not a ridiculous devotion to say a pray before a game
at Tables; for even in *sortilegies* and matters of
greatest uncertainty, there is a settled and preordered
course of effects. It is we that are blind, not Fortune:
because our Eye is too dim to discover the mystery of
her effects, we foolishly paint her blind, and hoodwink
the Providence of the Almighty. I cannot justifie that
contemptible Proverb, *That fools only are Fortunate*;
or that insolent Paradox, *That a wise man is out of the
reach of Fortune*; much less those opprobrious epithets
of Poets, *Whore, Bawd,* and *Strumpet*. 'Tis, I confess,
the common fate of men of singular gifts of mind to be
destitute of those of Fortune, which doth not any way
deject the Spirit of wiser judgments, who throughly
understand the justice of this proceeding; and being
inrich'd with higher donatives, cast a more careless eye
on these vulgar parts of felicity. It is a most unjust
ambition to desire to engross the mercies of the
Almighty, not to be content with the goods of mind,

SECT.
18

without a possession of those of body or Fortune: and it is an error worse than heresie, to adore these complemental and circumstantial pieces of felicity, and undervalue those perfections and essential points of happiness wherein we resemble our Maker. To wiser desires it is satisfaction enough to deserve, though not to enjoy the favours of Fortune; let Providence provide for Fools: 'tis not partiality, but equity in God, who deals with us but as our natural Parents; those that are able of Body and Mind, he leaves to their deserts; to those of weaker merits he imparts a larger portion, and pieces out the defect of one, by the access of the other. Thus have we no just quarrel with Nature, for leaving us naked; or to envy the Horns, Hoofs, Skins, and Furs of other Creatures, being provided with Reason, that can supply them all. We need not labour with so many Arguments to confute Judicial Astrology; for if there be a truth therein, it doth not injure Divinity: if to be born under *Mercury* disposeth us to be witty, under *Jupiter* to be wealthy; I do not owe a Knee unto those, but unto that merciful Hand that hath ordered my indifferent and uncertain nativity unto such benevolous Aspects. Those that hold that all things are governed by Fortune, had not erred, had they not persisted there: The *Romans* that erected a temple to Fortune, acknowledged therein, though in a blinder way, somewhat of Divinity; for in a wise supputation all things begin and end in the Almighty. There is a nearer way to Heaven than *Homer's* Chain; an easy Logick may conjoin heaven and Earth, in one Argument, and with less than a *Sorites* resolve all things unto God. For though we christen effects by their most sensible and nearest Causes, yet is God the true and infallible Cause of all, whose concourse though it be general, yet doth it subdivide it self into the particular Actions of every thing, and is that Spirit, by which each singular Essence not only subsists, but performs its operation.

THE bad construction, and perverse comment on these pair of second Causes, or visible hands of God, have perverted the Devotion of many unto Atheism; who, forgetting the honest Advisoes of Faith, have listened unto the conspiracy of Passion and Reason. I have therefore always endeavoured to compose those Feuds and angry Dissensions between Affection, Faith and Reason: For there is in our Soul a kind of Triumvirate, or triple Government of three Competitors, which distracts the Peace of this our Common-wealth, not less than did that other the State of *Rome*.

As Reason is a Rebel unto Faith, so Passion unto Reason: As the Propositions of Faith seem absurd unto Reason, so the Theorems of Reason unto Passion, and both unto Reason; yet a moderate and peaceable discretion may so state and order the matter, that they may be all Kings, and yet make but one Monarchy, every one exercising his Soveraignty and Prerogative in a due time and place, according to the restraint and limit of circumstance. There is, as in Philosophy, so in Divinity, sturdy doubts and boisterous Objections, wherewith the unhappiness of our knowledge too nearly acquainteth us. More of these no man hath known than my self, which I confess I conquered, not in a martial posture, but on my Knees. For our endeavours are not only to combat with doubts, but always to dispute with the Devil: the villany of that Spirit takes a hint of Infidelity

SECT.
19

from our Studies, and by demonstrating a naturality in one way, makes us mistrust a miracle in another. Thus having perused the *Archidoxes* and read the secret Sympathies of things, he would disswade my belief from the miracle of the Brazen Serpent, make me conceit that Image worked by Sympathy, and was but an *Ægyptian* trick to cure their Diseases without a miracle. Again, having seen some experiments of *Bitumen*, and having read far more of *Naphtha*, he whispered to my curiosity the fire of the Altar might be natural ; and bid me mistrust a miracle in *Elias*, when he entrenched the Altar round with Water : for that inflamable substance yields not easily unto Water, but flames in the Arms of its Antagonist. And thus would he inveagle my belief to think the combustion of *Sodom* might be natural, and that there was an Asphaltick and Bituminous nature in that Lake before the Fire of *Gomorrah*. I know that *Manna* is now plentifully gathered in *Calabria* ; and *Josephus* tells me, in his days it was as plentiful in *Arabia* ; the Devil therefore made the *quære*, Where was then the miracle in the days of *Moses* : the *Israelite* saw but that in his time, the Natives of those Countries behold in ours. Thus the Devil played at Chess with me, and yielding a Pawn, thought to gain a Queen of me, taking advantage of my honest endeavours ; and whilst I laboured to raise the structure of my Reason, he strived to undermine the edifice of my Faith.

SECT.
20

NEITHER had these or any other ever such advantage of me, as to incline me to any point of Infidelity or desperate positions of Atheism ; for I have been these many years of opinion there was never any. Those that held Religion was the difference of Man from Beasts, have spoken probably, and proceed upon a principle as inductive as the other. That doctrine of *Epicurus*, that denied the Providence of God, was no Atheism, but a magnificent and high strained conceit of his Majesty, which he deemed too sublime to mind the trivial Actions of those inferiour Creatures. That fatal Necessity of the Stoicks, is nothing but the immutable Law of his will. Those that heretofore denied the Divinity of the Holy Ghost, have been condemned, but as Hereticks ; and those that now deny our Saviour (though more than Hereticks) are not so much as Atheists: for though they deny two persons in the Trinity, they hold as we do, there is but one God.

That Villain and Secretary of Hell, that composed that miscreant piece of the Three Impostors, though divided from all Religions, and was neither Jew, Turk, nor Christian, was not a positive Atheist. I confess every country hath its *Machiavel*, every Age its *Lucian*, whereof common Heads must not hear, nor more advanced Judgments too rashly venture on: It is the Rhetorick of Satan, and may pervert a loose or prejudicate belief.

I CONFESS I have perused them all, and can discover nothing that may startle a discreet belief; yet are there heads carried off with the Wind and breath of such motives. I remember a Doctor in Physick of *Italy*, who could not perfectly believe the immortality of the Soul, because *Galen* seemed to make a doubt thereof. With another I was familiarly acquainted in *France*, a Divine, and a man of singular parts, that on the same point was so plunged and gravelled with [1]three lines of *Seneca*, that

SECT. 21

[1] *Post Mortem nihil est,*

c

SECT.
21

*ipsaque
Mors nihil.
Mors indi-
vidua est,
noxia cor-
pori, nec
patiens ani-
mæ ... Toti
morimur,
nullaque
pars manet
nostri.*

all our Antidotes, drawn from both Scripture and
Philosophy, could not expel the poyson of his errour.
There are a set of Heads, that can credit the relations
of Mariners, yet question the Testimonies of St. *Paul*;
and peremptorily maintain the traditions of *Ælian* or
Pliny, yet in Histories of Scripture raise Queries and
Objections, believing no more than they can parallel
in humane Authors. I confess there are in Scripture
Stories that do exceed the Fables of Poets, and to a
captious Reader sound like *Garagantua* or *Bevis*:
Search all the Legends of times past, and the fabulous
conceits of these present, and 'twill be hard to find one
that deserves to carry the Buckler unto *Sampson*; yet
is all this of an easie possibility, if we conceive a divine
concourse, or an influence but from the little Finger of
the Almighty. It is impossible that either in the discourse of man, or in the infallible Voice of God, to the
weakness of our apprehensions, there should not appear
irregularities, contradictions, and antinomies: my self
could shew a Catalogue of doubts, never yet imagined
nor questioned, as I know, which are not resolved at
the first hearing; not fantastick Queries or Objections
of Air; for I cannot hear of Atoms in Divinity. I can
read the History of the Pigeon that was sent out of
the Ark, and returned no more, yet not question how
she found out her Mate that was left behind: That
Lazarus was raised from the dead, yet not demand
where in the interim his Soul awaited; or raise a
Law-case, whether his Heir might lawfully detain his
inheritance bequeathed unto him by his death, and he,
though restored to life, have no Plea or Title unto his
former possessions. Whether *Eve* was framed out of
the left side of *Adam*, I dispute not; because I stand
not yet assured which is the right side of a man, or

whether there be any such distinction in Nature: that
she was edified out of the Rib of *Adam*, I believe, yet
raise no question who shall arise with that Rib at the
Resurrection. Whether *Adam* was an Hermaphrodite,
as the Rabbins contend upon the Letter of the Text,
because it is contrary to reason, there should be an
Hermaphrodite before there was a Woman; or a composition of two Natures before there was a second composed. Likewise, whether the World was created in
Autumn, Summer, or the Spring, because it was created
in them all; for whatsoever Sign the Sun possesseth,
those four Seasons are actually existent: It is the Nature
of this Luminary to distinguish the several Seasons of
the year, all which it makes at one time in the whole
Earth, and successive in any part thereof. There are
a bundle of curiosities, not only in Philosophy, but in
Divinity, proposed and discussed by men of most supposed abilities, which indeed are not worthy our vacant
hours, much less our serious Studies. Pieces only fit
to be placed in *Pantagruel's* Library, or bound up with *In Rabbe-*
Tartaretus, *De modo Cacandi.* *lais.*

THESE are niceties that become not those that SECT.
peruse so serious a Mystery: There are 22
others more generally questioned and called
to the Bar, yet methinks of an easie and possible truth.
'Tis ridiculous to put off, or down the general Flood
of *Noah* in that particular inundation of *Deucalion*:
that there was a Deluge once, seems not to me so
great a Miracle, as that there is not one always. How
all the kinds of Creatures, not only in their own bulks,
but with a competency of food and sustenance, might
be preserved in one Ark, and within the extent of
three hundred Cubits, to a reason that rightly examines

it, will appear very feasible. There is another secret not contained in the Scripture, which is more hard to comprehend, and put the honest Father to the refuge of a Miracle: and that is, not only how the distinct pieces of the World, and divided Islands should be first planted by men, but inhabited by Tigers, Panthers, and Bears. How *America* abounded with Beasts of prey, and noxious Animals, yet contained not in it that necessary Creature, a Horse, is very strange. By what passage those, not only Birds, but dangerous and unwelcome Beasts, came over: How there be Creatures there (which are not found in this Triple Continent); all which must needs be strange unto us, that hold but one Ark, and that the Creatures began their progress from the Mountains of *Ararat*: They who to salve this would make the Deluge particular, proceed upon a principle that I can no way grant; not only upon the negative of holy Scriptures, but of mine own Reason, whereby I can make it probable, that the World was as well peopled in the time of *Noah,* as in ours; and fifteen hundred years to people the World, as full a time for them, as four thousand years since have been to us. There are other assertions and common Tenents drawn from Scripture, and generally believed as Scripture, whereunto notwithstanding, I would never betray the liberty of my Reason. 'Tis a Paradox to me, that *Methusalem* was the longest liv'd of all the Children of *Adam*: and no man will be able to prove it; when from the process of the Text, I can manifest it may be otherwise. That *Judas* perished by hanging himself, there is no certainty in Scripture: though in one place it seems to affirm it, and by a doubtful word hath given occasion to translate it; yet in another place, in a more punctual

description, it makes it improbable, and seems to overthrow it. That our Fathers, after the Flood, erected
the Tower of *Babel* to preserve themselves against a
second Deluge, is generally opinioned and believed,
yet is there another intention of theirs expressed in
Scripture : Besides, it is improbable from the circumstance of the place, that is, a plain in the Land of
Shinar : These are no points of Faith, and therefore
may admit a free dispute. There are yet others, and
those familiarly concluded from the Text, wherein
(under favour) I see no consequence : the Church of
Rome, confidently proves the opinion of Tutelary
Angels, from that Answer when *Peter* knockt at the
Door ; *'Tis not he, but his Angel;* that is, might some
say, his Messenger, or some body from him ; for so the
Original signifies, and is as likely to be the doubtful
Families meaning. This exposition I once suggested
to a young Divine, that answered upon this point ; to
which I remember the *Franciscan* Opponent replyed
no more, but That it was a new, and no authentick
interpretation.

THESE are but the conclusions and fallible
discourses of man upon the Word of God,
for such I do believe the holy Scriptures :
yet were it of man, I could not chuse but say, it was
the singularest and superlative piece that hath been
extant since the Creation : were I a Pagan, I should
not refrain the Lecture of it ; and cannot but commend
the judgment of *Ptolomy*, that thought not his Library
compleat without it. The Alcoran of the *Turks*
(I speak without prejudice) is an ill composed Piece,
containing in it vain and ridiculous Errors in Philosophy, impossibilities, fictions, and vanities beyond

SECT.
23

laughter, maintained by evident and open Sophisms, the Policy of Ignorance, deposition of Universities, and banishment of Learning, that hath gotten Foot by Arms and violence: This without a blow, hath disseminated it self through the whole Earth. It is not unremarkable what *Philo* first observed, That the Law of *Moses* continued two thousand years without the least alteration; whereas, we see, the Laws of other Common-weals do alter with occasions; and even those, that pretended their Original from some Divinity, to have vanished without trace or memory. I believe besides *Zoroaster*, there were divers that writ before *Moses*, who, notwithstanding, have suffered the common fate of time. Mens Works have an age like themselves; and though they out-live their Authors, yet have they a stint and period to their duration: This only is a work too hard for the teeth of time, and cannot perish but in the general Flames, when all things shall confess their Ashes.

SECT.
24

I HAVE heard some with deep sighs lament the lost lines of *Cicero*; others with as many groans deplore the combustion of the Library of *Alexandria*: for my own part, I think there be too many in the World, and could with patience behold the urn and ashes of the *Vatican*, could I, with a few others, recover the perished leaves of *Solomon*. I would not omit a Copy of *Enoch's* Pillars, had they many nearer Authors than *Josephus*, or did not relish somewhat of the Fable. Some men have written more than others have spoken; [1]*Pineda* quotes more Authors in one work, than are necessary in a whole World. Of those three great inventions in *Germany*, there are two which are not without their incommodities, and

[1] Pineda *in his* Monarchica Ecclesiastica *quotes one thousand and forty Authors.*

'tis disputable whether they exceed not their use and commodities. 'Tis not a melancholy *Utinam* of my own, but the desires of better heads, that there were a general Synod; not to unite the incompatible difference of Religion, but for the benefit of learning, to reduce it as it lay at first, in a few, and solid Authors; and to condemn to the fire those swarms & millions of *Rhapsodies* begotten only to distract and abuse the weaker judgements of Scholars, and *to maintain the trade and mystery of Typographers*.

I CANNOT but wonder with what exception the Samaritans could confine their belief to the Pentateuch, or five Books of *Moses*. I am ashamed at the Rabbinical Interpretation of the Jews, upon the Old Testament, as much as their defection from the New. And truly it is beyond wonder, how that contemptible and degenerate issue of *Jacob*, once so devoted to Ethnick Superstition, and so easily seduced to the Idolatry of their Neighbours, should now in such an obstinate and peremptory belief adhere unto their own Doctrine, expect impossibilities, and, in the face and eye of the Church, persist without the least hope of Conversion. This is a vice in them, that were a vertue in us; for obstinacy in a bad Cause is but constancy in a good. And herein I must accuse those of my own Religion; for there is not any of such a fugitive Faith, such an unstable belief, as a Christian; none that do so oft transform themselves, not unto several shapes of Christianity and of the same Species, but unto more unnatural and contrary Forms, of Jew and Mahometan; that, from the name of Saviour, can condescend to the bare term of Prophet; and from an old belief that he is come, fall

SECT.
25

to a new expectation of his coming. It is the promise of Christ to make us all one Flock; but how and when this Union shall be, is as obscure to me as the last day. Of those four Members of Religion we hold a slender proportion; there are, I confess, some new additions, yet small to those which accrew to our Adversaries, and those only drawn from the revolt of Pagans, men but of negative Impieties, and such as deny Christ, but because they never heard of him: but the Religion of the Jew is expressly against the Christian, and the Mahometan against both. For the Turk, in the bulk he now stands, he is beyond all hope of conversion; if he fall asunder, there may be conceived hopes, but not without strong improbabilities. The Jew is obstinate in all fortunes; the persecution of fifteen hundred years hath but confirmed them in their Errour: they have already endured whatsoever may be inflicted, and have suffered, in a bad cause, even to the condemnation of their enemies. Persecution is a bad and indirect way to plant Religion: It hath been the unhappy method of angry Devotions, not only to confirm honest Religion, but wicked Heresies, and extravagant Opinions. It was the first stone and Basis of our Faith; none can more justly boast of Persecutions, and glory in the number and valour of Martyrs; for, to speak properly, those are true and almost only examples of fortitude: Those that are fetch'd from the field, or drawn from the actions of the Camp, are not oft-times so truely precedents of valour as audacity, and at the best attain but to some bastard piece of fortitude: If we shall strictly examine the circumstances and requisites which *Aristotle* requires to true and perfect valour, we shall find the name only in his Master *Alexander*, and as little in that Roman Worthy,

Julius Cæsar ; and if any, in that easie and active way
have done so nobly as to deserve that name, yet in the
passive and more terrible piece these have surpassed,
and in a more heroical way may claim the honour of
that Title. 'Tis not in the power of every honest
Faith to proceed thus far, or pass to Heaven through
the flames ; every one hath it not in that full measure,
nor in so audacious and resolute a temper, as to endure
those terrible tests and trials ; who notwithstanding,
in a peaceable way do truely adore their Saviour,
and have (no doubt) a Faith acceptable in the eyes
of God.

NOW as all that dye in the War are not
termed Souldiers ; so neither can I properly
term all those that suffer in matters of
Religion, Martyrs. The Council of *Constance* condemns *John Huss* for an Heretick ; the Stories of his
own Party stile him a Martyr : He must needs offend
the Divinity of both, that says he was neither the
one nor the other : There are many (questionless)
canonised on earth, that shall never be Saints in
Heaven ; and have their names in Histories and
Martyrologies, who in the eyes of God are not so
perfect Martyrs, as was that wise Heathen *Socrates*,
that suffered on a fundamental point of Religion, the
Unity of God. I have often pitied the miserable
Bishop that suffered in the cause of *Antipodes*, yet
cannot chuse but accuse him of as much madness, for
exposing his living on such a trifle ; as those of ignorance and folly, that condemned him. I think my
conscience will not give me the lye, if I say there are
not many extant that in a noble way fear the face of
death less than myself ; yet, from the moral duty I owe

SECT.
26

to the Commandment of God, and the natural respects that I tender unto the conservation of my essence and being, I would not perish upon a Ceremony, Politick points, or indifferency: nor is my belief of that untractible temper, as not to bow at their obstacles, or connive at matters wherein there are not manifest impieties: The leaven therefore and ferment of all, not only Civil, but Religious actions, is Wisdom; without which, to commit our selves to the flames is Homicide, and (I fear) but to pass through one fire into another.

SECT.
27

THAT Miracles are ceased, I can neither prove, nor absolutely deny, much less define the time and period of their cessation: that they survived Christ, is manifest upon the Record of Scripture: that they out-lived the Apostles also, and were revived at the Conversion of Nations, many years after, we cannot deny, if we shall not question those Writers whose testimonies we do not controvert in points that make for our own opinions; therefore that may have some truth in it that is reported by the Jesuites of their Miracles in the *Indies*; I could wish it were true, or had any other testimony than their own Pens. They may easily believe those Miracles abroad, who daily conceive a greater at home, the transmutation of those visible elements into the Body and Blood of our Saviour: for the conversion of Water into Wine, which he wrought in *Cana*, or what the Devil would have had him done in the Wilderness, of Stones into Bread, compared to this, will scarce deserve the name of a Miracle. Though indeed to speak properly, there is not one Miracle greater than another, they being the extraordinary effects of the Hand of

God, to which all things are of an equal facility; and
to create the World as easie as one single Creature.
For this is also a Miracle, not onely to produce effects
against, or above Nature, but before Nature; and to
create Nature as great a Miracle as to contradict or
transcend her. We do too narrowly define the Power
of God, restraining it to our capacities. I hold that
God can do all things; how he should work contradictions, I do not understand, yet dare not therefore
deny. I cannot see why the Angel of God should
question *Esdras* to recal the time past, if it were
beyond his own power; or that God should pose
mortality in that, which he was not able to perform
himself. I will not say God cannot, but he will not
perform many things, which we plainly affirm he
cannot: this I am sure is the mannerliest proposition,
wherein, notwithstanding, I hold no Paradox. For
strictly his power is the same with his will, and they
both with all the rest do make but one God.

THEREFORE that Miracles have been, I do
believe; that they may yet be wrought by
the living, I do not deny: but have no confidence in those which are fathered on the dead; and this
hath ever made me suspect the efficacy of reliques, to
examine the bones, question the habits and appur-
tenances of Saints, and even of Christ himself. I
cannot conceive why the Cross that *Helena* found, and
whereon Christ himself dyed, should have power to
restore others unto life: I excuse not *Constantine* from
a fall off his Horse, or a mischief from his enemies,
upon the wearing those nails on his bridle, which our
Saviour bore upon the Cross in his hands. I compute
among *Piæ fraudes*, nor many degrees before con-

SECT.
28

secrated Swords and Roses, that which *Baldwyn,* King of *Jerusalem,* return'd the *Genovese* for their cost and pains in his War, to wit, the ashes of *John* the Baptist. Those that hold the sanctity of their Souls doth leave behind a tincture and sacred faculty on their bodies, speak naturally of Miracles, and do not salve the doubt. Now one reason I tender so little Devotion unto Reliques, is, I think, the slender and doubtful respect I have always held unto Antiquities: for that indeed which I admire, is far before Antiquity, that is, Eternity; and that is, God himself; who, though he be styled the ancient of days, cannot receive the adjunct of Antiquity, who was before the World, and shall be after it, yet is not older than it; for in his years there is no Climacter; his duration is Eternity, and far more venerable than Antiquity.

SECT.
29

BUT above all things I wonder how the curiosity of wiser heads could pass that great and indisputable Miracle, the cessation of Oracles; and in what swoun their Reasons lay, to content themselves, and sit down with such a far-fetch'd and ridiculous reason as *Plutarch* alleadgeth for it. The Jews, that can believe the supernatural Solstice of the Sun in the days of *Joshua,* have yet the impudence to deny the Eclipse, which every Pagan confessed, at his death: but for this, it is evident beyond all contradiction,[1] the Devil himself confessed it. Certainly it is not a warrantable curiosity, to examine the verity of Scripture by the concordance of humane history, or seek to confirm the Chronicle of *Hester* or *Daniel* by the authority of *Megasthenes* or *Herodotus.* I confess, I have had an unhappy curiosity this way, till I laughed my self out of it with a piece of *Justine,*

[1] *In his Oracle to* Augustus.

where he delivers that the Children of *Israel* for being scabbed were banished out of *Egypt*. And truely since I have understood the occurrences of the World, and know in what counterfeit shapes, and deceitful vizards times present represent on the stage things past; I do believe them little more then things to come. Some have been of my opinion, and endeavoured to write the History of their own lives; wherein *Moses* hath outgone them all, and left not onely the story of his life, but as some will have it, of his death also.

IT is a riddle to me, how this story of Oracles hath not worm'd out of the World that doubtful conceit of Spirits and Witches; how so many learned heads should so far forget their Metaphysicks, and destroy the ladder and scale of creatures, as to question the existence of Spirits: for my part, I have ever believed, and do now know, that there are Witches: they that doubt of these, do not onely deny them, but spirits; and are obliquely and upon consequence a sort not of Infidels, but Atheists. Those that to confute their incredulity desire to see apparitions, shall questionless never behold any, nor have the power to be so much as Witches; the Devil hath them already in a heresie as capital as Witchcraft; and to appear to them, were but to convert them. Of all the delusions wherewith he deceives mortality, there is not any that puzleth me more than the Legerdemain of *Changelings*; I do not credit those transformations of reasonable creatures into beasts, or that the Devil hath a power to transpeciate a man into a Horse, who tempted Christ (as a trial of his Divinity) to convert but stones into bread. I could believe that Spirits use

SECT.
30

with man the act of carnality, and that in both sexes;
I conceive they may assume, steal, or contrive a
body, wherein there may be action enough to content decrepit lust, or passion to satisfie more active
veneries ; yet in both, without a possibility of
generation : and therefore that opinion that Antichrist
should be born of the Tribe of *Dan*, by conjunction
with the Devil, is ridiculous, and a conceit fitter for a
Rabbin than a Christian.   I hold that the Devil doth
really possess some men, the spirit of Melancholly
others, the spirit of Delusion others ; that as the Devil
is concealed and denyed by some, so God and good
Angels are pretended by others whereof the late defection of the Maid of *Germany* hath left a pregnant
example.

SECT. AGAIN, I believe that all that use sorceries,
31   incantations, and spells, are not Witches,
             or, as we term them, Magicians ; I conceive
there is a traditional Magick, not learned immediately
from the Devil, but at second hand from his Scholars,
who having once the secret betrayed, are able, and do
emperically practise without his advice, they both
proceeding upon the principles of Nature ; where
actives, aptly conjoyned to disposed passives, will
under any Master produce their effects.   Thus I
think at first a great part of Philosophy was Witchcraft, which being afterward derived to one another,
proved but Philosophy, and was indeed no more but
the honest effects of Nature : What invented by us is
Philosophy, learned from him is Magick.   We do
surely owe the discovery of many secrets to the discovery of good and bad Angels.   I could never pass
that sentence of *Paracelsus*, without an asterisk, or

annotation; [1] *Ascendens constellatum multa revelat,* *quærentibus magnalia naturæ,* i.e. *opera Dei.* I do think that many mysteries ascribed to our own inventions, have been the courteous revelations of Spirits; for those noble essences in Heaven bear a friendly regard unto their fellow Natures on Earth; and therefore believe that those many prodigies and ominous prognosticks, which fore-run the ruines of States, Princes, and private persons, are the charitable premonitions of good Angels, which more careless enquiries term but the effects of chance and nature.

[1] *Thereby is meant our good Angel appointed us from our Nativity.*

NOW, besides these particular and divided Spirits, there may be (for ought I know) an universal and common Spirit to the whole World. It was the opinion of *Plato,* and it is yet of the *Hermetical* Philosophers: if there be a common nature that unites and tyes the scattered and divided individuals into one species, why may there not be one that unites them all? However, I am sure there is a common Spirit that plays within us, yet makes no part of us; and that is the Spirit of God, the fire and scintillation of that noble and mighty Essence, which is the life and radical heat of Spirits, and those essences that know not the vertue of the Sun, a fire quite contrary to the fire of Hell: This is that gentle heat that broodeth on the waters, and in six days hatched the World; this is that irradiation that dispels the mists of Hell, the clouds of horrour, fear, sorrow, despair; and preserves the region of the mind in serenity: Whatsoever feels not the warm gale and gentle ventilation of this Spirit, (though I feel his pulse) I dare not say he lives; for truely without this, to me there is no heat

SECT.
32

under the Tropick; nor any light, though I dwelt in the body of the Sun.

> *As when the labouring Sun hath wrought his track*
> *Up to the top of lofty* Cancers *back,*
> *The ycie Ocean cracks, the frozen pole*
> *Thaws with the heat of the Celestial coale;*
> *So when thy absent beams begin t' impart*
> *Again a Solstice on my frozen heart,*
> *My winter's ov'r; my drooping spirits sing,*
> *And every part revives into a Spring.*
> *But if thy quickening beams a while decline,*
> *And with their light bless not this Orb of mine,*
> *A chilly frost surpriseth every member,*
> *And in the midst of* June *I feel* December.
> *O how this earthly temper doth debase*
> *The noble Soul in this her humble place.*
> *Whose wingy nature ever doth aspire*
> *To reach that place whence first it took its fire.*
> *These flames I feel, which in my heart do dwell,*
> *Are not thy beams, but take their fire from Hell.*
> *O quench them all, and let thy light divine*
> *Be as the Sun to this poor Orb of mine;*
> *And to thy sacred Spirit convert those fires,*
> *Whose earthly fumes choak my devout aspires.*

SECT. 33 THEREFORE for Spirits, I am so far from denying their existence, that I could easily believe, that not onely whole Countries, but particular persons, have their Tutelary and Guardian Angels: It is not a new opinion of the Church of *Rome*, but an old one of *Pythagoras* and *Plato*; there is no heresie in it; and if not manifestly defin'd in Scripture, yet is it an opinion of a good and wholesome use in the course and actions of a mans life, and would serve as an *Hypothesis* to salve many doubts, whereof common Philosophy affordeth no solution. Now if you demand my opinion and Metaphysicks of their natures, I confess them very shallow, most of them in a negative way, like that of God; or in a

comparative, between our selves and fellow-creatures;
for there is in this Universe a Stair, or manifest Scale
of creatures, rising not disorderly, or in confusion, but
with a comely method and proportion. Between creatures of meer existence and things of life, there is a large
disproportion of nature; between plants and animals
or creatures of sense, a wider difference; between them
and man, a far greater: and if the proportion hold
one, between Man and Angels there should be yet a
greater. We do not comprehend their natures, who
retain the first definition of *Porphyry*, and distinguish
them from our selves by immortality; for before his
Fall, 'tis thought, Man also was Immortal; yet must
we needs affirm that he had a different essence from
the Angels; having therefore no certain knowledge of
their Natures, 'tis no bad method of the Schools, whatsoever perfection we find obscurely in our selves, in a
more compleat and absolute way to ascribe unto them.
I believe they have an extemporary knowledge, and
upon the first motion of their reason do what we
cannot without study or deliberation; that they know
things by their forms, and define by specifical difference
what we describe by accidents and properties; and
therefore probabilities to us may be demonstrations
unto them: that they have knowledge not onely of
the specifical, but numerical forms of individuals, and
understand by what reserved difference each single
Hypostasis (besides the relation to its species) becomes
its numerical self. That as the Soul hath a power to
move the body it informs, so there's a faculty to move
any, though inform none; ours upon restraint of time,
place, and distance; but that invisible hand that conveyed *Habakkuk* to the Lyons Den, or *Philip* to *Azotus*,
infringeth this rule, and hath a secret conveyance,

D

wherewith mortality is not acquainted : if they have that intuitive knowledge, whereby as in reflexion they behold the thoughts of one another, I cannot peremptorily deny but they know a great part of ours. They that to refute the Invocation of Saints, have denied that they have any knowledge of our affairs below, have proceeded too far, and must pardon my opinion, till I can thoroughly answer that piece of Scripture, *At the conversion of a sinner the Angels in Heaven rejoyce.* I cannot with those in that great Father securely interpret the work of the first day, *Fiat lux,* to the creation of Angels, though I confess there is not any creature that hath so neer a glympse of their nature, as light in the Sun and Elements. We stile it a bare accident, but where it subsists alone, 'tis a spiritual Substance, and may be an Angel : in brief, conceive light invisible, and that is a Spirit.

SECT.
34
THESE are certainly the Magisterial and master-pieces of the Creator, the Flower, or (as we may say) the best part of nothing, actually existing, what we are but in hopes and probability ; we are onely that amphibious piece between a corporal and spiritual Essence, that middle form that links those two together, and makes good the Method of God and Nature, that jumps not from extreams, but unites the incompatible distances by some middle and participating natures : that we are the breath and similitude of God, it is indisputable, and upon record of holy Scripture ; but to call ourselves a Microcosm, or little World, I thought it only a pleasant trope of Rhetorick, till my neer judgement and second thoughts told me there was a real truth therein : for first we are a rude mass, and in the rank of creatures, which onely

are, and have a dull kind of being, not yet privileged
with life, or preferred to sense or reason ; next we live
the life of Plants, the life of Animals, the life of Men,
and at last the life of Spirits, running on in one mysterious nature those five kinds of existences, which
comprehend the creatures not onely of the World, but
of the Universe ; thus is man that great and true
Amphibium, whose nature is disposed to live not onely
like other creatures in divers elements, but in divided
and distinguished worlds : for though there be but one
to sense, there are two to reason, the one visible, the
other invisible, whereof *Moses* seems to have left description, and of the other so obscurely, that some
parts thereof are yet in controversie. And truely for
the first chapters of *Genesis*, I must confess a great
deal of obscurity ; though Divines have to the power
of humane reason endeavoured to make all go in a
literal meaning, yet those allegorical interpretations
are also probable, and perhaps the mystical method
of *Moses* bred up in the Hieroglyphical Schools of the
Egyptians.

NOW for that immaterial world, methinks we
need not wander so far as beyond the first
moveable ; for even in this material Fabrick
the spirits walk as freely exempt from the affection of
time, place, and motion, as beyond the extreamest circumference : do but extract from the corpulency of
bodies, or resolve things beyond their first matter, and
you discover the habitation of Angels, which if I call
the ubiquitary and omnipresent essence of God, I hope
I shall not offend Divinity : for before the Creation of
the World God was really all things. For the Angels
he created no new World, or determinate mansion, and

therefore they are everywhere where is his Essence, and do live at a distance even in himself. That God made all things for man, is in some sense true, yet not so far as to subordinate the Creation of those purer Creatures unto ours, though as ministring Spirits they do, and are willing to fulfil the will of God in these lower and sublunary affairs of man : God made all things for himself, and it is impossible he should make them for any other end than his own Glory ; it is all he can receive, and all that is without himself : for honour being an external adjunct, and in the honourer rather than in the person honoured, it was necessary to make a Creature, from whom he might receive this homage ; and that is in the other world Angels, in this, Man ; which when we neglect, we forget the very end of our Creation, and may justly provoke God, not onely to repent that he hath made the World, but that he hath sworn he would not destroy it. That there is but one World, is a conclusion of Faith. *Aristotle* with all his Philosophy hath not been able to prove it, and as weakly that the world was eternal ; that dispute much troubled the Pen of the Philosophers, but *Moses* decided that question, and all is salved with the new term of a Creation, that is, a production of something out of nothing; and what is that ? Whatsoever is opposite to something ; or more exactly, that which is truely contrary unto God ; for he onely is, all others have an existence with dependency, and are something but by a distinction ; and herein is Divinity conformant unto Philosophy, and generation not onely founded on contrarieties, but also creation ; God being all things, is contrary unto nothing, out of which were made all things, and so nothing became something, and *Omneity* informed *Nullity* into an Essence.

THE whole Creation is a Mystery, and particularly that of Man; at the blast of his mouth were the rest of the Creatures made, and at his bare word they started out of nothing: but in the frame of Man (as the Text describes it) he played the sensible operator, and seemed not so much to create, as make him; when he had separated the materials of other creatures, there consequently resulted a form and soul; but having raised the walls of man, he has driven to a second and harder creation of a substance like himself, an incorruptible and immortal Soul. For these two affections we have the Philosophy and opinion of the Heathens, the flat affirmative of *Plato*, and not a negative from *Aristotle*: there is another scruple cast in by Divinity (concerning its production) much disputed in the *Germane* auditories, and with that indifferency and equality of arguments, as leave the controversie undetermined. I am not of *Paracelsus* mind, that boldly delivers a receipt to make a man without conjunction; yet cannot but wonder at the multitude of heads that do deny traduction, having no other argument to confirm their belief, then that Rhetorical sentence, and *Antimetathesis* of *Augustine*, *Creando infunditur, infundendo creatur*: either opinion will consist well enough with Religion; yet I should rather incline to this, did not one objection haunt me, not wrung from speculations and subtilties, but from common sense and observation; not pickt from the leaves of any Author, but bred amongst the weeds and tares of mine own brain: And this is a conclusion from the equivocal and monstrous productions in the copulation of Man with Beast: for if the Soul of man be not transmitted, and transfused in the seed of the Parents, why are not those productions

meerly beasts, but have also an impression and tincture
of reason in as high a measure, as it can evidence it
self in those improper Organs? Nor truely can I
peremptorily deny, that the Soul in this her sublunary estate, is wholly, and in all acceptions in-
organical, but that for the performance of her ordinary
actions, there is required not onely a symmetry and
proper disposition of Organs, but a Crasis and temper
correspondent to its operations. Yet is not this mass
of flesh and visible structure the instrument and proper
corps of the Soul, but rather of Sense, and that the
hand of Reason. In our study of Anatomy there is a
mass of mysterious Philosophy, and such as reduced
the very Heathens to Divinity: yet amongst all those
rare discourses, and curious pieces I find in the Fabrick
of man, I do not so much content my self, as in that I
find not, there is no Organ or Instrument for the
rational soul: for in the brain, which we term the seat
of reason, there is not any thing of moment more than
I can discover in the crany of a beast: and this is a
sensible and no inconsiderable argument of the in-
organity of the Soul, at least in that sense we usually
so conceive it. Thus we are men, and we know not
how; there is something in us that can be without us,
and will be after us, though it is strange that it hath
no history, what it was before us, nor cannot tell how
it entred in us.

SECT.
37

NOW for these walls of flesh, wherein the
Soul doth seem to be immured, before
the Resurrection, it is nothing but an
elemental composition, and a Fabrick that must fall
to ashes. *All flesh is grass*, is not onely metaphorically, but litterally, true; for all those creatures we

behold, are but the herbs of the field, digested into flesh in them, or more remotely carnified in our selves. Nay further, we are what we all abhor, *Anthropophagi* and Cannibals, devourers not onely of men, but of our selves; and that not in an allegory, but a positive truth : for all this mass of flesh which we behold, came in at our mouths; this frame we look upon, hath been upon our trenchers; in brief, we have devour'd our selves. I cannot believe the wisdom of *Pythagoras* did ever positively, and in a literal sense, affirm his *Metempsychosis*, or impossible transmigration of the Souls of men into beasts : of all Metamorphoses, or transmigrations, I believe only one, that is of *Lots* wife; for that of *Nebuchodonosor* proceeded not so far; in all others I conceive there is no further verity than is contained in their implicite sense and morality. I believe that the whole frame of a beast doth perish, and is left in the same state after death as before it was materialled unto life; that the souls of men know neither contrary nor corruption; that they subsist beyond the body, and outlive death by the priviledge of their proper natures, and without a Miracle; that the Souls of the faithful, as they leave Earth, take possession of Heaven: that those apparitions and ghosts of departed persons are not the wandring souls of men, but the unquiet walks of Devils, prompting and suggesting us unto mischief, blood, and villany; instilling and stealing into our hearts that the blessed spirits are not at rest in their graves, but wander sollicitous of the affairs of the World; but that those phantasms appear often, and do frequent Cœmeteries, Charnel-houses, and Churches, it is because those are the dormitories of the dead, where the Devil like an insolent Champion beholds with pride the spoils and Trophies of his Victory over *Adam*.

THIS is that dismal conquest we all deplore, that makes us so often cry (*O*) *Adam, quid fecisti* ? I thank God I have not those strait ligaments, or narrow obligations to the World, as to dote on life, or be convulst and tremble at the name of death : Not that I am insensible of the dread and horrour thereof, or by raking into the bowels of the deceased, continual sight of Anatomies, Skeletons, or Cadaverous reliques, like Vespilloes, or Grave-makers, I am become stupid, or have forgot the apprehension of Mortality ; but that marshalling all the horrours, and contemplating the extremities thereof, I find not any thing therein able to daunt the courage of a man, much less a well-resolved Christian : And therefore am not angry at the errour of our first Parents, or unwilling to bear a part of this common fate, and like the best of them to dye, that is, to cease to breathe, to take a farewel of the elements, to be a kind of nothing for a moment, to be within one instant of a spirit. When I take a full view and circle of my self, without this reasonable moderator, and equal piece of Justice, Death, I do conceive my self the miserablest person extant ; were there not another life that I hope for, all the vanities of this World should not intreat a moment's breath from me : could the Devil work my belief to imagine I could never dye, I would not outlive that very thought ; I have so abject a conceit of this common way of existence, this retaining to the Sun and Elements, I cannot think this is to be a man, or to live according to the dignity of humanity : in exspectation of a better, I can with patience embrace this life, yet in my best meditations do often defie death : I honour any man that contemns it, nor can I highly love any that is afraid of it : this

makes me naturally love a Souldier, and honour those
tattered and contemptible Regiments, that will dye at
the command of a Sergeant. For a Pagan there may
be some motives to be in love with life; but for a
Christian to be amazed at death, I see not how he can
escape this Dilemma, that he is too sensible of this
life, or hopeless of the life to come.

SOME Divines count Adam 30 years old at
his creation, because they suppose him
created in the perfect age and stature of
man. And surely we are all out of the computation
of our age, and every man is some months elder than
he bethinks him; for we live, move, have a being, and
are subject to the actions of the elements, and the
malice of diseases, in that other world, the truest
Microcosm, the Womb of our Mother. For besides
that general and common existence we are conceived
to hold in our Chaos, and whilst we sleep within the
bosome of our causes, we enjoy a being and life in
three distinct worlds, wherein we receive most manifest
graduations : In that obscure World and womb of our
mother, our time is short, computed by the Moon ; yet
longer then the days of many creatures that behold the
Sun, our selves being not yet without life, sense, and
reason; though for the manifestation of its actions, it
awaits the opportunity of objects, and seems to live
there but in its root and soul of vegetation; entring
afterwards upon the scene of the World, we arise up
and become another creature, performing the reasonable actions of man, and obscurely manifesting that
part of Divinity in us, but not in complement and perfection, till we have once more cast our secondine, that
is, this slough of flesh, and are delivered into the last

SECT.
39

world, that is, that ineffable place of *Paul*, that proper
ubi of spirits. The smattering I have of the Philosophers Stone (which is something more then the perfect
exaltation of Gold) hath taught me a great deal of
Divinity, and instructed my belief, how that immortal
spirit and incorruptible substance of my Soul may lye
obscure, and sleep a while within this house of flesh.
Those strange and mystical transmigrations that I
have observed in Silk-worms, turned my Philosophy into
Divinity. There is in these works of nature, which
seem to puzzle reason, something Divine, and hath more
in it then the eye of a common spectator doth discover.

SECT.
40

I AM naturally bashful, nor hath conversation,
age or travel, been able to effront, or enharden
me; yet I have one part of modesty which I
have seldom discovered in another, that is, (to speak
truely) I am not so much afraid of death, as ashamed
thereof; 'tis the very disgrace and ignominy of our
natures, that in a moment can so disfigure us, that our
nearest friends, Wife, and Children stand afraid and
start at us. The Birds and Beasts of the field, that
before in a natural fear obeyed us, forgetting all
allegiance, begin to prey upon us. This very conceit
hath in a tempest disposed and left me willing to be
swallowed up in the abyss of waters; wherein I had
perished unseen, unpityed, without wondering eyes,
tears of pity, Lectures of mortality, and none had said,
Quantum mutatus ab illo! Not that I am ashamed of
the Anatomy of my parts, or can accuse Nature for
playing the bungler in any part of me, or my own
vitious life for contracting any shameful disease upon
me, whereby I might not call my self as wholesome a
morsel for the worms as any.

SOME upon the courage of a fruitful issue, wherein, as in the truest Chronicle, they seem to outlive themselves, can with greater patience away with death. This conceit and counterfeit subsisting in our progenies, seems to me a meer fallacy, unworthy the desires of a man, that can but conceive a thought of the next World; who, in a nobler ambition, should desire to live in his substance in Heaven, rather than his name and shadow in the earth. And therefore at my death I mean to take a total adieu of the world, not caring for a Monument, History, or Epitaph, not so much as the memory of my name to be found any where, but in the universal Register of God. I am not yet so Cynical, as to approve the [1]Testament of *Diogenes*, nor do I altogether allow that *Rodomontado* of *Lucan*;

—— Cælo tegitur, qui non habet urnam.

He that unburied lies wants not his Herse,
For unto him a Tomb's the Universe.

But commend in my calmer judgement, those ingenuous intentions that desire to sleep by the urns of their Fathers, and strive to go the neatest way unto corruption. I do not envy the temper of Crows and Daws, nor the numerous and weary days of our Fathers before the Flood. If there be any truth in Astrology, I may outlive a Jubilee; as yet I have not seen one revolution of Saturn, nor hath my pulse beat thirty years; and yet excepting one, have seen the Ashes, & left under ground all the Kings of *Europe*; have been contemporary to three Emperours, four Grand Signiours, and as many Popes: methinks I have outlived my self, and begin to be weary of the Sun; I have shaken hands with delight: in my warm blood

SECT.
41

[1] *Who willed his friend not to bury him, but hang him up with a staff in his hand to fright away the crows.*

and Canicular days, I perceive I do anticipate the vices of age; the World to me is but a dream or mock-show, and we all therein but Pantalones and Anticks, to my severer contemplations.

SECT.
42

IT is not, I confess, an unlawful prayer to desire to surpass the days of our Saviour, or wish to outlive that age wherein he thought fittest to dye; yet if (as Divinity affirms) there shall be no gray hairs in Heaven, but all shall rise in the perfect state of men, we do but outlive those perfections in this World, to be recalled unto them by a greater Miracle in the next, and run on here but to be retrograde hereafter. Were there any hopes to outlive vice, or a point to be super-annuated from sin, it were worthy our knees to implore the days of *Methuselah*. But age doth not rectifie, but incurvate our natures, turning bad dispositions into worser habits, and (like diseases) brings on incurable vices; for every day as we grow weaker in age, we grow stronger in sin; and the number of our days doth make but our sins innumerable. The same vice committed at sixteen, is not the same, though it agree in all other circumstances, at forty, but swells and doubles from the circumstance of our ages, wherein, besides the constant and inexcusable habit of transgressing, the maturity of our judgement cuts off pretence unto excuse or pardon : every sin the oftner it is committed, the more it acquireth in the quality of evil; as it succeeds in time, so it proceeds in degrees of badness; for as they proceed they ever multiply, and like figures in Arithmetick, the last stands for more than all that went before it. And though I think no man can live well once, but he that could live twice, yet for my own part I would not live over my hours past, or begin again the thred of my days : not upon *Cicero's* ground, because I have lived them well, but for fear I should live them worse : I find my growing Judgment daily instruct me how to be better, but my untamed affections and confirmed vitiosity makes me daily do worse; I find in my confirmed age the same sins I discovered in my youth ; I committed many then because I was a Child, and because I commit them still, I am yet an infant. Therefore I perceive a man may be twice a Child before the days of dotage ; and stands in need of *Æsons* Bath before threescore.

AND truely there goes a great deal of providence to produce a mans life unto threescore : there is more required than an able temper for those years ; though the radical humour contain in it sufficient oyl for seventy, yet I perceive in some it gives no light past thirty : men assign not all the causes of long life, that write whole Books thereof. They that found themselves on the radical balsome, or vital sulphur of the parts, determine not why *Abel* lived not so long as *Adam.* There is therefore a secret glome or bottome of our days : 'twas his wisdom to determine them, but his perpetual and waking providence that fulfils and accomplisheth them ; wherein the spirits, our selves, and all the creatures of God in a secret and disputed way do execute his will. Let them not therefore complain of immaturity that die about thirty ; they fall but like the whole World, whose solid and well-composed substance must not expect the duration and period of its constitution : when all things are compleated in it, its age is accomplished ; and the last and general fever may as naturally destroy

SECT.
43

it before six thousand, as me before forty; there is therefore some other hand that twines the thread of life than that of Nature : we are not onely ignorant in Antipathies and occult qualities; our ends are as obscure as our beginnings; the line of our days is drawn by night, and the various effects therein by a pensil that is invisible; wherein though we confess our ignorance, I am sure we do not err if we say it is the hand of God.

SECT. 44

I AM much taken with two verses of *Lucan*, since I have been able not onely as we do at School, to construe, but understand.

> *Victurosque Dei celant ut vivere durent,*
> *Felix esse mori.*
>
> *We're all deluded, vainly searching ways*
> *To make us happy by the length of days;*
> *For cunningly to make's protract this breath,*
> *The Gods conceal the happiness of Death.*

There be many excellent strains in that Poet, wherewith his Stoical Genius hath liberally supplied him; and truely there are singular pieces in the Philosophy of *Zeno*, and doctrine of the Stoicks, which I perceive, delivered in a Pulpit, pass for current Divinity: yet herein are they in extreams, that can allow a man to be his own *Assassine*, and so highly extol the end and suicide of *Cato* ; this is indeed not to fear death, but yet to be afraid of life. It is a brave act of valour to contemn death; but where life is more terrible than death, it is then the truest valour to dare to live ; and herein Religion hath taught us a noble example : For all the valiant acts of *Curtius*, *Scevola*, or *Codrus*, do not parallel or match that one of *Job* ; and sure there is no torture to the rack of a disease, nor any Ponyards in death it self like those in the way or prologue to it. *Emori nolo, sed me esse mortuum nihil curo*; I would not die, but care not to be dead. Were I of *Cæsar's* Religion, I should be of his desires, and wish rather to go off at one blow, then to be sawed in pieces by the grating torture of a disease. Men that look no farther than their outsides, think health an appurtenance unto life, and quarrel with their constitutions for being sick; but I, that have examined the parts of man, and know upon what tender filaments that Fabrick hangs, do wonder that we are not always so; and considering the thousand doors that lead to death, do thank my God that we can die but once. 'Tis not onely the mischief of diseases, and villany of poysons, that make an end of us; we vainly accuse the fury of Guns, and the new inventions of death; it is in the power of every hand to destroy us, and we are beholding unto every one we meet, he doth not kill us. There is therefore but one comfort left, that, though it be in the power of the weakest arm to take away life, it is not in the strongest to deprive us of death : God would not exempt himself from that, the misery of immortality in the flesh; he undertook not that was immortal. Certainly there is no happiness within this circle of flesh, nor is it in the Opticks of these eyes to behold felicity; the first day of our Jubilee is Death; the Devil hath therefore failed of his desires; we are happier with death than we should have been without it : there is no misery but in himself, where there is no end of misery; and so indeed in his own sense the Stoick is in the right. He forgets that he can dye who complains of misery; we are in the power of no calamity while death is in our own.

NOW besides the literal and positive kind of death, there are others whereof Divines make mention, and those I think, not meerly Metaphorical, as mortification, dying unto sin and the World ; therefore, I say, every man hath a double Horoscope, one of his humanity, his birth ; another of his Christianity, his baptism, and from this do I compute or calculate my Nativity ; not reckoning those *Horæ combustæ* and odd days, or esteeming my self any thing, before I was my Saviours, and inrolled in the Register of Christ : Whosoever enjoys not this life, I count him but an apparition, though he wear about him the sensible affections of flesh. In these moral acceptions, the way to be immortal is to dye daily ; nor can I think I have the true Theory of death, when I contemplate a skull, or behold a Skeleton with those vulgar imaginations it casts upon us ; I have therefore enlarged that common *Memento mori*, into a more Christian memorandum, *Memento quatuor Novissima*, those four inevitable points of us all, Death, Judgement, Heaven, and Hell. Neither did the contemplations of the Heathens rest in their graves, without further thought of Rhadamanth or some judicial proceeding after death, though in another way, and upon suggestion of their natural reasons. I cannot but marvail from what *Sibyl* or Oracle they stole the Prophesie of the worlds destruction by fire, or whence *Lucan* learned to say,

> *Communis mundo superest rogus, ossibus astra*
> *Misturus.*
> *There yet remains to th' World one common Fire,*
> *Wherein our bones with stars shall make one Pyre.*

I believe the World grows near its end, yet is neither old nor decayed, nor shall ever perish upon the ruines of its own Principles. As the work of Creation was above nature, so its adversary annihilation ; without which the World hath not its end, but its mutation. Now what force should be able to consume it thus far, without the breath of God, which is the truest consuming flame, my Philosophy cannot inform me. Some believe there went not a minute to the Worlds creation, nor shall there go to its destruction ; those six days, so punctually described, make not to them one moment, but rather seem to manifest the method and Idea of the great work of the intellect of God, than the manner how he proceeded in its operation. I cannot dream that there should be at the last day any such Judicial proceeding, or calling to the Bar, as indeed the Scripture seems to imply, and the literal Commentators do conceive : for unspeakable mysteries in the Scriptures are often delivered in a vulgar and illustrative way ; and being written unto man, are delivered, not as they truely are, but as they may be understood ; wherein notwithstanding the different interpretations according to different capacities may stand firm with our devotion, nor be any way prejudicial to each single edification.

NOW to determine the day and year of this inevitable time, is not onely convincible and statute-madness, but also manifest impiety : How shall we interpret *Elias* 6000 years, or imagine the secret communicated to a Rabbi, which God hath denyed unto his Angels ? It had been an excellent Quære to have posed the Devil of *Delphos*, and must needs have forced him to some strange amphibology ; it hath not onely mocked the predictions of sundry Astrologers in Ages past, but the prophesies of many melancholy heads in these present, who neither under-

SECT.
46

E

standing reasonably things past or present, pretend a knowledge of things to come; heads ordained onely to manifest the incredible effects of melancholy, and to fulfil old prophecies rather than be the authors of new. *In those days there shall come* Wars and rumours of Wars, to me seems no prophecy, but a constant truth, in all times verified since it was pronounced: There shall be signs in the Moon and Stars; how comes he then like a Thief in the night, when he gives an item of his coming? That common sign drawn from the revelation of Antichrist, is as obscure as any: in our common compute he hath been come these many years; but for my own part to speak freely, I am half of opinion that Antichrist is the Philosophers stone in Divinity; for the discovery and invention thereof, though there be prescribed rules and probable inductions, yet hath hardly any man attained the perfect discovery thereof. That general opinion that the World grows neer its end, hath possessed all ages past as neerly as ours; I am afraid that the Souls that now depart, cannot escape that lingring expostulation of the Saints under the Altar, *Quousque, Domine? How long, O Lord?* and groan in the expectation of that great Jubilee.

In those days there shall come lyars and false prophets.

SECT. 47

THIS is the day that must make good that great attribute of God, his Justice; that must reconcile those unanswerable doubts that torment the wisest understandings, and reduce those seeming inequalities, and respective distributions in this world, to an equality and recompensive Justice in the next. This is that one day, that shall include and comprehend all that went before it; wherein, as in the last scene, all the Actors must enter, to compleat and make up the Catastrophe of this great piece. This is the day whose memory hath onely power to make us honest in the dark, and to be vertuous without a witness. *Ipsa sui pretium virtus sibi*, that Vertue is her own reward, is but a cold principle, and not able to maintain our variable resolutions in a constant and setled way of goodness. I have practised that honest artifice of *Seneca*, and in my retired and solitary imaginations, to detain me from the foulness of vice, have fancied to my self the presence of my dear and worthiest friends, before whom I should lose my head, rather than be vitious: yet herein I found that there was nought but moral honesty, and this was not to be vertuous for his sake who must reward us at the last. I have tryed if I could reach that great resolution of his, to be honest without a thought of Heaven or Hell; and indeed I found, upon a natural inclination, and inbred loyalty unto virtue, that I could serve her without a livery; yet not in that resolved and venerable way, but that the frailty of my nature, upon * easie temptation, might be induced to forget her. The life therefore and spirit of all our actions, is the resurrection, and a stable apprehension that our ashes shall enjoy the fruit of our pious endeavours: without this, all Religion is a fallacy, and those impieties of *Lucian, Euripides,* and *Julian,* are no blasphemies, but subtle verities, and Atheists have been the onely Philosophers.

H OW shall the dead arise, is no question of my Faith; to believe only possibilities, is not Faith, but meer Philosophy. Many things are true in Divinity, which are neither inducible by reason, nor confirmable by sense; and many things in

SECT. 48

* *Insert* any, 1672.

Philosophy confirmable by sense, yet not inducible by reason. Thus it is impossible by any solid or demonstrative reasons to perswade a man to believe the conversion of the Needle to the North; though this be possible and true, and easily credible, upon a single experiment unto the sense. I believe that our estranged and divided ashes shall unite again; that our separated dust after so many Pilgrimages and transformations into the parts of Minerals, Plants, Animals, Elements, shall at the Voice of God return into their primitive shapes, and joyn again to make up their primary and predestinate forms. As at the Creation there was a separation of that confused mass into its pieces; so at the destruction thereof there shall be a separation into its distinct individuals. As at the Creation of the World, all the distinct species that we behold lay involved in one mass, till the fruitful Voice of God separated this united multitude into its several species: so at the last day, when those corrupted reliques shall be scattered in the Wilderness of forms, and seem to have forgot their proper habits, God by a powerful Voice shall command them back into their proper shapes, and call them out by their single individuals: Then shall appear the fertility of *Adam*, and the magick of that sperm that hath dilated into so many millions. I have often beheld as a miracle, that artificial resurrection and revivification of *Mercury*, how being mortified into a thousand shapes, it assumes again its own, and returns into its numerical self. Let us speak naturally, and like Philosophers, the forms of alterable bodies in these sensible corruptions perish not; nor as we imagine, wholly quit their mansions, but retire and contract themselves into their secret and unaccessible parts, where they may best protect themselves from the action of their Antagonist. A plant or vegetable consumed to ashes, by a contemplative and school-Philosopher seems utterly destroyed, and the form to have taken his leave for ever: But to a sensible Artist the forms are not perished, but withdrawn into their incombustible part, where they lie secure from the action of that devouring element. This is made good by experience, which can from the Ashes of a Plant revive the plant, and from its cinders recal it into its stalk and leaves again. What the Art of man can do in these inferiour pieces, what blasphemy is it to affirm the finger of God cannot do in these more perfect and sensible structures? This is that mystical Philosophy, from whence no true Scholar becomes an Atheist, but from the visible effects of nature grows up a real Divine, and beholds not in a dream, as *Ezekiel*, but in an ocular and visible object the types of his resurrection.

NOW, the necessary Mansions of our restored selves, are those two contrary and incompatible places we call Heaven and Hell; to define them, or strictly to determine what and where these are, surpasseth my Divinity. That elegant Apostle which seemed to have a glimpse of Heaven, hath left but a negative description thereof; *which neither eye hath seen, nor ear hath heard, nor can enter into the heart of man*: he was translated out of himself to behold it; but being returned into himself, could not express it. St. *John's* description by Emerals, Chrysolites, and precious Stones, is too weak to express the material Heaven we behold. Briefly therefore, where the Soul hath the full measure and complement of happiness; where the boundless appetite of that

SECT.
49

spirit remains compleatly satisfied, that it can neither
desire addition nor alteration; that I think is truly
Heaven : and this can onely be in the injoyment of
that essence, whose infinite goodness is able to terminate the desires of it self, and the unsatiable wishes of
ours ; wherever God will thus manifest himself, there is
Heaven though within the circle of this sensible world.
Thus the Soul of man may be in Heaven any where, even
within the limits of his own proper body ; and when it
ceaseth to live in the body, it may remain in its own
soul, that is, its Creator : and thus we may say that
St. *Paul*, whether in the body, or out of the body, was
yet in Heaven. To place it in the Empyreal, or beyond the tenth sphear, is to forget the world's destruction ; for when this sensible world shall be destroyed,
all shall then be here as it is now there, an Empyreal
Heaven, a *quasi* vacuity ; when to ask where Heaven is,
is to demand where the Presence of God is, or where we
have the glory of that happy vision. *Moses* that was
bred up in all the learning of the *Egyptians*, committed
a gross absurdity in Philosophy, when with these eyes
of flesh he desired to see God, and petitioned his
Maker, that is, truth it self, to a contradiction. Those
that imagine Heaven and Hell neighbours, and conceive a vicinity between those two extreams, upon
consequence of the Parable, where *Dives* discoursed
with *Lazarus* in *Abraham's* bosome, do too grosly conceive of those glorified creatures, whose eyes shall
easily out-see the Sun, and behold without a perspec-
tive the extreamest distances : for if there shall be
in our glorified eyes, the faculty of sight and reception
of objects, I could think the visible species there to be
in as unlimitable a way as now the intellectual. I
grant that two bodies placed beyond the tenth sphear,

or in a vacuity, according to *Aristotle*'s Philosophy, could not behold each other, because there wants a body or Medium to hand and transport the visible rays of the object unto the sense; but when there shall be a general defect of either Medium to convey, or light to prepare and dispose that Medium, and yet a perfect vision, we must suspend the rules of our Philosophy, and make all good by a more absolute piece of opticks.

I CANNOT tell how to say that fire is the essence of Hell: I know not what to make of Purgatory, or conceive a flame that can either prey upon, or purifie the substance of a Soul: those flames of sulphur mention'd in the Scriptures, I take not to be understood of this present Hell, but of that to come, where fire shall make up the complement of our tortures, and have a body or subject wherein to manifest its tyranny. Some who have had the honour to be textuary in Divinity, are of opinion it shall be the same specifical fire with ours. This is hard to conceive, yet can I make good how even that may prey upon our bodies, and yet not consume us: for in this material World there are bodies that persist invincible in the powerfullest flames; and though by the action of fire they fall into ignition and liquation, yet will they never suffer a destruction. I would gladly know how *Moses* with an actual fire calcin'd, or burnt the Golden Calf into powder: for that mystical metal of Gold, whose solary and celestial nature I admire, exposed unto the violence of fire, grows onely hot, and liquifies, but consumeth not; so when the consumable and volatile pieces of our bodies shall be refined into a more impregnable and fixed temper, like Gold, though they suffer from the action of flames, they

SECT.
50

SECT.
50

shall never perish, but lye immortal in the arms of fire.
And surely if this frame must suffer onely by the action
of this element, there will many bodies escape, and not
onely Heaven, but Earth will not be at an end, but
rather a beginning. For at present it is not earth, but
a composition of fire, water, earth, and air; but at that
time, spoiled of these ingredients, it shall appear in a
substance more like it self, its ashes. Philosophers that
opinioned the worlds destruction by fire, did never
dream of annihilation, which is beyond the power of
sublunary causes; for the last * action of that element
is but vitrification, or a reduction of a body into glass;
and therefore some of our Chymicks facetiously affirm,
that at the last fire all shall be christallized and reverberated into glass, which is the utmost action of that
element. Nor need we fear this term annihilation, or
wonder that God will destroy the works of his Creation:
for man subsisting, who is, and will then truely appear,
a Microcosm, the world cannot be said to be destroyed.
For the eyes of God, and perhaps also of our glorified
selves, shall as really behold and contemplate the World
in its Epitome or contracted essence, as now it doth at
large and in its dilated substance. In the seed of a
Plant to the eyes of God, and to the understanding of
man, there exists, though in an invisible way, the perfect leaves, flowers, and fruit thereof: (for things that
are in *posse* to the sense, are actually existent to the
understanding). Thus God beholds all things, who
contemplates as fully his works in their Epitome, as in
their full volume; and beheld as amply the whole
world in that little compendium of the sixth day, as in
the scattered and dilated pieces of those five before.

* Last and proper, 1672.

MEN commonly set forth the torments of Hell
by fire, and the extremity of corporal afflictions, and describe Hell in the same method
that *Mahomet* doth Heaven. This indeed makes a
noise, and drums in popular ears; but if this be the
terrible piece thereof, it is not worthy to stand in
diameter with Heaven, whose happiness consists in
that part that is best able to comprehend it, that
immortal essence, that translated divinity and colony
of God, the Soul. Surely though we place Hell under
Earth, the Devil's walk and purlue is about it: men
speak too popularly who place it in those flaming
mountains, which to grosser apprehensions represent
Hell. The heart of man is the place the Devils dwell
in; I feel sometimes a Hell within my self; *Lucifer*
keeps his Court in my breast; *Legion* is revived in me.
There are as many Hells, as *Anaxagoras* conceited
worlds; there was more than one Hell in *Magdalene*,
when there were seven Devils; for every Devil is an
Hell unto himself; he holds enough of torture in his
own *ubi*, and needs not the misery of circumference to
afflict him. And thus a distracted Conscience here, is
a shadow or introduction unto Hell hereafter. Who
can but pity the merciful intention of those hands that
do destroy themselves? the Devil, were it in his power,
would do the like; which being impossible, his miseries
are endless, and he suffers most in that attribute
wherein he is impassible, his immortality.

I THANK God that with joy I mention it, I was
never afraid of Hell, nor never grew pale at the
description of that place; I have so fixed my contemplations on Heaven, that I have almost forgot the
Idea of Hell, and am afraid rather to lose the Joys of

the one, than endure the misery of the other : to be deprived of them is a perfect Hell, and needs methinks no addition to compleat our afflictions ; that terrible term hath never detained me from sin, nor do I owe any good action to the name thereof ; I fear God, yet am not afraid of him ; his mercies make me ashamed of my sins, before his Judgements afraid thereof : these are the forced and secondary method of his wisdom, which he useth but as the last remedy, and upon provocation ; a course rather to deter the wicked, than incite the virtuous to his worship. I can hardly think there was ever any scared into Heaven ; they go the fairest way to Heaven that would serve God without a Hell; other Mercenaries, that crouch into him in fear of Hell, though they term themselves the servants, are indeed but the slaves of the Almighty.

SECT.
53

AND to be true, and speak my soul, when I survey the occurrences of my life, and call into account the Finger of God, I can perceive nothing but an abyss and mass of mercies, either in general to mankind, or in particular to my self : and whether out of the prejudice of my affection, or an inverting and partial conceit of his mercies, I know not ; but those which others term crosses, afflictions, judgements, misfortunes, to me who inquire farther into them then their visible effects, they both appear, and in event have ever proved, the secret and dissembled favours of his affection. It is a singular piece of Wisdom to apprehend truly, and without passion, the Works of God, and so well to distinguish his Justice from his Mercy, as not miscall those noble Attributes : yet it is likewise an honest piece of Logick, so to dispute and argue the proceedings of

God, as to distinguish even his judgments into mercies.
For God is merciful unto all, because better to the
worst, than the best deserve ; and to say he punisheth
none in this world, though it be a Paradox, is no
absurdity. To one that hath committed Murther, if
the Judge should only ordain a Fine, it were a madness
to call this a punishment, and to repine at the sentence,
rather than admire the clemency of the Judge. Thus
our offences being mortal, and deserving not onely
Death, but Damnation ; if the goodness of God be
content to traverse and pass them over with a loss,
misfortune, or disease ; what frensie were it to term
this a punishment, rather than an extremity of mercy ;
and to groan under the rod of his Judgements, rather
than admire the Scepter of his Mercies ? Therefore to
adore, honour, and admire him, is a debt of gratitude
due from the obligation of our nature, states, and conditions ; and with these thoughts, he that knows them
best, will not deny that I adore him. That I obtain
Heaven, and the bliss thereof, is accidental, and not
the intended work of my devotion ; it being a felicity
I can neither think to deserve, nor scarce in modesty
to expect. For these two ends of us all, either as
rewards or punishments, are mercifully ordained and
disproportionably disposed unto our actions ; the one
being so far beyond our deserts, the other so infinitely
below our demerits.

THERE is no Salvation to those that believe **SECT.**
not in *Christ*, that is, say some, since his **54**
Nativity, and as Divinity affirmeth, before
also ; which makes me much apprehend the ends of
those honest Worthies and Philosophers which dyed
before his Incarnation. It is hard to place those

Souls in Hell, whose worthy lives do teach us Virtue on Earth: methinks amongst those many subdivisions of Hell, there might have been one Limbo left for these. What a strange vision will it be to see their Poetical fictions converted into Verities, and their imagined and fancied Furies into real Devils? how strange to them will sound the History of *Adam*, when they shall suffer for him they never heard of? when they who derive their genealogy from the Gods, shall know they are the unhappy issue of sinful man? It is an insolent part of reason, to controvert the Works of God, or question the Justice of his proceedings. Could Humility teach others, as it hath instructed me, to contemplate the infinite and incomprehensible distance betwixt the Creator and the Creature; or did we seriously perpend that one simile of St. *Paul, Shall the Vessel say to the Potter, Why hast thou made me thus?* it would prevent these arrogant disputes of reason, nor would we argue the definitive sentence of God, either to Heaven or Hell. Men that live according to the right rule and law of reason, live but in their own kind, as beasts do in theirs; who justly obey the prescript of their natures, and therefore cannot reasonably demand a reward of their actions, as onely obeying the natural dictates of their reason. It will therefore, and must at last appear, that all salvation is through *Christ*; which verity I fear these great examples of virtue must confirm, and make it good, how the perfectest actions of earth have no title or claim unto Heaven.

NOR truely do I think the lives of these or of any other, were ever correspondent, or in all points conformable unto their doctrines. It is evident that *Aristotle* transgressed the rule of his own Ethicks; the Stoicks that condemn passion, and command a man to laugh in *Phalaris* his Bull, could not endure without a groan a fit of the Stone or Colick. The *Scepticks* that affirmed they knew nothing, even in that opinion confute themselves, and thought they knew more than all the World beside. *Diogenes* I hold to be the most vain-glorious man of his time, and more ambitious in refusing all Honours, than *Alexander* in rejecting none. Vice and the Devil put a Fallacy upon our Reasons, and provoking us too hastily to run from it, entangle and profound us deeper in it. The Duke of *Venice*, that weds himself unto the Sea by a Ring of Gold, I will not argue of prodigality, because it is a solemnity of good use and consequence in the State: but the Philosopher that threw his money into the Sea to avoid Avarice, was a notorious prodigal. There is no road or ready way to virtue; it is not an easie point of art to disentangle our selves from this riddle, or web of Sin: To perfect virtue, as to Religion, there is required a *Panoplia*, or compleat armour; that whilst we lye at close ward against one Vice, we lye not open to the venny of another. And indeed wiser discretions that have the thred of reason to conduct them, offend without pardon; whereas, under-heads may stumble without dishonour. There go so many circumstances to piece up one good action, that it is a lesson to be good, and we are forced to be virtuous by the book. Again, the Practice of men holds not an equal pace, yea, and often runs counter to their Theory; we naturally know what is good, but naturally pursue what is evil: the Rhetorick wherewith I perswade another, cannot perswade my self: there is a depraved appetite in us, that will with patience hear the learned instructions of Reason, but yet perform no farther than agrees to its own irregular humour. In brief, we all are monsters, that is, a composition of Man and Beast; wherein we must endeavour to be as the Poets fancy that wise man *Chiron*, that is, to have the region of Man above that of Beast, and Sense to sit but at the feet of Reason. Lastly, I do desire with God that all, but yet affirm with men, that few shall know Salvation; that the bridge is narrow, the passage strait unto life: yet those who do confine the Church of God, either to particular Nations, Churches or Families, have made it far narrower then our Saviour ever meant it.

SECT.
56

THE vulgarity of those judgements that wrap the Church of God in *Strabo's* cloak, and restrain it unto *Europe*, seem to me as bad Geographers as *Alexander*, who thought he had Conquer'd all the World, when he had not subdued the half of any part thereof. For we cannot deny the Church of God both in *Asia* and *Africa*, if we do not forget the Peregrinations of the Apostles, the deaths of the Martyrs, the Sessions of many, and, even in our reformed judgement, lawful Councils, held in those parts in the minority and nonage of ours. Nor must a few differences, more remarkable in the eyes of man than perhaps in the judgement of God, excommunicate from Heaven one another, much less those Christians who are in a manner all Martyrs, maintaining their Faith, in the noble way of persecution, and serving God

in the Fire, whereas we honour him in the Sunshine.
'Tis true, we all hold there is a number of Elect, and
many to be saved ; yet take our Opinions together, and
from the confusion thereof there will be no such thing
as salvation, nor shall any one be saved. For first, the
Church of *Rome* condemneth us, we likewise them ; the
Sub-reformists and Sectaries sentence the Doctrine of
our Church as damnable; the Atomist, or Familist,
reprobates all these ; and all these, them again. Thus
whilst the Mercies of God do promise us Heaven, our
conceits and opinions exclude us from that place.
There must be, therefore, more than one St. *Peter* :
particular Churches and Sects usurp the gates of
Heaven, and turn the key against each other : and thus
we go to Heaven against each others wills, conceits and
opinions ; and with as much uncharity as ignorance,
do err I fear in points not only of our own, but one
anothers salvation.

I BELIEVE many are saved, who to man seem
reprobated ; and many are reprobated, who in the
opinion and sentence of man, stand elected : there
will appear at the Last day, strange and unexpected
examples both of his Justice and his Mercy ; and
therefore to define either, is folly in man, and insolency
even in the Devils : those acute and subtil spirits in all
their sagacity, can hardly divine who shall be saved ;
which if they could Prognostick, their labour were at
an end ; nor need they compass the earth seeking whom
they may devour. Those who upon a rigid application
of the Law, sentence *Solomon* unto damnation, condemn not onely him, but themselves, and the whole
World : for by the Letter and written Word of God,
we are without exception in the state of Death ; but

SECT.
57

there is a prerogative of God, and an arbitrary pleasure above the Letter of his own Law, by which
alone we can pretend unto Salvation, and through
which *Solomon* might be as easily saved as those who
condemn him.

SECT.
58

THE number of those who pretend unto Salvation, and those infinite swarms who think to
pass through the eye of this Needle, have
much amazed me. That name and compellation of
little Flock, doth not comfort, but deject my Devotion;
especially when I reflect upon mine own unworthiness,
wherein, according to my humble apprehensions,
I am below them all. I believe there shall never
be an Anarchy in Heaven, but as there are Hier-
archies amongst the Angels, so shall there be degrees
of priority amongst the Saints. Yet is it (I protest)
beyond my ambition to aspire unto the first ranks;
my desires onely are, and I shall be happy therein,
to be but the last man, and bring up the Rere in
Heaven.

SECT.
59

AGAIN, I am confident and fully perswaded, yet
dare not take my oath, of my Salvation: I
am as it were sure, and do believe without all
doubt, that there is such a City as *Constantinople*; yet
for me to take my Oath thereon were a kind of Perjury,
because I hold no infallible warrant from my own sense
to confirm me in the certainty thereof: And truly,
though many pretend an absolute certainty of their
Salvation, yet when an humble Soul shall contemplate
our own unworthiness, she shall meet with many
doubts, and suddenly find how little we stand in need

of the Precept of St. *Paul, Work out your salvation with fear and trembling.* That which is the cause of my Election, I hold to be the cause of my Salvation, which was the mercy and beneplacit of God, before I was, or the foundation of the World. *Before Abraham was, I am,* is the saying of Christ; yet is it true in some sense, if I say it of myself; for I was not onely before myself, but *Adam,* that is, in the Idea of God, and the decree of that Synod held from all Eternity. And in this sense, I say, the World was before the Creation, and at an end before it had a beginning; and thus was I dead before I was alive: though my grave be *England,* my dying place was Paradise: and *Eve* miscarried of me, before she conceiv'd of Cain.

INSOLENT zeals that do decry good Works, and rely onely upon Faith, take not away merit: for depending upon the efficacy of their Faith, they enforce the condition of God, and in a more sophistical way do seem to challenge Heaven. It was decreed by God, that only those that lapt in the water like Dogs, should have the honour to destroy the *Midianites*; yet could none of those justly challenge, or imagine he deserved that honour thereupon. I do not deny, but that true Faith, and such as God requires, is not onely a mark or token, but also a means of our Salvation; but where to find this, is as obscure to me, as my last end. And if our Saviour could object unto his own Disciples and Favourites, a Faith, that, to the quantity of a grain of Mustard-seed, is able to remove Mountains; surely that which we boast of, is not any thing, or at the most, but a remove from nothing. This is the Tenor of my belief; wherein, though there

SECT
60

F

be many things singular, and to the humour of my irregular self; yet if they square not with maturer Judgements I disclaim them, and do no further favour them, than the learned and best judgements shall authorize them.

THE SECOND PART

NOW for that other Virtue of Charity, without SECT. which Faith is a meer notion, and of no 1 existence, I have ever endeavoured to nourish the merciful disposition and humane inclination I borrowed from my Parents, and regulate it to the written and prescribed Laws of Charity; and if I hold the true Anatomy of my self, I am delineated and naturally framed to such a piece of virtue. For I am of a constitution so general, that it comforts and sympathizeth with all things; I have no antipathy, or rather Idio-syncrasie, in dyet, humour, air, any thing: I wonder not at the *French* for their dishes of Frogs, Snails, and Toadstools, nor at the Jews for Locusts and Grasshoppers; but being amongst them, make them my common Viands, and I find they agree with my Stomach as well as theirs. I could digest a Sallad gathered in a Churchyard, as well as in a Garden. I cannot start at the presence of a Serpent, Scorpion, Lizard, or Salamander: at the sight of a Toad or Viper, I find in me no desire to take up a stone to destroy them. I feel not in my self those common Antipathies that I can discover in others: Those National repugnances do not touch me, nor do I behold with prejudice the *French, Italian, Spaniard,* or *Dutch*; but where I find their actions in balance with my Country-men's, I honour, love, and

embrace them in the same degree. I was born in the
eighth Climate, but seem for to be framed and constellated unto all: I am no Plant that will not prosper
out of a Garden: All places, all airs make unto me one
Countrey; I am in *England*, every where, and under
any Meridian. I have been shipwrackt, yet am not
enemy with the Sea or Winds; I can study, play, or
sleep in a Tempest. In brief, I am averse from
nothing; my Conscience would give me the lye if I
should absolutely detest or hate any essence but the
Devil; or so at least abhor any thing, but that we
might come to composition. If there be any among
those common objects of hatred I do contemn and
laugh at, it is that great enemy of Reason, Virtue and
Religion, the Multitude; that numerous piece of monstrosity, which taken asunder seem men, and the
reasonable creatures of God; but confused together,
make but one great beast, and a monstrosity more
prodigious than Hydra: it is no breach of Charity to
call these Fools; it is the style all holy Writers have
afforded them, set down by *Solomon* in Canonical
Scripture, and a point of our Faith to believe so.
Neither in the name of Multitude do I onely include
the base and minor sort of people; there is a rabble
even amongst the Gentry, a sort of Plebeian heads,
whose fancy moves with the same wheel as these; men
in the same Level with Mechanicks, though their
fortunes do somewhat guild their infirmities, and their
purses compound for their follies. But as in casting
account, three or four men together come short in
account of one man placed by himself below them:
So neither are a troop of these ignorant Doradoes, of
that true esteem and value, as many a forlorn person,
whose condition doth place him below their feet. Let

us speak like Politicians, there is a Nobility without
Heraldry, a natural dignity, whereby one man is ranked
with another; another filed before him, according to
the quality of his Desert, and preheminence of his
good parts: Though the corruption of these times,
and the byas of present practice wheel another way.
Thus it was in the first and primitive Commonwealths,
and is yet in the integrity and Cradle of well-order'd
Polities, till corruption getteth ground, ruder desires
labouring after that which wiser considerations contemn; every one having a liberty to amass and heap
up riches, and they a licence or faculty to do or
purchase any thing.

THIS general and indifferent temper of mine
doth more neerly dispose me to this noble
virtue. It is a happiness to be born and
framed unto virtue, and to grow up from the seeds of
nature, rather than the inoculation and forced graffs of
education: yet if we are directed only by our particular
Natures, and regulate our inclinations by no higher
rule than that of our reasons, we are but Moralists;
Divinity will still call us Heathens. Therefore this
great work of charity must have other motives, ends,
and impulsions: I give no alms only to satisfie the
hunger of my Brother, but to fulfil and accomplish the
Will and Command of my God: I draw not my purse
for his sake that demands it, but his that enjoyned it;
I relieve no man upon the Rhetorick of his miseries,
nor to content mine own commiserating disposition:
for this is still but moral charity, and an act that
oweth more to passion than reason. He that relieves
another upon the bare suggestion and bowels of pity,
doth not this so much for his sake, as for his own;

SECT.
2

for by compassion we make others misery our own, and
so by relieving them, we relieve our selves also. It
is as erroneous a conceit to redress other Mens misfortunes upon the common considerations of merciful
natures, that it may be one day our own case; for this
is a sinister and politick kind of charity, whereby we
seem to bespeak the pities of men in the like occasions:
and truly I have observed that those professed Elee-
mosynaries, though in a croud or multitude, do yet
direct and place their petitions on a few and selected
persons : there is surely a Physiognomy, which those
experienced and Master Mendicants observe ; whereby
they instantly discover a merciful aspect, and will
single out a face, wherein they spy the signatures
and marks of Mercy: for there are mystically in our
faces certain Characters which carry in them the motto
of our Souls, wherein he that can read *A. B. C.* may
read our natures. I hold moreover that there is a
Phytognomy, or Physiognomy, not only of Men but of
Plants and Vegetables ; and in every one of them, some
outward figures which hang as signs or bushes of their
inward forms. The Finger of God hath left an Inscription upon all his works, not graphical, or composed
of Letters, but of their several forms, constitutions,
parts, and operations ; which aptly joyned together do
make one word that doth express their natures. By
these Letters God calls the Stars by their names ; and
by this Alphabet *Adam* assigned to every creature a
name peculiar to its nature. Now there are, besides
these Characters in our Faces, certain mystical figures
in our Hands, which I dare not call meer dashes, strokes
a la volee, or at random, because delineated by a Pencil
that never works in vain ; and hereof I take more particular notice, because I carry that in mine own hand,

which I could never read of, nor discover in another.
Aristotle I confess, in his acute and singular Book of
Physiognomy, hath made no mention of Chiromancy;
yet I believe the *Egyptians*, who were neerer addicted
to those abstruse and mystical sciences, had a knowledge therein; to which those vagabond and counterfeit
Egyptians did after pretend, and perhaps retained a
few corrupted principles, which sometimes might verifie
their prognosticks.

It is the common wonder of all men, how among
so many millions of faces, there should be none
alike: Now contrary, I wonder as much how there
should be any. He that shall consider how many
thousand several words have been carelesly and without study composed out of 24 Letters; withal, how
many hundred lines there are to be drawn in the
Fabrick of one Man; shall easily find that this variety
is necessary: And it will be very hard that they shall
so concur, as to make one portract like another. Let
a Painter carelesly limb out a million of Faces, and
you shall find them all different; yea let him have his
Copy before him, yet after all his art there will remain
a sensible distinction; for the pattern or example of
every thing is the perfectest in that kind, whereof we
still come short, though we transcend or go beyond it,
because herein it is wide, and agrees not in all points
unto the Copy. Nor doth the similitude of Creatures
disparage the variety of Nature, nor any way confound
the Works of God. For even in things alike there is
diversity; and those that do seem to accord, do
manifestly disagree. And thus is man like God; for
in the same things that we resemble him, we are utterly
different from him. There was never any thing so like
another, as in all points to concur; there will ever

some reserved difference slip in, to prevent the identity, without which, two several things would not be alike, but the same, which is impossible.

BUT to return from Philosophy to Charity: I hold not so narrow a conceit of this virtue, as to conceive that to give Alms is onely to be Charitable, or think a piece of Liberality can comprehend the Total of Charity. Divinity hath wisely divided the act thereof into many branches, and hath taught us in this narrow way, many paths unto goodness: as many ways as we may do good, so many ways we may be charitable: there are infirmities, not onely of Body, but of Soul, and Fortunes, which do require the merciful hand of our abilities. I cannot contemn a man for ignorance, but behold him with as much pity as I do *Lazarus*. It is no greater Charity to cloath his body, than apparel the nakedness of his Soul. It is an honourable object to see the reasons of other men wear our Liveries, and their borrowed understandings do homage to the bounty of ours: It is the cheapest way of beneficence, and like the natural charity of the Sun, illuminates another without obscuring it self. To be reserved and caitiff in this part of goodness, is the sordidest piece of covetousness, and more contemptible than pecuniary Avarice. To this (as calling my self a Scholar) I am obliged by the duty of my condition: I make not therefore my head a grave, but a treasure of knowledge; I intend no Monopoly, but a community in learning; I study not for my own sake only, but for theirs that study not for themselves. I envy no man that knows more than my self, but pity them that know less. I instruct no man as an exercise of my knowledge,

or with an intent rather to nourish and keep it alive
in mine own head, then beget and propagate it in his;
and in the midst of all my endeavours, there is but
one thought that dejects me, that my acquired parts
must perish with my self, nor can be Legacied among
my honoured Friends. I cannot fall out, or contemn
a man for an errour, or conceive why a difference in
Opinion should divide an affection: For Controversies,
Disputes, and Argumentations, both in Philosophy and
in Divinity, if they meet with discreet and peaceable
natures, do not infringe the Laws of Charity: in all
disputes, so much as there is of passion, so much there
is of nothing to the purpose; for then Reason, like a
bad Hound, spends upon a false Scent, and forsakes
the question first started. And this is one reason why
Controversies are never determined; for though they
be amply proposed, they are scarce at all handled,
they do so swell with unnecessary Digressions; and the
Parenthesis on the party, is often as large as the main
discourse upon the subject. The Foundations of Religion are already established, and the Principles of
Salvation subscribed unto by all: there remains not
many controversies worth a Passion, and yet never any
disputed without, not only in Divinity, but inferiour
Arts: What a βατραχομυομαχία and hot skirmish is
betwixt S. and T. in *Lucian*: How do Grammarians
hack and slash for the Genitive case in *Jupiter*? How
do they break their own pates to salve that of *Priscian*!
Si foret in terris, rideret Democritus. Yea, even
amongst wiser militants, how many wounds have been
given, and credits slain, for the poor victory of an
opinion, or beggerly conquest of a distinction? Scholars
are men of Peace, they bear no Arms, but their tongues
are sharper than Actus his razor; their Pens carry

SECT.
3

farther, and give a lowder report than Thunder: I had rather stand the shock of a Basilisco, than the fury of a merciless Pen. It is not meer Zeal to Learning, or Devotion to the Muses, that wiser Princes Patron the Arts, and carry an indulgent aspect unto Scholars; but a desire to have their names eternized by the memory of their writings, and a fear of the revengeful Pen of succeeding ages: for these are the men, that when they have played their parts, and had their *exits*, must step out and give the moral of their Scenes, and deliver unto Posterity an Inventory of their Virtues and Vices. And surely there goes a great deal of Conscience to the compiling of an History: there is no reproach to the scandal of a Story; it is such an authentick kind of falshood, that with authority belies our good names to all Nations and Posterity.

SECT.
4

THERE is another offence unto Charity, which no Author hath ever written of, and few take notice of; and that's the reproach, not of whole professions, mysteries and conditions, but of whole Nations; wherein by opprobrious Epithets we miscal each other, and by an uncharitable Logick, from a disposition in a few, conclude a habit in all.

> *Le mutin Anglois, & le bravache Escossois;*
> *Le bougre Italian, & le fol François;*
> *Le poultron Romain, le larron de Gascongne,*
> *L'Espagnol superbe, & l'Aleman yvrongne.*

St. *Paul*, that calls the *Cretians* lyars, doth it but indirectly, and upon quotation of their own Poet. It is as bloody a thought in one way, as *Nero's* was in another. For by a word we wound a thousand, and at one blow assassine the honour of a Nation. It is as compleat a piece of madness to miscal and rave

against the times, or think to recal men to reason, by
a fit of passion : *Democritus,* that thought to laugh the times into goodness, seems to me as deeply Hypochondriack, as *Heraclitus* that bewailed them. It moves not my spleen to behold the multitude in their proper humours, that is, in their fits of folly and madness, as well understanding that wisdom is not prophan'd unto the World, and 'tis the priviledge of a few to be Vertuous. They that endeavour to abolish Vice, destroy also Virtue ; for contraries, though they destroy one another, are yet in life of one another. Thus Virtue (abolish vice) is an Idea ; again, the community of sin doth not disparage goodness ; for when Vice gains upon the major part, Virtue, in whom it remains, becomes more excellent ; and being lost in some, multiplies its goodness in others, which remain untouched, and persist intire in the general inundation. I can therefore behold Vice without a Satyr, content only with an admonition, or instructive reprehension, for Noble Natures, and such as are capable of goodness, are railed into vice, that might as easily be admonished into virtue ; and we should be all so far the Orators of goodness, as to protract her from the power of Vice, and maintain the cause of injured truth. No man can justly censure or condemn another, because indeed no man truly knows another. This I perceive in my self ; for I am in the dark to all the world, and my nearest friends behold me but in a cloud : those that know me but superficially, think less of me than I do of my self ; those of my neer acquaintance think more ; God, who truly knows me, knows that I am nothing ; for he only beholds me and all the world ; who looks not on us through a derived ray, or a trajection of a sensible species, but beholds the substance without the helps of

accidents, and the forms of things, as we their operations. Further, no man can judge another, because no
man knows himself; for we censure others but as they
disagree from that humour which we fancy laudible in
our selves, and commend others but for that wherein
they seem to quadrate and consent with us. So that
in conclusion, all is but that we all condemn, Self-love.
'Tis the general complaint of these times, and perhaps
of those past, that charity grows cold; which I perceive
most verified in those which most do manifest the fires
and flames of zeal; for it is a virtue that best agrees
with coldest natures, and such as are complexioned for
humility. But how shall we expect Charity towards
others, when we are uncharitable to our selves? Charity
begins at home, is the voice of the World; yet is every
man his greatest enemy, and as it were, his own Executioner. *Non occides,* is the Commandment of God,
yet scarce observed by any man; for I perceive every
man is his own *Atropos,* and lends a hand to cut the
thred of his own days. *Cain* was not therefore the
first Murtherer, but *Adam,* who brought in death;
whereof he beheld the practice and example in his own
son *Abel,* and saw that verified in the experience of
another, which faith could not perswade him in the
Theory of himself.

SECT.
5

THERE is, I think, no man that apprehends his
own miseries less than my self, and no man
that so neerly apprehends anothers. I could
lose an arm without a tear, and with few groans, methinks, be quartered into pieces; yet can I weep most
seriously at a Play, and receive with true passion, the
counterfeit grief of those known and professed Impostures. It is a barbarous part of inhumanity to add

unto any afflicted parties misery, or indeavour to multiply in any man, a passion, whose single nature is already above his patience : this was the greatest affliction of *Job* ; and those oblique expostulations of his Friends, a deeper injury than the down-right blows of the Devil. It is not the tears of our own eyes only, but of our friends also, that do exhaust the current of our sorrows ; which falling into many streams, runs more peaceably, and is contented with a narrower channel. It is an act within the power of charity, to translate a passion out of one brest into another, and to divide a sorrow almost out of it self; for an affliction, like a dimension, may be so divided, as if not indivisible, at least to become insensible. Now with my friend I desire not to share or participate, but to engross, his sorrows; that by making them mine own, I may more easily discuss them; for in mine own reason, and within my self, I can command that, which I cannot intreat without my self, and within the circle of another. I have often thought those noble pairs and examples of friendship not so truly Histories of what had been, as fictions of what should be ; but I now perceive nothing in them but possibilities, nor any thing in the Heroick examples of *Damon* and *Pythias*, *Achilles* and *Patroclus*, which methinks upon some grounds I could not perform within the narrow compass of my self. That a man should lay down his life for his Friend, seems strange to vulgar affections, and such as confine themselves within that Worldly principle, Charity begins at home. For mine own part I could never remember the relations that I held unto my self, nor the respect that I owe unto my own nature, in the cause of God, my Country, and my Friends. Next to these three I do embrace my self:

I confess I do not observe that order that the Schools ordain our affections, to love our Parents, Wives, Children, and then our Friends; for excepting the injunctions of Religion, I do not find in my self such a necessary and indissoluble Sympathy to all those of my blood. I hope I do not break the fifth Commandment, if I conceive I may love my friend before the nearest of my blood, even those to whom I owe the principles of life: I never yet cast a true affection on a woman, but I have loved my friend as I do virtue, my soul, my God. From hence me thinks I do conceive how God loves man, what happiness there is in the love of God. Omitting all other, there are three most mystical unions, two natures in one person; three persons in one nature; one soul in two bodies. For though indeed they be really divided, yet are they so united, as they seem but one, and make rather a duality than two distinct souls.

SECT. 6

THERE are wonders in true affection; it is a body of *Enigma's*, mysteries, and riddles; wherein two so become one, as they both become two: I love my friend before my self, and yet methinks I do not love him enough: some few months hence, my multiplied affection will make me believe I have not loved him at all: when I am from him, I am dead till I be with him; when I am with him, I am not satisfied, but would still be nearer him. United souls are not satisfied with imbraces, but desire to be truly each other; which being impossible, their desires are infinite, and must proceed without a possibility of satisfaction. Another misery there is in affection, that whom we truly love like our own, we forget their looks, nor can our memory retain the Idea of their faces; and it is no wonder, for they are our selves, and our affection makes their looks our own. This noble affection falls not on vulgar and common constitutions, but on such as are mark'd for virtue: he that can love his friend with this noble ardour, will in a competent degree affect all. Now if we can bring our affections to look beyond the body, and cast an eye upon the soul, we have found out the true object, not only of friendship, but Charity; and the greatest happiness that we can bequeath the soul, is that wherein we all do place our last felicity, Salvation; which though it be not in our power to bestow, it is in our charity and pious invocations to desire, if not procure and further. I cannot contentedly frame a prayer for my self in particular, without a catalogue for my friends; nor request a happiness wherein my sociable disposition doth not desire the fellowship of my neighbour. I never hear the Toll of a passing Bell, though in my mirth, without my prayers and best wishes for the departing spirit: I cannot go to cure the body of my patient, but I forget my profession, and call unto God for his soul: I cannot see one say his prayers, but in stead of imitating him, I fall into a supplication for him, who perhaps is no more to me than a common nature: and if God hath vouchsafed an ear to my supplications, there are surely many happy that never saw me, and enjoy the blessing of mine unknown devotions. To pray for Enemies, that is, for their salvation, is no harsh precept, but the practice of our daily and ordinary devotions. I cannot believe the story of the Italian: our bad wishes and uncharitable desires proceed no further than this life; it is the Devil, and the uncharitable votes of Hell, that desire our misery in the World to come.

TO do no injury, nor take none, was a principle, which to my former years, and impatient affections, seemed to contain enough of Morality; but my more setled years, and Christian constitution, have fallen upon severer resolutions. I can hold there is no such thing as injury; that if there be, there is no such injury as revenge, and no such revenge as the contempt of an injury: that to hate another, is to malign himself; that the truest way to love another, is to despise our selves. I were unjust unto mine own Conscience, if I should say I am at variance with any thing like my self. I find there are many pieces in this one fabrick of man; this frame is raised upon a mass of Antipathies: I am one methinks, but as the World; wherein notwithstanding there are a swarm of distinct essences, and in them another World of contrarieties; we carry private and domestick enemies within, publick and more hostile adversaries without. The Devil, that did but buffet St. *Paul*, plays methinks at sharp with me. Let me be nothing, if within the compass of my self I do not find the battail of *Lepanto*, Passion against Reason, Reason against Faith, Faith against the Devil, and my Conscience against all. There is another man within me, that's angry with me, rebukes, commands, and dastards me. I have no Conscience of Marble, to resist the hammer of more heavy offences; nor yet too soft and waxen, as to take the impression of each single peccadillo or scape of infirmity: I am of a strange belief, that it is as easie to be forgiven some sins, as to commit some others. For my Original sin, I hold it to be washed away in my Baptism, for my actual transgressions, I compute and reckon with God, but from my last repentance, Sacrament, or general absolution; and therefore am not terrified with the sins or madness of my youth. I thank the goodness of God, I have no sins that want a name; I am not singular in offences; my transgressions are Epidemical, and from the common breath of our corruption. For there are certain tempers of body, which matcht with an humorous depravity of mind, do hatch and produce vitiosities, whose newness and monstrosity of nature admits no name; this was the temper of that Lecher that carnal'd with a Statua, and constitution of *Nero* in his Spintrian recreations. For the Heavens are not only fruitful in new and unheard-of stars, the Earth in plants and animals; but mens minds also in villany and vices: now the dulness of my reason, and the vulgarity of my disposition, never prompted my invention, nor sollicited my affection unto any of those; yet even those common and quotidian infirmities that so necessarily attend me, and do seem to be my very nature, have so dejected me, so broken the estimation that I should have otherwise of my self, that I repute my self the most abjectest piece of mortality. Divines prescribe a fit of sorrow to repentance; there goes indignation, anger, sorrow, hatred, into mine; passions of a contrary nature, which neither seem to sute with this action, nor my proper constitution. It is no breach of charity to our selves, to be at variance with our Vices; nor to abhor that part of us, which is an enemy to the ground of charity our God; wherein we do but imitate our great selves the world, whose divided Antipathies and contrary faces do yet carry a charitable regard unto the whole by their particular discords, preserving the common harmony, and keeping in fetters those powers, whose rebellions once Masters, might be the ruine of all.

I THANK God, amongst those millions of Vices I do inherit and hold from *Adam*, I have escaped one, and that a mortal enemy to Charity, the first and father-sin*, not onely of man, but of the devil, Pride; a vice whose name is comprehended in a Monosyllable, but in its nature not circumscribed with a World. I have escaped it in a condition that can hardly avoid it. Those petty acquisitions and reputed perfections that advance and elevate the conceits of other men, add no feathers unto mine. I have seen a Grammarian towr and plume himself over a single line in *Horace*, and shew more pride in the construction of one Ode, than the Author in the composure of the whole book. For my own part, besides the *Jargon* and *Patois* of several Provinces, I understand no less than six Languages; yet I protest I have no higher conceit of my self, than had our Fathers before the confusion of *Babel*, when there was but one Language in the World, and none to boast himself either Linguist or Critick. I have not onely seen several Countries, beheld the nature of their Climes, the Chorography of their Provinces, Topography of their Cities, but understood their several Laws, Customs, and Policies; yet cannot all this perswade the dulness of my spirit unto such an opinion of my self, as I behold in nimbler and conceited heads, that never looked a degree beyond their Nests. I know the names, and somewhat more, of all the constellations in my Horizon; yet I have seen a prating Mariner, that could onely name the pointers and the North Star, out-talk me, and conceit

* Farther-sin, 1682.

himself a whole Sphere above me. I know most of the Plants of my Countrey, and of those about me; yet methinks I do not know so many as when I did but know a hundred, and had scarcely ever Simpled further than *Cheap-side*. For indeed, heads of capacity, and such as are not full with a handful, or easie measure of knowledge, think they know nothing, till they know all; which being impossible, they fall upon the opinion of *Socrates*, and only know they know not any thing. I cannot think that *Homer* pin'd away upon the riddle of the fishermen; or that *Aristotle*, who understood the uncertainty of knowledge, and confessed so often the reason of man too weak for the works of nature, did ever drown himself upon the flux and reflux of *Euripus*. We do but learn to-day, what our better advanced judgements will unteach to-morrow; and *Aristotle* doth but instruct us, as *Plato* did him; that is, to confute himself. I have run through all sorts, yet find no rest in any: though our first studies and *junior* endeavours may style us Peri-pateticks, Stoicks, or Academicks, yet I perceive the wisest heads prove, at last, almost all Scepticks, and stand like *Janus* in the field of knowledge. I have therefore one common and authentick Philosophy I learned in the Schools, whereby I discourse and satisfie the reason of other men; another more reserved, and drawn from experience, whereby I content mine own. *Solomon*, that complained of ignorance in the height of knowledge, hath not only humbled my conceits, but discouraged my endeavours. There is yet another conceit that hath sometimes made me shut my books, which tells me it is a vanity to waste our days in the blind pursuit of knowledge; it is but attending a little longer, and we shall enjoy that by instinct and infusion

which we endeavour at here by labour and inquisition.
It is better to sit down in a modest ignorance, and rest
contented with the natural blessing of our own reasons,
than buy the uncertain knowledge of this life, with sweat
and vexation, which Death gives every fool *gratis*, and
is an accessary of our glorification.

SECT.
9

I WAS never yet once, and commend their resolutions who never marry twice : not that I disallow
of second marriage; as neither in all cases, of
Polygamy, which considering some times, and the unequal number of both sexes, may be also necessary.
The whole World was made for man, but the twelfth
part of man for woman : Man is the whole World, and
the Breath of God ; Woman the Rib and crooked piece
of man. I could be content that we might procreate
like trees, without conjunction, or that there were any
way to perpetuate the World without this trivial and
vulgar way of coition; it is the foolishest act a wise
man commits in all his life; nor is there any thing
that will more deject his cool'd imagination, when he
shall consider what an odd and unworthy piece of folly
he hath committed. I speak not in prejudice, nor am
averse from that sweet Sex, but naturally amorous of
all that is beautiful; I can look a whole day with
delight upon a handsome Picture, though it be but of
an Horse. It is my temper, and I like it the better, to
affect all harmony; and sure there is musick even in
the beauty, and the silent note which *Cupid* strikes,
far sweeter than the sound of an instrument. For
there is a musick where ever there is a harmony, order
or proportion; and thus far we may maintain the
musick of the Sphears : for those well-ordered motions,
and regular paces, though they give no sound unto the

ear, yet to the understanding they strike a note most full of harmony. Whosoever is harmonically composed, delights in harmony; which makes me much distrust the symmetry of those heads which declaim against all Church-Musick. For my self, not only from my obedience, but my particular Genius, I do embrace it: for even that vulgar and Tavern-Musick, which makes one man merry, another mad, strikes in me a deep fit of devotion, and a profound contemplation of the first Composer. There is something in it of Divinity more than the ear discovers: it is an Hieroglyphical and shadowed lesson of the whole World, and creatures of God; such a melody to the ear, as the whole World well understood, would afford the understanding. In brief, it is a sensible fit of that harmony, which intellectually sounds in the ears of God. I will not say with *Plato*, the soul is an harmony, but harmonical, and hath its nearest sympathy unto Musick: thus some whose temper of body agrees, and humours the constitution of their souls, are born Poets, though indeed all are naturally inclined unto Rhythme. [1] This made *Tacitus* in the very first line of his Story, fall upon a verse, and *Cicero* the worst of Poets, but [2] declaiming for a Poet, falls in the very first sentence upon a perfect [3] Hexameter. I feel not in me those sordid and unchristian desires of my profession; I do not secretly implore and wish for Plagues, rejoyce at Famines, revolve Ephemerides and Almanacks, in expectation of malignant Aspects, fatal Conjunctions, and Eclipses: I rejoyce not at unwholesome Springs, nor unseasonable Winters; my Prayer goes with the Husbandman's; I desire every thing in its proper season, that neither men nor the times be put out of temper. Let me be sick my self, if sometimes the

[1] *Urbem Romam in principio Reges habuere.*

[2] *Pro Archiâ poëtâ.*

[3] *In qua me non inficior mediocriter esse.*

malady of my patient be not a disease unto me; I
desire rather to cure his infirmities than my own necessities: where I do him no good, methinks it is scarce
honest gain; though I confess 'tis but the worthy
salary of our well-intended endeavours. I am not only
ashamed, but heartily sorry, that besides death, there
are diseases incurable; yet not for my own sake, or that
they be beyond my Art, but for the general cause and
sake of humanity, whose common cause I apprehend as
mine own. And to speak more generally, those three
Noble Professions which all civil Commonwealths do
honour, are raised upon the fall of *Adam*, and are not
exempt from their infirmities; there are not only diseases
incurable in Physick, but cases indissolvable in Laws,
Vices incorrigible in Divinity: if general Councils may
err, I do not see why particular Courts should be
infallible; their perfectest rules are raised upon the
erroneous reasons of Man; and the Laws of one, do
but condemn the rules of another; as *Aristotle* oft-
times the opinions of his Predecessours, because,
though agreeable to reason, yet were not consonant to
his own rules, and Logick of his proper Principles.
Again, to speak nothing of the Sin against the Holy
Ghost, whose cure not onely, but whose nature is
unknown; I can cure the Gout or Stone in some, sooner
than Divinity Pride or Avarice in others. I can cure
Vices by Physick, when they remain incurable by
Divinity; and shall obey my Pills, when they contemn
their precepts. I boast nothing, but plainly say, we all
labour against our own cure; for death is the cure of
all diseases. There is no Catholicon or universal
remedy I know but this, which, though nauseous to
queasie stomachs, yet to prepared appetites is Nectar,
and a pleasant potion of immortality.

F OR my Conversation, it is like the Sun's with all men, and with a friendly aspect to good and bad. Methinks there is no man bad, and the worst, best; that is, while they are kept within the circle of those qualities, wherein they are good; there is no man's mind of such discordant and jarring a temper, to which a tunable disposition may not strike a harmony. *Magnæ virtutes, nec minora vitia;* it is the posie of the best natures, and may be inverted on the worst; there are in the most depraved and venemous dispositions, certain pieces that remain untoucht, which by an *Antiperistasis* become more excellent, or by the excellency of their antipathies are able to preserve themselves from the contagion of their enemy vices, and persist intire beyond the general corruption. For it is also thus in nature. The greatest Balsomes do lie enveloped in the bodies of most powerful Corrosives; I say moreover, and I ground upon experience, that poisons contain within themselves their own Antidote, and that which preserves them from the venome of themselves, without which they were not deleterious to others onely, but to themselves also. But it is the corruption that I fear within me, not the contagion of commerce without me. 'Tis that unruly regiment within me, that will destroy me; 'tis I that do infect my self; the man without a Navel yet lives in me; I feel that original canker corrode and devour me; and therefore *Defenda me Dios de me,* Lord deliver me from my self, is a part of my Letany, and the first voice of my retired imaginations. There is no man alone, because every man is a *Microcosm,* and carries the whole World about him; *Nunquam minus solus quàm cum solus,* though it be the Apothegme of a wise man, is yet true in the mouth of a fool; indeed, though in a Wilderness, a man is never alone, not only because he is with himself and his own thoughts, but because he is with the Devil, who ever consorts with our solitude, and is that unruly rebel that musters up those disordered motions which accompany our sequestred imaginations. And to speak more narrowly, there is no such thing as solitude, nor any thing that can be said to be alone and by itself, but God, who is his own circle, and can subsist by himself; all others, besides their dissimilary and Heterogeneous parts, which in a manner multiply their natures, cannot subsist without the concourse of God, and the society of that hand which doth uphold their natures. In brief, there can be nothing truly alone and by it self, which is not truly one; and such is only God: All others do transcend an unity, and so by consequence are many.

SECT
11

NOW for my life, it is a miracle of thirty years, which to relate, were not a History, but a piece of Poetry, and would sound to common ears like a Fable; for the World, I count it not an Inn, but an Hospital; and a place not to live, but to dye in. The world that I regard is my self; it is the Microcosm of my own frame that I cast mine eye on; for the other, I use it but like my Globe, and turn it round sometimes for my recreation. Men that look upon my outside, perusing only my condition and Fortunes, do err in my Altitude, for I am above *Atlas* his shoulders. The earth is a point not only in respect of the Heavens above us, but of that heavenly and celestial part within us: that mass of Flesh that circumscribes me, limits not my mind: that surface that tells the Heavens it hath an end, cannot persuade me I have any: I take my circle to be above three hundred and sixty; though the number of the Ark do measure my body, it comprehendeth not my mind : whilst I study to find how I am a Microcosm, or little World, I find my self something more than the great. There is surely a piece of Divinity in us, something that was before the Elements, and owes no homage unto the Sun. Nature tells me I am the Image of God, as well as Scripture : he that understands not thus much, hath not his introduction or first lesson, and is yet to begin the Alphabet of man. Let me not injure the felicity of others, if I say I am as happy as any : *Ruat cœlum, Fiat voluntas tua*, salveth all ; so that whatsoever happens, it is but what our daily prayers desire. In brief, I am content, and what should providence add more ? Surely this is it we call Happiness, and this do I enjoy ; with this I am happy in a dream, and as content to enjoy a happiness in a fancy, as others in a more apparent truth and realty. There is surely a neerer apprehension of any thing that delights us in our dreams, than in our waked senses ; without this I were unhappy : for my awaked judgment discontents me, ever whispering unto me, that I am from my friend ; but my friendly dreams in night requite me, and make me think I am within his arms. I thank God for my happy dreams, as I do for my good rest, for there is a satisfaction in them unto reasonable desires, and such as can be content with a fit of happiness. And surely it is not a melancholy conceit to think we are all asleep in this World, and that the conceits of this life are as meer dreams to those of the next, as the Phantasms of the night, to the conceits of the day. There is an equal delusion in both, and the one doth but seem to be the embleme or picture of the other ; we are somewhat more than our selves in our sleeps, and the slumber of the body seems

to be but the waking of the soul.   It is the ligation of
sense, but the liberty of reason, and our waking conceptions do not match the Fancies of our sleeps.   At
my Nativity, my Ascendant was the watery sign of
Scorpius; I was born in the Planetary hour of *Saturn*,
and I think I have a piece of that Leaden Planet in
me.   I am no way facetious, nor disposed for the mirth
and galliardize of company; yet in one dream I can
compose a whole Comedy, behold the action, apprehend the jests, and laugh my self awake at the conceits
thereof: were my memory as faithful as my reason is
then fruitful, I would never study but in my dreams;
and this time also would I chuse for my devotions : but
our grosser memories have then so little hold of our
abstracted understandings, that they forget the story,
and can only relate to our awaked souls, a confused
and broken tale of that that hath passed.   *Aristotle*,
who hath written a singular Tract of Sleep, hath not
methinks throughly defined it; nor yet *Galen*, though
he seem to have corrected it; for those *Noctambuloes*
and night-walkers, though in their sleep, do yet injoy
the action of their senses : we must therefore say that
there is something in us that is not in the jurisdiction
of *Morpheus*; and that those abstracted and ecstatick
souls do walk about in their own corps, as spirits with
the bodies they assume; wherein they seem to hear,
and feel, though indeed the Organs are destitute of
sense, and their natures of those faculties that should
inform them.   Thus it is observed, that men sometimes upon the hour of their departure, do speak and
reason above themselves; for then the soul beginning
to be freed from the ligaments of the body, begins to
reason like her self, and to discourse in a strain above
mortality.

WE term sleep a death, and yet it is waking
that kills us, and destroys those spirits that
are the house of life. 'Tis indeed a part
of life that best expresseth death; for every man
truely lives, so long as he acts his nature, or some way
makes good the faculties of himself: *Themistocles*
therefore that slew his Soldier in his sleep, was a
merciful Executioner: 'tis a kind of punishment the
mildness of no laws hath invented; I wonder the fancy
of *Lucan* and *Seneca* did not discover it. It is that
death by which we may be literally said to dye daily;
a death which *Adam* dyed before his mortality; a
death whereby we live a middle and moderating point
between life and death; in fine, so like death, I dare
not trust it without my prayers, and an half adieu
unto the World, and take my farewell in a Colloquy
with God.

The night is come, like to the day;
Depart not thou great God away.
Let not my sins, black as the night,
Eclipse the lustre of thy light.
Keep still in my Horizon; for to me
The Sun makes not the day, but thee.
Thou whose nature cannot sleep,
On my temples centry keep;
Guard me 'gainst those watchful foes,
Whose eyes are open while mine close.
Let no dreams my head infest,
But such as Jacob's temples blest.
While I do rest, my Soul advance;
Make my sleep a holy trance.
That I may, my rest being wrought,
Awake into some holy thought;
And with as active vigour run
My course, as doth the nimble Sun.
Sleep is a death; O make me try,
By sleeping, what it is to die:
And as gently lay my head
On my grave, as now my bed.

Howere I rest, great God, let me
Awake again at last with thee.
And thus assur'd, behold I lie
Securely, or to awake or die.
These are my drowsie days ; in vain
I do now wake to sleep again :
O come that hour, when I shall never
Sleep again, but wake for ever.

This is the Dormative I take to bedward; I need no
other *Laudanum* than this to make me sleep; after
which, I close mine eyes in security, content to take
my leave of the Sun, and sleep unto the resurrection.

SECT.
13

THE method I should use in distributive Justice,
I often observe in commutative; and keep a
Geometrical proportion in both; whereby be-
coming equable to others, I become unjust to my self,
and supererogate in that common principle, *Do unto
others as thou wouldst be done unto thy self.* I was not
born unto riches, neither is it I think my Star to be
wealthy; or if it were, the freedom of my mind, and
frankness of my disposition, were able to contradict
and cross my fates. For to me avarice seems not so
much a vice, as a deplorable piece of madness; to
conceive ourselves Urinals, or be perswaded that we are
dead, is not so ridiculous, nor so many degrees beyond
the power of Hellebore, as this. The opinion of
Theory, and positions of men, are not so void of
reason as their practised conclusions: some have held
that Snow is black, that the earth moves, that the
Soul is air, fire, water; but all this is Philosophy,
and there is no *delirium*, if we do but speculate the
folly and indisputable dotage of avarice, to that
subterraneous Idol, and God of the Earth. I do
confess I am an Atheist; I cannot perswade myself to

honour that the World adores; whatsoever virtue its
prepared substance may have within my body, it hath
no influence nor operation without: I would not
entertain a base design, or an action that should call
me villain, for the Indies; and for this only do I love
and honour my own soul, and have methinks two arms
too few to embrace myself. *Aristotle* is too severe,
that will not allow us to be truely liberal without
wealth, and the bountiful hand of Fortune; if this be
true, I must confess I am charitable only in my liberal
intentions, and bountiful well-wishes. But if the
example of the Mite be not only an act of wonder, but
an example of the noblest Charity, surely poor men
may also build Hospitals, and the rich alone have
not erected Cathedrals. I have a private method
which others observe not; I take the opportunity of
my self to do good; I borrow occasion of Charity
from mine own necessities, and supply the wants of
others, when I am in most need my self; for it is
an honest stratagem to make advantage of our selves,
and so to husband the acts of vertue, that where they
were defective in one circumstance, they may repay
their want, and multiply their goodness in another.
I have not *Peru* in my desires, but a competence, and
ability to perform those good works to which he hath
inclined my nature. He is rich, who hath enough to
be charitable; and it is hard to be so poor, that a
noble mind may not find a way to this piece of goodness. *He that giveth to the poor, lendeth to the Lord*;
there is more Rhetorick in that one sentence, than in
a Library of Sermons; and indeed if those Sentences
were understood by the Reader, with the same Em-
phasis as they are delivered by the Author, we needed
not those Volumes of instructions, but might be honest

by an Epitome. Upon this motive only I cannot behold a Beggar without relieving his Necessities with my Purse, or his Soul with my Prayers; these scenical and accidental differences between us, cannot make me forget that common and untoucht part of us both; there is under these *Cantoes* and miserable outsides, these mutilate and semi-bodies, a soul of the same alloy with our own, whose Genealogy is God as well as ours, and in as fair a way to Salvation as our selves. Statists that labour to contrive a Common-wealth without our poverty, take away the object of charity, not understanding only the Common-wealth of a Christian, but forgetting the prophecie of Christ.

SECT. 14

NOW there is another part of charity, which is the Basis and Pillar of this, and that is the love of God, for whom we love our neighbour; for this I think charity, to love God for himself, and our neighbour for God. All that is truly amiable is God, or as it were a divided piece of him, that retains a reflex or shadow of himself. Nor is it strange that we should place affection on that which is invisible; all that we truly love is thus; what we adore under affection of our senses, deserves not the honour of so pure a title. Thus we adore virtue, though to the eyes of sense she be invisible: thus that part of our noble friends that we love, is not that part that we imbrace, but that insensible part that our arms cannot embrace. God being all goodness, can love nothing but himself, and the traduction of his holy Spirit. Let us call to assize the loves of our parents, the affection of our wives and children, and they are all dumb shows and dreams, without reality, truth or constancy: for first, there is a strong bond of affection between us and our Parents; yet how easily dissolved? We betake our selves to a woman, forget our mother in a wife, and the womb that bare us, in that that shall bear our Image: this woman blessing us with children, our affection leaves the level it held before, and sinks from our bed unto our issue and picture of Posterity, where affection holds no steady mansion. They, growing up in years, desire our ends; or applying themselves to a woman, take a lawful way to love another better than our selves. Thus I perceive a man may be buried alive, and behold his grave in his own issue.

I CONCLUDE therefore and say, there is no happiness under (or as *Copernicus* will have it, above) the Sun, nor any Crambe in that repeated verity and burthen of all the wisdom of *Solomon, All is vanity and vexation of Spirit.* There is no felicity in that the World adores: *Aristotle* whilst he labours to refute the Idea's of *Plato*, falls upon one himself: for his *summum bonum* is a *Chimæra,* and there is no such thing as his Felicity. That wherein God himself is happy, the holy Angels are happy, in whose defect the Devils are unhappy; that dare I call happiness: whatsoever conduceth unto this, may with an easy Metaphor deserve that name: whatsoever else the World terms Happiness, is to me a story out of *Pliny*, a tale of *Boccace* or *Malizspini*; an apparition or neat delusion, wherein there is no more of Happiness, than the name. Bless me in this life with but peace of my Conscience, command of my affections, the love of thy self and my dearest friends, and I shall be happy enough to pity *Cæsar*. These are, O Lord, the humble desires of my

SECT.
15

most reasonable ambition, and all I dare call happiness on earth ; wherein I set no rule or limit to thy Hand or Providence ; dispose of me according to the wisdom of thy pleasure. Thy will be done, though in my own undoing.

FINIS

PSEUDODOXIA EPIDEMICA

OR ENQUIRIES
INTO VERY MANY RECEIVED
TENENTS AND COMMONLY
PRESUMED TRUTHS

TO THE READER

WOULD Truth dispense, we could be content, with Plato, *that knowledge were but remembrance; that intellectual acquisition were but reminiscential evocation, and new Impressions but the colouring of old stamps which stood pale in the soul before. For what is worse, knowledge is made by oblivion, and to purchase a clear and warrantable body of Truth, we must forget and part with much we know. Our tender Enquiries taking up Learning at large, and together with true and assured notions, receiving many, wherein our reviewing judgments do find no satisfaction. And therefore in this* Encyclopædie *and round of Knowledge, like the great and exemplary Wheels of Heaven, we must observe two Circles: that while we are daily carried about, and whirled on by the swing and rapt of the one, we may maintain a natural and proper course, in the slow and sober wheel of the other. And this we shall more readily perform, if we timely survey our knowledge; impartially singling out those encroachments, which junior compliance and popular credulity hath admitted. Whereof at present we have endeavoured a long and serious* Adviso; *proposing not only a large and copious List, but from experience and reason attempting their decisions.*

And first we crave exceeding pardon in the audacity

of the Attempt, humbly acknowledging a work of such concernment unto truth, and difficulty in it self, did well deserve the conjunction of many heads. And surely more advantageous had it been unto Truth, to have fallen into the endeavors of some co-operating advancers, that might have performed it to the life, and added authority thereto; which the privacy of our condition, and unequal abilities cannot expect. Whereby notwithstanding we have not been diverted; nor have our solitary attempts been so discouraged, as to dispair the favourable look of Learning upon our single and unsupported endeavours.

Nor have we let fall our Pen, upon discouragement of Contradiction, Unbelief and Difficulty of disswasion from radicated beliefs, and points of high prescription, although we are very sensible, how hardly teaching years do learn, what roots old age contracteth unto errors, and how such as are but acorns in our younger brows, grow Oaks in our elder heads, and become inflexible unto the powerfullest arm of reason. Although we have also beheld, what cold requitals others have found in their several redemptions of Truth; and how their ingenuous Enquiries have been dismissed with censure, and obloquie of singularities.

Some consideration we hope from the course of our Profession, which though it leadeth us into many truths that pass undiscerned by others, yet doth it disturb their Communications, and much interrupt the office of our Pens in their well intended Transmissions. And therefore surely in this work attempts will exceed performances; it being composed by snatches of time, as medical vacations, and the fruitless importunity of Uroscopy would permit us. And therefore also, perhaps it hath not found that regular and constant stile, those infallible

Inspection of Urines.

experiments and those assured determinations, which the subject sometime requireth, and might be expected from others, whose quiet doors and unmolested hours afford no such distractions. Although whoever shall indifferently perpend the exceeding difficulty, which either the obscurity of the subject, or unavoidable paradoxology must often put upon the Attemptor, he will easily discern, a work of this nature is not to be performed upon one legg; and should smel of oyl, if duly and deservedly handled.

Our first intentions considering the common interest of Truth, resolved to propose it unto the Latine republique and equal Judges of Europe, *but owing in the first place this service unto our Country, and therein especially unto its ingenuous Gentry, we have declared our self in a language best conceived. Although I confess the quality of the Subject will sometimes carry us into expressions beyond meer English apprehensions. And indeed, if elegancy still proceedeth, and English Pens maintain that stream, we have of late observed to flow from many; we shall within few years be fain to learn Latine to understand English, and a work will prove of equal facility in either. Nor have we addressed our Pen or Stile unto the people (whom Books do not redress, and are this way incapable of reduction), but unto the knowing and leading part of Learning. As well understanding (at least probably hoping) except they be watered from higher regions, and fructifying meteors of Knowledge, these weeds must lose their alimental sap, and wither of themselves. Whose conserving influence, could our endeavours prevent; we should trust the rest unto the sythe of* Time, *and hopefull dominion of Truth.*

We hope it will not be unconsidered, that we find no open tract, or constant manuduction in this Labyrinth;

but are oft-times fain to wander in the America *and untravelled parts of Truth. For though not many years past, Dr.* Primrose *hath made a learned Discourse of vulgar Errors in Physick, yet have we discussed but two or three thereof.* Scipio Mercurii *hath also left an excellent tract in* Italian, *concerning popular Errors; but confining himself only unto those in Physick, he hath little conduced unto the generality of our doctrine.* Laurentius Ioubertus, *by the same Title led our expectation into thoughts of great relief; whereby notwithstanding we reaped no advantage; it answering scarce at all the promise of the inscription. Nor perhaps (if it were yet extant) should we find any farther Assistance from that ancient piece of* Andreas, *pretending the same Title. And therefore we are often constrained to stand alone against the strength of opinion, and to meet the* Goliah *and Giant of Authority, with contemptible pibbles, and feeble arguments, drawn from the scrip and slender stock of our selves. Nor have we indeed scarce named any Author whose name we do not honour; and if detraction could invite us, discretion surely would contain us from any derogatory intention, where highest Pens and friendliest eloquence must fail in commendation.*

And therefore also we cannot but hope the equitable considerations, and candour of reasonable minds. We cannot expect the frown of Theology *herein; nor can they which behold the present state of things, and controversie of points so long received in Divinity, condemn our sober Enquiries in the doubtfull appertinancies of Arts, and Receptaries of Philosophy. Surely Philologers and Critical Discoursers, who look beyond the shell and obvious exteriours of things, will not be angry with our narrower explorations. And we cannot doubt, our Brothers in Physick (whose knowledge in Naturals*

περὶ τῶν
ψευδῶς
πεπιστευ-
μένων,
Athenæi,
lib. 7.

will lead them into a nearer apprehension of many things delivered) will friendly accept, if not countenance our endeavours. Nor can we conceive it may be unwelcome unto those honoured Worthies, who endeavour the advancement of Learning: as being likely to find a clearer progression, when so many rubs are levelled, and many untruths taken off, which passing as principles with common beliefs, disturb the tranquility of Axioms, which otherwise might be raised. And wise men cannot but know, that arts and learning want this expurgation: and if the course of truth be permitted unto its self, like that of time and uncorrected computations, it cannot escape many errors, which duration still enlargeth.

Lastly, we are not Magisterial in opinions, nor have we Dictator-like obtruded our conceptions; but in the humility of Enquiries or disquisitions, have only proposed them unto more ocular discerners. And therefore opinions are free, and open it is for any to think or declare the contrary. And we shall so far encourage contradiction, as to promise no disturbance, or re-oppose any Pen, that shall fallaciously or captiously refute us; that shall only lay hold of our lapses, single out Digressions, Corollaries, or Ornamental conceptions, to evidence his own in as indifferent truths. And shall only take notice of such, whose experimental and judicious knowledge shall solemnly look upon it; not only to destroy of ours, but to establish of his own; not to traduce or extenuate, but to explain and dilucidate, to add and ampliate, according to the laudable custom of the Ancients in their sober promotions of Learning. Unto whom notwithstanding, we shall not contentiously rejoin, or only to justifie our own, but to applaud or confirm his maturer assertions; and shall confer what is in us unto his name and honour; Ready to be swallowed in any worthy enlarger: as having acquired our end, if any way, or under any name we may obtain a work, so much desired, and yet desiderated of Truth.

THOMAS BROWN.

THE POSTSCRIPT

Readers,

TO enform you of the Advantages of the present Impression, and disabuse your expectations of any future Enlargements; these are to advertise thee, that this Edition comes forth with very many Explanations, Additions, and Alterations throughout, besides that of one entire Chapter: But that now this Work is compleat and perfect, expect no further Additions.

THE FIRST BOOK
OR GENERAL PART

CHAPTER I
Of the Causes of Common Errors.

THE First and Father-cause of common Error, is, The common infirmity of Human Nature; of whose deceptible condition, although perhaps *The Introduction.* there should not need any other eviction, than the frequent Errors we shall our selves commit, even in the express declarement hereof: yet shall we illustrate the same from more infallible constitutions, and persons presumed as far from us in condition, as time, that is, our first and ingenerated forefathers. From whom as we derive our Being, and the several wounds of constitution; so, may we in some manner excuse our infirmities in the depravity of those parts, whose Traductions were pure in them, and their Originals but once removed from God. Who notwithstanding (if posterity may take leave to judge of the fact, as they are assured to suffer in the punishment) were grossly deceived, in their perfection; *Matter of* and so weakly deluded in the clarity of their under- *great dispute, how* standing, that it hath left no small obscurity in ours, *our first parents* How error should gain upon them. *could be so*

For first, They were deceived by Satan; and that not *deceived.* in an invisible insinuation; but an open and discoverable

121

CHAP.
I

apparition, that is, in the form of a Serpent; whereby although there were many occasions of suspition, and such as could not easily escape a weaker circumspection, yet did the unwary apprehension of *Eve* take no advantage thereof. It hath therefore seemed strange unto some, she should be deluded by a Serpent, or subject her reason to a beast, which God had subjected unto hers. It hath empuzzled the enquiries of others to apprehend, and enforced them unto strange conceptions, to make out, how without fear or doubt she could discourse with such a creature, or hear a Serpent speak, without suspition of Imposture. The wits of others have been so bold, as to accuse her simplicity, in receiving his Temptation so coldly; and when such specious effects of the Fruit were Promised, as to make them like God; not to desire, at least not to wonder he pursued not that benefit himself. And had it been their own case, would perhaps have replied, If the tast of this Fruit maketh the eaters like *Gods*, why remainest thou a Beast? If it maketh us but *like Gods*, we are so already. If thereby our eyes shall be opened hereafter, they are at present quick enough, to discover thy deceit; and we desire them no opener, to behold our own shame. If to know good and evil be our advantage, although we have Free-will unto both, we desire to perform but one; We know 'tis good to obey the commandement of God, but evil if we transgress it.

They were deceived by one another, and in the greatest disadvantage of Delusion, that is, the stronger by the weaker: For *Eve* presented the Fruit, and *Adam* received it from her. Thus the *Serpent* was cunning enough, to begin the deceit in the weaker, and the weaker of strength, sufficient to consummate the fraud in the stronger. Art and fallacy was used unto her; a

naked offer proved sufficient unto him : So his superstruction was his Ruine, and the fertility of his Sleep
an issue of Death unto him.   And although the condition of Sex, and posteriority of Creation, might
somewhat extenuate the Error of the Woman: Yet
was it very strange and inexcusable in the Man ; especially, if as some affirm, he was the wisest of all men
since ; or if, as others have conceived, he was not
ignorant of the Fall of the Angels, and had thereby
Example and punishment to deterr him.

CHAP.
I

Adam *sup-
posed by some
to have been
the wisest
man that
ever was.*

They were deceived from themselves, and their own
apprehensions ; for *Eve* either mistook, or traduced the
commandment of God.   *Of every Tree of the Garden
thou mayest freely eat, but of the Tree of knowledge of
good and evil thou shalt not eat: for in the day thou
eatest thereof, thou shalt surely die.*   Now *Eve* upon
the question of the *Serpent*, returned the Precept in
different terms : *You shall not eat of it, neither shall
you touch it, less perhaps you die.*   In which delivery,
there were no less than two mistakes, or rather additional mendacities ; for the Commandment forbad not
the touch of the Fruit ; and positively said, *Ye shall
surely die :* but she extenuating, replied, *ne fortè mori-
amini, lest perhaps ye die.*   For so in the vulgar translation it runneth, and so it is expressed in the *Thargum*
or Paraphrase of *Jonathan.*   And therefore although
it be said, and that very truely, *that the Devil was a
lyer from the beginning*, yet was the Woman herein
the first express beginner : and falsified twice, before
the reply of *Satan.*   And therefore also, to speak
strictly, the sin of the Fruit was not the first Offence :
They first transgressed the Rule of their own Reason ;
and after the Commandment of God.

Adam *and
Eve how
they fell.*

They were deceived through the Conduct of their

Senses, and by Temptations from the Object it self whereby although their intellectuals had not failed in the Theory of truth, yet did the inservient and brutal Faculties controll the suggestion of Reason : Pleasure and Profit already overswaying the instructions of Honesty, and Sensuality perturbing the reasonable commands of Vertue. For so it is delivered in the Text : That when the Woman saw, *that the Tree was good for food*, and *that it was pleasant unto the eye*, and *a Tree to be desired to make one wise, she took of the fruit thereof and did eat.* Now hereby it appeareth, that *Eve*, before the Fall, was by the same and beaten away of allurements inveigled, whereby her posterity hath been deluded ever since ; that is, those three delivered by St. *John, The lust of the flesh, the lust of the eye, and the pride of life* : Where indeed they seemed as weakly to fail, as their debilitated posterity, ever after. Whereof notwithstanding, some in their imperfection, have resisted more powerful temptations ; and in many moralities condemned the facility of their seductions.

Again, they might, for ought we know, be still deceived in the unbelief of their Mortality, even after they had eat of the Fruit : For, *Eve* observing no immediate execution of the Curse, she delivered the Fruit unto *Adam* : who, after the tast thereof, perceiving himself still to live, might yet remain in doubt, whether he had incurred Death ; which perhaps he did not indubitably believe, until he was after convicted in the visible example of *Abel*. For he that would not believe the Menace of God at first, it may be doubted whether, before an ocular example, he believed the

Curse at last. And therefore they are not without all reason, who have disputed the Fact of *Cain* : that is, although he purposed to do mischief, whether he

intended to kill his Brother; or designed that, whereof CHAP.
he had not beheld an example in his own kind. There   I
might be somewhat in it, that he would not have done,
or desired undone, when he brake forth as desperately,
as before he had done uncivilly, *My iniquity is greater
than can be forgiven me.*

Some nicities I confess there are which extenuate,
but many more that aggravate this Delusion; which
exceeding the bounds of this Discourse, and perhaps
our Satisfaction, we shall at present pass over. And
therefore whether the Sin of our First Parents were the
greatest of any since; whether the transgression of *Eve*
seducing, did not exceed that of *Adam* seduced; or
whether the resistibility of his Reason, did not equiva-
lence the facility of her Seduction; we shall refer it to the
Schoolman; Whether there was not in *Eve* as great
injustice in deceiving her husband, as imprudence in
being deceived her self; especially, if foretasting the
Fruit, her eyes were opened before his, and she knew
the effect of it, before he tasted of it; we leave it unto
the *Moralist*. Whether the whole relation be not
Allegorical, that is, whether the temptation of the
Man by the Woman, be not the seduction of the
rational and higher parts by the inferiour and feminine
faculties; or whether the Tree in the midst of
the Garden, were not that part in the Center of the
body, in which was afterward the appointment of Cir-
cumcision in Males, we leave it unto the *Thalmudist*. *The* Thalmu-
Whether there were any Policy in the Devil to tempt dist's *Allegories upon*
them before the Conjunction, or whether the Issue *the History*
before tentation, might in justice have suffered with *of* Adam *and*
Eve's *Fall.*
those after, we leave it unto the *Lawyer*. Whether *Adam*
foreknew the advent of Christ, or the reparation of his
Error by his Saviour; how the execution of the Curse

should have been ordered, if, after *Eve* had eaten, *Adam* had yet refused. Whether if they had tasted the Tree of life, before that of Good and Evil, they had yet suffered the curse of Mortality: or whether the efficacy of the one had not over-powred the penalty of the other, we leave it unto GOD. For he alone can truly determine these, and all things else; Who as he hath proposed the World unto our disputation, so hath he reserved many things unto his own resolution; whose determination we cannot hope from flesh, but must with reverence suspend unto that great Day, whose justice shall either condemn our curiosities, or resolve our disquisitions.

Lastly, Man was not only deceivable in his Integrity, but the Angels of light in all their Clarity. He that said, He would be like the highest did erre, if in some way he conceived himself so already: but in attempting so high an effect from himself, he mis-understood the nature of God, and held a false apprehension of his own; whereby vainly attempting not only insolencies, but impossibilities, he deceived himself as low as Hell. In brief, there is nothing infallible but GOD, who cannot possibly erre. For things are really true as they correspond unto his conception; and have so much verity as they hold of conformity unto that Intellect, in whose *Idea* they had their first determinations. And therefore being the Rule, he cannot be Irregular; nor, being Truth it self, conceaveably admit the impossible society of Error.

CHAPTER II

A further Illustration of the same.

BEING thus deluded before the Fall, it is no wonder if their conceptions were deceitful, and could scarce speak without an Error after. For, what is very remarkable (and no man that I know hath yet observed) in the relations of Scripture before the Flood, there is but one speech delivered by Man, wherein there is not an erroneous conception; and, strictly examined, most hainously injurious unto truth. The pen of *Moses* is brief in the account before the Flood, and the speeches recorded are but six. The first is that of *Adam*, when upon the expostulation of God, he replied; *I heard thy voice in the Garden, and because I was naked I hid my self.* In which reply, there was included a very gross Mistake, and, if with pertinacity maintained, a high and capital Error. For thinking by this retirement to obscure himself from God, he infringed the omnisciency and essential Ubiquity of his Maker, Who as he created all things, so is he beyond and in them all, not only in power, as under his subjection, or in his presence, as being in his cognition; but in his very Essence, as being the soul of their causalities, and the essential cause of their existencies. Certainly, his posterity at this distance and after so perpetuated an impairment, cannot but condemn the poverty of his conception, that thought to obscure himself from his Creator in the shade of the Garden, who had beheld him before in the darkness of his Chaos, and the great obscurity of Nothing; that thought to fly from God, which could not fly himself;

or imagined that one tree should conceal his nakedness from Gods eye, as another had revealed it unto his own. Those tormented Spirits that wish the mountains to cover them, have fallen upon desires of minor absurdity, and chosen ways of less improbable concealment. Though this be also as ridiculous unto reason, as fruitless unto their desires; for he that laid the foundations of the Earth, cannot be excluded the secrecy of the Mountains; nor can there any thing escape the perspicacity of those eyes which were before light, and in whose opticks there is no opacity. This is the consolation of all good men, unto whom his Ubiquity affordeth continual comfort and security : And this is the affliction of Hell, unto whom it affordeth despair, and remediless calamity. For those restless Spirits that fly the face of the Almighty, being deprived the fruition of his eye, would also avoid the extent of his hand ; which being impossible, their sufferings are desperate, and their afflictions without evasion ; until they can get out of *Trismegistus* his Circle, that is, to extend their wings above the Universe, and pitch beyond Ubiquity.

The Second is that Speech of *Adam* unto God ; *The woman whom thou gavest me to be with me, she gave me of the Tree, and I did eat.* This indeed was an unsatisfactory reply, and therein was involved a very impious Error, as implying God the Author of sin, and accusing his Maker of his transgression. As if he had said, If thou hadst not given me a woman, I had not been deceived : Thou promisedst to make her a help, but she hath proved destruction unto me : Had I remained alone, I had not sinned ; but thou gavest me a Consort, and so I became seduced. This was a bold and open accusation of God, making the fountain of good, the contriver of evil, and the forbidder of the crime an

abettor of the fact prohibited. Surely, his mercy was
great that did not revenge the impeachment of his
justice ; And his goodness to be admired, that it refuted
not his argument in the punishment of his excusation,
and only pursued the first transgression without a
penalty of this the second.

The third was that of *Eve* ; *The Serpent beguiled me,
and I did eat.* In which reply, there was not only a very
feeble excuse, but an erroneous translating her own
offence upon another ; Extenuating her sin from that
which was an aggravation, that is, to excuse the Fact at
all, much more upon the suggestion of a beast, which
was before in the strictest terms prohibited by her
God. For although we now do hope the mercies of
God will consider our degenerated integrities unto
some minoration of our offences ; yet had not the sincerity of our first parents so colourable expectations,
unto whom the commandment was but single, and their
integrities best able to resist the motions of its transgression. And therefore so heinous conceptions have
risen hereof, that some have seemed more angry therewith, than God himself : Being so exasperated with
the offence, as to call in question their salvation, and
to dispute the eternal punishment of their Maker.
Assuredly with better reason may posterity accuse
them than they the Serpent or one another ; and the
displeasure of the *Pelagians* must needs be irreconcilable,
who peremptorily maintaining they can fulfil the whole
Law, will insatisfactorily condemn the non-observation
of one.

The fourth, was that speech of *Cain* upon the demand
of God, *Where is thy brother ?* and he said, *I know not.*
In which Negation, beside the open impudence, there
was implied a notable Error ; for returning a lie unto

CHAP.
II

his Maker, and presuming in this manner to put off the Searcher of hearts, he denied the omnisciency of God, whereunto there is nothing concealable. The answer oı Satan in the case of *Job*, had more of truth, wisdom, and Reverence, this; *Whence comest thou Satan?* and he said, *From compassing of the Earth.* For though an enemy of God, and hater of all Truth, his wisdom will hardly permit him to falsifie with the All-mighty. For well understanding the Omniscience of his nature, he is not so ready to deceive himself, as to falsifie unto him whose cognition is no way deludable. And therefore when in the tentation of Christ he played upon the fallacy, and thought to deceive the Author of Truth, the Method of this proceeding arose from the uncertainty of his Divinity; whereof had he remained assured, he had continued silent; nor would his discretion attempt so unsucceedable a temptation. And so again at the last day, when our offences shall be drawn into accompt, the subtilty of that Inquisitor shall not present unto God a bundle of calumnies or confutable accusations, but will discreetly offer up unto his Omnisciency, a true and undeniable list of our transgressions.

The Devill knew not our Saviour to be God when he tempted him.

The fifth is another reply of *Cain* upon the denouncement of his curse, *My iniquity is greater then can be forgiven*: For so it is expressed in some Translations. The assertion was not only desperate, but the conceit erroneous, overthrowing that glorious Attribute of God, his Mercy, and conceiving the sin of murder unpardonable. Which how great soever, is not above the repentance of man; but far below the mercies of God, and was (as some conceive) expiated in that punishment he suffered temporally for it. There are but two examples of this error in holy Scripture, and they both for Murder, and both as it were of the same

person; for Christ was mystically slain in *Abel*, and
therefore *Cain* had some influence on his death as well
as *Judas*; but the sin had a different effect on *Cain*,
from that it had on *Judas*; and most that since have
fallen into it. For they like *Judas* desire death, and
not unfrequently pursue it: *Cain* on the contrary grew
afraid thereof, and obtained a securement from it.
Assuredly, if his despair continued, there was punishment enough in life, and Justice sufficient in the mercy
of his protection. For the life of the desperate equalls
the anxieties of death; who in uncessant inquietudes
but act the life of the damned, and anticipate the
desolations of Hell. 'Tis indeed a sin in man, but a
punishment only in Devils, who offend not God but
afflict themselves, in the appointed despair of his
mercies. And as to be without hope is the affliction of
the damned, so is it the happiness of the blessed; who
having all their expectations present, are not distracted
with futurities: So is it also their felicity to have no
Faith; for enjoying the beatifical vision, there is
nothing unto them inevident; and in the fruition of
the object of Faith, they have received the full evacuation of it.

The last speech was that of *Lamech, I have slain a man
to my wound, and a young man to my hurt*: If *Cain* be
avenged seven fold, truly *Lamech* seventy and seven fold.
Now herein there seems to be a very erroneous Illation:
from the Indulgence of God unto *Cain*, concluding an
immunity unto himself; that is, a regular protection from
a single example, and an exemption from punishment in
a fact that naturally deserved it. The Error of this
offender was contrary to that of *Cain*, whom the *Rabbins*
conceive that *Lamech* at this time killed. He despaired
in Gods mercy in the same Fact, where this presumed

Cain, *as the
Rabbins
think, was
the man
slain by*
Lamech,
Gen. 4, 23.

of it; he by a decollation of all hope annihilated his mercy, this by an immoderancy thereof destroyed his Justice. Though the sin were less, the Error was as great; For as it is untrue, that his mercy will not forgive offenders, or his benignity co-operate to their conversions; So is it also of no less falsity to affirm His justice will not exact account of sinners, or punish such as continue in their transgressions.

Thus may we perceive, how weakly our Fathers did Erre before the Floud, how continually and upon common discourse they fell upon Errors after; it is therefore no wonder we have been erroneous ever since. And being now at greatest distance from the beginning of Error, are almost lost in its dissemination, whose waies are boundless, and confess no circumscription.

CHAPTER III

Of the second cause of Popular Errors; the erroneous disposition of the People.

HAVING thus declared the infallible nature of Man even from his first production, we have beheld the general cause of Error. But as for popular Errors, they are more neerly founded upon an erroneous inclination of the people; as being the most deceptable part of Mankind and ready with open armes to receive the encroachments of Error. Which condition of theirs although deducible from many Grounds, yet shall we evidence it but from a few, and such as most neerly and undeniably declare their natures.

How unequal discerners of truth they are, and

openly exposed unto Error, will first appear from their
unqualified intellectuals, unable to umpire the difficulty of its dissensions. For Error, to speak largely,
is a false judgment of things, or, an assent unto
falsity. Now whether the object whereunto they deliver up their assent be true or false, they are incom-
petent judges.

For the assured truth of things is derived from the
principles of knowledge, and causes which determine
their verities. Whereof their uncultivated understandings, scarce holding any theory, they are but bad discerners of verity ; and in the numerous track of Error,
but casually do hit the point and unity of truth.

Their understanding is so feeble in the discernment of
falsities, and averting the Errors of reason, that it sub-
mitteth unto the fallacies of sense, and is unable to
rectifie the Error of its sensations. Thus the greater
part of Mankind having but one eye of Sense and Reason, *Arguments*
conceive the Earth far bigger than the Sun, the fixed *of sensitive*
quality most
Stars lesser than the Moon, their figures plain, and their *prevailing*
spaces from Earth equidistant. For thus their Sense *upon vulgar*
capacities.
informeth them, and herein their reason cannot Rectifie
them ; and therefore hopelesly continuing in mistakes,
they live and die in their absurdities ; passing their days
in perverted apprehensions, and conceptions of the
World, derogatory unto God, and the wisdom of the
Creation.

Again, being so illiterate in the point of intellect,
and their sense so incorrected, they are farther indisposed ever to attain unto truth ; as commonly proceeding
in those wayes, which have most reference unto sense,
and wherein there lyeth most notable and popular
delusion.

For being unable to wield the intellectuall arms of

Fable.

reason, they are fain to betake themselves unto wasters, and the blunter weapons of truth : affecting the gross and sensible ways of Doctrine, and such as will not consist with strict and subtile Reason. Thus unto them a piece of Rhetorick is a sufficient argument of Logick ; an Apologue of *Esop,* beyond a Syllogysm in *Barbara* ; parables than propositions, and proverbs more powerful than demonstrations. And therefore are they led rather by Example, than Precept ; receiving perswasions from visible inducements, before electual instructions. And therefore also they judge of human actions by the event ; for being uncapable of operable circumstances, or rightly to judge the prudentiality of affairs, they only gaze upon the visible success, and therefore condemn or cry up the whole progression. And so from this ground in the Lecture of holy Scripture, their apprehensions are commonly confined unto the literal sense of the Text, from whence have ensued the gross and duller sort of Heresies. For not attaining the deuteroscopy, and second intention of the words, they are fain to omit the Superconsequencies, Coherencies, Figures, or Tropologies ; and are not sometime perswaded by fire beyond their literalities. And therefore also things invisible, but into intellectual discernments, to humour the grossness of their comprehensions, have been degraded from their proper forms, and God Himself dishonoured into manual expressions. And so likewise being unprovided, or unsufficient for higher speculations, they will always betake themselves unto sensible representations, and can hardly be restrained the dulness of Idolatry : A sin or folly not only derogatory unto God but men ; overthrowing their Reason, as well as his Divinity. In brief, a reciprocation, or rather, an inversion of the Creation, making

God one way, as he made us another; that is, after our
Image, as he made us after His own.

Moreover, their understanding thus weak in it self,
and perverted by sensible delusions, is yet farther impaired by the dominion of their appetite; that is, the
irrational and brutal part of the soul, which lording it
over the soveraign faculty, interrupts the actions of
that noble part, and choaks those tender sparks, which
Adam hath left them of reason. And therefore they
do not only swarm with Errors, but vices depending
thereon. Thus they commonly affect no man any
further than he deserts his reason, or complies with
their aberrancies. Hence they imbrace not vertue for
it self, but its reward; and the argument from pleasure
or Utility is far more powerful, than that from vertuous
Honesty: which *Mahomet* and his contrivers well understood, when he set out the felicity of his Heaven, by
the contentments of flesh, and the delights of sense,
slightly passing over the accomplishment of the Soul,
and the beatitude of that part which Earth and visibilities too weakly affect. But the wisdom of our
Saviour, and the simplicity of his truth proceeded
another way; defying the popular provisions of happiness from sensible expectations; placing his felicity in
things removed from sense, and the intellectual enjoyment of God. And therefore the doctrine of the one
was never afraid of Universities, or endeavoured the
banishment of learning, like the other. And though
Galen doth sometimes nibble at *Moses*, and, beside the
Apostate Christian, some *Heathens* have questioned his *Julian.*
Philosophical part, or treaty of the Creation: Yet is
there surely no reasonable *Pagan*, that will not admire
the rational and well grounded precepts of Christ;
whose life, as it was conformable unto his Doctrine, so

was that unto the highest rules of Reason; and must therefore flourish in the advancement of learning, and the perfection of parts best able to comprehend it.

Again, Their individual imperfections being great, they are moreover enlarged by their aggregation; and being erroneous in their single numbers, once hudled together, they will be Error it self. For being a confusion of knaves and fools, and a farraginous concurrence of all conditions, tempers, sexes, and ages; it is but natural if their determinations be monstrous, and many wayes inconsistent with Truth. And therefore wise men have alwaies applauded their own judgment, in the contradiction of that of the people; and their soberest adversaries, have ever afforded them the stile of fools and mad men; and, to speak impartially, their actions have made good these *Epithets*. Had *Orestes* been Judge, he would not have acquitted that *Lystrian* rabble of madness, who, upon a visible miracle, falling into so high a conceit of *Paul* and *Barnabas*, that they termed the one *Jupiter*, the other *Mercurius*; that they brought Oxen and Garlands, and were hardly restrained from sacrificing unto them; did notwithstanding suddenly after fall upon *Paul*, and having stoned him drew him for dead out of the City. It might have hazarded the sides of *Democritus*, had he been present at that tumult of *Demetrius*; when the people flocking together in great numbers, some crying one thing, and some another, and the assembly was confused, and the most part knew not wherefore they were come together; notwithstanding, all with one voice for the space of two hours cried out, Great is *Diana* of the *Ephesians*. It had overcome the patience of *Job*, as it did the meekness of *Moses*, and would surely have mastered any, but the longanimity, and lasting sufferance of God; had

Non sani
esse homi-
nis, non
sanus juret
Orestes.

they beheld the Mutiny in the wilderness, when, after
ten great Miracles in *Egypt*, and some in the same
place, they melted down their stoln ear-rings into a
Calf, and monstrously cryed out; *These are thy Gods,*
O Israel, *that brought thee out of the land of* Egypt. It
much accuseth the impatience of *Peter*, who could not
endure the staves of the multitude, and is the greatest
example of lenity in our Saviour, when he desired of
God forgiveness unto those, who having one day brought
him into the City in triumph, did presently after, act
all dishonour upon him, and nothing could be heard
but, *Crucifige*, in their Courts. Certainly he that con-
sidereth these things in God's peculiar people will
easily discern how little of truth there is in the wayes
of the Multitude; and though sometimes they are
flattered with that *Aphorism*, will hardly believe, The
voice of the people to be the voice of God.

Lastly, being thus divided from truth in themselves,
they are yet farther removed by advenient deception.
For true it is (and I hope I shall not offend their
vulgarities,) if I say, they are daily mocked into Error
by subtler devisors, and have been expressly deluded by
all professions and ages. Thus the *Priests* of Elder
time, have put upon them many incredible conceits,
not only deluding their apprehensions with Ariolation,
South-saying, and such oblique Idolatries, but winning
their credulities unto the literal and down-right adorement of Cats, Lizzards, and Beetles. And thus also in
some Christian Churches, wherein is presumed an irre-
provable truth, if all be true that is suspected, or half
what is related; there have not wanted many strange
deceptions, and some thereof are still confessed by the
name of Pious Frauds. Thus *Theudas* an Impostor was
able to lead away Four thousand into the Wilderness,

and the delusions of *Mahomet* almost the fourth part of *Mankind.* Thus all Heresies, how gross soever, have found a welcome with the people. For thus, many of the Jews were wrought into belief that *Herod* was the *Messias* ; and *David George* of *Leyden and Arden,* were not without a party amongst the people, who maintained the same opinion of themselves almost in our days.

Physitians (many at least that make profession thereof) beside divers less discoverable wayes of fraud, have made them believe, there is the book of fate, or *The* Author's the power of *Aarons* breast-plate, in Urins. And there- *Censure* fore hereunto they have recourse, as unto the Oracle of *upon Judg-* life, the great determinator of Virginity, Conception, *ment by* *Urine.* Fertility, and the Inscrutable infirmities of the whole Body. For as though there were a seminality in Urine, or that, like the Seed, it carried with it the *Idea* of every part, they foolishly conceive, we visibly behold therein the Anatomy of every particle, and can thereby indigitate their Diseases : And running into any demands, expect from us a sudden resolution in things, whereon the Devil of *Delphos* would demurr ; and we know hath taken respite of some dayes to answer easier questions.

Saltimbancoes, Quacksalvers, and *Charlatans,* deceive *Places in* them in lower degrees. Were *Esop* alive, the *Piazza* *Venice and* and *Pont-Neuf* could not but speak their fallacies ; *Paris, where* *Mounte-* mean while there are too many, whose cries cannot *banks play* conceal their mischief. For their Impostures are full *their pranks.* of cruelty, and worse than any other ; deluding not only unto pecuniary defraudations, but the irreparable deceit of death.

Astrologers, which pretend to be of *Cabala* with the Starrs (such I mean as abuse that worthy Enquiry)

have not been wanting in their deceptions; who having
won their belief unto principles whereof they make
great doubt themselves, have made them believe that
arbitrary events below, have necessary causes, above;
whereupon their credulities assent unto any Prognosticks; and daily swallow the Predictions of men, which,
considering the independency of their causes, and con-
tigency in their Events, are only in the prescience
of God.

Fortune-tellers, Juglers, Geomancers, and the like
incantory Impostors, though commonly men of Inferiour
rank, and from whom without Illumination they can
expect no more than from themselves, do daily and
professedly delude them. Unto whom (what is deplorable in Men and Christians) too many applying themselves, betwixt jest and earnest, betray the cause of
Truth, and sensibly make up the legionary body of Error.

Statists and *Politicians*, unto whom *Ragione di Stato*,
is the first Considerable, as though it were their business to deceive the people, as a Maxim, do hold, that
truth is to be concealed from them; unto whom
although they reveal the visible design, yet do they
commonly conceal the capital intention. And therefore have they ever been the instruments of great
designes, yet seldom understood the true intention of
any, accomplishing the drifts of wiser heads, as inanimate and ignorant Agents, the general design of the
World; who though in some Latitude of sense, and in
a natural cognition perform their proper actions, yet
do they unknowingly concurr unto higher ends, and *The people*
blindly advance the great intention of Nature. Now *of* Rome,
how far they may be kept in ignorance a greater ex- *suffered to*
ample there is in the people of *Rome*; who never knew *right name*
the true and proper name of their own City. For, *of their City.*

CHAP.
III

beside that common appellation received by the
Citizens, it had a proper and secret name concealed
from them : *Cujus alterum nomen discere secretis Cere-
moniarum nefas habetur,* saith *Plinie*; lest the name
thereof being discovered unto their enemies, their
Penates and Patronal God might be called forth by
charms and incantations. For according unto the
tradition of *Magitians*, the tutelary Spirits will not
remove at common appellations, but at the proper
names of things whereunto they are Protectors.

Thus having been deceived by themselves, and continually deluded by others, they must needs be stuffed
with Errors, and even over-run with these inferiour
falsities ; whereunto whosoever shall resign their
reasons, either from the Root of deceit in themselves,
or inability to resist such trivial deceptions from others,
although their condition and fortunes may place them
many Spheres above the multitude; yet are they still
within the line of Vulgarity, and Democratical enemies
of truth.

CHAPTER IV

Of the nearer and more Immediate Causes of
popular Errors, both in the wiser and
common sort, Misapprehension, Fallacy,
or false Deduction, Credulity, Supinity,
Adherence unto Antiquity, Tradition and
Authority.

THE first is a mistake, or a misconception of
things, either in their first apprehensions,
or secondary relations. So *Eve* mistook the
Commandment, either from the immediate injunction

of God, or from the secondary narration of her CHAP.
Husband. So might the Disciples mistake our IV
Saviour, in his answer unto *Peter* concerning the death
of *John*, as is delivered, *John* 21. Peter *seeing* John,
said unto Jesus, *Lord, and what shall this man do?*
Jesus *saith, If I will, that he tarry till I come, what is*
that unto thee? *Then went this saying abroad among*
the brethren, that that Disciple should not die. Thus
began the conceit and opinion of the *Centaures*: that *The belief of*
is, in the mistake of the first beholders, as is declared *Centaures*
by *Servius*; when some young *Thessalians* on horse- *occasioned.*
back were beheld afar off, while their horses watered,
that is, while their heads were depressed, they were
conceived by the first Spectators, to be but one animal;
and answerable hereunto have their pictures been drawn
ever since.

And, as simple mistakes commonly beget fallacies,
so men rest not in false apprehensions, without absurd
and inconsequent deductions; from fallacious foundations, and misapprehended *mediums*, erecting conclusions no way inferrible from their premises. Now the
fallacies whereby men deceive others, and are deceived
themselves, the Ancients have divided into Verbal and
Real. Of the Verbal, and such as conclude from mistakes of the Word, although there be no less than six,
yet are there but two thereof worthy our notation, and
unto which the rest may be referred; that is the fallacy
of Equivocation and Amphibology which conclude from *Equivoca-*
the ambiguity of some one word, or the ambiguous *tion and Am-*
phibologie,
Syntaxis of many put together. From this fallacy *how they*
differ.
arose that calamitous Error of the Jews, misappre-
hending the Prophesies of their *Messias*, and expound-
ing them always unto literal and temporal expectations.
By this way many Errors crept in and perverted the

Pythagoras,
*his Allegori-
cal precepts
moralized.*

πᾶν δειλοι
κυαμῶν ἄπο
χεῖρας ἔχεσθε.

Doctrine of *Pythagoras*, whilst men received his Precepts in a different sense from his intention; converting Metaphors into proprieties, and receiving as literal expressions, obscure and involved truths. Thus when he enjoyned his Disciples, an abstinence from Beans, many conceived they were with severity debarred the use of that pulse; which notwithstanding could not be his meaning; for as *Aristoxenus*, who wrote his life averreth, he delighted much in that kind of food himself. But herein, as *Plutarch* observeth, he had no other intention than to dissuade men from Magistracy, or undertaking the publick offices of state; for by beans was the Magistrate elected in some parts of *Greece*; and, after his daies, we read in *Thucydides*, of the Councel of the bean in *Athens*. The same word also in Greek doth signifie a Testicle, and hath been thought by some an injunction only of Continency, as *Aul. Gellius* hath expounded, and as *Empedocles* may also be interpreted: that is, *Testiculis miseri dextras subducite*; and might be the original intention of *Pythagoras*; as having a notable hint hereof in Beans, from the natural signature of the venereal organs of both Sexes. Again, his injunction is, not to harbour Swallows in our Houses: Whose advice notwithstanding we do not contemn, who daily admit and cherish them: For herein a caution is only implied, not to entertain ungrateful and thankless persons, which like the Swallow are no way commodious unto us; but having made use of our habitations, and served their own turns, forsake us. So he commands to deface the Print of a Cauldron in the ashes, after it hath boiled. Which strictly to observe were condemnable superstition: But hereby he covertly adviseth us not to persevere in anger; but after our choler hath boiled,

to retain no impression thereof. In the like sense are
to be received, when he adviseth his Disciples to give
the right hand but to few, to put no viands in a
Chamber-pot, not to pass over a Balance, not to rake
up fire with a Sword, or piss against the Sun. Which
ænigmatical deliveries comprehend useful verities, but
being mistaken by literal Expositors at the first, they
have been mis-understood by most since, and may be
occasion of Error to Verbal capacities for ever.

This fallacy in the first delusion Satan put upon
Eve, and his whole tentation might be the same continued; so when he said, *Ye shall not die*, that was, in
his equivocation, ye shall not incurr a present death,
or a destruction immediately ensuing your transgression. *Your eyes shall be opened*; that is, not to the
enlargement of your knowledge, but discovery of your
shame and proper confusion; *You shall know good
and evil*; that is, you shall have knowledge of good by
its privation, but cognisance of evil by sense and visible
experience. And the same fallacy or way of deceit, so
well succeeding in Paradise, he continued in his Oracles
through all the World. Which had not men more
warily understood, they might have performed many
acts inconsistent with his intention. *Brutus* might
have made haste with *Tarquine* to have kissed his
own Mother. The *Athenians* might have built them
wooden Walls, or doubled the Altar at *Delphos*.

The circle of this fallacy is very large; and herein
may be comprised all Ironical mistakes, for intended
expressions receiving inverted significations; all deductions from Metaphors, Parables, Allegories, unto
real and rigid interpretations. Whereby have risen
not only popular Errors in Philosophy, but vulgar and *De hæresi-*
senseless Heresies in Divinity; as will be evident unto *bus.*

any that shall examine their foundations, as they stand
related by *Epiphanius, Austin,* or *Prateolus.*

Other wayes there are of deceit ; which consist not
in false apprehension of Words, that is, Verbal expressions or sentential significations, but fraudulent
deductions, or inconsequent illations, from a false conception of things. Of these extradictionary and real
fallacies, *Aristotle* and *Logicians* make in number six,
but we observe that men are most commonly deceived
by four thereof: those are, *Petitio principii, A dicto
secundum quid ad dictum simpliciter, A non causa pro
causa* ; And, *fallacia consequentis.*

The first is, *Petitio principii.* Which fallacy is committed, when a question is made a *medium,* or we
assume a *medium* as granted, whereof we remain as
unsatisfied as of the question. Briefly, where that is
assumed as a Principle to prove another thing, which
is not conceded as true it self. By this fallacy was
Eve deceived, when she took for granted, a false assertion of the Devil ; *Ye shall not surely die ; for God doth
know that in the day ye shall eat thereof, your eyes shall
be opened, and you shall be as Gods.* Which was but a
bare affirmation of Satan, without proof or probable
inducement, contrary unto the command of God, and
former belief of her self. And this was the Logick of the
Jews when they accused our *Saviour* unto *Pilate* ; who
demanding a reasonable impeachment, or the allega-
tion of some crime worthy of Condemnation ; they
only replied, *If he had not been worthy of Death, we
would not have brought Him before thee.* Wherein
there was neither accusation of the person, nor satisfaction of the Judge ; who well understood, a bare
accusation was not presumption of guilt, and the
clamours of the people no accusation at all. The same

Fallacy is sometime used in the dispute, between *Job* and his friends; they often taking that for granted which afterward he disproveth.

The second is, *A dicto secundum quid ad dictum simpliciter*, when from that which is but true in a qualified sense, an inconditional and absolute verity is inferred; transferring the special consideration of things unto their general acceptions, or concluding from their strict acception, unto that without all limitation. This fallacy men commit when they argue from a particular to a general; as when we conclude the vices or qualities of a few, upon a whole Nation. Or from a part unto the whole. Thus the Devil argues with our Saviour: and by this, he would perswade Him he might be secure, if he cast himself from the Pinnacle: For, said he, it is written, *He shall give his Angels charge con-* Psal. 91. *cerning thee, and in their hands they shall bear thee up, lest at any time thou dash thy foot against a stone.* But this illation was fallacious, leaving one part of the Text, *He shall keep thee in all thy wayes*; that is, in the wayes of righteousness, and not of rash attempts: so he urged a part for the whole, and inferred more in the conclusion, than was contained in the premises. By the same fallacy we proceed, when we conclude from the sign unto the thing signified. By this incroachment, Idolatry first crept in, men converting the symbolical use of Idols into their proper Worship, and receiving the representation of things as the substance and thing it self. So the Statue of *Belus* at first erected in his memory, was in after-times adored as a Divinity. And so also in the Sacrament of the *The Original of Idolatry.* *Eucharist*, the Bread and Wine which were but the signals or visible signs, were made the things signified, and worshipped as the Body of Christ. And hereby

K

generally men are deceived that take things spoken in some Latitude without any at all. Hereby the *Jews* were deceived concerning the commandment of the Sabbath, accusing our Saviour *for healing the sick*, and his Disciples *for plucking the ears of Corn upon that day*. And by this deplorable mistake they were deceived unto destruction, upon the assault of *Pompey* the great, made upon that day; by whose superstitious observation they could not defend themselves, or perform any labour whatever.

The Alcoran *endures neither Wine nor Universities.*   The third is, *A non causa pro causa*, when that is pretended for a cause which is not, or not in that sense which is inferred. Upon this consequence the law of *Mahomet* forbids the use of Wine; and his Successors abolished Universities. By this also many Christians have condemned literature, misunderstanding the counsel of Saint *Paul*, who adviseth no further than to beware of Philosophy. On this Foundation were built the conclusions of Southsayers in their Augurial, and Tripudiary divinations; collecting presages from voice or food of Birds, and conjoyning Events unto causes of no connection. Hereupon also are grounded the gross mistakes, in the cure of many diseases: not only from the last medicine, and sympathetical Receipts, but Amulets, Charms, and all incantatory applications; deriving effects not only from inconcurring causes, but things devoid of all efficiency whatever.

The fourth is, the Fallacy of the Consequent; which if strictly taken, may be a fallacious illation in reference unto antecedency, or consequency; as to conclude from the position of the antecedent to the position of the consequent, or from the remotion of the consequent to the remotion of the antecedent. This is usually committed, when in connexed Propositions the Terms adhere contingently. This is frequent in Oratory illations; and thus the *Pharisees*, because He conversed with Publicans and Sinners, accused the holiness of Christ. But if this Fallacy be largely taken, it is committed in any vicious illation, offending the rules of good consequence; and so it may be very large, and comprehend all false illations against the settled Laws of Logick: But the most usual inconsequencies are from particulars, from negatives, and from affirmative conclusions in the second figure, wherein indeed offences are most frequent, and their discoveries not difficult.

CHAPTER V

Of Credulity and Supinity.

A THIRD cause of common Errors is the Credulity of men, that is, an easie assent to what is obtruded, or a believing at first ear, what is delivered by others. This is a weakness in the understanding, without examination assenting unto things, which from their Natures and Causes do carry no perswasion; whereby men often swallow falsities for truths, dubiosities for certainties, feasibilities for possibilities, and things impossible as possibilities themselves. Which, though the weakness of the Intellect, and most discoverable in vulgar heads; yet hath it sometime fallen upon wiser brains, and greater advancers of Truth. Thus many wise *Athenians* so far forgot their Philosophy, and the nature of humane production, that they descended unto belief, that the original of their Nation was from the Earth, and had no other beginning than the seminality and womb of their great Mother. Thus is it not without wonder, how those learned *Arabicks* so tamely delivered up their belief unto the absurdities of the *Alcoran.* How the noble *Geber,* *Avicenna,* and *Almanzor,* should rest satisfied in the nature and causes of Earthquakes, delivered from the doctrine of their *Prophet*; that is, from the motion of a great Bull, upon whose horns all the earth is poised. How their faiths could decline so low, as to concede their generations in Heaven, to be made by the smell of a Citron, or that the felicity of their Paradise should consist in a Jubile of copulation, that is, a coition of one act prolonged unto fifty years. Thus is it almost beyond wonder, how the belief of reasonable creatures, should ever submit unto Idolatry : and the credulity of those men scarce credible (without presumption of a second Fall) who could believe a Deity in the work of their own hands. For although in that ancient and diffused adoration of Idols, unto the *Priests* and subtiler heads, the worship perhaps might be symbolical, and as those Images some way related unto their Deities; yet was the Idolatry direct and down-right in the People; whose credulity is illimitable, who may be made believe that any thing is God ; and may be made believe there is no God at all.

Obstinate and irrational Scepticism, justly censured.

And as Credulity is the cause of Error, so Incredulity oftentimes of not enjoying truth ; and that not only an obstinate incredulity, whereby we will not acknowledge assent unto what is reasonably inferred, but any Academical reservation in matters of easie truth, or rather sceptical infidelity against the evidence of reason and sense. For these are conceptions befalling wise men, as absurd as the apprehensions of fools, and the credulity of the people which promiscuously swallow any thing.

For this is not only derogatory unto the wisdom of God,
who hath proposed the World unto our knowledge, and
thereby the notion of Himself; but also detractory
unto the intellect, and sense of man expressly disposed
for that inquisition. And therefore, *hoc tantum scio,
quod nihil scio,* is not to be received in an absolute sense,
but is comparatively expressed unto the number of
things whereof our knowledge is ignorant. Nor will it
acquit the insatisfaction of those which quarrel with all
things, or dispute of matters, concerning whose verities
we have conviction from reason, or decision from the
inerrable and requisite conditions of sense. And therefore if any affirm, the earth doth move, and will not
believe with us, it standeth still; because he hath
probable reasons for it, and I no infallible sense,
nor reason against it, I will not quarrel with his
assertion. But if, like *Zeno,* he shall walk about,
and yet deny there is any motion in Nature, surely
that man was constituted for *Anticera,* and were a fit
companion for those, who having a conceit they are
dead, cannot be convicted into the society of the
living.

The fourth is a Supinity, or neglect of Enquiry, even
of matters whereof we doubt; rather believing, than
going to see; or doubting with ease and *gratis,* than
believing with difficulty or purchase. Whereby, either
from a temperamental inactivity, we are unready to put
in execution the suggestions or dictates of reason ; or by
a content and acquiescence in every species of truth, we
embrace the shadow thereof, or so much as may palliate
its just and substantial acquirements. Had our fore-
Fathers sat down in these resolutions, or had their
curiosities been sedentary, who pursued the knowledge
of things through all the corners of nature, the face of

truth had been obscure unto us, whose lustre in some part their industries have revealed.

Certainly the sweat of their labours was not salt unto them, and they took delight in the dust of their endeavours. For questionless, in Knowledge there is no slender difficulty; and Truth, which wise men say doth lye in a Well, is not recoverable by exantlation. It were some extenuation of the Curse, if *in sudore vultus tui* were confinable unto corporal exercitations, and there still remained a Paradise, or unthorny place of knowledge. But now our understandings being eclipsed, as well as our tempers infirmed, we must betake our selves to wayes of reparation, and depend upon the illumination of our endeavours. For, thus we may in some measure repair our primary ruines, and build our selves Men again. And though the attempts of some have been precipitous, and their Enquiries so audacious, as to come within command of the flaming swords, and lost themselves in attempts above humanity; yet have the Enquiries of most defected by the way, and tired within the sober circumference of Knowledge.

And this is the reason, why some have transcribed any thing; and although they cannot but doubt thereof, yet neither make Experiment by sense, or Enquiry by reason; but live in doubts of things, whose satisfaction is in their own power; which is indeed the inexcusable part of our ignorance, and may perhaps fill up the charge of the last day. For, not obeying the dictates of Reason, and neglecting the cries of Truth, we fail not only in the trust of our undertakings, but in the intention of man it self. Which although more venial in ordinary constitutions, and such as are not framed beyond the capacity of beaten notions, yet will inexcusably condemn some men, who having received excellent

endowments, have yet sate down by the way, and frus-   CHAP.
trated the intention of their habilities. For certainly,   V
as some men have sinned in the principles of humanity,
and must answer, for not being men, so others offend,
if they be not more. *Magis extra vitia, quam cum vir-
tutibus,* would commend those: These are not excusable without an Excellency. For, great constitutions,
and such as are constellated unto knowledge, do nothing
till they out-do all; they come short of themselves, if
they go not beyond others; and must not sit down under
the degree of Worthies. God expects no lustre from
the minor Stars; but if the Sun should not illuminate
all, it were a sin in Nature. *Ultimus bonorum,* will not
excuse every man, nor is it sufficient for all to hold the
common level: Mens names should not only distinguish
them: A man should be something, that men are not,
and individual in somewhat beside his proper Name.
Thus while it exceeds not the bounds of reason and
modesty, we cannot condemn singularity. *Nos numerus
sumus,* is the Motto of the multitude, and for that
reason are they Fools. For things as they recede from
unity, the more they approach to imperfection, and
Deformity; for they hold their perfection in their
Simplicities, and as they nearest approach unto God.

Now as there are many great Wits to be condemned,
who have neglected the increment of Arts, and the
sedulous pursuit of knowledge; so are there not a few
very much to be pitied, whose industry being not
attended with natural parts, they have sweat to little
purpose, and rolled the stone in vain. Which chiefly
proceedeth from natural incapacity, and genial indis-   *Universities why many*
position, at least, to those particulars whereunto they   *times full of*
apply their endeavours. And this is one reason why,   *Scholars, and empty*
though Universities be full of men, they are oftentimes   *of Learning.*

empty of learning: Why, as there are some men do much without learning, so others but little with it, and few that attain to any measure of it. For many heads that undertake it, were never squared, nor timber'd for it. There are not only particular men, but whole Nations indisposed for learning; whereunto is required, not only education, but a pregnant *Minerva*, and

The natural genius or inclination, how much to be regarded in the choice of a Profession.

teeming Constitution. For the Wisdom of God hath divided the *Genius* of men according to the different affairs of the World: and varied their inclination according to the variety of Actions to be performed therein. Which they who consider not, rudely rushing upon professions and ways of life, unequal to their natures; dishonour, not only themselves and their Functions, but pervert the harmony of the whole World. For, if the World went on as God hath ordained it, and were every one imployed in points concordant to their Natures, Professions; Arts and Commonwealths would rise up of themselves; nor needed we a Lanthorn to find a man in *Athens*.

CHAPTER VI

Of adherence unto Antiquity.

Immoderate respect unto Antiquity, a general cause of Error.

BUT the mortallest enemy unto Knowledge, and that which hath done the greatest execution upon truth, hath been a peremptory adhesion unto Authority, and more especially, the establishing of our belief upon the dictates of Antiquity. For (as every capacity may observe) most men of Ages present, so superstitiously do look on Ages past, that the Authorities of the one, exceed the reasons of the other: Whose persons indeed being far removed from

our times, their works, which seldom with us pass un-
controuled, either by contemporaries, or immediate
successors, are now become out of the distance of
Envies : and the farther removed from present times,
are conceived to approach the nearer unto truth it self.
Now hereby methinks we manifestly delude our selves,
and widely walk out of the track of Truth.

For first, Men hereby impose a Thraldom on their
Times, which the ingenuity of no Age should endure,
or indeed, the presumption of any did ever yet enjoyn.
Thus *Hippocrates* about 2000 years ago, conceived it
no injustice, either to examine or refute the Doctrines
of his Predecessors : *Galen* the like, and *Aristotle* the
most of any. Yet did not any of these conceive themselves infallible, or set down their dictates as verities
irrefragable, but when they deliver their own Inventions, or reject other mens Opinions, they proceed with
Judgment and Ingenuity ; establishing their assertion,
not only with great solidity, but submitting them also
unto the correction of future discovery.

Secondly, Men that adore times past, consider not
that those times were once present ; that is, as our own
are at this instant, and we our selves unto those to
come, as they unto us at present, as we relye on them,
even so will those on us, and magnifie us hereafter, who
at present condemn our selves. Which very absurdity
is daily committed amongst us, even in the esteem and
censure of our own times. And to speak impartially,
old Men, from whom we should expect the greatest
example of Wisdom, do most exceed in this point of
folly ; commending the days of their youth, which
they scarce remember, at least well understood not ; extolling those times their younger years have heard their
Fathers condemn, and condemning those times the

gray heads of their posterity shall commend. And thus is it the humour of many heads, to extol the days of their Fore-fathers, and declaim against the wickedness of times present. Which notwithstanding they cannot handsomly do, without the borrowed help and Satyrs of times past; condemning the vices of their own times, by the expressions of vices in times which they commend; which cannot but argue the community of vice in both. *Horace* therefore, *Juvenal,* and *Persius* were no Prophets, although their lines did seem to indigitate and point at our times. There is a certain list of vices committed in all Ages, and declaimed against by all Authors, which will last as long as humane nature; which digested into common places, may serve for any Theme, and never be out of date until Dooms-day.

Thirdly, The Testimonies of Antiquity and such as pass oraculously amongst us, were not, if we consider them, always so exact, as to examine the doctrine they delivered. For some, and those the acutest of them, have left unto us many things of falsity; controlable, not only by critical and collective reason, but common and Country observation.

Hereof there want not many examples in *Aristotle,* through all his Book of Animals; we shall instance onely in three of his Problems, and all contained under one Section. The first enquireth, why a Man doth cough, but not an Oxe or Cow; whereas, notwithstanding the contrary is often observed by Husbandmen, and stands confirmed by those who have expressly treated *De Re Rustica,* and have also delivered divers remedies for it. Why Juments, as Horses, Oxen, and Asses, have no eructation or belching, whereas indeed the contrary is often observed, and also delivered by

Columella. And thirdly, Why Man alone hath gray hairs? whereas it cannot escape the eyes, and ordinary observation of all men, as Horses, Dogs, and Foxes, wax gray with age in our Countries; and in the colder Regions, many other Animals without it. And though favourable constructions may somewhat extenuate the rigour of these concessions, yet will scarce any palliate that in the fourth of his Meteors, that Salt is easiest dissolvable in cold water: Nor that of *Diascorides,* that Quicksilver is best preserved in Vessels of Tin and Lead.

Other Authors write often dubiously even in matters wherein is expected a strict and definite truth; extenuating their affirmations, with *aiunt, ferunt, fortasse*: as *Diascorides, Galen, Aristotle,* and many more. Others by hear-say; taking upon trust most they have delivered, whose Volumes are meer Collections, drawn from the mouths or leaves of other Authors; as may be observed in *Plinie, Elian, Athenæus,* and many more. Not a few transcriptively, subscribing their Names unto other mens endeavours, and meerly transcribing almost all they have written. The *Latines* transcribing the *Greeks,* the *Greeks* and *Latines,* each other.

Thus hath *Justine* borrowed all from *Trogus Pompeius,* and *Julius Solinus,* in a manner transcribed *Plinie.* Thus have *Lucian* and *Apuleius* served *Lucius Pratensis*: men both living in the same time, and both transcribing the same Author, in those famous Books, entituled *Lucius* by the one, and *Aureus Asinus* by the other. In the same measure hath *Simocrates* in his Tract *De Nilo,* dealt with *Diodorus Siculus,* as may be observed in that work annexed unto *Herodotus,* and translated by *Jungermannus.* Thus *Eratosthenes* wholly translated *Timotheus de Insulis,* not reserving the very Preface.

The Antiquity, and some notable instances of Plagiarism, that is, of transcribing or filching Authors.

The same doth *Strabo* report of *Eudorus*, and *Ariston*, in a Treatise entituled *De Nilo*. *Clemens Alexandrinus* hath observed many examples hereof among the *Greeks*; and *Pliny* speaketh very plainly in his Preface, that conferring his Authors, and comparing their works together, he generally found those that went before *verbatim* transcribed, by those that followed after, and their Originals never so much as mentioned. To omit how much the wittiest piece of *Ovid* is beholden unto *Parthenius Chius*; even the magnified *Virgil* hath borrowed, almost in all his Works; his *Eclogues* from *Theocritus*, his *Georgicks* from *Hesiod* and *Aratus*, his *Æneads* from *Homer*, the second Book whereof containing the exploit of *Sinon* and the *Trojan* Horse (as *Macrobius* observeth) he hath *verbatim* derived from *Pisander*. Our own Profession is not excusable herein. Thus *Oribasius*, *Ætius*, and *Ægineta*, have in a manner transcribed *Galen*. But *Marcellus Empericus*, who hath left a famous Work *De Medicamentis*, hath word for word transcribed all *Scribonius Largus*, *De Compositione Medicamentorum*, and not left out his very Peroration. Thus may we perceive the Ancients were but men, even like our selves. The practice of transcription in our days, was no Monster in theirs: *Plagiarie* had not its Nativity with Printing, but began in times when thefts were difficult, and the paucity of Books scarce wanted that Invention.

Nor did they only make large use of other Authors, but often without mention of their names. *Aristotle*, who seems to have borrowed many things from *Hippocrates*, in the most favourable construction, makes mention but once of him, and that by the by, and without reference unto his present Doctrine. *Virgil*, so much beholding unto *Homer*, hath not his name in all

His Metamorphosis.

In his Politicks.

his Works: and *Plinie*, who seems to borrow many
Authors out of *Dioscorides*, hath taken no notice of
him. I wish men were not still content to plume themselves with others Feathers. Fear of discovery, not
single ingenuity affords Quotations rather than Tran-
scriptions; wherein notwithstanding the Plagiarisme
of many makes little consideration, whereof though
great Authors may complain, small ones cannot but
take notice.

Fourthly, While we so eagerly adhere unto Antiquity,
and the accounts of elder times, we are to consider the
fabulous condition thereof. And that we shall not deny,
if we call to mind the Mendacity of *Greece*, from whom we
have received most relations, and that a considerable part
of ancient Times, was by the *Greeks* themselves termed
μυθικόν, that is, made up or stuffed out with Fables.
And surely the fabulous inclination of those days, was
greater then any since; which swarmed so with Fables,
and from such slender grounds, took hints for fictions,
poysoning the World ever after; wherein how far they
exceeded, may be exemplified from *Palephatus*, in his
Book of *Fabulous Narrations*. That Fable of *Orpheus*
who by the melody of his Musick, made Woods and
Trees to follow him, was raised upon a slender foundation; for there were a crew of mad women, retired
unto a Mountain from whence being pacified by his
Musick, they descended with boughs in their hands,
which unto the fabulosity of those times proved a
sufficient ground to celebrate unto all posterity the
Magick of *Orpheus* Harp, and its power to attract the
senseless Trees about it. That *Medea* the famous
Sorceress could renew youth, and make old men young
again, was nothing else, but that from the knowledge
of Simples she had a Receit to make white hair black,

*An ancient
Author who
writ Περì
ἀπίστων, sive
de incredi-
bilibus,
whereof some
part is yet
extant.*

*The Fable
of Orpheus
his Harp,
etc. whence
occasioned.*

and reduce old heads, into the tincture of youth again. The Fable of *Gerion* and *Cerberus* with three heads, was this : *Gerion* was of the City *Tricarinia*, that is, of three heads, and *Cerberus* of the same place was one of his Dogs, which running into a Cave upon pursuit of his Masters Oxen, *Hercules* perforce drew him out of that place, from whence the conceits of those days affirmed no less, then that *Hercules* descended into Hell, and brought up *Cerberus* into the habitation of the living. Upon the like grounds was raised the figment of *Briareus*, who dwelling in a City called *Hecatonchiria*, the fansies of those times assigned him an hundred hands. 'Twas ground enough to fansie wings unto *Dædalus*, in that he stole out of a Window from *Minos*, and sailed away with his son *Icarus* : who steering his course wisely, escaped ; but his son carrying too high a sail was drowned. That *Niobe* weeping over her children, was turned into a Stone, was nothing else, but that during her life she erected over their Sepultures a Marble Tomb of her own. When *Acteon* had undone himself with Dogs, and the prodigal attendants of hunting, they made a solemn story how he was devoured by his Hounds. And upon the like grounds was raised the Anthropophagie of *Diomedes* his horses. Upon as slender foundation was built the Fable of the *Minotaure* ; for one *Taurus* a servant of *Minos* gat his Mistris *Pasiphae* with child, from whence the Infant was named *Minotaurus*. Now this unto the fabulosity of those times was thought sufficient to accuse *Pasiphae* of Beastiality, or admitting conjunction with a Bull ; and in succeeding ages gave a hint of depravity unto *Domitian* to act the Fable into reality. In like manner, as *Diodorus* plainly delivereth, the famous Fable of *Charon* had its Nativity ; who being

no other but the common Ferry-man of *Egypt*, that
wafted over the dead bodies from *Memphis*, was made
by the *Greeks* to be the Ferry-man of Hell, and solemn
stories raised after of him. Lastly, we shall not need
to enlarge, if that be true which grounded the generation of *Castor* and *Helen* out of an Egg, because they
were born and brought up in an upper room, according
unto the Word ὠὸν, which with the *Lacædemonians*
had also that signification.

Fifthly, We applaud many things delivered by
the Ancients, which are in themselves but ordinary,
and come short of our own Conceptions. Thus we
usually extol, and our Orations cannot escape the sayings
of the wise men of *Greece*. *Nosce teipsum*, of *Thales*:
Nosce tempus, of *Pittacus*: *Nihil nimis*, of *Cleobulus*;
which notwithstanding to speak indifferently, are but
vulgar precepts in Morality, carrying with them
nothing above the line, or beyond the extemporary
sententiosity of common conceits with us. Thus we
magnifie the Apothegms or reputed replies of Wisdom,
whereof many are to be seen in *Laertius*, more in
Lycosthenes, not a few in the second Book of *Macrobius*,
in the salts of *Cicero*, *Augustus*, and the Comical wits of
those times: in most whereof there is not much to
admire, and are methinks exceeded, not only in the
replies of wise men, but the passages of society, and
urbanities of our times. And thus we extol their
Adages, or Proverbs; and *Erasmus* hath taken great
pains to make collections of them, whereof notwithstanding, the greater part will, I believe, unto indifferent
Judges be esteemd no extraordinaries: and may be
parallel'd, if not exceeded, by those of more unlearned
Nations, and many of our own.

Sixthly, We urge Authorities in points that need

not, and introduce the testimony of ancient Writers, to confirm things evidently believed, and whereto no reasonable hearer but would assent without them; such as are, *Nemo mortalium omnibus horis sapit. Virtute nil præstantius, nil pulchrius. Omnia vincit amor. Præclarum quiddam veritas.* All which, although things known and vulgar, are frequently urged by many men, and though trivial verities in our mouths, yet, noted from *Plato, Ovid,* or *Cicero,* they become reputed elegancies. For many hundred to instance but in one we meet with while we are writing. *Antonius Guevara* that elegant *Spaniard,* in his Book entituled, *The Dial of Princes,* beginneth his Epistle thus. *Apolonius Thyaneus,* disputing with the Scholars of *Hiarchas,* said, that among all the affections of nature, nothing was more natural, then the desire all have to preserve life. Which being a confessed Truth, and a verity acknowledged by all, it was a superfluous affectation to derive its Authority from *Apolonius,* or seek a confirmation thereof as far as *India,* and the learned Scholars of *Hiarchas.* Which whether it be not all one to strengthen common Dignities and Principles known by themselves, with the Authority of Mathematicians; or think a man should believe, the whole is greater then its parts, rather upon the Authority of *Euclide,* then if it were propounded alone; I leave unto the second and wiser cogitations of all men. 'Tis sure a Practice that savours much of Pedantry; a reserve of Puerility we have not shaken off from School; where being seasoned with Minor sentences, by a neglect of higher Enquiries, they prescribe upon our riper ears, and are never worn out but with our Memories.

A pedantical vanity to quote Authors in matters of common sense or of familiar acknowledgement.

Lastly, While we so devoutly adhere unto Antiquity in some things, we do not consider we have deserted

them in several others. For they indeed have not onely
been imperfect, in the conceit of some things, but either
ignorant or erroneous in many more. They understood
not the motion of the eighth sphear from West to
East, and so conceived the longitude of the Stars invariable. They conceived the torrid Zone unhabitable,
and so made frustrate the goodliest part of the Earth.
But we now know 'tis very well empeopled, and the
habitation thereof esteemed so happy, that some have
made it the proper seat of Paradise ; and been so far
from judging it unhabitable, that they have made it the
first habitation of all. Many of the Ancients denied
the *Antipodes*, and some unto the penalty of contrary
affirmations ; but the experience of our enlarged navigations, can now assert them beyond all dubitation.
Having thus totally relinquisht them in some things,
it may not be presumptuous, to examine them in others ;
but surely most unreasonable to adhere to them in all, as
though they were infallible, or could not err in any way.

*CHAP.
VI*

*Some re-
markable
mistakes
among the
Ancients.*

CHAPTER VII

Of Authority.

NOR is onely a resolved prostration unto Antiquity
a powerful enemy unto knowledge, but any
confident adherence unto Authority, or resig-
nation of our judgements upon the testimony of Age
or Author whatsoever.

For first, to speak generally an argument from
Authority to wiser examinations, is but a weaker kind of
proof ; it being but a topical probation, and as we term
it, an inartificial argument, depending upon a naked
asseveration : wherein neither declaring the causes,

*Authority
(simply)
but a mean
argument
especially.*

affections or adjuncts of what we believe, it carrieth not with it the reasonable inducements of knowledge. And therefore, *Contra negantem principia, Ipse dixit*, or *Oportet discentem credere*, although Postulates very accommodable unto *Junior* indoctrinations; yet are their Authorities but temporary, and not to be imbraced beyond the minority of our intellectuals. For our advanced beliefs are not to be built upon dictates, but having received the probable inducements of truth, we become emancipated from testimonial engagements, and are to erect upon the surer base of reason.

Secondly, Unto reasonable perpensions it hath no place in some Sciences, small in others, and suffereth many restrictions, even where it is most admitted. It is of no validity in the Mathematicks, especially the *In the Mathe-maticks.* mother part thereof, Arithmetick and Geometry. For these Sciences concluding from dignities and principles known by themselves: receive not satisfaction from probable reasons, much less from bare and peremptory asseverations. And therefore if all *Athens* should decree, that in every Triangle, two sides, which soever be taken, are greater then the side remaining, or that in rectangle triangles the square which is made of the side that subtendeth the right angle, is equal to the squares which are made of the sides containing the right angle: although there be a certain truth therein, Geometricians notwithstanding would not receive satisfaction without demonstration thereof. 'Tis true, by the vulgarity of Philosophers, there are many points believed without probation; nor if a man affirm from *Ptolomy*, that the Sun is bigger then the Earth, shall he probably meet with any contradiction: whereunto notwithstanding Astronomers will not assent without some convincing argument or demonstrative proof thereof. And therefore certainly of all men a Philosopher should be no swearer; for an oath which is the end of controversies in Law, cannot determine any here; nor are the deepest Sacraments or desperate imprecations of any force to perswade, where reason only, and necessary *mediums* must induce. CHAP. VII

In Natural Philosophy more generally pursued amongst us, it carrieth but slender consideration; for that also proceeding from setled Principles, therein is expected a satisfaction from scientifical progressions, and such as beget a sure rational belief. For if Authority might have made out the assertions of Philosophy, we might have held that Snow was black, that the Sea was but the sweat of the Earth, and many of the like absurdities. Then was *Aristotle* injurious to fall upon *Melissus*, to reject the assertions of *Anaxagoras, Anaximander,* and *Empedocles*; then were we also ungrateful unto himself; from whom our *Junior* endeavours embracing many things on his authority, our mature and secondary enquiries, are forced to quit those receptions, and to adhere unto the nearer account of Reason. And although it be not unusual, even in Philosophical Tractates to make enumeration of Authors, yet are there reasons usually introduced, and to ingenious Readers do carry the stroke in the perswasion. And surely if we account it reasonable among our selves, and not injurious unto rational Authors, no farther to abet their Opinions then as they are supported by solid Reasons: certainly with more excusable reservation may we shrink at their bare testimonies; whose argument is but precarious, and subsists upon the charity of our assentments. *And Physick.*

In Morality, Rhetorick, Law and History, there is I confess a frequent and allowable use of testimony; and yet herein I perceive, it is not unlimitable, but admitteth many restrictions. Thus in Law both Civil and Divine : that is onely esteemed a legal testimony, which receives comprobation from the mouths of at least two witnesses ; and that not only for prevention of calumny, but assurance against mistake ; whereas notwithstanding the solid reason of one man, is as sufficient as the clamor of a whole Nation ; and with imprejudicate apprehensions begets as firm a belief as the authority or aggregated testimony of many hundreds. For reason being the very root of our natures, and the principles thereof common unto all, what is against the Laws of true reason, or the unerring understanding of any one, if rightly apprehended ; must be disclaimed by all Nations, and rejected even by mankind.

Again, A testimony is of small validity if deduced from men out of their own profession ; so if *Lactantius* affirm the Figure of the Earth is plain, or *Austin* deny there are *Antipodes* ; though venerable Fathers of the Church, and ever to be honoured, yet will not their Authorities prove sufficient to ground a belief thereon. Whereas notwithstanding the solid reason or confirmed experience of any man, is very approvable in what profession soever. So *Raymund Sebund* a Physitian of *Tholouze*, besides his learned Dialogues *De Natura Humana*, hath written a natural Theologie ; demonstrating therein the Attributes of God, and attempting the like in most points of Religion. So *Hugo Grotius* a Civilian, did write an excellent Tract of the verity of Christian Religion. Wherein most rationally delivering themselves, their works will be embraced by most that understand them, and their reasons enforce belief even from prejudicate Readers. Neither indeed have the Authorities of men been ever so awful ; but that by

some they have been rejected, even in their own professions. Thus *Aristotle* affirming the birth of the
Infant or time of its gestation, extendeth sometimes
unto the eleventh Month, but *Hippocrates*, averring
that it exceedeth not the tenth : *Adrian* the Emperour
in a solemn process, determined for *Aristotle* ; but
Justinian many years after, took in with *Hippocrates*
and reversed the Decree of the other. Thus have
Councils, not only condemned private men, but the
Decrees and Acts of one another. So *Galen* after all
his veneration of *Hippocrates*, in some things hath
fallen from him. *Avicen* in many from *Galen* ; and
others succeeding from him. And although the singularity of *Paracelsus* be intolerable, who sparing onely
Hippocrates, hath reviled not onely the Authors, but
almost all the learning that went before him ; yet is it
not much less injurious unto knowledge obstinately
and inconvincibly to side with any one. Which humour
unhappily possessing many, they have by prejudice
withdrawn themselves into parties, and contemning the
soveraignty of truth, seditiously abetted the private
divisions of error.

Moreover a testimony in points Historical, and where
it is of unavoidable use, is of no illation in the negative,
nor is it of consequence that *Herodotus* writing nothing
of *Rome*, there was therefore no such City in his time ;
or because *Dioscorides* hath made no mention of Uni-
corns horn, there is therefore no such thing in Nature.
Indeed, intending an accurate enumeration of Medical
materials, the omission hereof affords some probability,
it was not used by the Ancients, but will not conclude
the non-existence thereof. For so may we annihilate
many Simples unknown to his enquiries, as *Senna*,
Rhubarb, Bezoar, Ambregris, and divers others. Whereas

indeed the reason of man hath not such restraint; concluding not onely affirmatively but negatively; not onely affirming there is no magnitude beyond the last heavens, but also denying there is any vacuity within them. Although it be confessed, the affirmative hath the prerogative illation, and *Barbara* engrosseth the powerful demonstration.

Lastly, The strange relations made by Authors, may sufficiently discourage our adherence unto Authority; and which if we believe we must be apt to swallow any thing. Thus *Basil* will tell us, the Serpent went erect like Man, and that that Beast could speak before the Fall. *Tostatus* would make us believe that *Nilus* encreaseth every new Moon. *Leonardo Fioravanti* an Italian Physitian, beside many other secrets, assumeth unto himself the discovery of one concerning Pellitory of the Wall; that is, that it never groweth in the sight of the *North* star. *Doue si possa vedere la stella Tramontana*, wherein how wide he is from truth, is easily discoverable unto every one, who hath but Astronomy enough to know that Star. *Franciscus Sanctius* in a laudable Comment upon *Alciats* Emblems, affirmeth, and that from experience, a Nightingale hath no tongue. *Avem Philomelam lingua carere pro certo affirmare possum, nisi me oculi fallunt.* Which if any man for a while shall believe upon his experience, he may at his leisure refute it by his own. What fool almost would believe, at least, what wise man would relie upon that Antidote delivered by *Pierius* in his Hieroglyphicks against the sting of a Scorpion? that is, to sit upon an Ass with ones face toward his tail; for so the pain leaveth the Man, and passeth into the Beast. It were methinks but an uncomfortable receit for a Quartane Ague (and yet as good perhaps as many

others used) to have recourse unto the *Recipe* of *Sam-*
monicus; that is, to lay the fourth Book of *Homers*
Iliads under ones head, according to the precept of
that Physitian and Poet, *Mœoniæ Iliados quartum sup-*
pone trementi. There are surely few that have belief *An eye*
to swallow, or hope enough to experiment the Colly- *medicine.*
rium of *Albertus*; which promiseth a strange effect,
and such as Thieves would count inestimable, that is,
to make one see in the dark: yet thus much, according
unto his receit, will the right eye of an Hedge-hog boiled
in oyl, and preserved in a brazen vessel effect. As
strange it is, and unto vicious inclinations were worth
a nights lodging with *Lais*, what is delivered in *Kir-* *Ten*
anides; that the left stone of a Weesel, wrapt up in *thousand*
the skin of a she Mule, is able to secure incontinency *drachms.*
from conception.

These with swarms of others have men delivered in
their Writings, whose verities are onely supported by
their authorities: But being neither consonant unto
reason, nor correspondent unto experiment, their affirmations are unto us no axioms: We esteem thereof as
things unsaid, and account them but in the list of
nothing. I wish herein the *Chymists* had been more
sparing: who over-magnifying their preparations, in-
veigle the curiosity of many, and delude the security
of most. For if experiments would answer their en-
comiums, the Stone and Quartane Agues were not
opprobrious unto Physitians: we might contemn that
first and most uncomfortable Aphorism of *Hippocrates*, *Ars longa*
for surely that Art were soon attained, that hath so *vita brevis*
general remedies; and life could not be short, were
there such to prolong it.

CHAPTER VIII

A brief enumeration of Authors.

NOW for as much as we have discoursed of Authority, and there is scarce any tradition or popular error but stands also delivered by some good Author; we shall endeavour a short discovery of such, as for the major part have given authority hereto : who though excellent and useful Authors, yet being either transcriptive, or following common relations, their accounts are not to be swallowed at large, or entertained without all circumspection. In whom the *ipse dixit*, although it be no powerful argument in any, is yet less authentick then in many other, because they deliver not their own experiences, but others affirmations, and write from others, as later pens from them.

1. The first in order, as also in time shall be *Herodotus* of *Halicarnassus*, an excellent and very elegant Historian; whose Books of History were so well received in his own days, and at their rehearsal in the Olympick games, they obtained the names of the nine Muses; and continued in such esteem unto descending Ages, that *Cicero* termed him, *Historiarum parens.* And *Dionysius* his Countryman, in an Epistle to *Pompey*, after an express comparison, affords him the better of *Thucydides*; all which notwithstanding, he hath received from some, the stile of *Mendaciorum pater.* His Authority was much infringed by *Plutarch*, who being offended with him, as *Polybius* had been with *Philarcus* for speaking too coldly of his Countrymen, hath left a particular Tract, *De malignitate*

Herodoti. But in this latter Century, *Camerarius* and *Stephanus* have stepped in, and by their witty Apologies, effectually endeavoured to frustrate the Arguments of *Plutarch*, or any other. Now in this Author, as may be observed in our ensuing discourse, and is better discernable in the perusal of himself, there are many things fabulously delivered, and not to be accepted as truths : whereby nevertheless if any man be deceived, the Author is not so culpable as the Believer. For he indeed imitating the Father Poet, whose life he hath also written, and as *Thucydides* observeth, as well intending the delight as benefit of his Reader, hath besprinkled his work with many fabulosities ; whereby if any man be led into error, he mistaketh the intention of the Author, who plainly confesseth he writeth many things by hear-say, and forgetteth a very considerable caution of his ; that is, *Ego quæ fando cognovi, exponere narratione mea debeo omnia : credere autem esse vera omnia, non debeo.*

2. In the second place is *Ctesias* the Cnidian, Physitian unto *Artaxerxes* King of *Persia*, his Books are often recited by ancient Writers, and by the industry of *Stephanus* and *Rhodomanus*, there are extant some fragments thereof in our days ; he wrote the History of *Persia*, and many narrations of *India*. In the first, as having a fair opportunity to know the truth, and as *Diodorus* affirmeth the perusal of *Persian* Records, his testimony is acceptable. In his *Indian* Relations, wherein are contained strange and incredible accounts, he is surely to be read with suspension. These were they which weakned his authority with former ages ; for as we may observe, he is seldom mentioned, without a derogatory Parenthesis in any Author. *Aristotle* besides the frequent undervaluing of his authority, in

his Books of Animals gives him the lie no less then twice, concerning the seed of Elephants. *Strabo* in his eleventh Book hath left a harder censure of him. *Equidem facilius Hesiodo & Homero, aliquis fidem adhibuerit, itémque Tragicis Poetis, quam Ctesiœ, Herodoto, Hellanico & eorum similibus.* But *Lucian* hath spoken more plainer then any. *Scripsit Ctesias de Indorum regione, deque iis quœ apud illos sunt, ea quœ nec ipse vidit, neque ex ullius sermone audivit.* Yet were his relations taken up by some succeeding Writers, and many thereof revived by our Countryman, Sir *John Mandevil,* Knight, and Doctor in Physick; who after thirty years peregrination died at *Liege,* and was there honourably interred. He left a Book of his Travels, which hath been honoured with the translation of many Languages, and now continued above three hundred years; herein he often attesteth the fabulous relations of *Ctesias,* and seems to confirm the refuted accounts of Antiquity. All which may still be received in some acceptions of morality, and to a pregnant invention, may afford commendable mythologie; but in a natural and proper exposition, it containeth impossibilities, and things inconsistent with truth.

3. There is a Book *De mirandis auditionibus,* ascribed unto *Aristotle*; another *De mirabilibus narrationibus,* written long after by *Antigonus,* another also of the same title by *Plegon Trallianus,* translated by *Xilander,* and with the Annotations of *Meursius,* all whereof make good the promise of their titles, and may be read with caution. Which if any man shall likewise observe in the Lecture of *Philostratus,* concerning the life of *Apollonius,* and even in some passages of the sober and learned *Plutarchus*; or not only in ancient Writers,

but shall carry a wary eye on *Paulus Venetus*, *Jovius*, CHAP.
Olaus Magnus, *Nierembergius*, and many other : I think VIII
his circumspection is laudable, and he may thereby
decline occasion of Error.

4. *Dioscorides Anazarbeus*, he wrote many Books in
Physick, but six thereof *De Materia Medica*, have
found the greatest esteem : he is an Author of good
antiquity and use, preferred by *Galen* before *Cratevas*,
Pamphilus, and all that attempted the like description
before him ; yet all he delivereth therein is not to be
conceived Oraculous. For beside that, following the
wars under *Anthony*, the course of his life would not
permit a punctual *Examen* in all ; there are many
things concerning the nature of Simples, traditionally
delivered, and to which I believe he gave no assent
himself. It had been an excellent Receit, and in his
time when Saddles were scarce in fashion of very great
use, if that were true which he delivers, that *Vitex*, or
Agnus Castus held only in the hand, preserveth the
rider from galling. It were a strange effect, and *A like*
Whores would forsake the experiment of *Savine*, if *opinion*
that were a truth which he delivereth of Brake or *of Elder.*
female Fearn, that onely treading over it, it causeth
a sudden abortion. It were to be wished true, and
women would idolize him, could that be made out
which he recordeth of *Phyllon*, *Mercury*, and other
vegetables, that the juice of the male Plant drunk, or
the leaves but applied unto the genitals, determines
their conceptions unto males. In these relations
although he be more sparing, his predecessors were
very numerous ; and *Galen* hereof most sharply accuseth
Pamphilus. Many of the like nature we meet sometimes
in *Oribasius*, *Ætius*, *Trallianus*, *Serapion*, *Evax*, and
Marcellus, whereof some containing no colour of verity,

we may at first sight reject them; others which seem to carry some face of truth, we may reduce unto experiment. And herein we shall rather perform good offices unto truth, then any disservice unto their relators, who have well deserved of succeeding Ages; from whom having received the conceptions of former Times, we have the readier hint of their conformity with ours, and may accordingly explore and sift their verities.

5. *Plinius Secundus* of *Verona*; a man of great Eloquence, and industry indefatigable, as may appear by his writings, especially those now extant, and which are never like to perish, but even with learning it self; that is, his Natural History. He was the greatest Collector or Rhapsodist of the Latines, and as *Suetonius* observeth, he collected this piece out of two thousand Latine and Greek Authors. Now what is very strange, there is scarce a popular error passant in our days, which is not either directly expressed, or diductively contained in this Work; which being in the hands of most men, hath proved a powerful occasion of their propagation. Wherein notwithstanding the credulity of the Reader, is more condemnable than the curiosity of the Author: for commonly he nameth the Authors from whom he received those accounts, and writes but as he reads, as in his Preface to *Vespasian* he acknowledgeth.

Plinies Natural History collected out of 2000 *several Authors.*

6. *Claudius Ælianus*, who flourished not long after in the reign of *Trajan*, unto whom he dedicated his Tacticks; an elegant and miscellaneous Author, he hath left two Books which are in the hands of every one, his History of Animals, and his *Varia Historia*. Wherein are contained many things suspicious, not a few false, some impossible; he is much beholding unto

Ctesias, and in many uncertainties writes more confidently then *Pliny.*

7. *Julius Solinus,* who lived also about his time: He left a Work entituled *Polyhistor,* containing great variety of matter, and is with most in good request at this day. But to speak freely what cannot be concealed, it is but *Pliny* varied, or a transcription of his Natural History: nor is it without all wonder it hath continued so long, but is now likely, and deserves indeed to live for ever; not onely for the elegancy of the Text, but the excellency of the Comment, lately performed by *Salmasius,* under the name of *Plinian* Exercitations.

8. *Athenæus,* a delectable Author, very various, and justly stiled by *Casaubon, Græcorum Plinius.* There is extant of his, a famous Piece, under the name of *Deipnosophista,* or *Cæna Sapientum,* containing the Discourse of many learned men, at a Feast provided by *Laurentius.* It is a laborious Collection out of many Authors, and some whereof are mentioned no where else. It containeth strange and singular relations, not without some spice or sprinkling of all Learning. The Author was probably a better Grammarian then Philosopher, dealing but hardly with *Aristotle* and *Plato,* and betrayeth himself much in his Chapter *De Curiositate Aristotelis.* In brief, he is an Author of excellent use, and may with discretion be read unto great advantage: and hath therefore well deserved the Comments of *Casaubon* and *Dalecampius.* But being miscellaneous in many things, he is to be received with suspition; for such as amass all relations, must erre in some, and may without offence be unbelieved in many.

9. We will not omit the works of *Nicander,* a Poet of good antiquity: that is, his *Theriaca,* and *Alexi-*

pharmaca, Translated and Commented by *Gorræus* : for therein are contained several Traditions, and popular Conceits of venemous Beasts; which only deducted, the Work is to be embraced, as containing the first description of poysons and their antidotes, whereof *Dioscorides, Pliny,* and *Galen,* have made especial use in elder times; and *Ardoynus, Grevinus,* and others, in times more near our own. We might perhaps let pass *Oppianus,* that famous Cilician Poet. There are extant of his in Greek, four Books of Cynegeticks or Venation, five of Halieuticks or Piscation, commented and published by *Ritterhusius* ; wherein describing Beasts of venery and Fishes, he hath indeed but sparingly inserted the vulgar conceptions thereof. So that abating the annual mutation of Sexes in the *Hyæna,* the single Sex of the *Rhinoceros,* the Antipathy between two Drums, of a Lamb and a Wolfes skin, the informity of Cubs, the venation of *Centaures,* the copulation of the *Murena* and the Viper, with some few others, he may be read with great delight and profit. It is not without some wonder his Elegant Lines are so neglected. Surely *That write* hereby we reject one of the best Epick Poets, and much *Hexameters,* condemn the Judgement of *Antoninus,* whose apprehen- *or long* sions so honoured his Poems, that as some report, for *verses.* every verse, he assigned him a Stater of Gold.

10. More warily are we to receive the relations of *Philes,* who in *Greek Iambicks* delivered the proprieties of Animals, for herein he hath amassed the vulgar accounts recorded by the Ancients, and hath therein especially followed *Ælian.* And likewise *Johannes Tzetzes,* a Grammarian, who besides a Comment upon *Hesiod* and *Homer,* hath left us *Chiliads de Varia Historia*; wherein delivering the accounts of *Ctesias, Herodotus,* and most of the Ancients, he

is to be embraced with caution, and as a transcriptive
Relator.

11. We cannot without partiality omit all caution
even of holy Writers, and such whose names are venerable unto all posterity: not to meddle at all with
miraculous Authors, or any Legendary relators, we
are not without circumspection to receive some Books
even of authentick and renowned Fathers. So are we
to read the leaves of *Basil* and *Ambrose,* in their Books
entituled *Hexameron,* or *The Description of the Creation*;
Wherein delivering particular accounts of all the
Creatures, they have left us relations sutable to those
of *Ælian, Plinie,* and other Natural Writers ; whose
authorities herein they followed, and from whom most
probably they desumed their Narrations. And the
like hath been committed by *Epiphanius,* in his Physi-
ologie: that is, a Book he hath left concerning the
Nature of Animals. With no less caution must we
look on *Isidor* Bishop of *Sevil*; who having left in
twenty Books, an accurate work *De Originibus,* hath
to the Etymologie of Words, super-added their received Natures; wherein most generally he consents
with common Opinions and Authors which have
delivered them.

12. *Albertus* Bishop of *Ratisbone,* for his great
Learning and latitude of Knowledge, sirnamed *Magnus.* Besides Divinity, he hath written many Tracts
in Philosophy; what we are chiefly to receive with
caution, are his Natural Tractates, more especially
those of Minerals, Vegetables, and Animals, which are
indeed chiefly Collections out of *Aristotle, Ælian,* and
Pliny, and respectively contain many of our popular
Errors. A man who hath much advanced these
Opinions by the authority of his Name, and delivered

most Conceits, with strict Enquiry into few. In the same *Classis* may well be placed *Vincentius Belluacensis*, or rather he from whom he collected his *Speculum naturale*, that is, *Guilielmus de Conchis*; and also *Hortus Sanitatis*, and *Bartholomeus Glanvil*, sirnamed *Anglicus*, who writ *De proprietatibus Rerum*. Hither also may be referred *Kiranides*, which is a Collection out of *Harpocration* the Greek, and sundry Arabick Writers; delivering not onely the Natural but Magical propriety of things; a Work as full of Vanity as Variety; containing many relations, whose Invention is as difficult as their Beliefs, and their Experiments sometime as hard as either.

13. We had almost forgot *Jeronimus Cardanus* that famous Physician of *Milan*, a great Enquirer of Truth, but too greedy a Receiver of it. He hath left many excellent Discourses, Medical, Natural, and Astrological; the most suspicious are those two he wrote by admonition in a dream, that is *De Subtilitate & Varietate Rerum.* Assuredly this learned man hath taken many things upon trust, and although examined some, hath let slip many others. He is of singular use unto a prudent Reader; but unto him that onely desireth Hoties, or to replenish his head with varieties; like many others before related, either in the Original or confirmation, he may become no small occasion of Error.

14. Lastly, Authors are also suspicious, not greedily to be swallowed, who pretend to write of Secrets, to deliver Antipathies, Sympathies, and the occult abstrusities of things; in the list whereof may be accounted, *Alexis Pedimontanus, Antonius Mizaldus, Trinum Magicum,* and many others. Not omitting that famous Philosopher of *Naples, Baptista Porta*; in whose Works, although there be contained many excellent things,

and verified upon his own Experience; yet are there
many also receptary, and such as will not endure the
test. Who although he hath delivered many strange
Relations in his Phytognomia, and his Villa; yet hath
he more remarkably expressed himself in his Natural
Magick, and the miraculous effects of Nature. Which
containing various and delectable subjects, withall pro-
mising wondrous and easie effects, they are entertained
by Readers at all hands; whereof the major part sit
down in his authority, and thereby omit not onely the
certainty of Truth, but the pleasure of its Experiment.

Thus have we made a brief enumeration of these
Learned Men; not willing any to decline their Works
(without which it is not easie to attain any measure
of general Knowledge,) but to apply themselves with
caution thereunto. And seeing the lapses of these
worthy Pens, to cast a wary eye on those diminutive,
and pamphlet Treaties daily published amongst us.
Pieces maintaining rather Typography than Verity,
Authors presumably writing by Common Places, wherein for many years promiscuously amassing all that
makes for their subject, they break forth at last in
trite and fruitless Rhapsodies; doing thereby not only
open injury unto Learning, but committing a secret
treachery upon truth. For their relations falling upon
credulous Readers, they meet with prepared beliefs;
whose supinities had rather assent unto all, then adventure the trial of any.

Thus, I say, must these Authors be read, and thus
must we be read our selves; for discoursing of matters
dubious, and many convertible truths; we cannot without arrogancy entreat a credulity, or implore any
farther assent, then the probability of our Reasons,
and verity of experiments induce.

M

CHAPTER IX

Of the Same.

THERE are beside these Authors and such as have positively promoted errors, divers other which are in some way accessory; whose verities although they do not directly assert, yet do they obliquely concur unto their beliefs. In which account are many holy Writers, Preachers, Moralists, Rhetoricians, Orators and Poets; for they depending upon Invention, deduce their mediums from all things whatsoever; and playing much upon the simile, or illustrative argumentation: to induce their Enthymemes unto the people, they took up popular conceits, and from traditions unjustifiable or really false, illustrate matters of undeniable truth. Wherein although their intention be sincere, and that course not much condemnable; yet doth it notoriously strengthen common Errors, and authorise Opinions injurious unto truth.

Thus have some Divines drawn into argument the Fable of the *Phœnix*, made use of that of the *Salamander, Pelican, Basilisk*, and divers relations of *Plinie*; deducing from thence most worthy morals, and even upon our Saviour. Now although this be not prejudicial unto wiser Judgments, who are but weakly moved with such arguments, yet it is oft times occasion of Error unto vulgar heads, who expect in the Fable as equal a truth as in the Moral, and conceive that infallible Philosophy, which is in any sense delivered by Divinity. But wiser discerners do well understand, that every Art hath its own circle; that the effects of

things are best examined, by sciences wherein are CHAP.
delivered their causes; that strict and definitive IX
expressions, are alway required in Philosophy, but a *Expressions*
loose and popular delivery will serve oftentimes in *of holy Scrip-*
ture fitted
Divinity. As may be observed even in holy Scripture, *many times*
which often omitteth the exact account of things; *rather to*
popular and
describing them rather to our apprehensions, then *common ap-*
leaving doubts in vulgar minds, upon their unknown *prehension,*
then to the
and Philosophical descriptions. Thus it termeth the *exact Nature*
of things.
Sun and the Moon the two great lights of Heaven.
Now if any shall from hence conclude, the Moon is
second in magnitude unto the Sun, he must excuse my
belief; and it cannot be strange, if herein I rather
adhere unto the demonstration of *Ptolomy*, then the
popular description of *Moses*. Thus is it said, *Chron.*
2. 4. That *Solomon* made a molten Sea of ten Cubits
from brim to brim round in compass, and five Cubits
the height thereof, and a line of thirty Cubits did
compass it round about. Now in this description, the
circumference is made just treble unto the Diameter:
that is, as 10. to 30. or 7. to 21. But *Archimedes* *In his Cyclo-*
demonstrates, that the proportion of the Diameter *metria.*
unto the circumference, is as 7. unto almost 22. which
will occasion a sensible difference, that is almost a
Cubit. Now if herein I adhere unto *Archimedes* who
speaketh exactly, rather then the sacred Text which
speaketh largely; I hope I shall not offend Divinity:
I am sure I shall have reason and experience of every
circle to support me.

Thus Moral Writers, Rhetoricians and Orators make
use of several relations which will not consist with
verity. *Aristotle* in his Ethicks takes up the conceit
of the *Bever*, and the divulsion of his Testicles. The
tradition of the Bear, the Viper, and divers others are

frequent amongst Orators. All which although unto the illiterate and undiscerning hearers may seem a confirmation of their realities; yet is this no reasonable establishment unto others, who will not depend hereon otherwise then common Apologues: which being of impossible falsities, do notwithstanding include wholsome moralities, and such as expiate the trespass of their absurdities.

The Hieroglyphical doctrine of the Ægyptians (which in their four hundred years cohabitation some conjecture they learned from the Hebrews) hath much advanced many popular conceits. For using an Alphabet of things, and not of words, through the image and pictures thereof, they endeavoured to speak their hidden conceits in the letters and language of Nature. In pursuit whereof, although in many things, they exceeded not their true and real apprehensions; yet in some other they either framing the story, or taking up the tradition, conducible unto their intentions, obliquely confirmed many falsities; which as authentick and conceded truths did after pass unto the Greeks, from them unto other Nations, and are still retained by symbolical Writers, Emblematists, Heralds, and others. Whereof some are strictly maintained for truths, as naturally making good their artificial representations; others symbolically intended, are literally received, and swallowed in the first sense, without all gust of the second. Whereby we pervert the profound and mysterious knowledge of Ægypt; containing the Arcana's of Greek Antiquities, the Key of many obscurities and ancient learning extant. Famous herein in former Ages were *Heraiscus, Cheremon, Epius,* especially *Orus Apollo Niliacus*: who lived in the reign of *Theodosius,* and in Ægyptian language left two

Books of Hieroglyphicks, translated into Greek by
Philippus, and a large collection of all made after by
Pierius. But no man is likely to profound the Ocean
of that Doctrine, beyond that eminent example of
industrious Learning, *Kircherus*.

Painters who are the visible representers of things,
and such as by the learned sense of the eye endeavour
to inform the understanding, are not inculpable herein,
who either describing Naturals as they are, or actions
as they have been, have oftentimes erred in their
delineations. Which being the Books that all can
read, are fruitful advancers of these conceptions, especially in common and popular apprehensions: who being
unable for farther enquiry, must rest in the draught
and letter of their descriptions.

Lastly, Poets and Poetical Writers have in this
point exceeded others, trimly advancing the Ægyptian
notions of *Harpies*, *Phœnix*, *Gryphins*, and many more.
Now however to make use of Fictions, Apologues, and
Fables, be not unwarrantable, and the intent of these
inventions might point at laudable ends; yet do they
afford our junior capacities a frequent occasion of
error, setling impressions in our tender memories,
which our advanced judgments generally neglect to
expunge. This way the vain and idle fictions of the
Gentiles did first insinuate into the heads of Christians;
and thus are they continued even unto our days. Our
first and literary apprehensions being commonly instructed in Authors which handle nothing else; wherewith our memories being stuffed, our inventions become
pedantick, and cannot avoid their allusions; driving at
these as at the highest elegancies, which are but the
frigidities of wit, and become not the genius of manly
ingenuities. It were therefore no loss like that of

Galens Library, if these had found the same fate; and would in some way requite the neglect of solid Authors, if they were less pursued. For were a pregnant wit educated in ignorance hereof, receiving only impressions from realities; upon such solid foundations, it must surely raise more substantial superstructions, and fall upon very many excellent strains, which have been jusled off by their intrusions.

CHAPTER X

Of the last and common Promoter of false Opinions, the endeavours of Satan.

BUT beside the infirmities of humane Nature, the seed of Error within our selves, and the several ways of delusion from each other, there is an invisible Agent, and secret promoter without us, whose activity is undiscerned, and plays in the dark upon us; and that is the first contriver of Error, and professed opposer of Truth, the Devil. For though permitted unto his proper principles, *Adam* perhaps would have sinned without the suggestion of Satan: and from the transgressive infirmities of himself might have erred alone, as well as the Angels before him: And although also there were no Devil at all, yet there is now in our Natures a confessed sufficiency unto corruption, and the frailty of our own Oeconomie, were able to betray us out of Truth, yet wants there not another Agent, who taking advantage hereof proceedeth to obscure the diviner part, and efface all tract of its traduction. To attempt a particular of all his wiles, is too bold an Arithmetick for

The Devils method of propagating Error in the World.

man : what most considerably concerneth his popular
and practised ways of delusion, he first deceiveth
mankind in five main points concerning God and
himself.

And first his endeavours have ever been, and they
cease not yet to instill a belief in the mind of Man,
there is no God at all. And this he principally
endeavours to establish in a direct and literal apprehension ; that is, that there is no such reality existent,
that the necessity of his entity dependeth upon ours,
and is but a Political Chymera ; that the natural
truth of God is an artificial erection of Man, and the
Creator himself but a subtile invention of the Creature.
Where he succeeds not thus high, he labours to introduce a secondary and deductive Atheism; that although
men concede there is a God, yet should they deny his
providence. And therefore assertions have flown about,
that he intendeth only the care of the species or common
natures, but letteth loose the guard of individuals, and
single existencies therein : that he looks not below the
Moon, but hath designed the regiment of sublunary
affairs unto inferiour deputations. To promote which
apprehensions, or empuzzel their due conceptions, he
casteth in the notions of fate, destiny, fortune, chance,
and necessity ; terms commonly misconceived by vulgar
heads, and their propriety sometime perverted by the
wisest. Whereby extinguishing in minds the compen-
sation of vertue and vice, the hope and fear of Heaven
or Hell ; they comply in their actions unto the drift
of his delusions, and live like creatures without the
capacity of either.

Now hereby he not onely undermineth the Base of
Religion, and destroyeth the principle preambulous
unto all belief ; but puts upon us the remotest Error

CHAP.
X

from Truth. For Atheism is the greatest falsity, and to affirm there is no God, the highest lie in Nature. And therefore strictly taken, some men will say his labour is in vain; For many there are, who cannot conceive there was ever any absolute *Atheist*; or such as could determine there was no God, without all check from himself, or contradiction from his other opinions. And therefore those few so called by elder times, might be the best of *Pagans*; suffering that name rather in relation to the gods of the Gentiles, then the true Creator of all. A conceit that cannot befal his greatest enemy, or him that would induce the same in us; who hath a sensible apprehension hereof, for he believeth with trembling. To speak yet more strictly and conformably unto some Opinions, no creature can wish thus much; nor can the Will which hath a power to run into velleities, and wishes of impossibilities, have any *utinam* of this. For to desire there were no God, were plainly to unwish their own being; which must needs be annihilated in the substraction of that essence which substantially supporteth them, and restrains them from regression into nothing. And if as some contend, no creature can desire his own annihilation, that Nothing is not appetible, and not to be at all, is worse then to be in the miserablest condition of something; the Devil himself could not embrace that motion, nor would the enemy of God be freed by such a Redemption.

But coldly thriving in this design, as being repulsed by the principles of humanity, and the dictates of that production, which cannot deny its original, he fetcheth a wider circle; and when he cannot make men conceive there is no God at all, he endeavours to make them believe there is not one, but many: wherein he hath

been so successful with common heads, that he hath
led their belief thorow all the Works of Nature.

Now in this latter attempt, the subtilty of his cir-
cumvention, hath indirectly obtained the former. For
although to opinion there be many gods, may seem an
excess in Religion, and such as cannot at all consist
with Atheism, yet doth it deductively and upon inference include the same, for Unity is the inseparable and
essential attribute of Deity ; and if there be more then
one God, it is no Atheism to say there is no God at
all. And herein though *Socrates* only suffered, yet
were *Plato* and *Aristotle* guilty of the same Truth ;
who demonstratively understanding the simplicity of
perfection, and the indivisible condition of the first
causator, it was not in the power of Earth, or Areo-
pagy of Hell to work them from it. For holding an
[1]Apodictical knowledge, and assured science of its verity,
to perswade their apprehensions unto a plurality of
gods in the world, were to make *Euclide* believe there
were more than one Center in a Circle, or one right
Angle in a Triangle ; which were indeed a fruitless
attempt, and inferreth absurdities beyond the evasion
of Hell. For though Mechanick and vulgar heads
ascend not unto such comprehensions, who live not
commonly unto half the advantage of their principles ;
yet did they not escape the eye of wiser *Minerva's*, and
such as made good the genealogie of *Jupiters* brains ;
who although they had divers stiles for God, yet under
many appellations acknowledged one divinity : rather
conceiving thereby the evidence or acts of his power
in several ways and places, then a multiplication of
Essence, or real distraction of unity in any one.

Again, To render our errors more monstrous (and
what unto miracle sets forth the patience of God,) he

*Areopagus
the severe
Court of
Athens.*

[1] *Demon-
strative.*

hath endeavoured to make the world believe, that he was God himself; and failing of his first attempt to be but like the highest in Heaven, he hath obtained with men to be the same on Earth. And hath accordingly assumed the annexes of Divinity, and the prerogatives of the Creator, drawing into practice the operation of miracles, and the prescience of things to come. Thus hath he in a specious way wrought cures upon the sick : played over the wondrous acts of Prophets, and counterfeited many miracles of Christ and his Apostles. Thus hath he openly contended with God, and to this effect his insolency was not ashamed to play a solemn prize with *Moses*; wherein although his performance were very specious, and beyond the common apprehension of any power below a Deity; yet was it not such as could make good his Omnipotency. For he was wholly confounded in the conversion of dust into lice. An act Philosophy can scarce deny to be above the power of Nature, nor upon a requisite predisposition beyond the efficacy of the Sun. Wherein notwithstanding the head of the old Serpent was confessedly too weak for *Moses* hand, and the arm of his Magicians too short for the finger of God.

Thus hath he also made men believe that he can raise the dead, that he hath the key of life and death, and a prerogative above that principle which makes no regression from privations. The Stoicks that opinioned the souls of wise men dwelt about the Moon, and those of fools wandered about the Earth, advantaged the conceit of this effect; wherein the Epicureans, who held that death was nothing, nor nothing after death, must contradict their principles to be deceived. Nor could the Pythagoreans or such as maintained the transmigration of souls give easie admittance hereto:

for holding that separated souls successively supplied
other bodies, they could hardly allow the raising of
souls from other worlds, which at the same time, they
conceived conjoyned unto bodies in this.   More incon- *The Authors*
sistent with these Opinions, is the Error of Christians, *opinion, touching*
who holding the dead do rest in the Lord, do yet *Necromancy*
believe they are at the lure of the Devil; that he who *and apparitions of the*
is in bonds himself commandeth the fetters of the dead, *spirits of men*
and dwelling in the bottomless lake, the blessed from *departed.*
Abrahams bosome, that can believe the real resurrection of *Samuel*: or that there is any thing but delusion
in the practice of [1] Necromancy and popular raising of *[1]Divination*
Ghosts. *by the dead.*

He hath moreover endeavoured the opinion of Deity,
by the delusion of Dreams, and the discovery of things
to come in sleep, above the prescience of our waked
senses.   In this expectation he perswaded the credulity
of elder times to take up their lodging before his
temple, in skins of their own sacrifices : till his reser-
vedness had contrived answers, whose accomplishments
were in his power, or not beyond his presagement.
Which way, although it had pleased Almighty God,
sometimes to reveal himself, yet was the proceeding
very different.   For the revelations of Heaven are *How the*
conveyed by new impressions, and the immediate illu- *Devil works*
mination of the soul, whereas the deceiving spirit, *revelations*
by concitation of humours, produceth his conceited *or predic-*
phantasms, or by compounding the species already *tions.*
residing, doth make up words which mentally speak his
intentions.

But above all he most advanced his Deity in the
solemn practice of Oracles, wherein in several parts of
the World, he publikely professed his Divinity ; but
how short they flew of that spirit, whose omniscience,

they would resemble, their weakness sufficiently declared. What jugling there was therein, the Orator plainly confessed, who being good at the same game himself, could say that *Pythia* Philippised. Who can but laugh at the carriage of *Ammon* unto *Alexander*, who addressing unto him as a god, was made to believe, he was a god himself? How openly did he betray his Indivinity unto *Crœsus*, who being ruined by his Amphibology, and expostulating with him for so ungrateful a deceit, received no higher answer then the excuse of his impotency upon the contradiction of fate, and the setled law of powers beyond his power to controle! What more then sublunary directions, or such as might proceed from the Oracle of humane Reason, was in his advice unto the Spartans in the time of a great Plague; when for the cessation thereof, he wisht them to have recourse unto a Fawn, that is in open terms, unto one *Nebrus*, a good Physitian of those days? From no diviner a spirit came his reply unto *Caracalla*, who requiring a remedy for his Gout, received no other counsel then to refrain cold drink; which was but a dietetical caution, and such as without a journey unto *Æsculapius*, culinary prescription and kitchin Aphorisms might have afforded at home. Nor surely if any truth there were therein, of more then natural activity was his counsel unto *Democritus*; when for the Falling sickness he commended the Maggot in a Goats head. For many things secret are true; sympathies and antipathies are safely authentick unto us, who ignorant of their causes may yet acknowledge their effects. Beside, being a natural Magician he may perform many acts in ways above our knowledge, though not transcending our natural power, when our knowledge shall direct it. Part hereof hath been dis-

covered by himself, and some by humane indagation :
which though magnified as fresh inventions unto us,
are stale unto his cognition. I hardly believe he hath
from elder times unknown the verticity of the Loadstone; surely his perspicacity discerned it to respect
the North, when ours beheld it indeterminately. Many
secrets there are in Nature of difficult discovery unto
man, of easie knowledge unto Satan; whereof some
his vain glory cannot conceal, others his envy will not
discover.

Again, Such is the mysterie of his delusion, that
although he labour to make us believe that he is
God, and supremest nature whatsoever, yet would he
also perswade our beliefs, that he is less then Angels
or men; and his condition not onely subjected unto
rational powers, but the actions of things which have
no efficacy on our selves. Thus hath he inveigled no
small part of the world into a credulity of artificial
Magick : That there is an Art, which without compact
commandeth the powers of Hell; whence some have
delivered the polity of spirits, and left an account even
to their Provincial Dominions : that they stand in awe
of Charms, Spels, and Conjurations; that he is afraid
of letters and characters, of notes and dashes, which
set together do signifie nothing, not only in the dic-
tionary of man, but the subtiler vocabulary of Satan.
That there is any power in *Bitumen*, Pitch, or Brim- St. Johns
stone, to purifie the air from his uncleanness; that any *Wort, so
called by*
vertue there is in *Hipericon* to make good the name of *Magicians.*
fuga Dæmonis, any such Magick as is ascribed unto
the Root *Baaras* by *Josephus*, or *Cynospastus* by *Ælianus*, it is not easie to believe; nor is it naturally
made out what is delivered of *Tobias*, that by the fume
of a Fishes liver, he put to flight *Asmodeus*. That

*3 triangles
intersected
and made
of five lines.*

*Implying
Jehovah,
which in
Hebrew con-
sisteth of
four letters.*

they are afraid of the pentangle of *Solomon*, though so set forth with the body of man, as to touch and point out the five places wherein our Saviour was wounded, I know not how to assent. If perhaps he hath fled from holy Water, if he cares not to hear the sound of *Tetragrammaton*, if his eye delight not in the sign of the Cross; and that sometimes he will seem to be charmed with words of holy Scripture, and to flie from the letter and dead verbality, who must onely start at the life and animated interiors thereof: It may be feared they are but *Parthian* flights, *Ambuscado* retreats, and elusory tergiversations: Whereby to confirm our credulities, he will comply with the opinion of such powers, which in themselves have no activities. Whereof having once begot in our minds an assured dependence, he makes us relie on powers which he but precariously obeys; and to desert those true and only charms which Hell cannot withstand.

Lastly, To lead us farther into darkness, and quite to lose us in this maze of Error, he would make men believe there is no such creature as himself: and that he is not onely subject unto inferiour creatures, but in the rank of nothing. Insinuating into mens minds there is no Devil at all, and contriveth accordingly, many ways to conceal or indubitate his existency. Wherein beside that he annihilates the blessed Angels and Spirits in the rank of his Creation; he begets a security of himself, and a careless eye unto the last remunerations. And therefore hereto he inveigleth, not only *Sadduces* and such as retain unto the Church of God: but is also content that *Epicurus, Democritus,* or any Heathen should hold the same. And to this effect he maketh men believe that apparitions, and such as confirm his existence are either deceptions of

sight, or melancholly depravements of phansie. Thus
when he had not onely appeared but spake unto *Brutus*;
Cassius the Epicurian was ready at hand to perswade
him, it was but a mistake in his weary imagination,
and that indeed there were no such realities in nature.
Thus he endeavours to propagate the unbelief of
Witches, whose concession infers his co-existency; by
this means also he advanceth the opinion of total
death, and staggereth the immortality of the soul;
for, such as deny there are spirits subsistent without
bodies, will with more difficulty affirm the separated
existence of their own.

Now to induce and bring about these falsities, he
hath laboured to destroy the evidence of Truth, that
is the revealed verity and written Word of God. To
which intent he hath obtained with some to repudiate
the Books of *Moses*, others those of the Prophets, and
some both: to deny the Gospel and authentick Histories of Christ; to reject that of *John*, and to receive
that of *Judas*; to disallow all, and erect another of
Thomas. And when neither their corruption by *Valentinus* and *Arrius*, their mutilation by *Marcion*, *Manes*,
and *Ebion* could satisfie his design, he attempted the
ruine and total destruction thereof; as he sedulously
endeavoured, by the power and subtilty of *Julian*,
Maximinus, and *Dioclesian*.

But the longevity of that piece, which hath so long
escaped the common fate, and the providence of that
Spirit which ever waketh over it, may at last discourage
such attempts; and if not make doubtful its Mortality,
at least indubitably declare; this is a stone too big
for *Saturns* mouth, and a bit indeed Oblivion cannot
swallow.

And thus how strangely he possesseth us with Errors

may clearly be observed, deluding us into contradictory and inconsistent falsities; whilest he would make us believe, That there is no God. That there are many. That he himself is God. That he is less then Angels or Men. That he is nothing at all.

Nor hath he onely by these wiles depraved the conception of the Creator, but with such Riddles hath also entangled the Nature of our Redeemer. Some denying his Humanity, and that he was one of the Angels, as *Ebion*; that the Father and Son were but one person, as *Sabellius*. That his body was phantastical, as *Manes, Basilides, Priscillian, Jovinianus*; that he only passed through *Mary*, as *Utyches* and *Valentinus*. Some denying his Divinity; that he was begotten of humane principles, and the seminal Son of *Joseph*; as *Carpocras, Symmachus, Photinus*: that he was *Seth* the Son of *Adam*, as the *Sethians*: that he was less then Angels, as *Cherinthus*: that he was inferiour unto *Melchisedec*, as *Theodotus*: that he was not God, but God dwelt in him, as *Nicholaus*: and some embroyled them both. So did they which converted the Trinity into a Quaternity, and affirmed two persons in Christ, as *Paulus Samosatenus*: that held he was Man without a Soul, and that the Word performed that office in him, as *Apollinaris*: that he was both Son and Father, as *Montanus*: that *Jesus* suffered, but Christ remained impatible, as *Cherinthus*. Thus he endeavours to entangle Truths: And when he cannot possibly destroy its substance, he cunningly confounds its apprehensions; that from the inconsistent and contrary determinations thereof, consectary impieties, and hopeful conclusions may arise, there's no such thing at all.

CHAPTER XI

A further Illustration.

N OW although these ways of delusions most Christians have escaped, yet are there many other whereunto we are daily betrayed, and these we meet with in obvious occurrents of the world, wherein he induceth us, to ascribe effects unto causes of no cognation; and distorting the order and theory of causes perpendicular to their effects, he draws them aside unto things whereto they run parallel, and in their proper motions would never meet together.

Thus doth he sometime delude us in the conceits of Stars and Meteors, beside their allowable actions ascribing effects thereunto of independent causations. Thus hath he also made the ignorant sort believe that natural effects immediately and commonly proceed from supernatural powers : and these he usually drives from Heaven, his own principality the Air, and Meteors therein ; which being of themselves the effects of natural and created causes, and such as upon a due conjunction of actives and passives, without a miracle must arise unto what they appear; are always looked on by ignorant spectators as supernatural spectacles, and made the causes or signs of most succeeding contingencies. To behold a Rainbow in the night, is no prodigy unto a Philosopher. Then Eclipses of Sun or Moon, nothing is more natural. Yet with what superstition they have been beheld since the Tragedy of *Nicias* and his Army, many examples declare.

True it is, and we will not deny, that although these being natural productions from second and setled causes,

we need not alway look upon them as the immediate
hand of God, or of his ministring Spirits; yet do they
sometimes admit a respect therein; and even in their
naturals, the indifferency of their existencies contem-
porised unto our actions, admits a further consideration.

That two or three Suns or Moons appear in any
mans life or reign, it is not worth the wonder. But
that the same should fall out at a remarkable time, or
point of some decisive action; that the contingency
of the appearance should be confirmed unto that time;
that those two should make but one line in the Book
of Fate, and stand together in the great Ephemerides
of God; beside the Philosophical assignment of the
cause, it may admit a Christian apprehension in the
signality.

But above all he deceiveth us, when we ascribe the
effects of things unto evident and seeming causalities,
which arise from the secret and undiscerned action of
himself. Thus hath he deluded many Nations in his
Augurial and Extispicious inventions, from casual and
uncontrived contingencies divining events succeeding.
Which *Tuscan* superstition seizing upon *Rome*, hath
since possessed all *Europe*. When *Augustus* found
two galls in his sacrifice, the credulity of the City
concluded a hope of peace with *Anthony*; and the
conjunction of persons in choler with each other.
Because *Brutus* and *Cassius* met a Blackmore, and
Pompey had on a dark or sad coloured garment at
Pharsalia; these were presages of their overthrow.
Which notwithstanding are scarce Rhetorical sequels;
concluding Metaphors from realities, and from conceptions metaphorical inferring realities again.

Now these divinations concerning events, being in
his power to force, contrive, prevent, or further, they

must generally fall out conformably unto his predictions. When *Graccus* was slain, the same day the
Chickens refused to come out of the Coop : and *Claudius*
Pulcher underwent the like success, when he contemned
the Tripudiary Augurations : They died not because
the Pullets would not feed : but because the Devil
foresaw their death, he contrived that abstinence in
them. So was there no natural dependence of the
event. An unexpected way of delusion, and whereby
he more easily led away the incircumspection of their
belief. Which fallacy he might excellently have acted
before the death of *Saul*; for that being within his
power to foretell, was not beyond his ability to foreshew : and might have contrived signs thereof through
all the creatures, which visibly confirmed by the event,
had proved authentick unto those times, and advanced
the Art ever after.

He deludeth us also by Philters, Ligatures, Charms, *The danger*
ungrounded Amulets, Characters, and many superstitious *and delusion that is in*
ways in the cure of common diseases : seconding herein *cures by*
the expectation of men with events of his own contriv- *Charms, Amulets,*
ing. Which while some unwilling to fall directly upon *Ligatures,*
Magick, impute unto the power of imagination, or the *Characters, etc.*
efficacy of hidden causes, he obtains a bloody advan-
tage : for thereby he begets not only a false opinion,
but such as leadeth the open way of destruction. In
maladies admitting natural reliefs, making men rely
on remedies, neither of real operation in themselves,
nor more then seeming efficacy in his concurrence.
Which whensoever he pleaseth to withdraw, they stand
naked unto the mischief of their diseases : and revenge
the contempt of the medicines of the Earth which
God hath created for them. And therefore when
neither miracle is expected, nor connection of cause

unto effect from natural grounds concluded; however it be sometime successful, it cannot be safe to rely on such practises, and desert the known and authentick provisions of God. In which rank of remedies, if nothing in our knowledge or their proper power be able to relieve us, we must with patience submit unto that restraint, and expect the will of the Restrainer.

Now in these effects although he seems oft-times to imitate, yet doth he concur unto their productions in a different way from that spirit which sometime in natural means produceth effects above Nature. For whether he worketh by causes which have relation or none unto the effect, he maketh it out by secret and undiscerned ways of Nature. So when *Caius* the blind, in the reign of *Antoninus*, was commanded to pass from the right side of the Altar unto the left, to lay five fingers of one hand thereon, and five of the other upon his eys; although the cure succeeded and all the people wondered, there was not any thing in the action which did produce it, nor any thing in his power that could enable it thereunto. So for the same infirmity, when *Aper* was counselled by him to make a Collyrium or ocular medicine with the blood of a white Cock and Honey, and apply it to his eyes for three days: When *Julian* for his spitting of blood, was cured by Honey and Pine nuts taken from his Altar: When *Lucius* for the pain in his side, applied thereto the ashes from his Altar with wine; although the remedies were somewhat rational, and not without a natural vertue unto such intentions, yet need we not believe that by their proper faculties they produced these effects.

But the effects of powers Divine flow from another operation; who either proceeding by visible means or not, unto visible effects, is able to conjoin them by his co-operation. And therefore those sensible ways which seem of indifferent natures, are not idle ceremonies, but may be causes by his command, and arise unto productions beyond their regular activities. If *Nahaman* the Syrian had washed in *Jordan* without the command of the Prophet, I believe he had been cleansed by them no more then by the waters of *Damascus*. I doubt if any beside *Elisha* had cast in Salt, the waters of *Jericho* had not been made wholsome. I know that a decoction of wild gourd or Colocynthis (though somewhat qualified) will not from every hand be dulcified unto aliment by an addition of flower or meal. There was some natural vertue in the Plaister of figs applied unto *Ezechias*; we find that gall is very mundificative, and was a proper medicine to clear the eyes of *Tobit*: which carrying in themselves some action of their own, they were additionally promoted by that power, which can extend their natures unto the production of effects beyond their created efficiencies. And thus may he operate also from causes of no power unto their visible effects; for he that hath determined their actions unto certain effects, hath not so emptied his own, but that he can make them effectual unto any other.

Again, Although his delusions run highest in points of practice, whose errors draw on offensive or penal enormities, yet doth he also deal in points of speculation, and things whose knowledge terminates in themselves. Whose cognition although it seems indifferent, and therefore its aberration directly to condemn no man; yet doth he hereby preparatively dispose us unto errors, and deductively deject us into destructive conclusions.

That the Sun, Moon, and Stars are living creatures, endued with soul and life, seems an innocent Error, and an harmless digression from truth ; yet hereby he confirmed their Idolatry, and made it more plausibly embraced. For wisely mistrusting that reasonable spirits would never firmly be lost in the adorement of things inanimate, and in the lowest form of Nature ; he begat an opinion that they were living creatures, and could not decay for ever.

That spirits are corporeal, seems at first view a conceit derogative unto himself, and such as he should rather labour to overthrow ; yet hereby he establisheth the Doctrine of Lustrations, Amulets and Charms, as we have declared before.

That there are two principles of all things, one good, and another evil ; from the one proceeding vertue, love, light, and unity ; from the other, division, discord, darkness, and deformity, was the speculation of *Pythagoras, Empedocles,* and many ancient Philosophers, and was no more then *Oromasdes* and *Arimanius* of *Zoroaster.* Yet hereby he obtained the advantage of Adoration, and as the terrible principle became more dreadful then his Maker ; and therefore not willing to let it fall, he furthered the conceit in succeeding Ages, and raised the faction of *Manes* to maintain it.

That the feminine sex have no generative emission, affording no seminal Principles of conception ; was *Aristotles* Opinion of old, maintained still by some, and will be countenanced by him forever. For hereby he disparageth the fruit of the Virgin, frustrateth the fundamental Prophesie, nor can the seed of the Woman then break the head of the Serpent.

Nor doth he only sport in speculative Errors, which are of consequent impieties ; but the unquietness of his malice hunts after simple lapses, and such whose falsities do only condemn our understandings. Thus

if *Xenophanes* will say there is another world in the
Moon; If *Heraclitus* with his adherents will hold the
Sun is no bigger then it appeareth; If *Anaxagoras*
affirm that Snow is black; If any other opinion there
are no *Antipodes*, or that Stars do fall, he shall not
want herein the applause or advocacy of Satan. For
maligning the tranquility of truth, he delighteth to
trouble its streams; and being a professed enemy unto
God (who is truth it self) he promoteth any Error
as derogatory to his nature; and revengeth himself in
every deformity from truth. If therefore at any time
he speak or practise truth, it is upon design, and a
subtile inversion of the precept of God, to do good
that evil may come of it. And therefore sometime we
meet with wholsome doctrines from Hell; *Nosce teipsum*,
the Motto of *Delphos*, was a good precept in morality :
That a just man is beloved of the gods, an uncontrol-
able verity. 'Twas a good deed, though not well done,
which he wrought by *Vespasian*, when by the touch of
his foot he restored a lame man, and by the stroak of
his hand another that was blind, but the intention
hereof drived at his own advantage; for hereby he not
only confirmed the opinion of his power with the
people, but his integrity with Princes; in whose power
he knew it lay to overthrow his Oracles, and silence the
practice of his delusions.

But of such a diffused nature, and so large is the
Empire of Truth, that it hath place within the walls
of Hell, and the Devils themselves are daily forced to
practise it; not onely as being true themselves in a
Metaphysical verity, that is, as having their essence
conformable unto the Intellect of their Maker, but
making use of Moral and Logical verities; that is,
whether in the conformity of words unto things, or

things unto their own conceptions, they practise truth in common among themselves. For although without speech they intuitively conceive each other, yet do their apprehensions proceed through realities; and they conceive each other by species, which carry the true and proper notions of things conceived. And so also in Moral verities, although they deceive us, they lie unto each other; as well understanding that all community is continued by Truth, and that of Hell cannot consist without it.

To come yet nearer the point, and draw into a sharper angle; They do not only speak and practise truth, but may be said well-wishers hereunto, and in some sense do really desire its enlargement. For many things which in themselves are false, they do desire were true; He cannot but wish he were as he professeth, that he had the knowledge of future events; were it in his power, the Jews should be in the right, and the *Messias* yet to come. Could his desires effect it, the opinion of *Aristotle* should be true, the world should have no end, but be as immortal as himself. For thereby he might evade the accomplishment of those afflictions, he now but gradually endureth; for comparatively unto those flames, he is but yet in *Balneo*, then begins his *Ignis Rotæ*, and terrible fire, which will determine his disputed subtilty, and even hazard his immortality.

But to speak strictly, he is in these wishes no promoter of verity, but if considered some ways injurious unto truth; for (besides that if things were true, which now are false, it were but an exchange of their natures, and things must then be false, which now are true) the setled and determined order of the world would be perverted, and that course of things disturbed, which

seemed best unto the immutable contriver. For whilest
they murmur against the present disposure of things,
regulating determined realities unto their private opta-
tions, they rest not in their established natures; but
unwishing their unalterable verities, do tacitely desire
in them a deformity from the primitive Rule, and the
Idea of that mind that formed all things best. And *How the*
thus he offended truth even in his first attempt; For *Devils fell.*
not content with his created nature, and thinking it
too low, to be the highest creature of God, he offended
the Ordainer, not only in the attempt, but in the wish
and simple volition thereof.

THE SECOND BOOK

Of sundry popular Tenets concerning Mineral, and vegetable bodies, generally held for truth; which examined, prove either false, or dubious.

CHAPTER I

Of Crystal.

HEREOF the common Opinion hath been, and still remaineth amongst us, that Crystal is nothing else but Ice or Snow concreted, and by duration of time, congealed beyond liquation. Of which assertion, if prescription of time, and numerosity of Assertors, were a sufficient demonstration, we might sit down herein, as an unquestionable truth; nor should there need *ulterior* disquisition. For few Opinions there are which have found so many friends, or been so popularly received, through all Professions and Ages. *Pliny* is positive in this Opinion: *Crystallus sit gelu vehementius concreto:* the same is followed by *Seneca*, elegantly described by *Claudian*, not denied by *Scaliger*, some way affirmed by *Albertus, Brasavolus,* and directly by many others. The venerable Fathers of the Church have also assented hereto; As *Basil* in his *Hexameron, Isidore* in his Etymologies, and not only *Austin* a Latine Father, but *Gregory* the Great, and *Jerome* upon occasion of that term expressed in the first of *Ezekiel*.

All which notwithstanding, upon a strict enquiry, we find the matter controvertible, and with much more reason denied then is as yet affirmed. For though many have passed it over with easie affirmatives, yet are there also many Authors that deny it, and the exactest Mineralogists have rejected it. *Diodorus* in his eleventh Book denieth it, (if Crystal be there taken in its proper acception, as *Rhodiginus* hath used it, and not for a Diamond, as *Salmatius* hath expounded it) for in that place he affirmeth; *Crystallum esse lapidem ex aqua pura concretum, non tamen frigore sed divini caloris vi.* *Solinus* who transcribed *Pliny*, and therefore in almost all subscribed unto him, hath in this point dissented from him. *Putant quidam glaciem coire, et in Crystallum corporari, sed frustra.* *Mathiolus* in his Comment upon *Dioscorides*, hath with confidence rejected it. The same hath been performed by *Agricola de natura fossilium*; by *Cardan, Bœtius de Boot, Cæsius Bernardus, Sennertus*, and many more.

Now besides Authority against it, there may be many reasons deduced from their several differences which seem to overthrow it. And first, a difference is probable in their concretion. For if Crystal be a stone (as in the number thereof it is confessedly received,) it is not immediately concreted by the efficacy of cold, but rather by a Mineral spirit, and lapidifical principles of its own, and therefore while it lay *in solutis principiis*, and remained in a fluid Body, it was a subject very unapt for proper conglaciation; for Mineral spirits do generally resist and scarce submit thereto. So we observe that many waters and springs will never freeze,

and many parts in Rivers and Lakes, where there are
Mineral eruptions, will still persist without congelations, as we also observe in *Aqua fortis*, or any Mineral
solution, either of Vitriol, Alum, Salt-petre, Ammoniac,
or Tartar, which although to some degree exhaled, and
placed in cold Conservatories, will Crystallize and shoot
into white and glacious bodies; yet is not this a congelation primarily effected by cold, but an intrinsecal
induration from themselves; and a retreat into their
proper solidities, which were absorbed by the liquor,
and lost in a full imbibition thereof before. And so
also when wood and many other bodies do putrifie,
either by the Sea, other waters, or earths abounding
in such spirits; we do not usually ascribe their induration to cold, but rather unto salinous spirits, concretive
juices, and causes circumjacent, which do assimilate all
bodies not indisposed for their impressions.

But Ice is water congealed by the frigidity of the
air, whereby it acquireth no new form, but rather a
consistence or determination of its diffluency, and amit-
teth not its essence, but condition of fluidity. Neither
doth there any thing properly conglaciate but water,
or watery humidity; for the determination of quicksilver is properly fixation, that of milk coagulation,
and that of oyl and unctious bodies, only incrassation;
And therefore *Aristotle* makes a trial of the fertility of
humane seed, from the experiment of congelation; for
that (saith he) which is not watery and improlifical
will not conglaciate; which perhaps must not be taken
strictly, but in the germ and spirited particles: For
Eggs I observe will freeze, in the albuginous part thereof.
And upon this ground *Paracelsus* in his Archidoxis,
extracteth the magistery of wine; after four moneths
digestion in horse-dung, exposing it unto the extremity

of cold; whereby the aqueous parts will freeze, but the Spirit retire and be found congealed in the Center.

But whether this congelation be simply made by cold, or also by co-operation of any nitrous coagulum, or spirit of Salt the principle of concretion; whereby we observe that ice may be made with Salt and Snow by the fire side; as is also observable from Ice made by Saltpetre and water, duly mixed and strongly agitated at any time of the year, were a very considerable enquiry. For thereby we might clear the generation of Snow, Hail, and hoary Frosts, the piercing qualities of some winds, the coldness of Caverns, and some Cells. We might more sensibly conceive how Salt-petre fixeth the flying spirits of Minerals in Chymical Preparations, and how by this congealing quality it becomes an useful medicine in Fevers.

How to make Ice at any time of the year.

Again, The difference of their concretion is collectible from their dissolution; which being many ways performable in Ice, is few ways effected in Crystal. Now the causes of liquation are contrary to those of concretion; and as the Atoms and indivisible parcels are united, so are they in an opposite way disjoyned. That which is concreted by exsiccation or expression of humidity, will be resolved by humectation, as Earth, Dirt, and Clay; that which is coagulated by a fiery siccity, will suffer colliquation from an aqueous humidity, as Salt and Sugar, which are easily dissoluble in water, but not without difficulty in oyl, and well rectified spirits of Wine. That which is concreted by cold, will dissolve by a moist heat, if it consist of watery parts, as Gums, Arabick, Tragacanth, Ammoniac and others; in an airy heat or oyl, as all resinous bodies, Turpentine, Pitch, and Frankincense; in both, as gummy resinous bodies, Mastick, Camphire and Storax; in neither, as neutrals and bodies anomalous hereto, as Bdellium, Myrrhe, and others. Some by a violent dry heat, as Metals; which although corrodible by waters, yet will they not suffer a liquation from the powerfullest heat, communicable unto that element. Some will dissolve by this heat although their ingredients be earthy, as Glass, whose materials *The original* are fine Sand, and the ashes of Chali or Fearn; and so *ingredients* will Salt run with fire, although it be concreted by *of Glass.* heat. And this way may be effected a liquation in Crystal, but not without some difficulty; that is, calcination or reducing it by Art into a subtle powder; by which way and a vitreous commixture, Glasses are sometime made hereof, and it becomes the chiefest ground for artificial and factitious gemms. But the same way of solution is common also unto many Stones; and not onely Beryls and Cornelians, but Flints and Pebbles, are subject unto fusion, and will run like Glass in fire.

But Ice will dissolve in any way of heat, for it will dissolve with fire, it will colliquate in water, or warm oyl; nor doth it only submit unto an actual heat, but not endure the potential calidity of many waters. For it will presently dissolve in cold *Aqua fortis*, sp. of Vitriol, Salt, or Tartar, nor will it long continue its fixation in spirits of Wine, as may be observed in Ice injected therein.

Again, The concretion of Ice will not endure a dry attrition without liquation; for if it be rubbed long with a cloth, it melteth. But Crystal will calefie unto electricity, that is, a power to attract straws or light bodies, and convert the needle freely placed. Which is a declarement of very different parts, wherein we shall not inlarge, as having discoursed concerning such bodies in the Chap. of Electricks.

They are differenced by supernatation or floating
upon water; for Crystal will sink in water, as carrying
in its own bulk a greater ponderosity then the space in
any water it doth occupy; and will therefore only swim
in molten Metal and Quicksilver. But Ice will swim in
water of what thinness soever; and though it sink in
oyl, will float in spirits of Wine or *Aqua vitæ*. And
therefore it may swim in water, not only as being
water it self, and in its proper place, but perhaps as
weighing somewhat less then the water it possesseth.
And therefore as it will not sink unto the bottom, so
will it neither float above like lighter bodies, but being
near in weight, lie superficially or almost horizontally
unto it. And therefore also an Ice or congelation of
Salt or Sugar, although it descend not unto the bottom,
yet will it abate, and decline below the surface in thin
water, but very sensibly in spirits of Wine. For Ice
although it seemeth as transparent and compact as
Crystal, yet is it short in either; for its atoms are not
concreted into continuity, which doth diminish its
translucency; it is also full of spumes and bubbles,
which may abate its gravity. And therefore waters
frozen in Pans, and open Glasses, after their dissolution do commonly leave a froth and spume upon them,
which are caused by the airy parts diffused in the con-
gealable mixture which uniting themselves and finding
no passage at the surface, do elevate the mass, and
make the liquor take up a greater place then before:
as may be observed in Glasses filled with water, which
being frozen, will seem to swell above the brim. So
that if in this condensation any one affirmeth there is
also some rarefaction, experience may assert it.

They are distinguished in substance of parts and the
accidents thereof, that is, in colour and figure; for Ice

is a similar body, and homogeneous concretion, whose material is properly water, and but accidentally exceeding the simplicity of that element. But the body of Crystal is mixed; its ingredients many, and sensibly containeth those principles into which mixt bodies are reduced. For beside the spirit and mercurial principle it containeth a sulphur or inflamable part, and that in no small quantity; for besides its Electrick attraction, which is made by a sulphureous effluvium, it will strike fire upon percussion like many other stones, and upon collision with Steel actively send forth its sparks, not much inferiourly unto a flint. Now such bodies as strike fire have sulphureous or ignitible parts within them, and those strike best, which abound most in them. For these scintillations are not the accension of the air, upon the collision of two hard bodies, but rather the inflamable effluencies or vitrified sparks discharged from the bodies collided. For Diamonds, Marbles, Heliotropes and Agaths, though hard bodies, will not readily strike fire with a steel, much less with one another: Nor a Flint so readily with a Steel, if they both be very wet, for then the sparks are sometimes quenched in their eruption.

It containeth also a salt, and that in some plenty, which may occasion its fragility, as is also observable in Coral. This by the Art of Chymistry is separable, unto the operations whereof it is liable, with other concretions, as calcination, reverberation, sublimation, distillation: And in the preparation of Crystal, *Paracelsus* hath made a rule for that of Gemms. Briefly, it consisteth of parts so far from an Icie dissolution, that powerful menstruums are made for its emollition; whereby it may receive the tincture of Minerals, and so resemble Gemms, as *Boetius* hath declared in the

de Præparationibus.

distillation of Urine; spirits of Wine and Turpentine; and is not only triturable, and reducible into powder, by contrition, but will subsist in a violent fire, and endure a vitrification. Whereby are testified its earthly and fixed parts. For vitrification is the last work of fire, and a fusion of the Salt and Earth, which are the fixed elements of the composition, wherein the fusible Salt draws the Earth and infusible part into one continuum, and therefore ashes will not run from whence the Salt is drawn, as bone ashes prepared for the Test of Metals. Common fusion in Metals is also made by *The Physical causes of liquation or melting of Mettals, etc.* a violent heat, acting upon the volatile and fixed, the dry and humid parts of those bodies; which notwithstanding are so united, that upon attenuation from heat, the humid parts will not fly away, but draw the fixed ones into fluor with them. Ordinary liquation in wax and oily bodies is made by a gentler heat, where the oyl and salt, the fixed and fluid principles will not easily separate. All which, whether by vitrification, fusion or liquation, being forced into fluent consistencies, do naturally regress into their former solidities. Whereas the melting of Ice is a simple resolution, or return from solid to fluid parts, wherein it naturally resteth.

As for colour, although Crystal in his pellucid body seems to have none at all, yet in its reduction into powder, it hath a vail and shadow of blew; and in its courser pieces, is of a sadder hue then the powder of Venice glass; and this complexion it will maintain although it long endure the fire. Which notwithstanding needs not move us unto wonder; for vitrified and pellucid bodies, are of a clearer complexion in their continuities, then in their powders and Atomical divisions. So *Stibium* or glass of *Antimony*, appears

o

somewhat red in glass, but in its powder yellow; so painted glass of a sanguine red will not ascend in powder above a murrey.

As for the figure of Crystal (which is very strange, and forced *Pliny* to despair of resolution) it is for the most part hexagonal or six cornered; being built upon a confused matter, from whence as it were from a rcot angular figures arise, even as in the Amethyst and Basaltes. Which regular figuration hath made some opinion, it hath not its determination from circumscription, or as conforming unto contiguities, but rather from a seminal root, and formative principle of its own, even as we observe in several other concretions. So the stones which are sometime found in the gall of a man, are most triangular and pyramidal, although the figure of that part seems not to co-operate thereto. So the *Asteria* or *lapis stellaris*, hath on it the figure of a Star, so *Lapis Judaicus* hath circular lines in length all down its body, and equidistant, as though they had been turned by Art. So that we call a Fayrie stone, and is often found in *gravel pits* amongst us, being of an hemispherical figure, hath five double lines arising from the center of its basis, which if no accretion distract them, do commonly concur, and meet in the pole thereof. The figures are regular in many other stones, as in the Belemnites, *Lapis Anguinus, Cornu Ammonis*, and many more; as by those which have not the experience hereof may be observed in their figures expressed by Mineralogists. But Ice receiveth its figure according unto the surface wherein it concreteth, or the circumambiency which conformeth it. So it is plain upon the surface of water, but round in Hayl (which is also a glaciation,) and figured in its guttulous descent from the air, and so growing greater

In Stone-pits and Chalk-mines. Which seemeth to be Echinites decima Aldrovandi. Musæi Metallici, lib. 4. *Rather Echinometrites, as best resembling the Echinometra found commonly on our Sea-shore.*

or lesser according unto the accretion or pluvious
aggelation about the mother and fundamental Atomes
thereof; which seems to be some feathery particle of
Snow; although Snow it self be sexangular, or at least
of a starry and many-pointed figure.

They are also differenced in the places of their
generation; for though Crystal be found in cold
countries, and where Ice remaineth long, and the
air exceedeth in cold, yet is it also found in regions,
where Ice is seldom seen or soon dissolved; as *Pliny*
and *Agricola* relate of *Cyprus*, *Caramania* and an Island
in the Red sea; It hath been also found in the veins
of Minerals, sometimes agglutinated unto lead, sometimes in Rocks, opacous stones, and the marble face of *Wherein*
the Sculptor
Octavius Duke of *Parma*. It hath also constant veins; *found a*
as beside others, that of mount *Salvino* about the *piece of pure*
Crystal.
Territory of *Bergamo*; from whence if part be taken,
in no long tract of time out of the same place, as from
its mineral matrix, others are observed to arise. Which
made the learned *Cerautus* to conclude, *Videant hi an* *Mus. Cal*
sit glacies, an vero corpus fossile. It is also found in *ceolar.*
the veins of Minerals, in rocks, and sometime in common
earth. But as for Ice, it will not readily concrete but
in the approachment of the air, as we have made trial
in glasses of water, covered an inch with oyl, which
will not easily freeze in hard frosts of our climate.
For water commonly concreteth first in its surface, and
so conglaciates downward; and so will it do although
it be exposed in the coldest metal of lead, which well
accordeth with that expression of *Job, The waters are* *Chap.* 38.
hid as with a stone, and the face of the deep is frozen.
But whether water which hath been boiled or heated,
doth sooner receive this congelation, as commonly is
delivered, we rest in the experiment of *Cabeus,* who

hath rejected the same in his excellent discourse of Meteors.

They have contrary qualities elemental, and uses medicinal; for Ice is cold and moist, of the quality of water; but Crystal is cold and dry, according to the condition of earth. The use of Ice is condemned by most Physicians, that of Crystal commended by many. For although *Dioscorides* and *Galen* have left no mention thereof, yet hath *Mathiolus*, *Agricola*, and many commended it in dysenteries and fluxes; all for the increase of milk, most Chymists for the Stone, and some, as *Brassavolus* and *Bœtius*, as an antidote against poyson. Which occult and specifical operations are not expectable from Ice; for being but water congealed, it can never make good such qualities; nor will it reasonably admit of secret proprieties, which are the affections of forms, and compositions at distance from their elements.

What Crystal is.

Having thus declared what Crystal is not, it may afford some satisfaction to manifest what it is. To deliver therefore what with the judgement of approved Authors, and best reason consisteth, It is a Mineral body in the difference of stones, and reduced by some unto that subdivision, which comprehendeth gemms, transparent and resembling Glass or Ice, made of a lentous percolation of earth, drawn from the most pure and limpid juice thereof, owing unto the coldness of the earth some concurrence or coadjuvancy, but not immediate determination and efficiency, which are wrought by the hand of its concretive spirit, the seeds of petrification and Gorgon of it self. As sensible Philosophers conceive of the generation of Diamonds, Iris, Berils. Not making them of frozen icecles, or from meer aqueous and glaciable substances, condensing them by frosts into solidities, vainly to be expected even from Polary congelations: but from thin and finest earths, so well contempered and resolved, that transparency is not hindred; and containing lapidifical spirits, able to make good their solidities against the opposition and activity of outward contraries, and so leave a sensible difference between the bonds of glaciation, which in the mountains of Ice about the Northern Seas, are easily dissolved by ordinary heat of the Sun, and between the finer ligatures of petrification, whereby not only the harder concretions of Diamonds and Saphirs, but the softer veins of Crystal remain indissolvable in scorching Territories, and the *Negro* land of Congor.

And therefore I fear we commonly consider subterranities, not in contemplations sufficiently respective unto the Creation. For though *Moses* have left no mention of Minerals, nor made any other description then sutes unto the apparent and visible Creation, yet is there unquestionably, a very large Classis of Creatures in the Earth, far above the condition of elementarity. And although not in a distinct and indisputable way of vivency, or answering in all points the properties or affections of Plants, yet in inferiour and descending constitutions, they do like these contain specifical distinctions, and are determined by seminalities, that is, created and defined seeds committed unto the Earth from the beginning. Wherein although they attain not the indubitable requisites of Animation, yet have they a near affinity thereto. And though we want a proper name and expressive appellation, yet are they not to be closed up in the general name of concretions; or lightly passed over as only Elementary and Subterraneous mixtions.

The principle and most gemmary affection is its Tralucency: as for irradiancy or sparkling which is found in many gemms, it is not discoverable in this, for it cometh short of their compactness and durity: and therefore requireth not the Emery, as the Saphir, Granate, and Topaz, but will receive impression from Steel, in a manner like the Turchois. As for its diaphanity or perspicuity, it enjoyeth that most eminently; and the reason thereof is its continuity; as having its earthy and salinous parts so exactly resolved, that its body is left imporous and not discreted by atomical terminations. For, that continuity of parts is the cause of perspicuity, it is made perspicuous by two ways of experiment. That is, either in effecting transparency in those bodies which were not so before, or at least far short of the additional degree: So Snow becomes transparent upon liquation, so Horns and Bodies resolvable into continued parts or gelly. The like is observable in oyled paper, wherein the interstitial divisions being continuated by the accession of oyl, it becometh more transparent, and admits the visible rayes with less umbrosity. Or else the same is effected by rendring those bodies opacous, which were before pellucid and perspicuous.

Exact continuity of parts a cause of transparency in things, and why.

So Glass which was before diaphanous, being by powder reduced into multiplicity of superficies, becomes an opacous body, and will not transmit the light. So it is in Crystal powdered, and so it is also before; for if it be made hot in a crucible, and presently projected upon water, it will grow dim, and abate its diaphanity; for the water entering the body, begets a division of parts, and a termination of Atoms united before unto continuity.

The ground of this Opinion might be, first the con-

clusions of some men from experience; for as much as
Crystal is found sometimes in rocks, and in some places
not much unlike the stirious or stillicidious depend-
encies of Ice. Which notwithstanding may happen
either in places which have been forsaken or left bare
by the earth, or may be petrifications, or Mineral
indurations, like other gemms, proceeding from per-
colations of the earth disposed unto such concretions.

The second and most common ground is from the
name *Crystallus*, whereby in Greek both Ice and Crystal
are expressed; which many not duly considering, have
from their community of name, conceived a community of nature; and what was ascribed unto the
one, not unfitly appliable unto the other. But this is
a fallacy of Æquivocation, from a society in name
inferring an Identity in nature. By this fallacy was
he deceived that drank *Aqua fortis* for strong water.
By this are they deluded, who conceive *sperma Cæti*
which is found about the head, to be the spawn of the
Whale: Or take *sanguis draconis* (which is the gumme
of a tree,) to be the blood of a Dragon. By the same
Logick we may infer, the Crystalline humour of the eye,
or rather the Crystalline heaven above, to be of the
substance of Crystal here below; Or that God sendeth
down Crystal, because it is delivered in the vulgar
translation, Psal. 47. *Mittit Crystallum suum sicut
Buccellas.* Which translation although it literally
express the Septuagint; yet is there no more meant
thereby, than what our translation in plain English expresseth; that is, he casteth forth his Ice like morsels,
or what *Tremellius* and *Junius* as clearly deliver, *Agreement
Dejicit gelu suum sicut frusta, coram frigore ejus quis* *in name.*
consistet? which proper and latine expressions, had they
been observed in ancient translations, elder Expositors

had not been misguided by the Synonomy; nor had
they afforded occasion unto *Austin*, the Gloss, *Lyranus*,
and many others, to have taken up the common
conceit, and spoke of this Text conformably unto the
opinion rejected.

CHAPTER II

Concerning the Loadstone.

Of things particularly spoken thereof, evidently
or probably true.   Of things generally
believed, or particularly delivered, manifestly or probably false.   In the first of
the Magnetical vertue of the Earth, of the
four motions of the stone, that is, its Verticity or Direction, its Attraction or Coition,
its Declination, its Variation, and also of
its Antiquity.   In the second a rejection
of sundry opinions and relations thereof,
Natural, Medical, Historical, Magical.

*How the
earth is a
Magnetical
body.*

AND first we conceive the earth to be a Magnetical body.   A Magnetical body, we term
not onely that which hath a power attractive,
but that which seated in a convenient medium,
naturally disposeth it self to one invariable and fixed
situation.   And such a Magnetical vertue we conceive
to be in the Globe of the Earth, whereby as unto its
natural points and proper terms, it disposeth it self
unto the poles; being so framed, constituted, and
ordered unto these points, that those parts which are
now at the poles, would not naturally abide under

the Æquator, nor *Greenland* remain in the place of
Magellanica. And if the whole earth were violently
removed, yet would it not foregoe its primitive points,
nor pitch in the East or West, but return unto its
polary position again. For though by compactness or
gravity it may acquire the lowest place, and become
the center of the universe, yet that it makes good that
point, not varying at all by the accession of bodies
upon, or secession thereof from its surface, perturbing
the equilibration of either Hemisphere (whereby the
altitude of the stars might vary) or that it strictly
maintains the North and Southern points; that neither
upon the motions of the heavens, air, and winds
without, large eruptions and division of parts within,
its polary parts should never incline or veer unto the
Equator (whereby the latitude of places should also
vary) it cannot so well be salved from gravity as a
Magnetical verticity. This is probably, that foundation the wisdom of the Creator hath laid unto the
earth; in this sense we may more nearly apprehend,
and sensibly make out the expressions of holy Scripture,
as *Firmavit orbem terræ qui non commovebitur,* he hath
made the round world so sure that it cannot be moved:
as when it is said by *Job, Extendit Aquilonem super
vacuo, &c.* He stretcheth forth the North upon the
empty place, and hangeth the earth upon nothing.
And this is the most probable answer unto that great
question. Whereupon are the foundations of the
Earth fastened, or who laid the corner stone thereof?
Had they been acquainted with this principle, *Anaxagoras, Socrates,* and *Democritus,* had better made out
the ground of this stability; *Xenophanes* had not been
fain to say the Earth had no bottom; and *Thales
Milesius* to make it swim in water.

*The founda-
tion of the
Earths
stability.*

Psal. 93.

Job 38.

*The mag-
netical
vertue of
the Earth
diffused
extra se and
communi-
cated to
bodies ad-
jacent.*

Nor is the vigour of this great body included only in its self, or circumferenced by its surface, but diffused at indeterminate distances through the air, water, and all bodies circumjacent. Exciting and impregnating Magnetical bodies within its surface or without it, and performing in a secret and invisible way what we evidently behold effected by the Loadstone. For these effluxions penetrate all bodies, and like the species of visible objects are ever ready in the medium, and lay hold on all bodies proportionate or capable of their action, those bodies likewise being of a congenerous nature, do readily receive the impressions of their motor; and if not fettered by their gravity, conform themselves to situations, wherein they best unite unto their Animator. And this will sufficiently appear from the observations that are to follow, which can no better way be made out then by this we speak of, the Magnetical vigour of the Earth. Now whether these effluviums do flye by striated Atoms and winding particles as *Renatus des Cartes* conceiveth; or glide by streams attracted from either Pole and Hemisphere of the Earth unto the Equator, as Sir *Kenelm Digby* excellently declareth, it takes not away this vertue of the Earth, but more distinctly sets down the gests and progress thereof, and are conceits of eminent use to salve Magnetical Phenomena's. And as in Astronomy those hypotheses though never so strange are best

*Apparencies
observations.*

esteemed which best do salve apparencies; so surely in Philosophy those principles (though seeming monstrous) may with advantage be embraced, which best confirm

*The doctrine
of effluxions
acknow-
ledged by
the Author*

experiment, and afford the readiest reason of observation. And truly the doctrine of effluxions, their penetrating natures, their invisible paths, and insuspected effects, are very considerable; for besides this Mag-

netical one of the Earth, several effusions there may be
from divers other bodies, which invisibly act their parts
at any time, and perhaps through any medium; a part of
Philosophy but yet in discovery, and will, I fear, prove
the last leaf to be turned over in the Book of Nature.

First, Therefore it is true, and confirmable by every
experiment, that Steel and g*od* Iron never excited by
the Loadstone, discover in themselves a verticity; that
is, a directive or polary faculty, whereby, conveniently
placed, they do Septentrionate at one extream, and *Point to*
Australize at another. This is manifestable in long *the North.*
Point to
and thin plates of Steel perforated in the middle *the South.*
and equilibrated; or by an easier way in long wires
equiponderate with untwisted Silk and soft Wax; for
in this manner pendulous, they will conform themselves
Meridionally, directing one extream unto the North,
another to the South. The same is also manifest in
Steel wires thrust through little sphears or globes of
Cork and floated on the water, or in naked Needles
gently let fall thereon; for so disposed they will not
rest, until they have found out the Meridian, and as
near as they can lye parallel unto the Axis of the
Earth: Sometimes the eye, sometimes the point
Northward in divers Needles, but the same point
always in most: Conforming themselves unto the
whole Earth, in the same manner as they do unto
every Loadstone. For if a Needle untoucht be hanged
above a Loadstone, it will convert into a parallel position thereto; for in this situation it can best receive
its verticity and be excited proportionably at both
extreams. Now this direction proceeds not primitively
from themselves, but is derivative and contracted from
the Magnetical effluxions of the Earth; which they
have winded in their hammering and formation; or

else by long continuance in one position, as we shall declare hereafter.

It is likewise true what is delivered of Irons heated in the fire, that they contract a verticity in their refrigeration; for heated red hot and cooled in the Meridian from North to South, they presently contract a polary power, and being poised in air or water, convert that part unto the North which respected that point in its refrigeration, so that if they had no sensible verticity before, it may be acquired by this way; or if they had any, it might be exchanged by contrary position in the cooling. For by the fire they omit not onely many drossie and scorious parts, but whatsoever they had received either from the Earth or Loadstone; and so being naked and despoiled of all verticity, the Magnetical Atomes invade their bodies with more effect and agility.

Neither is it only true what *Gilbertus* first observed, that Irons refrigerated North and South acquire a Directive faculty; but if they be cooled upright and perpendicularly, they will also obtain the same. That part which is cooled toward the North on this side the Equator, converting it self unto the North, and attracting the South point of the Needle: the other and highest extream respecting the South, and attracting the Northern, according unto Laws Magnetical: For (what must be observed) contrary Poles or faces attract each other, as the North the South; and the like decline each other, as the North the North. Now on this side of the Equator, that extream which is next the Earth is animated unto the North, and the contrary unto the South; so that in coition it applies it self quite oppositely, the coition or attraction being contrary to the Verticity or Direction. Contrary, If we

speak according unto common use, yet alike, if we CHAP.
conceive the vertue of the North Pole to diffuse it self II
and open at the South, and the South at the North
again.

This polarity from refrigeration upon extremity and
in defect of a Loadstone might serve to invigorate and
touch a Needle any where; and this, allowing variation,
is also the readiest way at any season to discover the
North or South; and surely far more certain then what
is affirmed of the grains and circles in trees, or the *Some con-*
figure in the root of Fern. For if we erect a red hot *ceive that*
the figure
wire until it cool, then hang it up with wax and *of the Tree*
untwisted Silk, where the lower end and that which *or Spread-*
eagle in the
cooled next the earth doth rest, that is the Northern *root of*
point; and this we affirm will still be true whether it *Fern stands*
be cooled in the air or extinguished in water, oyl of *North and*
South, but
Vitriol, *Aqua fortis*, or Quicksilver. And this is also *not truly.*
evidenced in culinary utensils and Irons that often feel
the force of fire, as Tongs, Fire-shovels, Prongs, and
Andirons; all which acquire a Magnetical and polary
condition, and being suspended, convert their lower
extreams unto the North; with the same attracting
the Southern point of the Needle. For easier experiment, if we place a Needle touched at the foot of
Tongs or Andirons, it will obvert or turn aside its
lillie or North point, and conform its cuspis or South
extream unto the Andiron. The like verticity though
more obscurely is also contracted by Bricks and Tiles,
as we have made trial in some taken out of the backs
of chimneys. Now to contract this Direction, there
needs not a total ignition, nor is it necessary the
Irons should be red hot all over. For if a wire be
heated only at one end, according as that end is cooled
upward or downward, it respectively acquires a verti-

city, as we have declared in wires totally candent.
Nor is it absolutely requisite they should be cooled
perpendicularly, or strictly lie in the Meridian; for
whether they be refrigerated inclinatorily or somewhat
Æquinoxially, that is toward the Eastern or Western
points; though in a lesser degree, they discover some
verticity.

Nor is this onely true in Irons, but in the Loadstone
it self. For if a Loadstone be made red hot, it loseth
the magnetical vigour it had before in it self, and
acquires another from the Earth in its refrigeration;
for that part which cooleth toward the Earth will
acquire the respect of the North, and attract the
Southern point or cuspis of the Needle. The experiment hereof we made in a Loadstone of a parallelogram
or long square figure; wherein onely inverting the
extreams, as it came out of the fire, we altered the
poles or faces thereof at pleasure.

It is also true what is delivered of the Direction and
coition of Irons, that they contract a verticity by long
and continued position: that is, not onely being placed
from North to South, and lying in the Meridian, but respecting the Zenith and perpendicular unto the Center of
the Earth; as is manifest in bars of windows, casements,
hinges and the like. For if we present the Needle
unto their lower extreams, it wheels about and turns
its Southern point unto them. The same condition in
long time do Bricks contract which are placed in walls,
and therefore it may be a fallible way to find out the
Meridian by placing the Needle on a wall; for some
Bricks therein by a long and continued position, are
often magnetically enabled to distract the polarity of
the Needle. And therefore those Irons which are said
to have been converted into Loadstones; whether they

were real conversions, or onely attractive augmenta-
tions, might be much promoted by this position : as
the Iron cross of an hundred weight upon the Church
of St. *John* in *Ariminum*, or that Loadston'd Iron of
Cæsar Moderatus, set down by *Aldrovandus*.

CHAP. II
De miner.
l. 1.

Lastly, Irons do manifest a verticity not only upon
refrigeration and constant situation, but (what is
wonderful and advanceth the magnetical Hypothesis)
they evidence the same by meer position according as
they are inverted, and their extreams disposed respectively unto the Earth. For if an Iron or Steel not
firmly excited, be held perpendicularly or inclinatorily
unto the Needle, the lower end thereof will attract the
cuspis or Southern point ; but if the same extream be
inverted and held under the Needle, it will then attract
the lilly or Northern point ; for by inversion it changeth
its direction acquired before, and receiveth a new and
Southern polarity from the Earth, as being the upper
extream. Now if an Iron be touched before, it varieth
not in this manner ; for then it admits not this magnetical impression, as being already informed by the
Loadstone, and polarily determined by its preaction.

And from these grounds may we best determine
why the Northern Pole of the Loadstone attracteth a
greater weight than the Southern on this side the
Æquator ; why the stone is best preserved in a natural
and polary situation ; and why as *Gilbertus* observeth,
it respecteth that Pole out of the Earth, which it
regarded in its Mineral bed and subterraneous position.

It is likewise true and wonderful what is delivered
of the Inclination or Declination of the Loadstone ;
that is, the descent of the Needle below the plain of
the Horizon. For long Needles which stood before
upon their *axis*, *parallel* unto the Horizon, being

vigorously excited, incline and bend downward, depressing the North extream below the Horizon. That is the North on this, the South on the other side of the Equator; and at the very Line or middle circle stand without deflexion. And this is evidenced not onely from observations of the Needle in several parts of the earth, but sundry experiments in any part thereof, as in a long Steel wire, equilibrated or evenly ballanced in the air; for excited by a vigorous Loadstone it will somewhat depress its animated extream, and intersect the horizontal circumference. It is also manifest in a Needle pierced through a Globe of Cork so cut away and pared by degrees, that it will swim under water, yet sink not unto the bottom, which may be well effected; for if the Cork be a thought too light to sink under the surface, the body of the water may be attenuated with spirits of wine; if too heavy, it may be incrassated with salt; and if by chance too much be added, it may again be thinned by a proportionable addition of fresh water. If then the Needle be taken out, actively touched and put in again, it will depress and bow down its Northern head toward the bottom, and advance its Southern extremity toward the brim. This way invented by *Gilbertus* may seem of difficulty; the same with less labour may be observed in a needled sphere of Cork equally contiguous unto the surface of the water; for if the Needle be not exactly equiponderant, that end which is a thought too light, if touched becometh even; that Needle also which will but just swim under the water, if forcibly touched will sink deeper, and sometime unto the bottom. If likewise that inclinatory vertue be destroyed by a touch from the contrary Pole, that end which before was elevated will then decline, and this perhaps might be observed in some scales exactly ballanced, and in such Needles which for their bulk can hardly be supported by the water. For if they be powerfully excited and equally let fall, they commonly sink down and break the water at that extream whereat they were septentrionally excited : and by this way it is conceived there may be some fraud in the weighing of precious commodities, and such as carry a value in quarter-grains ; by placing a powerful Loadstone above or below, according as we intend to depress or elevate one extream.

Now if these Magnetical emissions be onely qualities, and the gravity of bodies incline them onely unto the earth ; surely that which alone moveth other bodies to descent, carrieth not the stroak in this, but rather the Magnetical alliciency of the Earth ; unto which with alacrity it applieth it self, and in the very same way unto the whole Earth, as it doth unto a single Loadstone. For if an untouched Needle be at a distance suspended over a Loadstone, it will not hang parallel, but decline at the North extream, and at that part will first salute its Director. Again, what is also wonderful, this inclination is not invariable ; for just under the line the Needle lieth parallel with the Horizon, but sailing North or South it beginneth to incline, and encreaseth according as it approacheth unto either Pole ; and would at last endeavour to erect it self. And this is no more then what it doth upon the Loadstone, and that more plainly upon the Terrella or spherical magnet Cosmographically set out with circles of the Globe. For at the Equator thereof, the Needle will stand rectangularly ; but approaching Northward toward the Tropick it will regard the stone obliquely, and when it attaineth the Pole, directly ;

P

and if its bulk be no impediment, erect it self and stand perpendicularly thereon. And therefore upon strict observation of this inclination in several latitudes and due records preserved, instruments are made whereby without the help of Sun or Star, the latitude of the place may be discovered; and yet it appears the observations of men have not as yet been so just and equal as is desirable; for of those Tables of declination which I have perused, there are not any two that punctually agree; though some have been thought exactly calculated, especially that which *Ridley* received from Mr. *Brigs*, in our time Geometry Professor in *Oxford*.

It is also probable what is delivered concerning the variation of the Compass that is the cause and ground thereof, for the manner as being confirmed by observation we shall not at all dispute. The variation of the Compass is an Arch of the Horizon intercepted between the true and Magnetical Meridian; or more plainly, a deflexion and siding East and West from the true Meridian. The true Meridian is a major Circle passing through the Poles of the World, and the Zenith or Vertex of any place, exactly dividing the East from the West. Now on this line the Needle exactly lieth not, but diverts and varieth its point, that is, the North point on this side the Equator, the South on the other; sometimes on the East, sometime toward the West, and in some few places varieth not at all. First, therefore it is observed that betwixt the Shore of *Ireland*, *France*, *Spain*, *Guiny*, and the *Azores*, the North point varieth toward the East, and that in some variety; at *London* it varieth eleven degrees, at *Antwerp* nine, at *Rome* but five: at some parts of the *Azores* it deflecteth not, but lieth in the true Meridian; on the other side of the *Azores*, and this side of the Equator, the North

What the variation of the Compass is.

point of the Needle wheeleth to the West; so that in
the latitude of 36 near the shore, the variation is about
eleven degrees; but on the other side the Equator, it
is quite otherwise: for about *Capo Frio* in *Brasilia*,
the South point varieth twelve degrees unto the West,
and about the mouth of the Straits of *Magellan* five or
six; but elongating from the coast of *Brasilia* toward
the shore of *Africa* it varieth Eastward, and arriving
at *Capo de las Agullas*, it resteth in the Meridian, and
looketh neither way.

Now the cause of this variation was thought by
Gilbertus to be the inequality of the Earth, variously
disposed, and indifferently intermixed with the Sea:
withal the different disposure of its Magnetical vigor
in the eminencies and stronger parts thereof. For the
Needle naturally endeavours to conform unto the
Meridian, but being distracted, driveth that way
where the greater and powerfuller part of the Earth is
placed. Which may be illustrated from what hath
been delivered and may be conceived by any that
understands the generalities of Geography. For
whereas on this side the Meridian, or the Isles of
Azores, where the first Meridian is placed, the Needle
varieth Eastward; it may be occasioned by that vast
Tract of Earth, that is, of *Europe, Asia,* and *Africa,*
seated toward the East, and disposing the Needle that
way. For arriving at some part of the *Azores*, or
Islands of Saint *Michael*, which have a middle situation
between these Continents, and that vast and almost
answerable Tract of *America*, it seemeth equally distracted by both; and diverting unto neither, doth
parallel and place it self upon the true Meridian. But
sailing farther, it veers its Lilly to the West, and
regardeth that quarter wherein the Land is nearer or

*The cause
of the varia
tion of the
Compass.*

greater; and in the same latitude as it approacheth the shore augmenteth its variation. And therefore as some observe, if *Columbus* or whosoever first discovered *America*, had apprehended the cause of this variation, having passed more then half the way, he might have been confirmed in the discovery, and assuredly foretold there lay a vast and mighty continent toward the West. The reason I confess and inference is good, but the instance perhaps not so. For *Columbus* knew not the variation of the compass, whereof *Sebastian Cabot* first took notice, who after made discovery in the Northern part of that continent. And it happened indeed that part of *America* was first discovered, which was on this side farthest distant, that is, *Jamaica, Cuba*, and the Isles in the Bay of *Mexico*. And from this variation do some new discoverers deduce a proba- bility in the attempts of the Northern passage toward the *Indies*.

Now because where the greater continents are joyned, the action and effluence is also greater; therefore those Needles do suffer the greatest variation which are in Countries which most do feel that action. And there- fore hath *Rome* far less variation then *London*; for on the West side of *Rome* are seated the great continents of *France, Spain, Germany*, which take off the exuper- ance, and in some way ballance the vigor of the Eastern parts. But unto *England* there is almost no Earth West, but the whole extent of *Europe* and *Asia* lieth Eastward; and therefore at *London* it varieth eleven degrees, that is almost one *Rhomb*. Thus also by reason of the great continent of *Brasilia, Peru*, and *Chili*, the Needle deflecteth toward the Land twelve degrees; but at the straits of *Magellan* where the Land is narrowed, and the Sea on the other side, it

varieth but five or six.   And so likewise, because the
Cape *de las Agullas* hath Sea on both sides near it, and
other Land remote, and as it were æquidistant from it,
therefore at that point the Needle conforms unto the
true Meridian, and is not distracted by the vicinity of
Adjacencies.   This is the general and great cause of
variation.   But if in certain Creeks and Vallies the
Needle prove irregular, and vary beyond expectation,
it may be imputed unto some vigorous part of the
Earth, or Magnetical eminence not far distant.   And
this was the invention of *D. Gilbert*, not many years
past, a Physician in *London*.   And therefore although
some assume the invention of its direction, and other
have had the glory of the Card; yet in the experiments, grounds, and causes thereof, *England* produced
the Father Philosopher, and discovered more in it then
Columbus or *Americus* did ever by it.

Unto this in great part true the reason of *Kircherus*
may be added: That this variation proceedeth not
only from terrestrious eminencies, and magnetical veins
of the Earth, laterally respecting the Needle, but the
different coagmentation of the Earth disposed unto
the Poles, lying under the Sea and Waters, which affect
the Needle with great or lesser variation, according to
the vigour or imbecility of these subterraneous lines, or
the entire or broken compagination of the magnetical
fabrick under it.   As is observable from several Loadstones placed at the bottom of any water, for a Loadstone or Needle upon the surface, will variously conform
it self, according to the vigour or faintness of the
Loadstones under it.

Thus also a reason may be alledged for the variation
of the variation, and why, according to observation,
the variation of the Needle hath after some years been

found to vary in some places. For this may proceed from mutations of the earth, by subterraneous fires, fumes, mineral spirits, or otherwise; which altering the constitution of the magnetical parts, in process of time, doth vary the variation over the place.

It is also probable what is conceived of its Antiquity, that the knowledge of its polary power and direction unto the North was unknown unto the Ancients; and though *Levinus Lemnius*, and *Cœlius Colcagninus*, are of another belief, is justly placed with new inventions by *Pancirollus*. For their *Achilles* and strongest argument is an expression in *Plautus*, a very Ancient author, and contemporary unto *Ennius*. *Hic ventus jam secundus est, cape modo versoriam.* Now this *versoriam* they construe to be the compass, which notwithstanding according unto *Pineda*, who hath discussed the point, *Turnebus*, *Cabeus*, and divers others, is better interpreted the rope that helps to turn the Ship, or as we say, doth make it tack about; the Compass declaring rather the Ship is turned, then conferring unto its conversion. As for the long expeditions and sundry voyages of elder times, which might confirm the Antiquity of this invention, it is not improbable they were performed by the help of Stars; and so might the Phœnicean navigators, and also *Ulisses* sail about the Mediterranean, by the flight of Birds, or keeping near the shore; and so might *Hanno* coast about *Africa*; or by the help of Oars, as is expressed in the voyage of *Jonah*. And whereas it is contended that this verticity was not unknown unto *Solomon*, in whom is presumed an universality of knowledge; it will as forcibly follow, he knew the Art of Typography, Powder and Guns, or had the Philosophers Stone, yet sent unto *Ophir* for Gold. It is not to be denied, that

beside his Political wisdom, his knowledge in Philosophy
was very large; and perhaps from his works therein,
the ancient Philosophers, especially *Aristotle*, who had
the assistance of *Alexanders* acquirements, collected
great observables. Yet if he knew the use of the
Compass, his Ships were surely very slow, that made a
three years voyage from *Eziongeber* in the red Sea
unto *Ophir*; which is supposed to be *Taprobana* or
Malaca in the *Indies*, not many moneths sail; and
since in the same or lesser time, *Drake* and *Candish*
performed their voyage about the Earth.

And as the knowledge of its verticity is **not** so old
as some conceive, so it is more ancient then most
believe; nor had its discovery with Guns, Printing, or
as many think, some years before the discovery of
America. For it was not unknown unto *Petrus Pere-
grinus* a Frenchman, who two hundred years since left
a Tract of the Magnet, and a perpetual motion to be
made thereby, preserved by *Gasserus*. *Paulus Venetus*,
and about five hundred years past *Albertus Magnus*
make mention hereof, and quote for it a Book of
Aristotle, *De Lapide*; which Book although we find in
the Catalogue of *Laertius*, yet with *Cabeus* we may
rather judge it to be the work of some Arabick Writer,
not many years before the days of *Albertus*.

Lastly, It is likewise true what some have delivered
of *Crocus Martis*, that is, Steel corroded with Vinegar,
Sulphur, or otherwise, and after reverberated by fire.
For the Loadstone will not at all attract it, nor will it
adhere, but lye therein like Sand. This to be understood of *Crocus Martis* well reverberated, and into a
violet colour: for common *chalybs præparatus*, or
corroded and powdered Steel, the Loadstone attracts
like ordinary filings of Iron; and many times most of

that which passeth for *Crocus Martis*. So that this way may serve as a test of its preparation ; after which it becometh a very good medicine in fluxes. The like may be affirmed of flakes of Iron that are rusty and begin to tend unto Earth ; for their cognation then expireth, and the Loadstone will not regard them.

And therefore this may serve as a trial of good Steel. The Loadstone taking up a greater mass of that which is most pure, it may also decide the conversion of Wood into Iron, as is pretended from some Waters : and the common conversion of Iron into Copper by the mediation of blew Coperose, for the Loadstone will not attract it. Although it may be questioned, whether in this operation, the Iron or Coperose be transmuted, as may be doubted from the cognation of Coperose with Copper ; and the quantity of Iron remaining after the conversion. And the same may be useful to some discovery concerning Vitriol or Coperose of Mars, by some called Salt of Steel, made by the spirits of Vitriol or Sulphur. For the corroded powder of Steel will after ablution be actively attracted by the Loadstone, and also remaineth in little diminished quantity. And therefore whether those shooting Salts partake but little of Steel, and be not rather the vitriolous spirits fixed into Salt by the effluvium or odor of Steel, is not without good question.

CHAPTER III

Concerning the Loadstone, therein of sundry common Opinions, and received several relations : Natural, Historical, Medical, Magical.

AND first not only a simple Heterodox, but a very hard Paradox, it will seem, and of great absurdity unto obstinate ears, if we say, attraction is unjustly appropriated unto the Loadstone, and that perhaps we speak not properly, when we say vulgarly and appropriately the Loadstone draweth Iron ; and yet herein we should not want experiment and great authority. The words of *Renatus des Cartes* in his Principles of Philosophy are very plain. *Præterea magnes trahet ferrum, sive potius magnes & ferrum ad invicem accedunt, neque enim ulla ibi tractio est.* The same is solemnly determined by *Cabeus. Nec magnes trahit proprie ferrum, nec ferrum ad se magnetem provocat, sed ambo pari conatu ad invicem confluunt.* Concordant hereto is the assertion of Doctor *Ridley,* Physitian unto the Emperour of *Russia,* in his Tract of Magnetical Bodies, defining Magnetical attraction to be a natural incitation and disposition conforming unto contiguity, an union of one Magnetical Body with another, and no violent haling of the weak unto the stronger. And this is also the doctrine of *Gilbertus,* by whom this motion is termed Coition, and that not made by any faculty attractive of one, but a Syndrome and concourse of each ; a Coition alway of their vigours, and also of their bodies, if bulk or impediment prevent not. And

Attraction reciprocal betwixt the Loadstone and Iron.

therefore those contrary actions which flow from oppo-site Poles or Faces, are not so properly expulsion and attraction, as *Sequela* and *Fuga,* a mutual flight and following. Consonant whereto are also the deter-mination of *Helmontius, Kircherus,* and *Licetus.*

The same is also confirmed by experiment; for if a piece of Iron be fastened in the side of a bowl or bason of water, a Loadstone swimming freely in a Boot of Cork, will presently make unto it. So if a Steel or Knife untouched, be offered toward the Needle that is touched, the Needle nimbly moveth toward it, and conformeth unto union with the Steel that moveth not. Again, If a Loadstone be finely filed, the Atoms or dust thereof will adhere unto Iron that was never touched, even as the powder of Iron doth also unto the Load-stone. And lastly, if in two Skiffs of Cork, a Load-stone and Steel be placed within the Orb of their activities, the one doth not move the other standing still, but both hoise sail and steer unto each other. So that if the Loadstone attract, the Steel hath also its attraction; for in this action the Alliciency is reciprocal, which joyntly felt, they mutually approach and run into each others arms.

And therefore surely more moderate expressions become this action, then what the Ancients have used, which some have delivered in the most violent terms of their language; so *Austin* calls it, *Mirabilem ferri raptorem*: *Hippocrates* λίθος τὸν σίδηρον ἁρπάζει, *Lapis qui ferrum rapit.* *Galen* disputing against *Epicurus* useth the term ἕλκειν, but this also is too violent: among the Ancients *Aristotle* spake most warily, ὅστις τὸν σίδηρον κινεῖ, *Lapis qui ferrum movet*: and in some tolerable acception do run the expressions of *Aquinas, Scaliger* and *Cusanus.*

Many relations are made, and great expectations are raised from the *Magnes Carneus*, or a Loadstone, that hath a faculty to attract not only iron but flesh; but this upon enquiry, and as *Cabeus* also observed, is nothing else but a weak and inanimate kind of Loadstone, veined here and there with a few magnetical and ferreous lines; but consisting of a bolary and clammy substance, whereby it adheres like *Hœmatites*, or *Terra Lemnia*, unto the Lips. And this is that stone which is to be understood, when Physitians joyn it with *Ætites*, or the Eagle stone, and promise therein a vertue against abortion.

There is sometime a mistake concerning the variation of the Compass, and therein one point is taken for another. For beyond that Equator some men account its variation by the diversion of the Northern point, whereas beyond that Circle the Southern point is Soveraign, and the North submits his preheminency. For in the Southern coast either of *America* or *Africa*, the Southern point deflects and varieth toward the Land, as being disposed and spirited that way by the Meridional and proper Hemisphere. And therefore on that side of the Earth the varying point is best accounted by the South. And therefore also the writings of some, and Maps of others, are to be enquired, that make the Needle decline unto the East twelve degrees at *Capo Frio*, and six at the straits of *Magellan*; accounting hereby one point for another, and preferring the North in the Liberties and Province of the South.

But certainly false it is what is commonly affirmed and believed, that Garlick doth hinder the attraction of the Loadstone, which is notwithstanding delivered by grave and worthy Writers, by *Pliny*, *Solinus*, *Ptolomy*, *Plutarch*, *Albertus*, *Mathiolus*, *Rueus*, *Langius*,

That Garlick hinders not the attraction of the Loadstone.

and many more. An effect as strange as that of *Homers Moly*, and the Garlick that *Mercury* bestowed upon *Ulysses*. But that it is evidently false, many experiments declare. For an Iron wire heated red hot and quenched in the juice of Garlick, doth notwithstanding contract a verticity from the Earth, and attracteth the Southern point of the Needle. If also the tooth of a Loadstone be covered or stuck in Garlick, it will notwithstanding attract; and Needles excited and fixed in Garlick until they begin to rust, do yet retain their attractive and polary respects.

Nor yet the Adamant or Diamond.

Of the same stamp is that which is obtruded upon us by Authors ancient and modern, that an Adamant or Diamond prevents or suspends the attraction of the Loadstone : as is in open terms delivered by *Pliny*. *Adamas dissidet cum Magnete lapide, ut juxta positus ferrum non patiatur abstrahi, aut si admotus magnes, apprehenderit, rapiat atque auferat.* For if a Diamond be placed between a Needle and a Loadstone, there will nevertheless ensue a Coition even over the body of the Diamond. And an easie matter it is to touch or excite a Needle through a Diamond, by placing it at the tooth of a Loadstone; and therefore the relation is false, or our estimation of these gemms untrue ; nor are they Diamonds which carry that name amongst us.

De genera-tione rerum.

It is not suddenly to be received what *Paracelsus* affirmeth, that if a Loadstone be anointed with Mercurial oyl, or onely put into Quicksilver, it omitteth its attraction for ever. For we have found that Loadstones and touched Needles which have laid long time in Quicksilver have not amitted their attraction. And we also find that red hot Needles or wires extinguished in Quicksilver, do yet acquire a verticity according to the Laws of position in extinction. Of greater repug-

nancy unto reason is that which he delivers concerning
its graduation, that heated in fire and often extinguished in oyl of Mars or Iron, it acquires an ability to
extract or draw forth a nail fastened in a wall; for, as
we have declared before, the vigor of the Loadstone is
destroyed by fire, nor will it be re-impregnated by any
other Magnete then the Earth.

Nor is it to be made out what seemeth very plausible,
and formerly hath deceived us, that a Loadstone will
not attract an Iron or Steel red hot. The falsity hereof
discovered first by *Kircherus*, we can confirm by iterated
experiment; very sensibly in armed Loadstones, and
obscurely in any other.

True it is, that besides fire some other wayes there
are of its destruction, as Age, Rust; and what is least
dreamt on, an unnatural or contrary situation. For
being impolarily adjoyned unto a more vigorous Loadstone, it will in a short time enchange its Poles; or
being kept in undue position, that is, not lying on the
Meridian, or else with its poles inverted, it receives in
longer time impair in activity, exchange of Faces; and
is more powerfully preserved by position then by the
dust of Steel. But the sudden and surest way is fire;
that is, fire not onely actual but potential; the one
surely and suddenly, the other slowly and imperfectly;
the one changing, the other destroying the figure. For
if distilled Vinegar or *Aqua fortis* be poured upon the
powder of Loadstone, the subsiding powder dryed,
retains some Magnetical vertue, and will be attracted
by the Loadstone: but if the menstruum or dissolvent
be evaporated to a consistence, and afterward doth
shoot into Icycles or Crystals, the Loadstone hath no
power upon them; and if in a full dissolution of Steel
a separation of parts be made by precipitation or

exhalation, the exsiccated powder hath lost its wings and ascends not unto the Loadstone. And though a Loadstone fired doth presently omit its proper vertue, and according to the position in cooling contracts a new verticity from the Earth ; yet if the same be laid awhile in *aqua fortis* or other corrosive water, and taken out before a considerable corrosion, it still reserves its attraction, and will convert the Needle according to former polarity. And that duly preserved from violent corrosion, or the natural disease of rust, it may long conserve its vertue, beside the Magnetical vertue of the Earth, which hath lasted since the Creation, a great example we have from the observation of our learned friend Mr. *Graves*, in an Ægyptian Idol cut out of Loadstone, and found among the *Mummies* ; which still retains its attraction, though probably taken out of the Mine about two thousand years ago.

In his learned Pyramido-graphia.

It is improbable what *Pliny* affirmeth concerning the object of its attraction, that it attracts not only ferreous bodies, but also *liquorem vitri* ; for in the body of Glass there is no ferreous or magnetical nature which might occasion attraction. For of the Glass we use, the purest is made of the finest sand and the ashes of Chali or Glaswort, and the courser or green sort of the ashes of Brake or other plants. True it is that in the making of Glass, it hath been an ancient practice to cast in pieces of magnet, or perhaps manganes : conceiving it carried away all ferreous and earthy parts, from the pure and running portion of Glass, which the Loadstone would not respect ; and therefore if that attraction were not rather Electrical then Magnetical, it was a wondrous effect what *Helmont* delivereth concerning a Glass wherein the Magistery of Loadstone was prepared, which after retained an attractive quality.

But whether the Magnet attracteth more then common Iron, may be tried in other bodies. It seems to attract the Smyris or Emery in powder; It draweth the shining or glassie powder brought from the *Indies*, and usually implied in writing-dust. There is also in Smiths Cinders by some adhesion of Iron whereby they appear as it were glazed, sometime to be found a magnetical operation; for some thereof applied have power to move the Needle. But whether the ashes of vegetables which grow over Iron Mines contract a magnetical quality, as containing some mineral particles, which by sublimation ascend unto their Roots, and are attracted together with their nourishment; according as some affirm from the like observations upon the Mines of Silver, Quick silver, and Gold, we must refer unto further experiment.

It is also improbable and something singular what some conceive, and *Eusebius Nierembergius*, a learned Jesuit of *Spain* delivers, that the body of man is magnetical, and being placed in a Boat, the Vessel will never rest untill the head respecteth the North. If this be true, the bodies of Christians do lye unnaturally in their Graves. King *Cheops* in his Tomb, and the *Jews* in their beds have fallen upon the natural position : who reverentially declining the situation of their Temple, nor willing to lye as that stood, do place their Beds from North to South, and delight to sleep Meridionally. This Opinion confirmed would much advance the Microcosmical conceit, and commend the Geography of *Paracelsus*, who according to the Cardinal points of the World divideth the body of man ; and therefore working upon humane ordure, and by long preparation rendring it odoriferous, he terms it *Zibeta Occidentalis*, Western *Civet* ; making the face the East, but the posteriours the *America* or Western part of his Microcosm. The verity hereof might easily be tried in *Wales*, where there are portable Boats, and made of Leather, which would convert upon the impulsion of any verticity; and seem to be the same whereof in his description of *Britain Cæsar* hath left some mention.

*Anagram-
matically.*

Another kind of verticity, is that which *Angelus doce mihi jus, alias, Michael Sundevogis,* in a Tract *De Sulphure,* discovereth in Vegetables, from sticks let fall or depressed under water; which equally framed and permitted unto themselves, will ascend at the upper end, or that which was vertical in their vegetation; wherein notwithstanding, as yet, we have not found satisfaction. Although perhaps too greedy of Magnalities, we are apt to make but favourable experiments concerning welcome Truths, and such desired verities.

*Horæ subse-
civæ.*

It is also wondrous strange what *Lælius Bisciola* reporteth, that if unto ten ounces of Loadstone one of Iron be added, it encreaseth not unto eleven, but weighs ten ounces still. A relation inexcusable in a work of leisurable hours: the examination being as ready as the relation, and the falsity tried as easily as delivered. Nor is it to be omitted what is taken up by the *Cæsius Bernardus* a late Mineralogist, and originally confirmed by *Porta,* that Needles touched with a *Diamond* contract a verticity, even as they do with a Loadstone, which will not consist with experiment. And therefore, as *Gilbertus* observeth, he might be deceived, in touching such Needles with *Diamonds,* which had a verticity before, as we have declared most Needles to have; and so had he touched them with Gold or Silver, he might have concluded a magnetical vertue therein.

In the same form may we place *Fracastorius* his attraction of silver, *Philostratus* his *Pantarbes*, *Apollodorus* and *Beda* his relation of the Loadstone that attracted onely in the night. But most inexcusable is *Franciscus Rueus*, a man of our own profession; who in his discourse of *Gemms* mentioned in the *Apocalyps*, undertakes a Chapter of the Loadstone. Wherein substantially and upon experiment he scarce delivereth any thing: making long enumeration of its traditional qualities, whereof he seemeth to believe many, and some above convicted by experience, he is fain to salve as impostures of the Devil. But *Bœtius de Boot* Physitian unto *Rodulphus* the second, hath recompenced this defect; and in his Tract *De Lapidibus & Gemmis*, speaks very materially hereof; and his Discourse is consonant unto Experience and Reason.

As for Relations Historical, though many there be of less account, yet two alone deserve consideration: The first concerneth magnetical Rocks, and attractive Mountains in several parts of the Earth. The other the Tomb of *Mahomet* and bodies suspended in the air. Of Rocks magnetical there are likewise two relations; for some are delivered to be in the *Indies*, and some in the extremity of the North, and about the very Pole. The Northern account is commonly ascribed unto *Olaus Magnus* Archbishop of *Upsale*, who out of his Predecessor *Joannes*, *Saxo*, and others, compiled a History of some Northern Nations; but this assertion we have not discovered in that Work of his which commonly passeth amongst us, and should believe his Geography herein no more then that in the first line of his Book; when he affirmeth that *Biarmia* (which is not seventy degrees in latitude) hath the Pole for its Zenith, and Equinoctial for the Horizon.

Now upon this foundation, how uncertain soever men have erected mighty illations, ascribing thereto the cause of the Needles direction, and conceiving the effluctions from these Mountains and Rocks invite the Lilly toward the North. Which conceit though countenanced by learned men, is not made out either by experience or reason, for no man hath yet attained or given a sensible account of the Pole by some degrees. It is also observed the Needle doth very much vary as it approacheth the Pole; whereas were there such direction from the Rocks, upon a nearer approachment it would more directly respect them. Beside, were there such magnetical Rocks under the Pole, yet being so far removed they would produce no such effect. For they that sail by the Isle of *Ilua* now called *Elba* in the Thuscan Sea which abounds in veins of Loadstone, observe no variation or inclination of the Needle; much less may they expect a direction from Rocks at the end of the Earth. And lastly, men that ascribe thus much unto Rocks of the North, must presume or discover the like magneticals at the South: For in the Southern Seas and far beyond the Equator, variations are large, and declinations as constant as in the Northern Ocean.

The other relation of Loadstone Mines and Rocks, in the shore of *India* is delivered of old by *Pliny*; wherein, saith he, they are so placed both in abundance and vigour, that it proves an adventure of hazard to pass those Coasts in a Ship with Iron nails. *Serapion* the Moor, an Author of good esteem and reasonable Antiquity, confirmeth the same, whose expression in the word *magnes* is this. The Mine of this Stone is in the Sea-coast of *India*, whereto when Ships approach, there is no Iron in them which flies not like a Bird

unto those Mountains; and therefore their ships are
fastened not with Iron but Wood, for otherwise they
would be torn to pieces. But this assertion, how
positive soever, is contradicted by all Navigators that
pass that way; which are now many, and of our own
Nation, and might surely have been controled by
Nearchus the Admiral of *Alexander*; who not knowing
the Compass, was fain to coast that shore.

CHAP.
III

*(Probably)
there be no
magnetical
Rocks.*

For the relation concerning *Mahomet*, it is generally
believed his Tomb at *Medina Talnabi*, in *Arabia*,
without any visible supporters hangeth in the air
between two Loadstones artificially contrived both
above and below; which conceit is fabulous and
evidently false from the testimony of Ocular Testators,
who affirm his Tomb is made of Stone, and lyeth upon
the ground; as beside others the learned *Vossius*
observeth from *Gabriel Sionita*, and *Joannes Hesronita*,
two *Maronites* in their relations hereof. Of such
intentions and attempt by *Mahometans* we read in
some Relators, and that might be the occasion of the
Fable, which by tradition of time and distance of
place enlarged into the Story of being accomplished.
And this hath been promoted by attempts of the like
nature; for we read in *Pliny* that one *Dinocrates* began
to Arch the Temple of *Arsinoe* in *Alexandria* with
Loadstone, that so her Statue might be suspended in
the air to the amazement of the beholders. And to
lead on our crudelity herein, confirmation may be
drawn from History and Writers of good authority.
So it is reported by *Ruffinus*, that in the Temple of
Serapis there was an Iron Chariot suspended by Loadstones in the air; which stones removed, the Chariot
fell and dashed into pieces. The like doth *Beda*
report of *Bellerophons* Horse, which framed of Iron,

*Mahomet's
tomb of
stone, and
built upon
the ground*

was placed between two Loadstones, with wings
expansed, pendulous in the air.

The verity of these Stories we shall not further
dispute, their possibility we may in some way determine; if we conceive what no man will deny, that
bodies suspended in the air have this suspension from
one or many Loadstones placed both above and below
it; or else by one or many placed only above it.
Likewise the body to be suspended in respect of the
Loadstone above, is either placed first at a pendulous
distance in the medium, or else attracted unto that
site by the vigor of the Loadstone. And so we first
affirm, that possible it is, a body may be suspended
between two Loadstones; that is, it being so equally
attracted unto both, that it determineth it self unto
neither. But surely this position will be of no duration; for if the air be agitated or the body waved
either way, it omits the equilibration, and disposeth
it self unto the nearest attractor. Again, It is not
impossible (though hardly feasible) by a single Loadstone to suspend an Iron in the air, the Iron being
artificially placed and at a distance guided toward the
stone, until it find the neutral point, wherein its
gravity just equals the magnetical quality, the one
exactly extolling as much as the other depresseth.
And lastly, Impossible it is that if an Iron rest upon
the ground, and a Loadstone be placed over it, it
should ever so arise as to hang in the way or medium;
for that vigor which at a distance is able to overcome
the resistance of its gravity and to lift it up from the
Earth, will as it approacheth nearer be still more able
to attract it; never remaining in the middle that
could not abide in the extreams. Now the way of
Baptista Porta that by a thred fastneth a Needle to a

Table, and then so guides and orders the same, that by the attraction of the Loadstone it abideth in the air, infringeth not this reason; for this is a violent retention, and if the thred be loosened, the Needle ascends and adheres unto the Attractor.

The third consideration concerneth Medical relations; wherein what ever effects are delivered, they are either derived from its mineral and ferreous condition, or else magnetical operation. Unto the ferreous and mineral quality pertaineth what *Dioscorides* an ancient Writer and Souldier under *Anthony* and *Cleopatra* affirmeth, that half a dram of Loadstone given with Honey and Water, proves a purgative medicine, and evacuateth gross humours. But this is a quality of great incertainty; for omitting the vehicle of Water and Honey, which is of a laxative power it self, the powder of some Loadstones in this dose doth rather *Powder of* constipate and binde, then purge and loosen the belly. *Loadstones,* And if sometimes it cause any laxity, it is probably in *of what operation.* the same way with Iron and Steel unprepared, which will disturb some bodies, and work by Purge and Vomit. And therefore, whereas it is delivered in a Book ascribed unto *Galen*, that it is a good medicine in dropsies, and evacuates the waters of persons so affected: It may I confess by siccity and astriction afford a confirmation unto parts relaxed, and such as be hydropically disposed; and by these qualities it may be useful in *Hernias* or *Ruptures*, and for these it is commended by *Ætius*, *Ægineta*, and *Oribatius*; who only affirm that it contains the vertue of *Hœmatites*, and being burnt was sometimes vended for it. Wherein notwithstanding there is an higher vertue; and in the same prepared, or in rich veins thereof, though crude, we have observed the effects of Chalybeat

Medicines; and the benefits of Iron and Steel in strong obstructions. And therefore that was probably a different vein of Loadstone, or infected with other mineral mixture, which the Ancients commended for a purgative medicine, and ranked the same with the violentest kinds thereof: with *Hippophae, Cneoron,* and *Thymelœa,* as we find it in *Hippocrates*; and might be somewhat doubtful, whether by the magnesian stone, he understood the Loadstone; did not *Achilles Statius* define the same, the Stone that loveth Iron.

De morbis internis.

To this mineral condition belongeth what is delivered by some, that wounds which are made with weapons excited by the Loadstone, contract a malignity, and become of more difficult cure; which nevertheless is not to be found in the incision of Chyrurgions with knives and lances touched; which leave no such effect behind them. Hither we also refer that affirmative, which sayes the Loadstone is poison; and therefore in the lists of poisons we find it in many Authors. But this our experience cannot confirm, and the practice of the King of *Zeilan* clearly contradicteth; who as *Garcias ab Horto,* Physitian unto the *Spanish* Viceroy delivereth, hath all his meat served up in dishes of Loadstone, and conceives thereby he preserveth the vigour of youth.

But surely from a magnetical activity must be made out what is let fall by *Ætius,* that a Loadstone held in the hand of one that is podagrical, doth either cure or give great ease in the Gout. Or what *Marcellus Empericus* affirmeth, that as an amulet, it also cureth the headach; which are but additions unto its proper nature, and hopeful enlargements of its allowed attraction. For perceiving its secret power to draw magnetical bodies, men have invented a new attraction, to

draw out the dolour and pain of any part. And from
such grounds it surely became a philter, and was
conceived a medicine of some venereal attraction; and
therefore upon this stone they graved the Image of
Venus, according unto that of *Claudian, Venerem magnetica gemma figurat.* Hither must we also refer what
is delivered concerning its power to draw out of the
body bullets and heads of arrows, and for the like
intention is mixed up in plaisters. Which course,
although as vain and ineffectual it be rejected by many
good Authors, yet is it not methinks so readily to be
denied, nor the Practice of many Physicians which
have thus compounded plaisters, thus suddenly to be
condemned, as may be observed in the *Emplastrum
divinum Nicolai,* the *Emplastrum nigrum* of *Augspurg,*
the *Opodeldoch* and *Attractivum* of *Paracelsus,* with
several more in the Dispensatory of *Wecker,* and
practice of *Sennertus.* The cure also of *Hernias,* or
Ruptures in *Pareus*: and the method also of curation
lately delivered by *Daniel Beckherus,** and approved by
the Professors of *Leyden,* that is, of a young man of
Spruceland that casually swallowed a knife about ten
inches long, which was cut out of his stomach, and the
wound healed up. In which cure to attract the knife
to a convenient situation, there was applied a plaister
made up with the powder of Loadstone. Now this
kind of practice *Libavius, Gilbertus,* and lately *Swick-
ardus* condemn, as vain, and altogether unuseful;
because a Loadstone in powder hath no attractive
power; for in that form it omits his polarly respects, and loseth those parts which are the rule of
attraction.

Wherein to speak compendiously, if experiment hath
not deceived us, we first affirm that a Loadstone in

CHAP.
III

*De cultri-
voro Prus-
siaco, 1636.
*The cure of
the Prussian
Knife.*

In his Ars
Magnetica.

powder omits not all attraction. For if the powder
of a rich vein be in a reasonable quantity presented
toward the Needle freely placed, it will not appear to
be void of all activity, but will be able to stir it. Nor
hath it only a power to move the Needle in powder
and by it self, but this will it also do, if incorporated
and mixed with plaisters; as we have made trial in
the *Emplastrum de Minia*, with half an ounce of the
mass, mixing a dram of Loadstone. For applying the
magdaleon or roal unto the Needle, it would both stir
and attract it; not equally in all parts, but more
vigorously in some, according unto the Mine of the
Stone, more plentifully dispersed in the mass. And
lastly, In the Loadstone powdered, the polary respects
are not wholly destroyed. For those diminutive particles are not atomical or meerly indivisible, but consist
of dimensions sufficient for their operations, though in
obscurer effects. Thus if unto the powder of Loadstone
or Iron we admove the North Pole of the Loadstone,
the Powders or small divisions will erect and conform
themselves thereto: but if the South Pole approach,
they will subside, and inverting their bodies, respect
the Loadstone with the other extream. And this will
happen not only in a body of powder together, but in
any particle or dust divided from it.

Now though we disavow not these plaisters, yet shall
we not omit two cautions in their use, that therein the
Stone be not too subtilly powdered, for it will better
manifest its attraction in a more sensible dimension.
That where is desired a speedy effect, it may be considered whether it were not better to relinquish the
powdered plaisters, and to apply an entire Loadstone
unto the part: And though the other be not wholly
ineffectual, whether this way be not more powerful,

and so might have been in the cure of the young man
delivered by *Beckerus*.

The last consideration concerneth Magical relations; in which account we comprehend effects derived and fathered upon hidden qualities, specifical forms, Antipathies and Sympathies, whereof from received grounds of Art, no reasons are derived. Herein relations are strange and numerous; men being apt in all Ages to multiply wonders, and Philosophers dealing with admirable bodies, as Historians have done with excellent men, upon the strength of their great atcheivements, ascribing acts unto them not only false but impossible; and exceeding truth as much in their relations, as they have others in their actions. Hereof we shall briefly mention some delivered by Authors of good esteem: whereby we may discover the fabulous inventions of some, the credulous supinity of others, and the great disservice unto truth by both: multiplying obscurities in Nature, and authorising hidden qualities that are false; whereas wise men are ashamed there are so many true.

And first, *Dioscorides* puts a shrewd quality upon it, and such as men are apt enough to experiment, who therewith discovers the incontinency of a wife, by placing the Loadstone under her pillow, whereupon she will not be able to remain in bed with her husband. The same he also makes a help unto thievery. For Thieves saith he, having a design upon a house, do make a fire at the four corners thereof, and cast therein the fragments of Loadstone: whence ariseth a fume that so disturbeth the inhabitants, that they forsake the house and leave it to the spoil of the Robbers. This relation, how ridiculous soever, hath *Albertus* taken up above a thousand years after, and *Marbodeus*

the Frenchman hath continued the same in Latine
Verse, which with the Notes of *Pictorius* is currant
unto our dayes. As strange must be the Lithomancy
or divination from this Stone, whereby as *Tzetzes*
delivers, *Helenus* the Prophet foretold the destruction
of *Troy* : and the Magick thereof not safely to be
believed, which was delivered by *Orpheus*, that sprinkled
with water it will upon a question emit a voice not
much unlike an Infant. But surely the Loadstone of
Laurentius Guascus the Physitian, is never to be
matched ; wherewith, as *Cardan* delivereth, whatsoever
Needles or Bodies were touched, the wounds and punc-
tures made thereby, were never felt at all. And yet
as strange is that which is delivered by some, that a
Loadstone preserved in the salt of a *Remora*, acquires
a power to attract gold out of the deepest Wells.
Certainly a studied absurdity, not casually cast out,
but plotted for perpetuity : for the strangeness of the
effect ever to be admired, and the difficulty of the trial
never to be convicted.

These conceits are of that monstrosity that they
refute themselves in their recitements. There is
another of better notice, and whispered thorow the
World with some attention ; credulous and vulgar
auditors readily believing it, and more judicious and
distinctive heads, not altogether rejecting it. The
conceit is excellent, and if the effect would follow,
somewhat divine ; whereby we might communicate
like spirits, and confer on earth with *Menippus* in the
Moon. And this is pretended from the sympathy of
two Needles touched with the same Loadstone, and
placed in the center of two Abecedary circles or rings,
with letters described round about them, one friend
keeping one, and another the other, and agreeing upon

an hour wherein they will communicate. For then, saith Tradition, at what distance of place soever, when one Needle shall be removed unto any letter, the other by a wonderful sympathy will move unto the same. But herein I confess my experience can find no truth; for having expressly framed two circles of Wood, and according to the number of the Latine letters divided each into twenty three parts, placing therein two stiles or Needles composed of the same steel, touched with the same Loadstone, and at the same point: of these two, whensoever I removed the one, although but at the distance of half a span, the other would stand like *Hercules* pillars, and if the Earth stand still, have surely no motion at all. Now as it is not possible that any body should have no boundaries, or Sphear of its activity, so it is improbable it should effect that at distance, which nearer hand it cannot at all perform.

Again, The conceit is ill contrived, and one effect inferred, whereas the contrary will ensue. For if the removing of one of the Needles from *A* to *B*, should have any action or influence on the other, it would not intice it from *A* to *B*, but repell it from *A* to *Z*: for Needles excited by the same point of the stone, do not attract, but avoid each other, even as these also do, when their invigorated extreams approach unto one other.

Lastly, Were this conceit assuredly true, yet were it not a conclusion at every distance to be tried by every head: it being no ordinary or Almanack business, but a Problem Mathematical, to finde out the difference of hours in different places; nor do the wisest exactly satisfie themselves in all. For the hours of several places anticipate each other, according unto their Longitudes, which are not exactly discovered of every place; and therefore the trial hereof at a considerable interval, is best performed at the distance of the *Antœci*; that is, such habitations as have the same Meridian and equal parallel, on different sides of the Æquator; or more plainly the same Longitude and the same Latitude unto the South, which we have in the North. For unto such situations it is noon and midnight at the very same time.

And therefore the Sympathy of these Needles is much of the same mould with that intelligence which is pretended from the flesh of one body transmuted by incision into another. For if by the Art of *Talia-cotius*, a permutation of flesh, or transmutation be made from one mans body into another, as if a piece of flesh be exchanged from the bicipital muscle of either parties arm, and about them both an Alphabet circumscribed; upon a time appointed as some conceptions affirm, they may communicate at what distance soever. For if the one shall prick himself in *A*, the other at the same time will have a sense thereof in the same part: and upon inspection of his arm perceive what letters the other points out in his. Which is a way of intelligence very strange: and would requite the lost Art of *Pythagoras*, who could read a reverse in the Moon.

De curtorum Chyrurgia.

Now this magnetical conceit how strange soever, might have some original in Reason; for men observing no solid body, whatsoever did interrupt its action, might be induced to believe no distance would terminate the same; and most conceiving it pointed unto the Pole of Heaven, might also opinion that nothing between could restrain it. Whosoever was the Author, the *Æolus* that blew it about was *Famianus Strada*, that Elegant Jesuit, in his Rhetorical prolusions, who chose out this subject to express the stile of *Lucretius*.

But neither *Baptista Porta, De Furtivis Literarum notis*; *Trithemius* in his Steganography, *Selenus* in his Cryptography, or *Nuncius inanimatus* make any consideration hereof, although they deliver many ways to communicate thoughts at distance. And this we will not deny may in some manner be effected by the Loadstone; that is, from one room into another; by placing a table in the wall common unto both, and writing thereon the same letters one against another: for upon the approach of a vigorous Loadstone unto a letter on this side, the Needle will move unto the same on the other. But this is a very different way from ours at present; and hereof there are many ways delivered, and more may be discovered which contradict not the rule of its operations.

CHAP.
III
Nunc. inanim. *by D.* Godwin
Bishop of Hereford.

As for *Unguentum Armarium*, called also *Magneticum*, it belongs not to this discourse, it neither having the Loadstone for its ingredient, nor any one of its actions: but supposeth other principles, as common and universal spirits, which convey the action of the remedy unto the part, and conjoins the vertue of bodies far disjoyned. But perhaps the cures it doth, are not worth so mighty principles; it commonly healing but simple wounds, and such as mundified and kept clean, do need no other hand then that of Nature, and the Balsam of the proper part. Unto which effect there being fields of Medicines, it may be a hazardous curiosity to rely on this; and because men say the effect doth generally follow, it might be worth the experiment to try, whether the same will not ensue, upon the same Method of cure, by ordinary Balsams, or common vulnerary plaisters.

Many other Magnetisms may be pretended, and the like attractions through all the creatures of Nature.

Whether the same be verified in the action of the
Sun upon inferiour bodies, whether there be *Æolian*
Magnets, whether the flux and reflux of the Sea be
caused by any Magnetism from the Moon; whether
the like be really made out, or rather Metaphorically
verified in the sympathies of Plants and Animals, might
afford a large dispute; and *Kircherus* in his *Catena
Magnetica* hath excellently discussed the same; which
work came late unto our hand, but might have much
advantaged this Discourse.

Other Discourses there might be made of the Loadstone: as Moral, Mystical, Theological; and some
have handsomely done them; as *Ambrose, Austine,
Gulielmus Parisiensis,* and many more, but these fall
under no Rule, and are as boundless as mens inventions.
And though honest minds do glorifie God hereby; yet
do they most powerfully magnifie him, and are to be
looked on with another eye, who demonstratively set
forth its Magnalities; who not from postulated or
precarious inferences, entreat a courteous assent; but
from experiments and undeniable effects, enforce the
wonder of its Maker.

CHAPTER IV

Of Bodies Electrical.

HAVING thus spoken of the Loadstone and
Bodies Magnetical, I shall in the next place
deliver somewhat of Electrical, and such as
may seem to have attraction like the other. Hereof
we shall also deliver what particularly spoken or not
generally known is manifestly or probably true, what

generally believed is also false or dubious. Now by
Electrical bodies, I understand not such as are Metal-
lical, mentioned by *Pliny*, and the Ancients; for their
Electrum was a mixture made of Gold, with the
Addition of a fifth part of Silver; a substance now
as unknown as true *Aurichalcum*, or *Corinthian* Brass,
and set down among things lost by *Pancirollus*. Nor
by Electrick Bodies do I conceive such only as take up
shavings, straws, and light bodies, in which number
the Ancients only placed *Jet* and *Amber*; but such as
conveniently placed unto their objects attract all bodies
palpable whatsoever. I say conveniently placed, that
is, in regard of the object, that it be not too ponderous,
or any way affixed; in regard of the Agent, that it be
not foul or sullied, but wiped, rubbed, and excitated;
in regard of both, that they be conveniently distant,
and no impediment interposed. I say, all bodies palpable, thereby excluding fire, which indeed it will not
attract, nor yet draw through it; for fire consumes its
effluxions by which it should attract.

Now although in this rank but two were commonly
mentioned by the Ancients, *Gilbertus* discovereth many
more; as *Diamonds*, *Saphyrs*, *Carbuncles*, *Iris*, *Opalls*,
Amethysts, *Beril*, *Crystal*, *Bristol-stones*, *Sulphur*, *Mastick*, hard *Wax*, hard *Rosin*, *Arsenic*, *Sal-gemm*, *Roch-
Allum*, common Glass, *Stibium*, or Glass of *Antimony*.
Unto these *Cabeus* addeth white *Wax*, *Gum Elemi*,
Gum Guaici, *Pix Hispanica*, and *Gipsum*. And unto
these we add *Gum Anime*, *Benjamin*, *Talcum*, *China-
dishes*, *Sandaraca*, *Turpentine*, *Styrax Liquida*, and
Caranna dried into a hard consistence. And the same
attraction we find, not onely in simple bodies, but
such as are much compounded; as in the *Oxycroceum*
plaister, and obscurely that *ad Herniam*, and *Gratia*

Dei; all which smooth and rightly prepared, will discover a sufficient power to stir the Needle, setled freely upon a well-pointed pin; and so as the Electrick may be applied unto it without all disadvantage.

But the attraction of these Electricks we observe to be very different. Resinous or unctuous bodies, and such as will flame, attract most vigorously, and most thereof without frication; as *Anime, Benjamin,* and most powerfully good hard Wax, which will convert the Needle almost as actively as the Loadstone. And we believe that all or most of this substance if reduced to hardness, tralucency or clearness, would have some attractive quality. But juices concrete, or Gums easily dissolving in water, draw not at all: as *Aloe, Opium, Sanguis Draconis, Lacca, Calbanum, Sagapenum.* Many stones also both precious and vulgar, although terse and smooth, have not this power attractive: as *Emeralds, Pearl, Jaspis, Corneleans, Agathe, Heliotropes, Marble, Alablaster, Touchstone, Flint,* and *Bezoar.* Glass attracts but weakly, though clear; some slick stones and thick Glasses indifferently: *Arsenic* but weakly, so likewise Glass of *Antimony,* but *Crocus Metallorum* not at all. Salts generally but weakly, as *Sal Gemma, Allum,* and also *Talke*; nor very discoverably by any frication, but if gently warmed at the fire, and wiped with a dry cloth, they will better discover their Electricities.

No Metal attracts, nor Animal concretion we know, although polite and smooth; as we have made trial in *Elks* Hoofs, Hawks-Talons, the Sword of a *Sword-fish, Tortois-shells, Sea-horse,* and *Elephants* Teeth, in Bones, in *Harts-horn,* and what is usually conceived *Unicorns-horn.* No Wood though never so hard and polished, although out of some thereof Electrick bodies proceed;

as *Ebony, Box, Lignum vitæ, Cedar, etc.* And although *Jet* and *Amber* be reckoned among *Bitumens*, yet neither do we find *Asphaltus*, that is, *Bitumens* of *Judea*, nor *Sea-cole*, nor *Camphire*, nor *Mummia* to attract, although we have tried in large and polished pieces. Now this attraction have we tried in straws and paleous bodies, in Needles of Iron, equilibrated, Powders of Wood and Iron, in Gold and Silver foliate. And not only in solid but fluent and liquid bodies, as oyls made both by expression and distillation; in Water, in spirits of Wine, *Vitriol* and *Aquafortis*.

But how this attraction is made, is not so easily determined; that 'tis performed by effluviums is plain, and granted by most; for Electricks will not commonly attract, except they grow hot or become perspirable. For if they be foul and obnubilated, it hinders their effluxion; nor if they be covered, though but with Linen or Sarsenet, or if a body be interposed, for that intercepts the effluvium. If also a powerful and broad Electrick of Wax or *Anime* be held over fine powder, the Atoms or small particles will ascend most numerously unto it; and if the Electrick be held unto the light, it may be observed that many thereof will fly, and be as it were discharged from the Electrick to the distance sometime of two or three inches. Which motion is performed by the breath of the effluvium issuing with agility; for as the Electrick cooleth, the projection of the Atoms ceaseth.

The manner hereof *Cabeus* wittily attempteth, affirming that this effluvium attenuateth and impelleth the neighbor air, which returning home in a gyration, carrieth with it the obvious bodies unto the Electrick. And this he labours to confirm by experiments; for if the straws be raised by a vigorous Electrick, they do

Cabeus his way for attraction in bodies Electrick.

R

appear to wave and turn in their ascents. If likewise the Electrick be broad, and the straws light and
chaffy, and held at a reasonable distance, they will not
arise unto the middle, but rather adhere toward the
Verge or Borders thereof. And lastly, if many straws
be laid together, and a nimble Electrick approach,
they will not all arise unto it, but some will commonly
start aside, and be whirled a reasonable distance from
it. Now that the air impelled returns unto its place
in a gyration or whirling, is evident from the Atoms
or Motes in the Sun. For when the Sun so enters a
hole or window, that by its illumination the Atoms or
Motes become perceptible, if then by our breath the
air be gently impelled, it may be perceived, that they
will circularly return and in a gyration unto their
places again.

*The way of
Sir Kenelm
Digby.*
Another way of their attraction is also delivered;
that is, by a tenuous emanation or continued effluvium,
which after some distance retracteth into it self; as is
observable in drops of Syrups, Oyl, and seminal Vis-
cosities, which spun at length, retire into their former
dimensions. Now these effluviums advancing from the
body of the Electrick, in their return do carry back the
bodies whereon they have laid hold within the Sphere
or Circle of their continuities; and these they do not
onely attract, but with their viscous arms hold fast a
good while after. And if any shall wonder why these
effluviums issuing forth impel and protrude not the
straw before they can bring it back, it is because the
effluvium passing out in a smaller thred and more
enlengthened filament, it stirreth not the bodies interposed, but returning unto its original, falls into a
closer substance, and carrieth them back unto it self.
And this way of attraction is best received, embraced

by Sir *Kenelm Digby* in his excellent Treaty of bodies,
allowed by *Des Cartes* in his principles of Philosophy,
as far and concerneth fat and resinous bodies, and with
exception of Glass, whose attraction he also deriveth
from the recess of its effluction. And this in some
manner the words of *Gilbertus* will bear : *Effluvia illa
tenuiora concipiunt & amplectuntur corpora, quibus
uniuntur, & electris tanquam extensis brachiis, & ad fontem propinquitate invalescentibus effluviis, deducuntur.*
And if the ground were true, that the Earth were an
Electrick body, and the air but the effluvium thereof,
we might have more reason to believe that from this
attraction, and by this effluction, bodies tended to the
Earth, and could not remain above it.

Our other discourse of Electricks concerneth a general
opinion touching *Jet* and *Amber*, that they attract all
light bodies, except *Ocymum* or *Basil*, and such as be
dipped in oyl or oyled; and this is urged as high as
Theophrastus : but *Scaliger* acquitteth him; And had
this been his assertion, *Pliny* would probably have taken
it up, who herein stands out, and delivereth no more but
what is vulgarly known. But *Plutarch* speaks positively
in his *Symposiacks*, that *Amber* attracteth all bodies,
excepting Basil and oyled substances. With *Plutarch*
consent many Authors both Ancient and Modern; but
the most inexcusable are *Lemnius* and *Rueus*, whereof
the one delivering the nature of Minerals mentioned in
Scripture, the infallible fountain of Truth, confirmeth
their vertues with erroneous traditions; the other
undertaking the occult and hidden Miracles of Nature,
accepteth this for one; and endeavoureth to alledge a
reason of that which is more then occult, that is, not
existent.

Now herein, omitting the authority of others, as the

Doctrine of experiment hath informed us, we first affirm, That *Amber* attracts not Basil, is wholly repugnant unto truth. For if the leaves thereof or dried stalks be stripped into small straws, they arise unto *Amber*, *Wax*, and other Electries, no otherwise then those of Wheat and Rye: nor is there any peculiar fatness or singular viscosity in that plant that might cause adhesion, and so prevent its ascension. But that *Jet* and *Amber* attract not straws oyled, is in part true and false. For if the straws be much wet or drenched in oyl, true it is that *Amber* draweth them not; for then the oyl makes the straws to adhere unto the part whereon they are placed, so that they cannot rise unto the Attractor; and this is true, not onely if they be soaked in Oyl, but spirits of Wine or Water. But if we speak of Straws or festucous divisions lightly drawn over with oyl, and so that it causeth no adhesion; or if we conceive an Antipathy between Oyl and *Amber*, the Doctrine is not true. For *Amber* will attract straws thus oyled, it will convert the Needles of Dials made either of Brass or Iron, although they be much oyled; for in these Needles consisting free upon their Center, there can be no adhesion. It will likewise attract Oyl it self, and if it approacheth unto a drop thereof, it becometh conical, and ariseth up unto it, for Oyl taketh not away his attraction, although it be rubbed over it. For if you touch a piece of Wax already excited with common Oyl, it will notwithstanding attract, though not so vigorously as before. But if you moisten the same with any Chymical Oyl, Water, or spirits of Wine, or only breath upon it, it quite omits its attraction, for either its influencies cannot get through, or will not mingle with those substances.

It is likewise probable the Ancients were mistaken
concerning its substance and generation; they conceiving it a vegetable concretion made of the gums of
Trees, especially *Pine* and *Poplar* falling into the water,
and after indurated or hardened, whereunto accordeth
the Fable of *Phaetons* sisters: but surely the concretion is Mineral, according as is delivered by *Boetius.*
For either it is found in Mountains and mediterraneous
parts; and so it is a fat and unctuous sublimation in
the Earth, concreted and fixed by salt and nitrous
spirits wherewith it meeteth. Or else, which is most
usual, it is collected upon the Sea-shore; and so it is
a fat and bituminous juice coagulated by the saltness
of the Sea. Now that salt spirits have a power to
congeal and coagulate unctuous bodies, is evident in
Chymical operations; in the distillations of *Arsenick,*
sublimate and *Antimony*; in the mixture of oyl of
Juniper, with the salt and acide spirit of *Sulphur,* for
thereupon ensueth a concretion unto the consistence of
Birdlime; as also in spirits of salt, or *Aqua fortis*
poured upon oyl of Olive, or more plainly in the
Manufacture of Soap. And many bodies will coagulate upon commixture, whose separated natures promise
no concretion. Thus upon a solution of *Tin* by *Aqua
fortis,* there will ensue a coagulation, like that of
whites of Eggs. Thus the volatile salt of Urine will *How the*
coagulate *Aqua vitæ,* or spirits of Wine; and thus *stone is
bred in the*
perhaps (as *Helmont* excellently declareth) the stones *Kidney or
Bladder.*
or calculous concretions in Kidney or Bladder may be
produced: the spirits or volatile salt of Urine conjoyning with the *Aqua vitæ* potentially lying therein; as
he illustrateth from the distillation of fermented Urine.
From whence ariseth an *Aqua vitæ* or spirit, which
the volatile salt of the same Urine will congeal; and

CHAP.
IV

Of a Bee and a Viper involved in Amber.
Mart. *l.* 4.

finding an earthy concurrence, strike into a lapideous substance.

Lastly, We will not omit what *Bellabonus* upon his own experiment writ from *Dantzich* unto *Mellichius*, as he hath left recorded in his Chapter, *De succino*, that the bodies of *Flies*, *Pismires*, and the like, which are said oft-times to be included in *Amber*, are not real but representative, as he discovered in several pieces broke for that purpose. If so, the two famous Epigrams hereof in *Martial* are but Poetical, the *Pismire* of *Brassavolus* imaginary, and *Cardans Mousoleum* for a Flie, a meer phansie. But hereunto we know not how to assent, as having met with some whose reals made good their representments.

CHAPTER V

Compendiously of sundry other common Tenents, concerning Mineral and Terreous Bodies, which examined, prove either false or dubious.

1. AND first we hear it in every mouth, and in many good Authors read it, That a *Diamond*, which is the hardest of stones, not yielding unto *Steel*, *Emery*, or any thing but its own powder, is yet made soft, or broke by the blood of a Goat. Thus much is affirmed by *Pliny*, *Solinus*, *Albertus*, *Cyprian*, *Austin*, *Isidore*, and many Christian Writers, alluding herein unto the heart of man and the precious bloud of our Saviour, who was typified by the Goat that was slain, and the scape-Goat in the Wilderness; and at the effusion of whose bloud, not

only the hard hearts of his enemies relented, but the
stony rocks and vail of the Temple were shattered.
But this I perceive is easier affirmed then proved.
For *Lapidaries,* and such as profess the art of cutting
this stone, do generally deny it; and they that seem
to countenance it, have in their deliveries so qualified
it, that little from thence of moment can be inferred
for it. For first, the holy Fathers, without a further
enquiry did take it for granted, and rested upon the
authority of the first deliverers. As for *Albertus,* he
promiseth this effect, but conditionally, not except the
Goat drink wine, and be fed with *Siler montanum,
petroselinum,* and such herbs as are conceived of power
to break the stone in the bladder. But the words of
Pliny, from whom most likely the rest at first derived
it, if strictly considered, do rather overthrow, then
any way advantage this effect. His words are these:
*Hircino rumpitur sanguine, nec aliter quam recenti,
calidoque macerata, & sic quoque multis ictibus, tunc
etiam præterquam eximias incudes malleosque ferreos
frangens.* That is, it is broken with Goats blood, but
not except it be fresh and warm, and that not without
many blows, and then also it will break the best Anvils
and Hammers of Iron. And answerable hereto, is the
assertion of *Isidore* and *Solinus.* By which account, a
Diamond steeped in Goats bloud, rather increaseth in
hardness, then acquireth any softness by the infusion;
for the best we have are comminuible without it; and
are so far from breaking hammers, that they submit
unto pistillation, and resist not an ordinary pestle.

Upon this conceit arose perhaps the discovery of
another; that the bloud of a Goat was soveraign for
the Stone, as it stands commended by many good Pulvis Lith-
Writers, and brings up the composition in the powder ontripticus.

of *Nicolaus*, and the Electuary of the Queen of *Colein*. Or rather because it was found an excellent medicine for the Stone, and its ability commended by some to dissolve the hardest thereof; it might be conceived by amplifying apprehensions, to be able to break a *Diamond*; and so it came to be ordered that the Goat should be fed with saxifragous herbs, and such as are conceived of power to break the stone. However it were, as the effect is false in the one, so is it surely very doubtful in the other. For although inwardly received it may be very diuretick, and expulse the stone in the Kidneys, yet how it should dissolve or break that in the bladder, will require a further dispute; and perhaps would be more reasonably tried by a warm injection thereof, then as it is commonly used. Wherein notwithstanding, we should rather rely upon the urine in a castlings bladder, a resolution of Crabs eyes, or the second distillation of Urine, as *Helmont* hath commended; or rather (if any such might be found) a Chylifactory menstruum or digestive preparation drawn from species or individuals, whose stomacks peculiarly dissolve lapideous bodies.

2. *That Glass is poison*, according unto common conceit, I know not how to grant. Not onely from the innocency of its ingredients, that is, fine Sand, and the ashes of Glass-wort of Fearn, which in themselves are harmless and useful : or because I find it by many commended for the Stone, but also from experience, as having given unto Dogs above a dram thereof, subtilly powdered in Butter and Paste, without any visible disturbance.

Why Glass is commonly held to be poysonous. The conceit is surely grounded upon the visible mischief of Glass grosly or coursly powdered, for that indeed is mortally noxious, and effectually used by

some to destroy Mice and Rats; for by reason of its
acuteness and angularity, it commonly excoriates the parts through which it passeth, and solicits them unto a continual expulsion. Whereupon there ensues fearful symptomes, not much unlike those which attend the action of poison. From whence notwithstanding, we cannot with propriety impose upon it that name, either by occult or elementary quality, which he that concedeth will much enlarge the Catalogue or Lists of Poisons. For many things, neither deleterious by substance or quality, are yet destructive by figure, or some occasional activity. So are Leeches destructive, and by some accounted poison; not properly, that is by temperamental contrariety, occult form, or so much as elemental repugnancy; but because being inwardly taken they fasten upon the veins, and occasion an effusion of bloud, which cannot be easily stanched. So a Sponge is mischievous, not in it self, for in its powder it is harmless: but because being received into the stomach it swelleth, and occasioning a continual distension, induceth a strangulation. So Pins, Needles, ears of Rye or Barley may be poison. So *Daniel* destroyed the Dragon by a composition of three things, whereof neither was poison alone, nor properly all together, that is, Pitch, Fat, and Hair, according as is expressed in the History. Then *Daniel* took Pitch, and Fat, and Hair, and did seeth them together, and made lumps thereof, these he put in the Dragons mouth, and so he burst asunder. That is, the Fat and Pitch being cleaving bodies, and the Hair continually extimulating the parts: by the action of the one, Nature was provoked to expell, but by the tenacity of the other forced to retain: so that there being left no passage in or out, the Dragon brake in pieces. It must therefore

be taken of grosly-powdered Glass, what is delivered
by *Grevinus*: and from the same must that mortal
dysentery proceed which is related by *Sanctorius*. And
in the same sense shall we only allow a *Diamond* to be
poison ; and whereby as some relate *Paracelsus* himself
was poisoned. So even the precious fragments and
cordial gems which are of frequent use in Physick, and
in themselves confessed of useful faculties, received
in gross and angular Powders, may so offend the
bowels, as to procure desperate languors, or cause most
dangerous fluxes.

That Glass may be rendred malleable and pliable
unto the hammer, many conceive, and some make
little doubt, when they read in *Dio*, *Pliny*, and *Petronius*, that one unhappily effected it for *Tiberius*.
Which notwithstanding must needs seem strange unto
such as consider, that bodies are ductile from a tenacious humidity, which so holdeth the parts together;
that though they dilate or extend, they part not from
each others. That bodies run into Glass, when the
volatile parts are exhaled, and the continuating humour
separated : the Salt and Earth, that is, the fixed parts
remaining. And therefore vitrification maketh bodies
brittle, as destroying the viscous humours which hinder
the disruption of parts. Which may be verified even
in the bodies of Metals. For Glass of Lead or Tin is
fragile, when that glutinous Sulphur hath been fired
out, which made their bodies ductile.

He that would most probably attempt it, must
experiment upon Gold. Whose fixed and flying parts
are so conjoined, whose Sulphur and continuating
principle is so united unto the Salt, that some may be
hoped to remain to hinder fragility after vitrification.
But how to proceed, though after frequent corrosion,

as that upon the agency of fire, it should not revive CHAP.
into its proper body before it comes to vitrifie, will   V
prove no easie discovery.

3. That Gold inwardly taken, either in substance,
infusion, decoction or extinction, is a cordial of great
efficacy, in sundry Medical uses, although a practice
much used, is also much questioned, and by no man
determined beyond dispute. There are hereof I
perceive two extream opinions; some excessively magnifying it, and probably beyond its deserts; others
extreamly vilifying it, and perhaps below its demerits.
Some affirming it a powerful Medicine in many diseases,
others averring that so used, it is effectual in none:
and in this number are very eminent Physicians,
Erastus, Duretus, Rondeletius, Brassavolus and many
other, who beside the strigments and sudorous adhe-
sions from mens hands, acknowledge that nothing
proceedeth from Gold in the usual decoction thereof.
Now the capital reason that led men unto this opinion,
was their observation of the inseparable nature of
Gold; it being excluded in the same quantity as it
was received, without alteration of parts, or diminution
of its gravity.

Now herein to deliver somewhat which in a middle
way may be entertained; we first affirm, that the
substance of Gold is invincible by the powerfullest
action of natural heat; and that not only alimentally
in a substantial mutation, but also medicamentally in
any corporeal conversion. As is very evident, not
only in the swallowing of golden bullets, but in the
lesser and foliate divisions thereof: passing the stomach
and guts even as it doth the throat, that is, without
abatement of weight or consistence. So that it entereth
not the veins with those electuaries, wherein it is

CHAP.
V

mixed : but taketh leave of the permeant parts, at the mouths of the *Meseraicks*, or Lacteal Vessels, and accompanieth the inconvertible portion unto the siege. Nor is its substantial conversion expectible in any composition or aliment wherein it is taken. And therefore that was truly a starving absurdity, which befel the wishes of *Midas*. And little credit there is to be given to the golden Hen, related by *Wendlerus*. So in the extinction of Gold, we must not conceive it parteth with any of its salt or dissoluble principle thereby, as we may affirm of Iron ; for the parts thereof are fixed beyond division, nor will they separate upon the strongest test of fire. This we affirm of pure Gold : for that which is currant and passeth in stamp amongst us, by reason of its allay, which is a proportion of Silver or Copper mixed therewith, is actually dequantitated by fire, and possibly by frequent extinction.

Secondly, Although the substance of Gold be not immuted or its gravity sensibly decreased, yet that from thence some vertue may proceed either in substantial reception or infusion we cannot safely deny. For possible it is that bodies may emit vertue and operation without abatement of weight ; as is evident in the Loadstone, whose effluencies are continual, and communicable without a minoration of gravity. And the like is observable in Bodies electrical, whose emissions are less subtile. So will a Diamond or Saphire emit an effluvium sufficient to move the Needle or a Straw, without diminution of weight. Nor will polished Amber although it send forth a gross and corporal exhalement, be found a long time defective upon the exactest scales. Which is more easily conceivable in a continued and tenacious effluvium, whereof a great part retreats into its body.

Thirdly, If amulets do work by emanations from their bodies, upon those parts whereunto they are appended, and are not yet observed to abate their weight; if they produce visible and real effects by imponderous and invisible emissions, it may be unjust to deny the possible efficacy of Gold, in the non-omission of weight, or deperdition of any ponderous particles.

Lastly, Since *Stibium* or Glass of Antimony, since also its *Regulus* will manifestly communicate unto Water or Wine, a purging and vomitory operation; and yet the body it self, though after iterated infusions, cannot be found to abate either vertue or weight: we shall not deny but Gold may do the like, that is, impart some effluences unto the infusion, which carry with them the separable subtilties thereof.

That therefore this Metal thus received, hath any undeniable effect, we shall not imperiously determine, although beside the former experiments, many more may induce us to believe it. But since the point is dubious and not yet authentically decided, it will be no discretion to depend on disputable remedies; but rather in cases of known danger, to have recourse unto medicines of known and approved activity. For, beside the benefit accruing unto the sick, hereby may be avoided a gross and frequent errour, commonly committed in the use of doubtful remedies, conjointly with those which are of approved vertues; that is to impute the cure unto the conceited remedy, or place it on that whereon they place their opinion. Whose operation although it be nothing, or its concurrence not considerable, yet doth it obtain the name of the whole cure: and carrieth often the honour of the capital energie, which had no finger in it.

Herein exact and critical trial should be made by publick enjoinment, whereby determination might be setled beyond debate: for since thereby not only the bodies of men, but great Treasures might be preserved, it is not only an errour of Physick, but folly of State, to doubt thereof any longer.

4. That a pot full of ashes, will still contain as much water as it would without them, although by *Aristotle* in his Problems taken for granted, and so received by most, is not effectable upon the strictest experiment I could ever make. For when the airy intersticies are filled, and as much of the salt of the ashes as the water will imbibe is dissolved, there remains a gross and terreous portion at the bottom, which will possess a space by it self, according whereto there will remain a quantity of Water not receivable; so will it come to pass in a pot of salt, although decrepitated; and so also in a pot of Snow. For so much it will want in reception, as its solution taketh up, according unto the bulk whereof, there will remain a portion of Water not to be admitted. So a Glass stuffed with pieces of Sponge will want about a sixth part of what it would receive without it. So Sugar will not dissolve beyond the capacity of the Water, nor a Metal in *aqua fortis* be corroded beyond its reception. And so a pint of salt of Tartar exposed unto a moist air until it dissolve, will make far more liquor, or as some term it oyl, then the former measure will contain.

Nor is it only the exclusion of air by water, or repletion of cavities possessed thereby, which causeth a pot of ashes to admit so great a quantity of Water, but also the solution of the salt of the ashes into the body of the dissolvent. So a pot of ashes will receive somewhat more of hot Water then of cold, for the

warm water imbibeth more of the Salt; and a vessel
of ashes more then one of pin-dust or filings of Iron;
and a Glass full of Water will yet drink in a proportion of Salt or Sugar without overflowing.

Nevertheless to make the experiment with most
advantage, and in which sense it approacheth nearest
the truth, it must be made in ashes throughly burnt
and well reverberated by fire, after the salt thereof
hath been drawn out by iterated decoctions. For then
the body being reduced nearer unto Earth, and emptied
of all other principles, which had former ingression
unto it, becometh more porous, and greedily drinketh
in water. He that hath beheld what quantity of
Lead the test of saltless ashes will imbibe, upon the
refining of Silver, hath encouragement to think it will
do very much more in water.

5. Of white powder and such as is discharged without *The Ingre-*
report, there is no small noise in the World : but how *dients of*
Gunpowder.
far agreeable unto truth, few I perceive are able to
determine. Herein therefore to satisfie the doubts of
some, and amuse the credulity of others, We first
• declare, that Gunpowder consisteth of three ingredients,
Salt-petre, Small-coal, and Brimstone. Salt-petre
although it be also natural and found in several places,
yet is that of common use an artificial Salt, drawn from
the infusion of salt Earth, as that of Stales, Stables,
Dove-houses, Cellers, and other covered places, where
the rain can neither dissolve, nor the Sun approach to
resolve it. Brimstone is a Mineral body of fat and
inflamable parts, and this is either used crude, and
called Sulphur Vive, and is of a sadder colour; or
after depuration, such as we have in magdeleons or
rolls, of a lighter yellow. Small-coal is known unto
all, and for this use is made of *Sallow, Willow, Alder,*

Hazel, and the like ; which three proportionably mixed, tempered, and formed into granulary bodies, do make up that Powder which is in use for Guns.

Now all these, although they bear a share in the discharge, yet have they distinct intentions, and different offices in the composition. From Brimstone proceedeth the piercing and powerful firing ; for Small-coal and Petre together will onely spit, nor vigorously continue the ignition. From Small-coal ensueth the black colour and quick accension ; for neither Brimstone nor Petre, although in Powder, will take fire like Small-coal, nor will they easily kindle upon the sparks of a Flint ; as neither will *Camphire*, a body very inflamable : but Small-coal is equivalent to Tinder, and serveth to light the Sulphur. It may also serve to diffuse the ignition through every part of the mixture ; and being of more gross and fixed parts, may seem to moderate the activity of Salt-petre, and prevent too hasty rarefaction. From Salt-petre proceedeth the force and the report ; for Sulphur and Small-coal mixed will not take fire with noise, or exilition, and Powder which is made of impure and greasie Petre hath but a weak emission, and giveth a faint report. And therefore in the three sorts of Powder the strongest containeth most Salt-petre, and the proportion thereof is about ten parts of Petre unto one of Coal and Sulphur.

But the immediate cause of the Report is the vehement commotion of the air upon the sudden and violent eruption of the Powder ; for that being suddenly fired, and almost altogether, upon this high rarefaction, requireth by many degrees a greater space then before its body occupied ; but finding resistance, it actively forceth his way, and by concusion of the air occasioneth the Report. Now with what violence it forceth upon

the air, may easily be conceived, if we admit what
Cardan affirmeth, that the Powder fired doth occupy
an hundred times a greater space then its own bulk;
or rather what *Snellius* more exactly accounteth; that
it exceedeth its former space no less then 12000 and
500 times. And this is the reason not only of this *The cause of Thunder.*
fulminating report of Guns, but may resolve the cause
of those terrible cracks, and affrighting noises of
Heaven; that is, the nitrous and sulphureous exhalations, set on fire in the Clouds; whereupon requiring a
larger place, they force out their way, not only with
the breaking of the cloud, but the laceration of the air
about it. When if the matter be spirituous, and the
cloud compact, the noise is great and terrible: If the
cloud be thin, and the Materials weak, the eruption is
languid, ending in coruscations and flashes without
noise, although but at the distance of two miles; which *The greatest distance of the Clouds.*
is esteemed the remotest distance of clouds. And
therefore such lightnings do seldom any harm. And
therefore also it is prodigious to have thunder in a
clear sky, as is observably recorded in some Histories.

From the like cause may also proceed subterraneous *The cause of Earth-quakes.*
Thunders and Earthquakes, when sulphureous and
nitreous veins being fired, upon rarefaction do force
their way through bodies that resist them. Where if
the kindled matter be plentiful, and the Mine close
and firm about it, subversion of Hills and Towns doth
sometimes follow: If scanty, weak, and the Earth
hollow or porous, there only ensueth some faint concussion or tremulous and quaking Motion. Surely, a main
reason why the Ancients were so imperfect in the
doctrine of Meteors, was their ignorance of Gunpowder and Fire-works, which best discover the causes
of many thereof.

Now therefore he that would destroy the report of Powder, must work upon the Petre; he that would exchange the colour, must think how to alter the Small-coal. For the one, that is, to make white Powder, it is surely many ways feasible: The best I know is by the powder of rotten Willows, Spunk, or Touch-wood prepared, might perhaps make it Russet: and some, as *Beringuccio* affirmeth, have promised to make it Red. All which notwithstanding doth little concern the Report, for that, as we have shewed, depends on another Ingredient. And therefore also under the colour of black, this principle is very variable; for it is made not onely by *Willow, Alder, Hazel*, etc. But some above all commend the coals of *Flax* and *Rushes*, and some also contend the same may be effected with Tinder.

In his
Pyrotechnia

As for the other, that is, to destroy the Report, it is reasonably attempted but two ways; either by quite leaving out, or else by silencing the Salt-petre. How to abate the vigour thereof, or silence its bombulation, a way is promised by *Porta*, not only in general terms by some fat bodies, but in particular by *Borax* and butter mixed in a due proportion; which saith he, will so go off as scarce to be heard by the discharger; and indeed plentifully mixed, it will almost take off the Report, and also the force of the charge. That it may be thus made without Salt-petre, I have met with but one example, that is, of *Alphonsus* Duke of *Ferrara*, who in the relation of *Brassavolus* and *Cardan*, invented such a Powder as would discharge a bullet without Report.

De examine Salium.

That therefore white Powder there may be, there is no absurdity; that also such a one as may give no report, we will not deny a possibility. But this how-

ever, contrived either with or without Salt-petre, will
surely be of little force, and the effects thereof no way
to be feared: For as it omits of Report so will it of
effectual exclusion, and so the charge be of little force
which is excluded. For thus much is reported of that
famous Powder of *Alphonsus*, which was not of force
enough to kill a Chicken, according to the delivery of
Brassavolus. *Jamque pulvis inventus est qui glandem
sine bombo projicit, nec tamen vehementer ut vel pullum
interficere possit.*

It is not to be denied, there are ways to discharge a
bullet, not only with Powder that makes no noise, but
without any Powder at all; as is done by Water and
Wind-guns, but these afford no fulminating Report,
and depend on single principles. And even in ordinary
Powder there are pretended other ways to alter the
noise and strength of the discharge; and the best, if
not only way, consists in the quality of the Nitre: for
as for other ways which make either additions or
alterations in the Powder, or charge, I find therein no
effect: That unto every pound of Sulphur, an adjection
of one ounce of Quick-silver, or unto every pound of
Petre, one ounce of *Sal Armoniac* will much intend
the force, and consequently the Report, as *Beringuccio*
hath delivered, I find no success therein. That a piece
of *Opium* will dead the force and blow, as some have
promised, I find herein no such peculiarity, no more
then in any Gum or viscose body: and as much effect
there is to be found from *Scammony*. That a bullet
dipped in oyl by preventing the transpiration of air,
will carry farther, and pierce deeper, as *Porta* affirmeth,
my experience cannot discern. That Quick-silver is more
destructive then shot, is surely not to be made out; for
it will scarce make any penetration, and discharged

from a Pistol, will hardly pierce through a Parch-
ment. That Vinegar, spirits of Wine, or the distilled
water of Orange-pills, wherewith the Powder is tempered, are more effectual unto the Report than common
Water, as some do promise, I shall not affirm; but
may assuredly more conduce unto the preservation and
durance of the Powder, as *Cataneo* hath well observed.

That the heads of arrows and bullets have been
discharged with that force, as to melt or grow red hot
in their flight, though commonly received, and taken
up by *Aristotle* in his Meteors, is not so easily allowable by any, who shall consider, that a Bullet of Wax
will mischief without melting; that an Arrow or
Bullet discharged against Linen or Paper do not set
them on fire; and hardly apprehend how an Iron
should grow red hot, since the swiftest motion at hand
will not keep one red that hath been made red by fire;
as may be observed in swinging a red hot Iron about,
or fastning it into a Wheel; which under that motion
will sooner grow cold then without it. That a Bullet
also mounts upward upon the horizontall or point-
blank discharge, many Artists do not allow: who
contend that it describeth a parabolical and bowing
line, by reason of its natural gravity inclining it always
downward.

But, Beside the prevalence from Salt-petre, as
Master-ingredient in the mixture; Sulphur may hold
a greater use in the composition and further activity
in the exclusion, then is by most conceived. For
Sulphur vive makes better Powder then common
Sulphur, which nevertheless is of a quick accension.
For Small-coal, Salt-petre, and *Camphire* made into
Powder will be of little force, wherein notwithstanding
there wants not the accending ingredient. And *Cam-*

phire though it flame well, yet will not flush so lively,
or defecate Salt-petre, if you inject it thereon, like
Sulphur; as in the preparation of *Sal prunellæ*. And
lastly, though many ways may be found to light this
Powder, yet is there none I know to make a strong
and vigorous Powder of Salt-petre, without the admix-
tion of Sulphur. *Arsenic* red and yellow, that is
Orpement and *Sandarach* may perhaps do something,
as being inflamable and containing Sulphur in them;
but containing also a salt, and mercurial mixtion, they
will be of little effect; and white or crystalline *Arsenic*
of less, for that being artificial, and sublimed with salt,
will not endure flammation.

This Antipathy or contention between Salt-petre
and Sulphur upon an actual fire, in their compleat and
distinct bodies, is also manifested in their preparations,
and bodies which invisibly contain them. Thus in the
preparation of *Crocus Metallorum*, the matter kindleth
and flusheth like Gunpowder, wherein notwithstanding,
there is nothing but *Antimony* and Salt-petre. But
this may proceed from the Sulphur of *Antimony*, not
enduring the society of Salt-petre; for after three or
four accensions, through a fresh addition of Petre, the
Powder will flush no more, for the sulphur of the
Antimony is quite exhaled. Thus Iron in *Aqua fortis*
will fall into ebullition, with noise and emication, as
also a crass and fumid exhalation, which are caused
from this combat of the sulphur of Iron with the acid
and nitrous spirits of *Aqua fortis*. So is it also in
Aurum fulminans, or Powder of Gold dissolved in
Aqua Regis, and precipitated with oyl of *Tartar*,
which will kindle without an actual fire, and afford
a report like Gun-powder; that is not as *Crollius* De consensu
affirmeth from any Antipathy between *Sal Armoniac* Chymico-
rum, etc.

and *Tartar*, but rather between the nitrous spirits of *Aqua Regis*, commixed *per minima* with the sulphur of Gold, as *Sennertus* hath observed.

6. That *Coral* (which is a *Lithophyton* or stone-plant, and groweth at the bottom of the Sea) is soft under Water, but waxeth hard in the air, although the assertion of *Dioscorides, Pliny,* and consequently *Solinus, Isidore, Rueus,* and many others, and stands believed by most, we have some reason to doubt, especially if we conceive with common Believers, a total softness at the bottom, and this induration to be singly made by the air, not only from so sudden a petrifaction and strange induration, not easily made out from the qualities of air, but because we find it rejected by experimental enquiries. *Johannes Beguinus* in his Chapter of the tincture of *Coral* undertakes to clear the World of this Error, from the express experiment of *John Baptista de Nicole*, who was Overseer of the gathering of *Coral* upon the Kingdom of *Thunis*. This Gentleman, saith he, desirous to find the nature of *Coral*, and to be resolved how it groweth at the bottom of the Sea, caused a man to go down no less then a hundred fathom, with express to take notice whether it were hard or soft in the place where it groweth. Who returning, brought in each hand a branch of *Coral*, affirming it was as hard at the bottom, as in the air where he delivered it. The same was also confirmed by a trial of his own, handling it a fathom under water before it felt the air. *Boetius* in his Tract *De Gemmis*, is of the same opinion, not ascribing its concretion unto the air, but the coagulating spirits of Salt, and lapidifical juice of the Sea, which entring the parts of that Plant, overcomes its vegetability, and converts it into a lapideous substance. And this,

In the French Copy.

How Coral of a Plant becomes a Stone.

saith he, doth happen when the Plant is ready to
decay; for all *Coral* is not hard, and in many concreted Plants some parts remain unpetrified, that is
the quick and livelier parts remain as Wood, and were
never yet converted. Now that Plants and ligneous
bodies may indurate under Water without approachment of air, we have experiment in *Coralline,* with
many Coralloidal concretions; and that little stony
Plant which Mr. *Johnson* nameth, *Hippuris coralloides,*
and *Gesner, foliis mansu Arenosis,* we have found in
fresh water, which is the less concretive portion of
that Element. We have also with us the visible
petrification of Wood in many waters, whereof so
much as is covered with water converteth into stone;
as much as is above it and in the air, retaineth the
form of Wood, and continueth as before.

Now though in a middle way we may concede, that
some are soft and others hard; yet whether all *Coral*
were first a woody substance, and afterward converted;
or rather some thereof were never such, but from the
sprouting spirit of Salt, were able even in their stony
natures to ramifie and send forth branches; as is observ- Gans
able in some stones, in silver and metallick bodies, is *Histor.*
not without some question. And such at least might *Coral.*
some of those be, which *Fiaroumti* observed to grow
upon Bricks at the bottom of the Sea, upon the coast
of *Barbarie.*

7. We are not throughly resolved concerning *Porcellane* or *China* dishes, that according to common belief
they are made of Earth, which lieth in preparation
about an hundred years under ground; for the relations
thereof are not onely divers, but contrary, and Authors
agree not herein. *Guido Pancirollus* will have them
made of Egg-shells, Lobster-shells, and *Gypsum* laid

*Of what
matter the
China dishes
be made.*

up in the Earth the space of 80 years : of the same affirmation is *Scaliger*, and the common opinion of most.
Ramuzius in his Navigations is of a contrary assertion,
that they are made out of Earth, not laid under ground,
but hardned in the Sun and Wind, the space of forty
years. But *Gonzales de Mendoza*, a man imployed
into *China* from *Philip* the second King of *Spain*, upon
enquiry and ocular experience, delivered a way different
from all these. For inquiring into the artifice thereof,
he found they were made of a Chalky Earth; which
beaten and steeped in water, affordeth a cream or fatness on the top, and a gross subsidence at the bottom ;
out of the cream or superfluitance, the finest dishes, saith
he, are made, out of the residence thereof the courser ;
which being formed, they gild or paint, and not after
an hundred years, but presently commit unto the fur-
nace. This, saith he, is known by experience, and
more probable then what *Odoardus Barbosa* hath
delivered, that they are made of shells, and buried
under earth an hundred years. And answerable in all
points hereto, is the relation of *Linschotten*, a diligent
enquirer, in his Oriental Navigations. Later confirmation may be had from *Alvarez* the Jesuit, who lived
long in those parts, in his relations of *China*. That
Porcellane Vessels were made but in one Town of the
Province of *Chiamsi* : That the earth was brought out
of other Provinces, but for the advantage of water,
which makes them more polite and perspicuous, they
were only made in this. That they were wrought and
fashioned like those of other Countries, whereof some
were tincted blew, some red, others yellow, of which
colour only they presented unto the King.

The latest account hereof may be found in the
voyage of the Dutch Embassadors sent from *Batavia*

unto the Emperour of *China*, printed in *French* 1665, which plainly informeth, that the Earth whereof *Porcellane* dishes are made, is brought from the Mountains of *Hoang*, and being formed into square loaves, is brought by water, and marked with the Emperours Seal: that the Earth it self is very lean, fine, and shining like Sand: and that it is prepared and fashioned after the same manner which the *Italians* observe in the fine Earthen Vessels of *Faventia* or *Fuenca*: that they are so reserved concerning that Artifice, that 'tis only revealed from Father unto Son: that they are painted with *Indico* baked in a fire for fifteen days together, and with very dry and not smoaking Wood: which when the Author had seen he could hardly contain from laughter at the common opinion above rejected by us.

Now if any enquire, why being so commonly made, and in so short a time, they are become so scarce, or not at all to be had? The Answer is given by these last Relators, that under great penalties it is forbidden to carry the first sort out of the Country. And of those surely the properties must be verified, which by *Scaliger* and others are ascribed unto China-dishes: That they admit no poison, that they strike fire, that they will grow hot no higher then the liquor in them ariseth. For such as pass amongst us, and under the name of the finest, will only strike fire, but not discover *Aconite*, *Mercury*, or *Arsenic*; but may be useful in dysenteries and fluxes beyond the other.

8. Whether a Carbuncle (which is esteemed the best and biggest of Rubies) doth flame in the dark, or shine like a coal in the night, though generally agreed on by common Believers, is very much questioned by many. By *Milius*, who accounts it a Vulgar Error ·

By the learned *Boetius*, who could not find it verified in that famous one of *Rodulphus*, which was as big as an Egg, and esteemed the best in *Europe*. Wherefore although we dispute not the possibility, and the like is said to have been observed in some Diamonds, yet whether herein there be not too high an apprehension, and above its natural radiancy, is not without just doubt : however it be granted a very splendid *Gem*, and whose sparks may somewhat resemble the glances of fire, and Metaphorically deserve that name. And therefore when it is conceived by some, that this Stone in the Brest-plate of *Aaron* respected the Tribe of *Dan*, who burnt the City of *Laish*; and *Sampson* of the same Tribe, who fired the Corn of the *Philistims*; in some sense it may be admitted, and is no intollerable conception.

As for that *Indian* Stone that shined so brightly in the Night, and pretended to have been shewn to many in the Court of *France*, as *Andreus Chioccus* hath declared out of *Thuanus*, it proved but an imposture, as that eminent Philosopher *Licetus* hath discovered, and therefore in the revised Editions of *Thuanus*, it is not to be found. As for the *Phosphorus* or *Bononian* Stone, which exposed unto the Sun, and then closely shut up, will afterward afford a light in the dark ; it is of unlike consideration, for that requireth calcination or reduction into a dry powder by fire, whereby it imbibeth the light in the vaporous humidity of the air about it, and therefore maintaineth its light not long, but goes out when the vaporous vehicle is consumed.

9. Whether the *Ætites* or *Eagle*-stone hath that eminent property to promote delivery or restrain abortion, respectively applied to lower or upward parts of

Licet de quæsit. per Epistolas.

Licet de lapide Bononiensi.

the body, we shall not discourage common practice by
our question : but whether they answer the account
thereof, as to be taken out of *Eagles* nests, co-operating
in Women unto such effects, as they are conceived
toward the young *Eagles* : or whether the single signature of one stone included in the matrix and belly of
another, were not sufficient at first, to derive this vertue
of the pregnant Stone, upon others in impregnation,
may yet be farther considered. Many sorts there are
of this ratling Stone, beside the *Geodes*, containing a
softer substance in it. Divers are found in *England*,
and one we met with on the Sea-shore, but because
many of eminent use are pretended to be brought from
Iseland, wherein are divers airies of *Eagles*, we cannot
omit to deliver what we received from a learned person
in that Country, *Ætites an in nidis Aquilarum aliquando* Theodorus
fuerit repertus, nescio. Nostra certè memoria, etiam Ionas Hitter-
inquirentibus non contigit invenisse, quare in fabulis dalæ Pastor.
habendum.

10. Terrible apprehensions and answerable unto their
names, are raised of *Fayrie* stones, and *Elves* spurs,
found commonly with us in Stone, Chalk, and Marl-
pits, which notwithstanding are no more than *Echinometrites* and *Belemnites*, the Sea-Hedge-Hog, and
the *Dart*-stone, arising from some siliceous Roots, and
softer then that of Flint, the Master-stone, lying more
regularly in courses, and arising from the primary and
strongest spirit of the Mine. Of the *Echinites*, such
as are found in Chalk-pits are white, glassie, and built
upon a Chalky inside ; some of an hard and flinty
substance, are found in Stone-pits and elsewhere.
Common opinion commendeth them for the Stone, but
are most practically used against Films in Horses eyes.

11. Lastly, He must have more heads than *Rome*

had Hills, that makes out half of those vertues ascribed unto stones, and their not only Medical, but Magical proprieties, which are to be found in Authors of great Name. In *Psellus, Serapion, Evax, Albertus, Aleazar, Marbodeus*; in *Maiolus, Rueus, Mylius,* and many more.

*Against
poison.
Provoking
Urine.
Against the
Falling
sickness.*

That *Lapis Lasuli* hath in it a purgative faculty we know; that *Bezoar* is Antidotal, *Lapis Judaicus* diuretical, *Coral* Antepileptical, we will not deny. That *Cornelians, Jaspis, Heliotropes,* and Blood-stones, may be of vertue to those intentions they are implied, experience and visible effects will make us grant. But that an *Amethyst* prevents inebriation, that an *Emerald* will break if worn in copulation. That a *Diamond* laid under the pillow, will betray the incontinency of a wife. That a *Saphire* is preservative against inchantments; that the fume of an *Agath* will avert a tempest, or the wearing of a *Crysoprase* make one out love with Gold; as some have delivered, we are yet, I confess, to believe, and in that infidelity are likely to end our days. And therefore, they which in the explication of the two Beryls upon the *Ephod,* or the twelve stones in the Rational or Brest-plate of *Aaron,* or those twelve which garnished the wall of the holy City in the Apocalyps, have drawn their significations from such as these; or declared their symbolical verities from such traditional falsities, have surely corrupted the sincerity of their Analogies, or misunderstood the mystery of their intentions.

Most men conceive that the twelve stones in *Aarons* brestplate made a Jewel surpassing any, and not to be parallel'd; which notwithstanding will hardly be made out from the description of the Text, for the names of the Tribes were engraven thereon, which must notably

abate their lustre. Beside, it is not clear made out
that the best of Gemms, a Diamond was amongst them; nor is to be found in the list thereof, set down by the *Jerusalem Thargum*, wherein we find the darker stones of *Sardius, Sardonix*, and *Jasper*; and if we receive them under those names wherein they are usually described, it is not hard to contrive a more illustrious and splendent Jewel. But being not ordained for meer lustre by diaphanous and pure tralucencies, their mysterious significations became more considerable then their Gemmary substances; and those no doubt did nobly answer the intention of the Institutor. Beside some may doubt whether there be twelve distinct species of noble tralucent Gemms in nature, at least yet known unto us, and such as may not be referred unto some of those in high esteem among us, which come short of the number of twelve; which to make up we must find out some others to match and join with the Diamond, *Beryl, Saphyr, Emerald, Amethyst, Topaz, Crysolit, Jacynth, Ruby*, and if we may admit it in this number, the Oriental Gianat.

CHAPTER VI

Of sundry Tenets concerning Vegetables or Plants, which examined, prove either false or dubious.

1. **M**ANY Mola's and false conceptions there are of *Mandrakes*, the first from great Antiquity, conceiveth the Root thereof resembleth the shape of Man; which is a conceit not to be made out by ordinary inspection, or any other eyes,

then such as regarding the Clouds, behold them in shapes conformable to pre-apprehensions.

Now whatever encouraged the first invention, there have not been wanting many ways of its promotion. The first a Catachrestical and far derived similitude it holds with Man; that is, in a bifurcation or division of the Root into two parts, which some are content to call Thighs; whereas notwithstanding they are oft-times three, and when but two, commonly so complicated and crossed, that men for this deceit are fain to effect their design in other plants; And as fair a resemblance is often found in *Carrots, Parsnips, Briony,* and many others. There are, I confess, divers Plants which carry about them not only the shape of parts, but also of whole Animals, but surely not all thereof, unto whom this conformity is imputed. Whoever shall peruse the signatures of *Crollius,* or rather the Phytognomy of *Porta,* and strictly observe how vegetable Realities are commonly forced into Animal Representations, may easily perceive in very many, the semblance is but postulatory, and must have a more assimilating phansie then mine to make good many thereof.

Μάνδρα,
Spelunca.

Illiterate heads have been led on by the name, which in the first syllable expresseth its Representation; but others have better observed the Laws of *Etymology,* and deduced it from a word of the same language, because it delighteth to grow in obscure and shady places; which derivation, although we shall not stand to maintain, yet the other seemeth answerable unto the Etymologies of many Authors, who often confound such nominal Notations. Not to enquire beyond our own profession, the Latine Physitians which most adhered unto the *Arabick* way, have often failed herein; particularly *Valescus de Tarranta,* a received Physitian,

*In the old
Edition.*

in whose *Philonium* or Medical practice these may be
observed : *Diarhea*, saith he, *Quia pluries venit in die.*
Herisepela, quasi hærens pilis, Emorrohis, ab emach
sanguis & morrohis quod est cadere.   Lithargia à Litos
quod est oblivio & Targus morbus, Scotomia à Scotus
quod est videre, & mias musca.   Opthalmia ab opus
Græce quod est succus, & Talmon quod est occulus.
Paralisis, quasi læsio partis.   Fistula à fos sonus &
stolon quod est emissio, quasi emissio soni vel vocis.
Which are derivations as strange indeed as the other,
and hardly to be parallel'd elsewhere ; confirming not
only the words of one language with another, but
creating such as were never yet in any.

The received distinction and common Notation by
Sexes, hath also promoted the conceit; for true it is,
that *Herbalists* from ancient times have thus distinguished them, naming that the Male, whose leaves are
lighter, and Fruit and Apples rounder ; but this is
properly no generative division, but rather some note
of distinction in colour, figure or operation.   For
though *Empedocles* affirm, there is a mixt, and undi-
vided Sex in Vegetables ; and *Scaliger* upon *Aristotle*,   De Plantis.
doth favourably explain that opinion ; yet will it not
consist with the common and ordinary acception, nor
yet with *Aristotles* definition.   For if that be Male
which generates in another, that Female which pro-
creates in it self; if it be understood of Sexes conjoined,
all Plants are Female ; and if of disjoined and con-
gressive generation, there is no Male or Female in
them at all.

But the Atlas or main Axis which supported this   *The impos-*
opinion, was dayly experience, and the visible testi-   *tures touch-*
mony of sense.   For many there are in several parts   *ing the*
of *Europe*, who carry about Roots and sell them unto   *Root of*
Mandrake.

ignorant people, which handsomely make out the shape of Man or Woman. But these are not productions of Nature, but contrivances of Art, as divers have noted, and *Mathiolus* plainly detected, who learned this way of Trumpery from a vagabond cheater lying under his cure for the French disease. His words were these, and may determine the point, *Sed profecto vanum & fabulosum, etc.* But this is vain and fabulous, which ignorant people, and simple women believe; for the roots which are carried about by impostors to deceive unfruitful women, are made of the roots of Canes, Briony and other plants : for in these yet fresh and virent, they carve out the figures of men and women, first sticking therein the grains of Barley or Millet, where they intend the hair should grow; then bury them in sand until the grains shoot forth their roots, which at the longest will happen in twenty days; they afterward clip and trim those tender strings in the fashion of beards and other hairy tegument. All which like other impostures once discovered is easily effected, and in the root of white *Briony* may be practised every spring.

What is therefore delivered in favour thereof, by Authors ancient or modern, must have its root in tradition, imposture, far derived similitude, or casual and rare contingency. So may we admit of the Epithet of *Pythagoras*, who calls it *Anthropomorphus*; and that of *Columella*, who terms it *Semihomo*; more applicable unto the Man-*Orchis*, whose flower represents a Man. Thus is *Albertus* to be received when he affirmeth, that *Mandrakes* represent man-kind with the distinction of either Sex. Under these restrictions may those Authors be admitted, which for this opinion are introduced by *Drusius*; nor shall we need to

Orchis
Anthropomorphus
cujus Icon
in Kircheri
Magia parastatica.
De mandragora.
De monstris.

question the monstrous root of *Briony* described in
Aldrovandus.

The second assertion concerneth its production. That it naturally groweth under Gallowses and places of execution, arising from fat or urine that drops from the body of the dead; a story somewhat agreeable unto the fable of the Serpents teeth sowed in the earth by *Cadmus*; or rather the birth of *Orion* from the urine of *Jupiter, Mercury,* and *Neptune.* Now this opinion seems grounded on the former, that is, a conceived similitude it hath with man; and therefore from him in some way they would make out its production: Which conceit is not only erroneous in the foundation, but injurious unto Philosophy in the superstruction. Making putrifactive generations, correspondent unto seminal productions, and conceiving in equivocal effects and univocal conformity unto the efficient. Which is so far from being verified of animals in their corruptive mutations into Plants, that they maintain not this similitude in their nearer translation into animals. So when the Oxe corrupteth into Bees, or the Horse into Hornets, they come not forth in the image of their originals. So the corrupt and excrementous humours in man are animated into Lice; and we may observe, *Generations* that Hogs, Sheep, Goats, Hawks, Hens, and others, *equivocal,* *are yet* have one peculiar and proper kind of vermine; not *commonly* resembling themselves according to seminal conditions, *regular and* *of a deter-* yet carrying a setled and confined habitude unto *minate form* their corruptive originals. And therefore come not *or species.* forth in generations erratical, or different from each other; but seem specifically and in regular shapes to attend the corruption of their bodies, as do more perfect conceptions, the rule of seminal productions.

The third affirmeth the roots of *Mandrakes* do make

T

a noise, or give a shriek upon eradication; which is indeed ridiculous, and false below confute: arising perhaps from a small and stridulous noise, which being firmly rooted, it maketh upon divulsion of parts. A slender foundation for such a vast conception: for such a noise we sometime observe in other Plants, in Parsenips, Liquorish, Eringium, Flags, and others.

The last concerneth the danger ensuing, That there follows an hazard of life to them that pull it up, that some evil fate pursues them, and they live not very long after. Therefore the attempt hereof among the Ancients, was not in ordinary way; but as *Pliny* informeth, when they intended to take up the root of this Plant, they took the wind thereof, and with a sword describing three circles about it, they digged it up, looking toward the *West*. A conceit not only injurious unto truth, and confutable by daily experience, but somewhat derogatory unto the providence of God; that is, not only to impose so destructive a quality on any Plant, but to conceive a Vegetable, whose parts are useful unto many, should in the only taking up prove mortal unto any. To think he suffereth the poison of *Nubia* to be gathered, *Napellus*, *Aconite*, and *Thora*, to be eradicated, yet this not to be moved. That he permitteth Arsenick and mineral poisons to be forced from the bowels of the Earth, yet not this from the surface thereof. This were to introduce a second forbidden fruit, and inhance the first malediction, making it not only mortal for *Adam* to taste the one, but capital unto his posterity to eradicate or dig up the other.

Now what begot, at least promoted so strange conceptions, might be the magical opinion hereof; this being conceived the Plant so much in use with *Circe*,

Granum
Nubiæ.

and therefore named *Circea*, as *Dioscorides* and *Theo-*
phrastus have delivered, which being the eminent
Sorcerers of elder story, and by the magick of simples
believed to have wrought many wonders: some men
were apt to invent, others to believe any tradition or
magical promise thereof.

Analogous relations concerning other plants, and such
as are of near affinity unto this, have made its currant
smooth, and pass more easily among us. For the same
effect is also delivered by *Josephus*, concerning the root
Baaras; by *Ælian* of *Cynospastus*; and we read in
Homer the very same opinion concerning Moly,

Μῶλυ δέ μιν καλέουσι θεοί· χαλεπὸν δέ τ' ὀρύσσειν
'Ανδράσι γε θνητοῖσι· θεοὶ δέ τε πάντα δύνανται.

The Gods it Moly call, whose Root to dig away,
Is dangerous unto Man ; but Gods, they all things may.

Now parallels or like relations alternately relieve
each other, when neither will pass asunder, yet are
they plausible together; their mutual concurrences
supporting their solitary instabilities.

Signaturists have somewhat advanced it ; who seldom
omitting what Ancients delivered ; drawing into inference received distinction of sex, not willing to examine
its humane resemblance; and placing it in the form
of strange and magical simples, have made men suspect
there was more therein, then ordinary practice allowed;
and so became apt to embrace whatever they heard or
read conformable unto such conceptions.

Lastly, The conceit promoteth it self: for concerning an effect whose trial must cost so dear, it fortifies
it self in that invention ; and few there are whose
experiment it need to fear. For (what is most contemptible) although not only the reason of any head,

but experience of every hand may well convict it, yet will it not by divers be rejected ; for prepossessed heads will ever doubt it, and timorous beliefs will never dare to trie it. So these Traditions how low and ridiculous soever, will find suspition in some, doubt in others, and serve as tests or trials of Melancholy and superstitious tempers for ever.

That Cinamon, Ginger, Clove, etc., are not of the same tree.

2. That Cinamon, Ginger, Clove, Mace, and Nutmeg, are but the several parts and fruits of the same tree, is the common belief of those which daily use them. Whereof to speak distinctly, Ginger is the root of neither Tree nor Shrub, but of an herbaceous Plant, resembling the Water Flower-De-luce, as *Garcias* first described ; or rather the common Reed, as *Lobelius* since affirmed. Very common in many parts of *India*, growing either from Root or Seed, which in *December* and *January* they take up, and gently dried, roll it up in earth, whereby occluding the pores, they conserve the natural humidity, and so prevent corruption.

Cinamon is the inward bark of a Cinamon Tree, whereof the best is brought from *Zeilan* ; this freed from the outward bark, and exposed unto the Sun, contracts into those folds wherein we commonly receive it. If it have not a sufficient isolation it looketh pale, and attains not its laudable colour ; if it be sunned too long, it suffereth a torrefaction, and descendeth somewhat below it.

Clove seems to be either the rudiment of a fruit, or the fruit it self growing upon the Clove tree, to be found but in few Countries. The most commendable is that of the Isles of *Molucca* ; it is first white, afterward green, which beaten down, and dried in the Sun, becometh black, and in the complexion we receive it.

Nutmeg is the fruit of a Tree differing from all these,

and as *Garcias* describeth it, somewhat like a Peach; growing in divers places, but fructifying in the Isle of *Banda*. The fruit hereof consisteth of four parts; the first or outward part is a thick and carnous covering like that of a Wal-nut. The second a dry and flosculous coat, commonly called Mace. The third a harder tegument or shell, which lieth under the Mace. The fourth a Kernel included in the shell, which is the same we call Nutmeg. All which both in their parts and order of disposure, are easily discerned in those fruits, which are brought in preserves unto us.

Now if because Mace and Nutmegs proceed from one Tree, the rest must bear them company; or because they are all from the *East Indies*, they are all from one Plant : the Inference is precipitous, nor will there such a Plant be found in the Herbal of Nature.

3. That Viscus Arboreus or Misseltoe is bred upon Trees, from seeds which Birds, especially Thrushes and Ring-doves let fall thereon, was the Creed of the Ancients, and is still believed among us, is the account of its production, set down by *Pliny*, delivered by *Virgil*, and subscribed by many more. If so, some reason must be assigned, why it groweth onely upon certain Trees, and not upon many whereon these Birds do light. For as Exotick observers deliver, it groweth upon Almond-trees, Chesnut, Apples, Oaks, and Pine-trees. As we observe in *England* very commonly upon Apple, Crabs, and White-thorn; sometimes upon Sallow, Hazel, and Oak : rarely upon Ash, Lime-tree, and Maple; never, that I could observe, upon Holly, Elm, and many more. Why it groweth not in all Countries and places where these Birds are found; for so *Brassavolus* affirmeth, it is not to be found in the Territory of *Ferrara*, and was fain to supply himself

from other parts of *Italy*. Why if it ariseth from a seed, if sown it will not grow again, as *Pliny* affirmeth, and as by setting the Berries thereof, we have in vain attempted its production; why if it cometh from seed that falleth upon the tree, it groweth often downwards, and puts forth under the bough, where seed can neither fall nor yet remain. Hereof beside some others, the Lord *Verulam* hath taken notice. And they surely speak probably who make it an arboreous excrescence, or rather superplant, bred of a viscous and superfluous sap which the tree it self cannot assimilate. And therefore sprouteth not forth in boughs and surcles of the same shape, and similary unto the Tree that beareth it; but in a different form, and secondary unto its specifical intention, wherein once failing, another form succeedeth: and in the first place that of Misseltoe, in Plants and Trees disposed to its production. And therefore also where ever it groweth, it is of constant shape, and maintains a regular figure; like other supercrescences, and such as living upon the stock of others, are termed parasitical Plants, as Polypody, Moss, the smaller Capillaries, and many more: So that several regions produce several Misseltoes; *India* one, *America* another, according to the law and rule of their degenerations.

What the Misseltoe in some Trees is.

Now what begot this conceit, might be the enlargement of some part of truth contained in its story. For certain it is, that some Birds do feed upon the berries of this Vegetable, and we meet in *Aristotle* with one kind of Trush called the Missel Trush, or feeder upon Misseltoe. But that which hath most promoted it, is a received proverb, *Turdus sibi malum cacat*; appliable unto such men as are authors of their own misfortunes. For according unto ancient tradition and *Plinies* rela-

'Ιξόβορος.

tion, the Bird not able to digest the fruit whereon she
feedeth; from her inconverted muting ariseth this
Plant, of the Berries whereof Birdlime is made, wherewith she is after entangled. But although Proverbs be
popular principles, yet is not all true that is proverbial;
and in many thereof, there being one thing delivered,
and another intended; though the verbal expression
be false, the Proverb is true enough in the verity of its
intention.

As for the Magical vertues in this Plant, and conceived efficacy unto veneficial intentions, it seemeth a
Pagan relique derived from the ancient *Druides*, the
great admirers of the Oak, especially the Misseltoe
that grew thereon; which according unto the particular of *Pliny*, they gathered with great solemnity.
For after sacrifice the Priest in a white garment
ascended the tree, cut down the Misseltoe with a
golden hook, and received it in a white coat; the
vertue whereof was to resist all poisons, and make
fruitful any that used it. Vertues not expected from
Classical practice; and did they fully answer their
promise which are so commended, in Epileptical intentions, we would abate these qualities. Country
practice hath added another, to provoke the after-
birth, and in that case the decoction is given unto
Cows. That the Berries are poison as some conceive,
we are so far from averring, that we have safely given
them inwardly; and can confirm the experiment of
Brassavolus, that they have some purgative quality.

*Paganish
superstition
about the
Misseltoe of
the Oak.*

4. The Rose of *Jericho*, that flourishes every year
just about Christmas Eve, is famous in Christian
reports; which notwithstanding we have some reason
to doubt, and are plainly informed by *Bellonius*, it is
but a Monastical imposture, as he hath delivered in his

observations, concerning the Plants in *Jericho*. That
which promoted the conceit, or perhaps begot its continuance, was a propriety in this Plant. For though it
be dry, yet will it upon imbibition of moisture dilate
its leaves, and explicate its flowers contracted, and
seemingly dried up. And this is to be effected not
only in the Plant yet growing, but in some manner
also in that which is brought exuccous and dry unto
us. Which quality being observed, the subtilty of
contrivers did commonly play this shew upon the Eve
of our Saviours Nativity, when by drying the Plant
again, it closed the next day, and so pretended a
double mystery : referring unto the opening and closing
of the womb of *Mary*.

Cap. 24.

φύτα τοῦ
ῥόδου.

There wanted not a specious confirmation from a
text in *Ecclesiasticus, Quasi palma exultata sum in Cades,
& quasi plantatio Rosœ in Jericho* : I was exalted like a
Palm-tree in *Engaddi,* and as a Rose in *Jericho*. The
sound whereof in common ears, begat an extraordinary
opinion of the Rose of that denomination. But herein
there seemeth a mistake : for by the Rose in the Text,
is implied the true and proper Rose, as first the Greek,
and ours accordingly rendreth it. But that which
passeth under this name, and by us is commonly called
the Rose of *Jericho*, is properly no Rose, but a small
thorny shrub or kind of Heath, bearing little white
flowers, far differing from the Rose ; whereof *Bellonius*
a very inquisitive *Herbalist,* could not find any in his
travels thorow *Jericho*. A Plant so unlike a Rose, it
hath been mistaken by some good *Simplist* for
Amomum ; which truly understood is so unlike a Rose,
that as *Dioscorides* delivers, the flowers thereof are like
the white Violet, and its leaves resemble *Briony*.

Suitable unto this relation almost in all points is

that of the Thorn at *Glassenbury,* and perhaps the
daughter hereof; herein our endeavours as yet have
not attained satisfaction, and cannot therefore enlarge.
Thus much in general we may observe, that strange
effects are naturally taken for miracles by weaker
heads, and artificially improved to that apprehension
by wiser. Certainly many precocious Trees, and such
as spring in the Winter, may be found in most parts
of *Europe,* and divers also in *England.* For most
Trees do begin to sprout in the Fall of the leaf or
Autumn, and if not kept back by cold and outward
causes, would leaf about the Solstice. Now if it
happen that any be so strongly constituted, as to make
this good against the power of Winter, they may produce their leaves or blossoms in that season. And
perform that in some singles, which is observable in
whole kinds; as in *Ivy,* which blossoms and bears at
least twice a year, and once in the Winter; as also in
Furz, which flowereth in that season.

CHAP.
VI

*Such a
Thorn there
is in* Parham
Park in
Suffolk, *and
elsewhere.*

5. That *ferrum Equinum,* or *Sferra Cavallo* hath a
vertue attractive of Iron, a power to break locks, and
draw off the shoes of a Horse that passeth over it;
whether you take it for one kind of *Securidaca,* or will
also take in *Lunaria,* we know it to be false: and
cannot but wonder at *Mathiolus,* who upon a parallel
in *Pliny* was staggered into suspension. Who notwithstanding in the imputed vertue to open things, close
and shut up, could laugh himself at that promise from
the herb *Æthiopis* or *Æthiopian* mullen; and condemn
the judgment of *Scipio,* who having such a picklock,
would spend so many years in battering the Gates of
Carthage. Which strange and Magical conceit, seems
to have no deeper root in reason, then the figure of
its seed; for therein indeed it somewhat resembles a

Horse-shoe; which notwithstanding *Baptista Porta* hath thought too low a signification, and raised the same unto a Lunary representation.

6. That *Bayes* will protect from the mischief of Lightning and Thunder, is a quality ascribed thereto, common with the Fig-tree, Eagle, and skin of a Seal. Against so famous a quality, *Vicomercatus* produceth experiment of a Bay-tree blasted in *Italy*. And therefore although *Tiberius* for this intent, did wear a Lawrel upon his Temples, yet did *Augustus* take a more probable course, who fled under arches and hollow vaults for protection. And though *Porta* conceive, because in a streperous eruption, it riseth against fire, it doth therefore resist lightning, yet is that no emboldning Illation. And if we consider the threefold effect of *Jupiters* Trisulk, to burn, discuss, and terebrate; and if that be true which is commonly delivered, that it will melt the blade, yet pass the scabbard; kill the child, yet spare the mother; dry up the wine, yet leave the hogshead entire: though it favour the amulet, it may not spare us; it will be unsure to rely on any preservative, 'tis no security to be dipped in Styx, or clad in the armour of *Ceneus*. Now that Beer, Wine, and other liquors, are spoiled with lightning and thunder, we conceive it proceeds not onely from noise and concussion of the air, but also noxious spirits, which mingle therewith, and draw them to corruption; whereby they become not only dead themselves, but sometime deadly unto others, as that which *Seneca* mentioneth; whereof whosoever drank, either lost his life, or else his wits upon it.

How Beer and Wine come to be spoiled by Lightning.

7. It hath much deceived the hope of good fellows, what is commonly expected of bitter Almonds, and though in *Plutarch* confirmed from the practice of

Claudius his Physitian, that Antidote against ebriety hath commonly failed. Surely men much versed in the practice do err in the theory of inebriation; conceiving in that disturbance the brain doth only suffer from exhalations and vaporous ascensions from the stomack, which fat and oyly substances may suppress. Whereas the prevalent intoxication is from the spirits of drink dispersed into the veins and arteries, from whence by common conveyances they creep into the brain, insinuate into its ventricles, and beget those vertigoes accompanying that perversion. And therefore the same effect may be produced by a Glister, the Head may be intoxicated by a medicine at the Heel. So the poisonous bites of Serpents, although on parts at distance from the head, yet having entered the veins, disturb the animal faculties, and produce the effects of drink, or poison swallowed. And so as the Head may be disturbed by the skin, it may the same way be relieved; as is observable in balneations, washings, and fomentations, either of the whole body, or of that part alone.

CHAPTER VII

Of some Insects, and the properties of several Plants.

1. FEW ears have escaped the noise of the Dead - watch, that is, the little clickling sound heard often in many rooms, somewhat resembling that of a Watch; and this is conceived to be of an evil omen or prediction of some persons death · wherein notwithstanding there is

nothing of rational presage or just cause of terrour unto melancholy and meticulous heads. For this noise is made by a little sheath-winged gray Insect found often in Wainscot, Benches, and Wood-work, in the Summer. We have taken many thereof, and kept them in thin boxes, wherein I have heard and seen them work and knack with a little *proboscis* or trunk against the side of the box, like a *Picus Martius*, or Woodpecker against a tree. It worketh best in warm weather, and for the most part giveth not over under nine or eleven stroaks at a time. He that could extinguish the terrifying apprehensions hereof, might prevent the passions of the heart, and many cold sweats in Grandmothers and Nurses, who in the sickness of children, are so startled with these noises.

2. The presage of the year succeeding, which is commonly made from Insects or little Animals in Oak apples, according to the kinds thereof, either Maggot, Fly, or Spider; that is, of Famine, War, or Pestilence; whether we mean that woody excrescence, which shooteth from the branch about *May*, or that round and Apple-like accretion which groweth under the leaf about the latter end of Summer, is I doubt too distinct, nor verifiable from event.

For Flies and Maggots are found every year, very seldom Spiders: And *Helmont* affirmeth he could never find the Spider and the Fly upon the same Trees, that is the signs of War and Pestilence, which often go together: Beside, that the Flies found were at first Maggots, experience hath informed us; for keeping these excrescencies, we have observed their conversions, beholding in Magnifying Glasses the daily progression thereof. As may be also observed in other Vegetable excretions, whose Maggots do terminate in Flies of constant shapes; as in the Nutgalls of the Out-landish Oak, and the Mossie tuft of the wild Briar; which having gathered in *November* we have found the little Maggots which lodged in wooden Cells all *Winter*, to turn into Flies in *June*.

We confess the opinion may hold some verity in the Analogy, or Emblematical phansie. For Pestilence is properly signified by the Spider, whereof some kinds are of a very venemous Nature. Famine by Maggots, which destroy the fruits of the Earth. And War not improperly by the Fly; if we rest in the phansie of *Homer*, who compares the valiant *Grecian* unto a Fly.

Some verity it may also have in it self, as truly declaring the corruptive constitution in the present sap and nutrimental juice of the Tree; and may consequently discover the disposition of that year, according to the plenty or kinds of these productions. For if the putrifying juices of bodies bring forth plenty of Flies and Maggots, they give forth testimony of *Abundance of Flies, Maggots,* common corruption, and declare that the Elements are *Maggots,* full of the seeds of putrifaction, as the great number *etc., what* of Caterpillars, Gnats, and ordinary Insects do also *may they* declare. If they run into Spiders, they give signs of *naturally signifie.* higher putrifaction, as plenty of Vipers and Scorpions are confessed to do; the putrifying Materials producing Animals of higher mischiefs, according to the advance and higher strain of corruption.

3. Whether all Plants have seed, were more easily determinable, if we could conclude concerning Harts-tongue, Fern, the Capillaries, Lunaria, and some others. But whether those little dusty particles, upon the lower side of the leaves, be seeds and seminal parts; or rather, as it is commonly conceived, excremental separations, we have not as yet been able to determine

by any germination or univocal production from them when they have been sowed on purpose : but having set the roots of Harts tongue in a garden, a year or two after there came up three or four of the same Plants, about two yards distance from the first. Thus much we observe, that they seem to renew yearly, and come not fully out till the Plant be in his vigour : and by the help of Magnifying Glasses we find these dusty Atoms to be round at first, and fully representing seeds, out of which at last proceed little Mites almost invisible ; so that such as are old stand open, as being emptied of some bodies formerly included ; which though discernable in Harts-tongue, is more notoriously discoverable in some differencies of Brake or Fern.

But exquisite Microscopes and Magnifying Glasses have at last cleared this doubt, whereby also long ago the noble *Fredericus Cæsius* beheld the dusts of Polypody as bigg as Pepper corns ; and as *Johannes Faber* testifieth, made draughts on Paper of such kind of seeds, as bigg as his Glasses represented them : and set down such Plants under the Classis of *Herbæ Tergifœtæ*, as may be observed in his notable Botanical Tables.

4. Whether the sap of Trees runs down to the roots in Winter, whereby they become naked and grow not; or whether they do not cease to draw any more, and reserve so much as sufficeth for conservation, is not a point indubitable. For we observe, that most Trees, as though they would be perpetually green, do bud at the Fall of the leaf, although they sprout not much forward untill the Spring, and warmer weather approacheth ; and many Trees maintain their leaves all Winter, although they seem to receive very small advantage in their growth. But that the sap doth powerfully rise in the Spring, to repair that moisture

whereby they barely subsisted in the Winter, and also to put the Plant in a capacity of fructification : he that hath beheld how many gallons of water may in a small time be drawn from a Birch-tree in the Spring, hath slender reason to doubt.

5. That *Camphire* Eunuchates, or begets in Men an impotency unto Venery, observation will hardly confirm ; and we have found it to fail in Cocks and Hens, though given for many days ; which was a more favourable trial then that of *Scaliger*, when he gave it unto a Bitch that was proud. For the instant turgescence is not to be taken off, but by Medicines of higher Natures ; and with any certainty but one way that we know, which notwithstanding, by suppressing that natural evacuation, may encline unto Madness, if taken in the Summer.

6. In the History of Prodigies we meet with many showrs of Wheat ; how true or probable, we have not room to debate. Only thus much we shall not omit to inform, That what was this year found in many places, and almost preached for Wheat rained from the clouds, was but the seed of Ivy-berries, which somewhat represent it ; and though it were found in Steeples and high places, might be conveyed thither, or muted out by Birds : for many feed thereon, and in the crops of some we have found no less then three ounces.

7. That every plant might receive a Name according unto the disease it cureth, was the wish of *Paracelsus*. A way more likely to multiply Empiricks then Herbalists ; yet what is practised by many is advantagious unto neither ; that is, relinquishing their proper appellations to re-baptize them by the name of Saints, Apostles, Patriarchs, and Martyrs, to call this the herb of *John*, that of *Peter*, this of *James*, or *Joseph*, that of

Mary or *Barbara*. For hereby apprehensions are made
additional unto their proper Natures; whereon superstitious practices ensue, and stories are framed
accordingly to make good their foundations.

8. We cannot omit to declare the gross mistake of
many in the Nominal apprehension of Plants; to instance but in few. An herb there is commonly called
Betonica Pauli, or *Pauls Betony*; hereof the People
have some conceit in reference to St. *Paul*; whereas
indeed that name is derived from *Paulus Ægineta*,
an ancient Physitian of *Ægina*, and is no more then
Speed-well, or *Fluellen*. The like expectations are
raised from *Herba Trinitatis*; which notwithstanding
obtaineth that name from the figure of its leaves, and
is one kind of Liverwort, or *Hepatica*. In *Milium
Solis*, the Epithete of the Sun hath enlarged its
opinion; which hath indeed no reference thereunto,
it being no more then *Lithospermon*, or *Grummel*, or
rather *Milium Soler*; which as *Serapion* from *Aben
Juliel* hath taught us, because it grew plentifully in
the Mountains of *Soler*, received that appellation. In
Jews-ears something is conceived extraordinary from
the Name, which is in propriety but *Fungus sambucinus*,
or an excrescence about the Roots of Elder, and concerneth not the Nation of the *Jews*, but *Judas Iscariot*,
upon a conceit, he hanged on this Tree; and is become
a famous Medicine in Quinsies, sore Throats, and
strangulations ever since. And so are they deceived
in the name of Horse-Raddish, Horse-Mint, Bull-rush,
and many more: conceiving therein some prenominal
consideration, whereas indeed that expression is but a
Grecism, by the prefix of *Hippos* and *Bous*, that is,
Horse and Bull, intending no more then Great.
According whereto the great Dock is called *Hippola-*

*Why the
Jews ear is
used for sore
Throats.*

pathum; and he that calls the Horse of *Alexander*, *Great-head*, expresseth the same which the *Greeks* do in *Bucephalus*.

9. Lastly, Many things are delivered and believed of other Plants, wherein at least we cannot but suspend. That there is a property in *Basil* to propagate Scorpions, and that by the smell thereof they are bred in the brains of men, is much advanced by *Hollerius*, who found•this Insect in the brains of a man that delighted much in this smell. Wherein beside that we find no way to conjoin the effect unto the cause assigned; herein the Moderns speak but timorously, and some of the Ancients quite contrarily. For, according unto *Oribasius*, Physitian unto *Julian*, The *Affricans*, Men best experienced in poisons, affirm, whosoever hath eaten *Basil*, although he be stung with a Scorpion, shall feel no pain thereby: which is a very different effect, and rather antidotally destroying, then seminally promoting its production.

That the leaves of *Catapucia* or Spurge, being plucked upward or downward, respectively perform their operations by Purge or Vomit, as some have written, and old wives still do preach, is a strange conceit, ascribing unto Plants positional operations, and after the manner of the Loadstone; upon the Pole whereof if a Knife be drawn from the handle unto the point, it will take up a Needle; but if drawn again from the point to the handle, it will attract it no more.

That Cucumbers are no commendable fruits, that being very waterish, they fill the veins with crude and windy serosities; that containing little Salt or spirit, they may also debilitate the vital acidity, and fermental faculty of the Stomach, we readily concede. But that they should be so cold, as be almost poison by that

U

quality, it will be hard to allow, without the contradiction of *Galen*: who accounteth them cold but in
the second degree, and in that Classis have most
Physitians placed them.

That Elder Berries are poison, as we are taught by
tradition, experience will unteach us. And beside the
promises of *Blochwitius*, the healthful effects thereof
daily observed will convict us.

That an Ivy Cup will separate Wine from Water, if
filled with both, the Wine soaking through, but the
Water still remaining, as after *Pliny* many have
averred, we know not how to affirm; who making
trial thereof, found both the liquors to soak indis-
tinctly through the bowl.

That Sheep do often get the Rot, by feeding in
boggy grounds where *Ros-solis* groweth, seems beyond
dispute. That this herb is the cause thereof, Shepherds
affirm and deny; whether it hath a cordial vertue by
sudden refection, sensible experiment doth hardly
confirm, but that it may have a Balsamical and resump-
tive Vertue, whereby it becomes a good Medicine in
Catarrhes and Consumptive dispositions, Practice and
Reason conclude. That the lentous drops upon it are
not extraneous, and rather an exudation from it self,
then a rorid concretion from without, beside other
grounds, we have reason to conceive; for having kept
the Roots moist and earthed in close chambers, they
have, though in lesser plenty, sent out these drops as
before.

That *Flos Affricanus* is poison, and destroyeth Dogs,
in two experiments we have not found.

That Yew and the Berries thereof are harmless,
we know.

That a Snake will not endure the shade of an Ash,

we can deny. Nor is it inconsiderable what is affirmed by *Bellonius*; for if his Assertion be true, our apprehension is oftentimes wide in ordinary simples, and in common use we mistake one for another. We know not the true Thyme; the Savourie in our Gardens is not that commended of old; and that kind of Hysop the Ancients used, is unknown unto us, who make great use of another.

We omit to recite the many Vertues, and endless faculties ascribed unto Plants, which sometime occur in grave and serious Authors; and we shall make a bad transaction for truth to concede a verity in half. To reckon up all, it were employment for *Archimedes*, who undertook to write the number of the Sands. Swarms of others there are, some whereof our future endeavours may discover; common reason I hope will save us a labour in many: Whose absurdities stand naked unto every eye; Errours not able to deceive the Embleme of Justice, and need no *Argus* to descry them. Herein there surely wants expurgatory animadversions, whereby we might strike out great numbers of hidden qualities; and having once a serious and conceded list, we might with more encouragement and safety attempt their Reasons.

THE THIRD BOOK

Of divers popular and received Tenets
concerning Animals, which examined,
prove either false or dubious.

CHAPTER I

Of the Elephant.

THE first shall be of the Elephant, whereof
there generally passeth an opinion it hath no
joints; and this absurdity is seconded with
another, that being unable to lie down, it sleepeth
against a Tree; which the Hunters observing, do saw
it almost asunder; whereon the Beast relying, by the
fall of the Tree, falls also down it self, and is able to
rise no more. Which conceit is not the daughter of
later times, but an old and gray-headed error, even in
the days of *Aristotle*, as he delivereth in his Book,
De incessu Animalium, and stands successively related
by several other authors: by *Diodorus Siculus*, *Strabo*,
Ambrose, *Cassiodore*, *Solinus*, and many more. Now
herein methinks men much forget themselves, not well
considering the absurdity of such assertions.

For first, they affirm it hath no joints, and yet
concede it walks and moves about; whereby they conceive there may be a progression or advancement made

in Motion without inflexion of parts. Now all progression or Animals locomotion being (as *Aristotle* teacheth) performed *tractu et pulsu*; that is, by drawing on, or impelling forward some part which was before in station, or at quiet; where there are no joints or flexures, neither can there be these actions. And this is true, not onely in Quadrupedes, Volatils, and Fishes, which have distinct and prominent Organs of Motion, Legs, Wings, and Fins; but in such also as perform their progression by the Trunk, as Serpents, Worms, and Leeches. Whereof though some want bones, and all extended articulations, yet have they arthritical Analogies, and by the motion of fibrous and musculous parts, are able to make progression. Which to conceive in bodies inflexible, and without all protrusion of parts, were to expect a Race from *Hercules* his pillars; or hope to behold the effects of *Orpheus* his Harp, when trees found joints, and danced after his Musick.

CHAP. I

How progression is made in animals.

Joint-like parts.

Again, While men conceive they never lie down, and enjoy not the position of rest, ordained unto all pedestrious Animals, hereby they imagine (what reason cannot conceive) that an Animal of the vastest dimension and longest duration, should live in a continual motion, without that alternity and vicissitude of rest whereby all others continue; and yet must thus much come to pass, if we opinion they lye not down and enjoy no decumbence at all. For station is properly no rest, but one kind of motion, relating unto that which Physitians (from *Galen*) do name extensive or tonical; that is, an extension of the muscles and organs of motion maintaining the body at length or in its proper figure.

Extensive or Tonical Motion, what?

Wherein although it seem to be unmoved, it is not

without all Motion; for in this position the muscles
are sensibly extended, and labour to support the body;
which permitted unto its proper gravity, would suddenly
subside and fall unto the earth; as it happeneth in
sleep, diseases, and death. From which occult action
and invisible motion of the muscles in station (as
Galen declareth) proceed more offensive lassitudes then
from ambulation. And therefore the Tyranny of some
have tormented men with long and enforced station,
and though *Ixion* and *Sisiphus* which always moved,
do seem to have the hardest measure; yet was not
Titius favoured, that lay extended upon *Caucasus*;
and *Tantalus* suffered somewhat more then thirst, that
stood perpetually in Hell. Thus *Mercurialis* in his
Gymnasticks justly makes standing one kind of exercise; and *Galen* when we lie down, commends unto us
middle figures, that is, not to lye directly, or at length,
but somewhat inflected, that the muscles may be at
rest; for such as he termeth *Hypobolemaioi* or figures, of
excess, either shrinking up or stretching out, are weari-
some positions, and such as perturb the quiet of those
parts. Now various parts do variously discover these
indolent and quiet positions, some in right lines, as
the wrists: some at right angles, as the cubit:
others at oblique angles, as the fingers and the
knees: all resting satisfied in postures of moderation, and none enduring the extremity of flexure or
extension.

Moreover men herein do strangely forget the obvious
relations of history, affirming they have no joints,
whereas they dayly read of several actions which are
not performable without them. They forget what is
delivered by *Xiphilinus*, and also by *Suetonius* in the
lives of *Nero* and *Galba*, that Elephants have been

instructed to walk on ropes, in publick shews before CHAP.
the people. Which is not easily performed by man, I
and requireth not only a broad foot, but a pliable
flexure of joints, and commandible disposure of all parts
of progression. They pass by that memorable place in
Curtius, concerning the Elephant of King *Porus, Indus
qui Elephantem regebat, descendere eum ratus, more solito
procumbere jussit in genua cœteri quoque (ita enim
instituti erant) demisere corpora in terram.* They De rebus
remember not the expression of *Osorius,* when he gestis
speaks of the Elephant presented to *Leo* the tenth, Emanuelis.
*Pontificem ter genibus flexis, et demisso corporis habitu
venerabundus salutavit.* But above all, they call not
to mind that memorable shew of *Germanicus,* wherein
twelve Elephants danced unto the sound of Musick,
and after laid them down in the *Tricliniums,* or places
of festival Recumbency.

They forget the Etymologie of the Knee, approved Γόνυ *from*
by some Grammarians. They disturb the position of γωνία.
the young ones in the womb : which upon extension of
legs is not easily conceivable ; and contrary unto the
general contrivance of Nature. Nor do they consider
the impossible exclusion thereof, upon extension and
rigour of the legs.

Lastly, they forget or consult not experience, whereof
not many years past, we have had the advantage in
England, by an Elephant shewn in many parts thereof,
not only in the posture of standing, but kneeling and
lying down. Whereby although the opinion at present
be well suppressed, yet from some strings of tradition,
and fruitful recurrence of errour, it is not improbable
it may revive in the next generation again. This being
not the first that hath been seen in *England* ; for
(besides some others) as *Polydore Virgil* relateth, *Lewis*

the French King sent one to Henry the third, and *Emanuel* of *Portugal* another to *Leo* the tenth into *Italy*, where notwithstanding the errour is still alive and epidemical, as with us.

Round, Pillar-like.
The hint and ground of this opinion might be the gross and somewhat Cylindrical composure of the legs, the equality and less perceptible disposure of the joints, especially in the former legs of this Animal; they appearing when he standeth, like Pillars of flesh, without any evidence of articulation. The different flexure and order of the joints might also countenance the same, being not disposed in the Elephant, as they are in other quadrupedes, but carry a nearer conformity unto those of Man; that is, the bought of the fore-legs, not directly backward, but laterally and somewhat inward; but the hough or suffraginous flexure behind rather outward. Somewhat different unto many other quadrupedes, as Horses, Camels, Deer, Sheep, and Dogs; for their fore-legs bend like our legs, and their hinder legs like our arms, when we move them to our shoulders. But quadrupedes oviparous, as Frogs, Lizards, Crocodiles, have their joints and motive flexures more analogously framed unto ours; and some among viviparous, that is, such thereof as can bring their fore-feet and meat therein unto their mouths, as most can do that have the clavicles or coller-bones: whereby their brests are broader, and their shoulders more asunder, as the Ape, the Monkey, the Squirrel and some others. If therefore any shall affirm the joints of Elephants are differently framed from most of other quadrupedes, and more obscurely and grosly almost then any, he doth herein no injury unto truth. But if *à dicto secundum quid ad dictum simpliciter*, he affirmeth also they have no articulations at all, he incurs the

controulment of reason, and cannot avoide the contradiction also of sense.

As for the manner of their venation, if we consult
historical experience, we shall find it to be otherwise
then as is commonly presumed, by sawing away of
Trees. The accounts whereof are to be seen at large
in *Johannes*, *Hugo*, *Edwardus Lopez*, *Garcias ab horto*,
Cadamustus, and many more.

Other concernments there are of the Elephant, which
might admit of discourse; and if we should question
the teeth of Elephants, that is, whether they be properly so termed, or might not rather be called horns:
it were no new enquiry of mine, but a Paradox as old
as *Oppianus*. Whether as *Pliny* and divers since affirm *Cyneget.*
it, that Elephants are terrified, and make away upon *lib. 2.*
the grunting of Swine, *Garcias ab horto* may decide,
who affirmeth upon experience, they enter their stalls,
and live promiscuously in the Woods of *Malavar*.
That the situation of the genitals is averse, and their
copulation like that which some believe of Camels, as
Pliny hath also delivered, is not to be received; for we
have beheld that part in a different position; and
their coition is made by supersaliency, like that of
horses, as we are informed by some who have beheld
them in that act. That some Elephants have not
only written whole sentences, as *Ælian* ocularly testifieth, but have also spoken, as *Oppianus* delivereth,
and *Christophorus à Costa* particularly relateth;
although it sound like that of *Achilles* Horse in *Homer*,
we do not conceive impossible. Nor beside the affinity *Some* Brutes
of reason in this Animal any such intollerable inca- *tolerably*
pacity in the organs of divers quadrupedes, whereby *well organ-*
they might not be taught to speak, or become imita- *speech and*
tors of speech like Birds. Strange it is how the *to reason.*

curiosity of men that have been active in the instruc-
tion of Beasts, have never fallen upon this artifice;
and among those, many paradoxical and unheard of
imitations, should not attempt to make one speak.
The Serpent that spake unto *Eve*, the Dogs and Cats
that usually speak unto Witches, might afford some
encouragement. And since broad and thick chops are
required in Birds that speak, since lips and teeth are
also organs of speech; from these there is also an
advantage in quadrupedes, and a proximity of reason
in Elephants and Apes above them all. Since also an
Echo will speak without any mouth at all, articulately
returning the voice of man, by only ordering the
vocal spirit in concave and hollow places; whether
the musculous and motive parts about the hollow
mouths of Beasts, may not dispose the passing spirit
into some articulate notes, seems a query of no great
doubt.

CHAPTER II

Of the Horse.

THE second Assertion, that an Horse hath no
gall, is very general, nor only swallowed by
the people, and common Farriers, but also
Veterinarians received by good *Veterinarians*, and some who have
or Farriers. laudably discoursed upon Horses. It seemeth also
very ancient; for it is plainly set down by *Aristotle*,
an Horse and all solid ungulous or whole hoofed
animals have no gall; and the same is also delivered
by *Pliny*, which notwithstanding we find repugnant
unto experience and reason. For first, it calls in

question the providence or wise provision of Nature;
who not abounding in superfluities, is neither deficient
in necessities. Wherein nevertheless there would be a
main defect, and her improvision justly accusable, if
such a feeding Animal, and so subject unto diseases
from bilious causes, should want a proper conveyance
for choler; or have no other receptacle for that humour
then the Veins, and general mass of bloud.

It is again controllable by experience, for we have
made some search and enquiry herein; encouraged by
Absyrtus a Greek Author, in the time of *Constantine,* Medicina
who in his Hippiatricks, obscurely assigneth the gall a equaria.
place in the liver; but more especially by *Carlo Ruini*
the *Bononian,* who in his *Anatomia del Cavallo,* hath
more plainly described it, and in a manner as I found
it. For in the particular enquiry into that part, in
the concave or simous part of the Liver, whereabout
the Gall is usually seated in quadrupedes, I discover an
hollow, long and membranous substance, of a pale
colour without, and lined with Choler and Gall within;
which part is by branches diffused into the lobes and
several parcels of the Liver; from whence receiving the
fiery superfluity, or cholerick remainder, by a manifest
and open passage, it conveyeth it into the *duodenum*
or upper gut, thence into the lower bowels; which is
the manner of its derivation in Man and other Animals.
And therefore although there be no eminent and
circular follicle, no round bag or vesicle which long
containeth this humour: yet is there a manifest
receptacle and passage of choler from the Liver into
the Guts: which being not so shut up, or at least not
so long detained, as it is in other Animals: procures
that frequent excretion, and occasions the Horse to
dung more often then many other, which considering

the plentiful feeding, the largeness of the guts, and their various circumvolution, was prudently contrived by providence in this Animal. For choler is the natural Glister, or one excretion whereby Nature excludeth another; which descending daily into the bowels, extimulates those parts, and excites them unto expulsion. And therefore when this humour aboundeth or corrupteth, there succeeds oft-times a *cholerica passio*, that is, a sudden and vehement Purgation upward and downward: and when the passage of gall becomes obstructed, the body grows costive, and the excrements of the belly white; as it happeneth in the Jaundice.

If any therefore affirm an Horse hath no gall, that is, no receptacle, or part ordained for the separation of Choler, or not that humour at all; he hath both sense and reason to oppose him. But if he saith it hath no bladder of Gall, and such as is observed in many other Animals, we shall oppose our sense, if we gain-say him. Thus must *Aristotle* be made out when he denieth this part, by this distinction we may relieve *Pliny* of a contradiction, who in one place affirming an Horse hath no gall, delivereth yet in another, that the gall of an Horse was accounted poison; and therefore at the sacrifices of Horses in *Rome*, it was unlawful for

the *Flamen* to touch it. But with more difficulty, or hardly at all is that reconcileable which is delivered by our Countryman, and received *Veterinarian*; whose words in his Master-piece, and Chapter of diseases from the Gall, are somewhat too strict, and scarce admit a Reconciliation. The fallacie therefore of this conceit is not unlike the former; *A dicto secundum quid ad dictum simpliciter.* Because they have not a bladder of gall, like those we usually observe in others, they have no gall at all. Which is a Paralogism not

admittible; a fallacy that dwels not in a cloud, and
needs not the Sun to scatter it.

CHAPTER III

Of the Dove.

THE third assertion is somewhat like the second, that a Dove or Pigeon hath no gall; which is affirmed from very great antiquity; for as *Pierius* observeth, from this consideration the Egyptians did make it the Hieroglyphick of Meekness. It hath been averred by many holy Writers, commonly delivered by *Postillers* and *Commentators*; who from the frequent mention of the Dove in the *Canticles*, the precept of our Saviour, to be wise as Serpents, and innocent as Doves: and especially the appearance of the Holy Ghost in the similitude of this Animal, have taken occasion to set down many affections of the Dove, and what doth most commend it, is, that it hath no gall. And hereof have made use not only Minor Divines, but *Cyprian, Austin, Isidore, Beda, Rupertus, Jansenius,* and many more.

Whereto notwithstanding we know not how to assent, it being repugnant unto the Authority and positive determination of ancient Philosophy. The affirmative of *Aristotle* in his History of Animals is very plain, *Fel aliis ventri, aliis intestino jungitur*: Some have the gall adjoined to the guts, as the Crow, the Swallow, Sparrow, and the Dove; the same is also attested by *Pliny,* and not without some passion by *Galen,* who in his Book *De Atra bile,* accounts him ridiculous that denies it.

It is not agreeable to the constitution of this

Animal, nor can we so reasonably conceive there wants
a Gall: that is, the hot and fiery humour in a body so
hot of temper, which Phlegm or Melancholy could not
effect.   Now of what complexion it is, *Julius Alexandrinus* declareth, when he affirmeth that some upon
the use thereof, have fallen into Feavers and Quinsies.
The temper of their Dung and intestinal Excretions do
also confirm the same; which Topically applied become
a *Phœnigmus* or Rubifying Medicine, and are of such
fiery parts, that as we read in *Galen*, they have of
themselves conceived fire, and burnt a house about
them.   And therefore when in the famine of *Samaria*
(wherein the fourth part of a Cab of Pigeons dung was
sold for five pieces of silver,) it is delivered by *Josephus*,
that men made use hereof in stead of common Salt:
although the exposition seem strange, it is more probable then many other.   For that it containeth very
much Salt, as beside the effects before expressed, is
discernable by taste, and the earth of Columbaries or
Dove-houses, so much desired in the artifice of Salt-
petre.   And to speak generally, the Excrement of
Birds hath more of Salt and acrimony, then that of
other pissing animals.   Now if because the Dove is of
a mild and gentle nature, we cannot conceive it should
be of an hot temper; our apprehensions are not
distinct in the measure of constitutions, and the

*Whence the
irascible,
whence the
concupiscible
Passions do
most arise.*

several parts which evidence such conditions.   For the
Irascible passions do follow the temper of the heart,
but the concupiscible distractions the crasis of the
liver.   Now many have hot livers, which have but cool
and temperate hearts; and this was probably the
temper of *Paris*, a contrary constitution to that of
Ajax, and both but short of *Medea*, who seemed to
exceed in either.

Lastly, it is repugnant to experience, for Anatomical
enquiry discovereth in them a gall: and that according
to the determination of *Aristotle*, not annexed unto the
liver, but adhering unto the guts: nor is the humour
contained in smaller veins, or obscurer capillations, but
in a vescicle, or little bladder, though some affirm it
hath no bag at all. And therefore the Hieroglyphick
of the Ægyptians, though allowable in the sense, is
weak in the foundation: who expressing meekness and
lenity by the portract of a Dove with a tail erected,
affirmed it had no gall in the inward parts, but only in
the rump, and as it were out of the body. And therefore also if they conceived their gods were pleased with
the sacrifice of this Animal, as being without gall, the
ancient Heathens were surely mistaken in the reason,
and in the very oblation. Whereas in the holocaust
or burnt-offering of *Moses*, the gall was cast away: for
as *Ben Maimon* instructeth, the inwards whereto the Levit. 1.
gall adhereth were taken out with the crop, according
unto the Law: which the Priest did not burn, but
cast unto the East, that is, behind his back, and
readiest place to be carried out of the Sanctuary. And
if they also conceived that for this reason they were
the Birds of *Venus*, and wanting the furious and dis- *Doves, the*
cording part, were more acceptable unto the Deity *Birds of*
of Love, they surely added unto the conceit, which *Venus, why!*
was at first venereal: and in this Animal may be
sufficiently made out from that conception.

The ground of this conceit is partly like the former,
the obscure situation of the gall, and out of the liver,
wherein it is commonly enquired. But this is a very
injust illation, not well considering with what variety
this part is seated in Birds. In some both at the
stomach and the liver, as in the Capriceps; in some at

Ἐγκρασίχολος.

the liver only, as in Cocks, Turkeys, and Pheasants; in others at the guts and liver, as in Hawks and Kites, in some at the guts alone, as Crows, Doves, and many more. And these perhaps may take up all the ways of situation, not only in Birds, but also other Animals; for what is said of the Anchovie, that answerable unto its name, it carrieth the gall in the head, is farther to be enquired. And though the discoloured particles in the skin of an Heron be commonly termed Galls, yet is not this Animal deficient in that part, but containeth it in the Liver. And thus when it is conceived that the eyes of *Tobias* were cured by the gall of the fish *Callyonimus*, or *Scorpius marinus*, commended to that effect by *Dioscorides*, although that part were not in the liver, yet there were no reason to doubt that probability. And whatsoever Animal it was, it may be received without exception, when it's delivered, the married couple as a testimony of future concord, did cast the gall of the sacrifice behind the Altar.

A strict and literal acception of a loose and tropical expression was a second ground hereof. For while some affirmed it had no gall, intending only thereby no evidence of anger or fury; others have construed it anatomically, and denied that part at all. By which illation we may infer, and that from sacred Text, a Pigeon hath no heart; according to that expression, *Factus est Ephraim sicut Columba seducta non habens Cor.* And so from the letter of the Scripture we may conclude it is no mild, but a fiery and furious animal, according to that of *Jeremy, Facta est terra in desolationem à facie iræ Columbæ*: and again, *Revertamur ad terram nativitatis nostræ à facie gladii Columbæ.* Where notwithstanding the Dove is not literally

Hosea 7.

Cap. 25.
Cap. 46.

intended; but thereby may be implied the *Babylonians*, whose Queen *Semiramis* was called by that name, and whose successors did bear the Dove in their Standard.　So is it proverbially said, *Formicæ sua bilis inest, habet et musca splenem*; whereas we know Philosophy doubteth these parts, nor hath *Anatomy* so clearly discovered them in those insects.

If therefore any affirm a Pigeon hath no gall, implying no more thereby then the lenity of this Animal, we shall not controvert his affirmation.　Thus may we make out the assertions of Ancient Writers, and safely receive the expressions of Divines and worthy Fathers. But if by a transition from Rhetorick to Logick, he shall contend, it hath no such part or humour, he committeth an open fallacy, and such as was probably first committed concerning *Spanish* Mares, whose swiftness tropically expressed from their generation by the wind; might after be grosly taken, and a real truth conceived in that conception.

CHAPTER IV

Of the Bever.

THAT a Bever to escape the Hunter, bites off his testicles or stones, is a Tenet very ancient; and hath had thereby advantage of propagation.　For the same we find in the Hieroglyphicks of the Egyptians in the Apologue of *Æsop*, an Author of great Antiquity, who lived in the beginning of the *Persian* Monarchy, and in the time of *Cyrus*: the same is touched by *Aristotle* in his Ethicks, but seriously delivered by *Ælian*, *Pliny*, and *Solinus*: the same we meet with in *Juvenal*, who by an

Æsops Apologues, of what antiquity.

handsome and Metrical expression more welcomly
engrafts it in our junior Memories:

> —— *imitatus Castora, qui se*
> *Eunuchum ipse facit, cupiens evadere damno*
> *Testiculorum, adeo medicatum intelligit inguen.*

It hath been propagated by Emblems: and some have
been so bad Grammarians as to be deceived by the
Name, deriving *Castor à castrando*, whereas the proper
Latine word is *Fiber*, and *Castor* but borrowed from
the Greek, so called *quasi γάϛωρ*, that is, *Animal
ventricosum*, from his swaggy and prominent belly.

Herein therefore to speak compendiously, we first
presume to affirm that from strict enquiry, we cannot
maintain the evulsion or biting off any parts, and this
is declarable from the best and most professed Writers:
for though some have made use hereof in a Moral or
Tropical way, yet have the professed Discoursers by
silence deserted, or by experience rejected this assertion. Thus was it in ancient times discovered, and
experimentally refuted by one *Sestius* a Physitian, as
it stands related by *Pliny*; by *Dioscorides*, who plainly
affirms that this tradition is false; by the discoveries
of Modern Authors, who have expressly discoursed
hereon, as *Aldrovandus, Mathiolus, Gesnerus, Bellonius*;
by *Olaus Magnus, Peter Martyr*, and others, who have
described the manner of their Venations in *America*;
they generally omitting this way of their escape, and
have delivered several other, by which they are daily
taken.

The original of the conceit was probably Hieroglyphical, which after became Mythological unto the
Greeks, and so set down by *Æsop*; and by process of
tradition, stole into a total verity, which was but par-
tially true, that is in its covert sense and Morality.

Now why they placed this invention upon the Bever
(beside the Medicable and Merchantable commodity
of *Castoreum*, or parts conceived to be bitten away)
might be the sagacity and wisdom of that Animal,
which from the works it performs, and especially its
Artifice in building, is very strange, and surely not to
be matched by any other. Omitted by *Plutarch*, *De
solertia Animalium*, but might have much advantaged
the drift of that Discourse.

If therefore any affirm a wise man should demean
himself like the Bever, who to escape with his life,
contemneth the loss of his genitals, that is in case of
extremity, not strictly to endeavour the preservation
of all, but to sit down in the enjoyment of the greater
good, though with the detriment and hazard of the
lesser; we may hereby apprehend a real and useful Truth.
In this latitude of belief, we are content to receive the
Fable of *Hippomanes*, who redeemed his life with the
loss of a Golden Ball; and whether true or false, we
reject not the Tragœdy of *Absyrtus*, and the dispersion
of his Members by *Medea*, to perplex the pursuit of her
Father. But if any shall positively affirm this act,
and cannot believe the Moral, unless he also credit the
Fable; he is surely greedy of delusion, and will hardly
avoid deception in theories of this Nature. The
Error therefore and Alogy in this opinion, is worse
then in the last; that is, not to receive Figures for
Realities, but expect a verity in Apologues; and
believe, as serious affirmations, confessed and studied
Fables.

Again, If this were true, and that the Bever in chase
makes some divulsion of parts, as that which we call
Castoreum; yet are not the same to be termed Testicles
or Stones; for these Cods or Follicles are found in

both Sexes, though somewhat more protuberant in the Male. There is hereto no derivation of the seminal parts, nor any passage from hence, unto the Vessels of Ejaculation: some perforations onely in the part it self, through which the humour included doth exudate: as may be observed in such as are fresh, and not much dried with age. And lastly, The Testicles properly so called, are of a lesser magnitude, and seated inwardly upon the loins: and therefore it were not only a fruitless attempt, but impossible act, to Eunuchate or castrate themselves: and might be an hazardous practice of Art, if at all attempted by others.

Now all this is confirmed from the experimental Testimony of five very memorable Authors: *Bellonius, Gesnerus, Amatus, Rondeletius,* and *Mathiolus*: who receiving the hint hereof from *Rondeletius* in the Anatomy of two Bevers, did find all true that had been delivered by him, whose words are these in his learned Book *De Piscibus: Fibri in inguinibus geminos tumores habent, utrinque vnicum, ovi Anserini magnitudine, inter hos est mentula in maribus, in fœminis pudendum, hi tumores testes non sunt, sed folliculi membrana contecti, in quorum medio singuli sunt meatus è quibus exudat liquor pinguis et cerosus, quem ipse Castor sæpe admoto ore lambit et exugit, postea veluti oleo, corporis partes oblinit: Hos tumores testes non esse hinc maxime colligitur, quod ab illis nulla est ad mentulam via neque ductus quo humor in mentulæ meatum derivitur, et foras emittatur; præterea quod testes intus reperiuntur, eosdem tumores Moscho animali inesse puto, è quibus odoratum illud plus emanat.* Then which words there can be no plainer, nor more evidently discovering the impropriety of this appellation. That which is included in the cod or visible bag about the groin, being not the

Testicle, or any spermatical part; but rather a collection of some superfluous matter deflowing from the body, especially the parts of nutrition as unto their proper emunctories; and as it doth in Musk and Civet Cats, though in a different and offensive odour; proceeding partly from its food, that being especially Fish; whereof this humour may be a garous excretion and olidous separation.

Most therefore of the Moderns before *Rondeletius*, and all the Ancients excepting *Sestius*, have misunderstood this part, conceiving *Castoreum* the Testicles of the *Bever*; as *Dioscorides*, *Galen*, *Ægineta*, *Ætius*, and others have pleased to name it. The Egyptians also failed in the ground of their Hieroglyphick, when they expressed the punishment of Adultery by the Bever depriving himself of his testicles, which was amongst them the penalty of such incontinency. Nor is *Ætius* perhaps, too strictly to be observed, when he prescribeth the stones of the Otter, or River-dog, as succedaneous unto *Castoreum*. But most inexcusable of all is *Pliny*; who having before him in one place the experiment of *Sestius* against it, sets down in another, that the *Bevers* of *Pontus* bite off their testicles: and in the same place affirmeth the like of the *Hyena*. Which was indeed well joined with the Bever, as having also a bag in those parts; if thereby we understand the *Hyena odorata*, or Civet Cat, as is delivered and graphically described by *Castellus*.

Castellus de Hyena odorifera.

Now the ground of this mistake might be the resemblance and situation of these tumours about those parts, wherein we observe the testicles in other animals. Which notwithstanding is no well founded illation, for the testicles are defined by their office, and not determined by place or situation; they having one office in all, but different seats in many. For beside that, no Serpent, or Fishes oviparous, that neither biped nor quadruped oviparous have testicles exteriourly, or prominent in the groin; some also that are viviparous contain these parts within, as beside this Animal, the Elephant and the Hedg-hog.

If any therefore shall term these testicles, intending metaphorically, and in no strict accception; his language is tolerable, and offends our ears no more then the Tropical names of Plants: when we read in Herbals, of Dogs, Fox, and Goat-stones. But if he insisteth thereon, and maintaineth a propriety in this language: our discourse hath overthrown his assertion, nor will Logic permit his illation; that is, from things alike, to conclude a thing the same; and from an accidental convenience, that is a similitude in place or figure, to infer a specifical congruity or substantial concurrence in Nature.

CHAPTER V

Of the Badger.

THAT a Brock or Badger hath the legs on one side shorter then of the other, though an opinion perhaps not very ancient, is yet very general; received not only by Theorists and unexperienced believers, but assented unto by most who have the opportunity to behold and hunt them daily. Which notwithstanding upon enquiry I find repugnant unto the three Determinators of Truth, Authority, Sense, and Reason. For first, *Albertus Magnus* speaks dubiously, confessing he could not confirm the verity hereof; but *Aldrovandus* plainly affirmeth, there can be no such inequality observed. And for my own part, upon indifferent enquiry, I cannot discover this difference, although the regardable side be defined, and the brevity by most imputed unto the left.

Again, It seems no easie affront unto Reason, and generally repugnant unto the course of Nature; for if we survey the total set of Animals, we may in their legs, or Organs of progression, observe an equality of length, and parity of Numeration; that is, not any to have an odd legg, or the supporters and movers of one side not exactly answered by the other. Although the hinder may be unequal unto the fore and middle legs, as in Frogs, Locusts, and Grasshoppers; or both unto the middle, as in some Beetles and Spiders, as is determined by *Aristotle, De incessu Animalium*. Perfect and viviparous quadrupeds, so standing in their position of proneness, that the opposite joints of Neighbour-legs consist in the same plane; and a line descending from their Navel intersects at right angles the axis of the Earth. It happeneth often I confess that a Lobster hath the Chely or great claw of one side longer then the other; but this is not properly their leg, but a part of apprehension, and whereby they hold or seiz upon their prey; for the legs and proper parts of progression are inverted backward, and stand in a position opposite unto these.

De incessu Animalium.

Lastly, The Monstrosity is ill contrived, and with some disadvantage; the shortness being affixed unto the legs of one side, which might have been more tolerably placed upon the thwart or Diagonial Movers. For the progression of quadrupeds being performed *per Diametrum*, that is the cross legs moving or resting together, so that two are always in motion, and two in

Diagonion, *a line drawn from the cross angles.*

CHAP. station at the same time; the brevity had been more
V tolerable in the cross legs. For then the Motion and
station had been performed by equal legs; whereas
herein they are both performed by unequal Organs,
and the imperfection becomes discoverable at every
hand.

CHAPTER VI

Of the Bear.

THAT a Bear brings forth her young informous
and unshapen, which she fashioneth after by
licking them over, is an opinion not only
vulgar, and common with us at present: but hath been
of old delivered by ancient Writers. Upon this foundation it was an Hieroglyphick with the Egyptians:
Aristotle seems to countenance it; *Solinus, Pliny,* and
Ælian directly affirm it, and *Ovid* smoothly delivereth it:

> *Nec catulus partu quem reddidit ursa recenti*
> *Sed male viva caro est, lambendo mater in artus*
> *Ducit, et in formam qualem cupit ipsa reducit.*

Which notwithstanding is not only repugnant unto
the sense of every one that shall enquire into it, but
the exact and deliberate experiment of three Authentick Philosophers. The first of *Mathiolus* in his
Comment on *Dioscorides,* whose words are to this
effect. In the Valley of *Anania* about *Trent,* in a
Bear which the Hunters eventerated or opened, I
beheld the young ones with all their parts distinct:
and not without shape, as many conceive; giving more
credit unto *Aristotle* and *Pliny,* then experience and
their proper senses. Of the same assurance was *Julius*

Scaliger in his Exercitations, *Ursam fœtus informes potius ejicere, quam parere, si vera dicunt, quos postea linctu effingat: Quid hujusce fabulæ authoribus fidei habendum ex hac historia cognosces; In nostris Alpibus venatores fœtum Ursam cepere, dissecta ea fœtus plane formatus intus inventus est.* And lastly, *Aldrovandus* who from the testimony of his own eyes affirmeth, that in the Cabinet of the Senate of *Bononia*, there was preserved in a Glass a Cub taken out of a Bear perfectly formed, and compleat in every part.

It is moreover injurious unto Reason, and much impugneth the course and providence of Nature, to conceive a birth should be ordained before there is a formation. For the conformation of parts is necessarily required, not onely unto the pre-requisites and previous conditions of birth, as Motion and Animation: but also unto the parturition or very birth it self. Wherein not only the Dam, but the younglings play their parts; and the cause and act of exclusion proceedeth from them both. For the exclusion of Animals is not meerly passive like that of Eggs, nor the total action of delivery to be imputed unto the Mother: but the first attempt beginneth from the Infant: which at the accomplished period attempteth to change his Mansion: and struling to come forth, dilacerates and breaks those parts which restrained him before.

Beside (what few take notice of) Men hereby do in an high measure vilifie the works of God, imputing that unto the tongue of a Beast, which is the strangest Artifice in all the acts of Nature; that is the formation *Formation in the Matrix, the* of the infant in the Womb, not only in Mankind, but all viviparous Animals. Wherein the plastick or for- *admirable work of Nature.* mative faculty, from matter appearing Homogeneous, and of a similar substance, erecteth Bones, Membranes, Veins, and Arteries: and out of these contriveth every part in number, place, and figure, according to the law of its species. Which is so far from being fashioned by any outward agent, that once omitted or perverted by a slip of the inward *Phidias*, it is not reducible by any other whatsoever. And therefore *Mirè me plasmaverunt manus tuæ*, though it originally respected the generation of Man, yet is it appliable unto that of other Animals; who entring the Womb in bare and simple Materials, return with distinction of parts, and the perfect breath of life. He that shall consider these alterations without, must needs conceive there have been strange operations within; which to behold, it were a spectacle almost worth ones beeing, a sight beyond all; except that Man had been created first, and might have seen the shew of five dayes after.

Now as the opinion is repugnant both unto sense and Reason, so hath it probably been occasioned from some slight ground in either. Thus in regard the Cub comes forth involved in the Chorion, a thick and tough Membrane obscuring the formation, and which the Dam doth after bite and tear asunder; the beholder at first sight conceives it a rude and informous lump of flesh, and imputes the ensuing shape unto the Mouthing of the Dam; which addeth nothing thereunto, but only draws the curtain, and takes away the vail which concealed the Piece before. And thus have some endeavoured to enforce the same from Reason; that is, the small and slender time of the Bears gestation, or going with her young; which lasting but few days (a Month some say) the exclusion becomes precipitous, and the young ones consequently informous; according to that of *Solinus, Trigesimus dies uterum liberat ursæ;*

unde evenit ut præcipitata fœcunditas informes creet CHAP.
partus. But this will overthrow the general Method VI
of Nature in the works of generation. For therein
the conformation is not only antecedent, but proportional unto the exclusion; and if the period of the
birth be short, the term of conformation will be as
sudden also. There may I confess from this narrow
time of gestation ensue a Minority or smalness in the
exclusion; but this however inferreth no informity,
and it still receiveth the Name of a natural and legiti-
mate birth; whereas if we affirm a total informity, it
cannot admit so forward a term as an Abortment, for Εκρυσις.
that supposeth conformation. So we must call this
constant and intended act of Nature, a slip or effluxion,
that is an exclusion before conformation: before the
birth can bear the name of the Parent, or be so much
as properly called an *Embryon.*

CHAPTER VII

Of the Basilisk.

MANY Opinions are passant concerning the
Basilisk or little King of Serpents, commonly
called the Cockatrice: some affirming, others
denying, most doubting the relations made hereof.
What therefore in these incertainties we may more
safely determine : that such an Animal there is, if we
evade not the testimony of Scripture and humane
Writers, we cannot safely deny. So it is said *Psalm* 91.
Super Aspidem et Basiliscum ambulabis, wherein the
Vulgar Translation retaineth the Word of the Septuagint, using in other places the Latine expression *Regulus,* as *Proverbs* 23. *Mordebit ut coluber, et sicut*

Regulus venena diffundet: and *Jeremy* 8. *Ecce ego
mittam vobis serpentes Regulos, etc.* That is, as ours
translate it, *Behold I will send Serpents, Cockatrices
among you which will not be charmed, and they shall
bite you.* And as for humane Authors, or such as have
discoursed of Animals, or Poisons, it is to be found
almost in all: in *Dioscorides, Galen, Pliny, Solinus,
Ælian, Ætius, Avicen, Ardoynus, Grevinus,* and many
more. In *Aristotle* I confess we find no mention
thereof, but *Scaliger* in his Comment and enumeration
of Serpents, hath made supply; and in his Exercitations delivereth that a Basilisk was found in *Rome,*
in the days of *Leo* the fourth. The like is reported
by *Sigonius*; and some are so far from denying one,
that they have made several kinds thereof: for such is
the *Catoblepas* of *Pliny* conceived to be by some, and
the *Dryinus* of *Ætius* by others.

But although we deny not the existence of the Basilisk, yet whether we do not commonly mistake in the
conception hereof, and call that a Basilisk which is
none at all, is surely to be questioned. For certainly
that which from the conceit of its generation we vulgarly call a Cockatrice, and wherein (but under a
different name) we intend a formal Identity and
adequate conception with the Basilisk; is not the
Basilisk of the Ancients, whereof such wonders are
delivered. For this of ours is generally described with
legs, wings, a Serpentine and winding tail, and a crist
or comb somewhat like a Cock. But the Basilisk of
elder times was a proper kind of Serpent, not above
three palms long, as some account; and differenced
from other Serpents by advancing his head, and some
white marks or coronary spots upon the crown, as all
authentick Writers have delivered.

Nor is this Cockatrice only unlike the Basilisk, but   CHAP.
of no real shape in Nature; and rather an Hierogly-   VII
phical fansie, to express different intentions, set forth
in different fashions. Sometimes with the head of a
Man, sometime with the head of an Hawk, as *Pierius*
hath delivered; and as with addition of legs the Heralds
and Painters still describe it. Nor was it only of old a
symbolical and allowable invention, but is now become
a manual contrivance of Art, and artificial imposure;
whereof besides others, *Scaliger* hath taken notice:
*Basilici formam mentiti sunt vulgo Gallinaceo similem,
et pedibus binis; neque enim absimiles sunt cæteris ser-
pentibus, nisi macula quasi in vertice candida, unde illi
nomen Regium;* that is, men commonly counterfeit
the form of a Basilisk with another like a Cock, and
with two feet; whereas they differ not from other
serpents, but in a white speck upon their Crown. Now
although in some manner it might be counterfeited in
Indian Cocks, and flying Serpents, yet is it commonly
contrived out of the skins of Thornbacks, Scaits, or
Maids, as *Aldrovand* hath observed, and also graphi- *By way of*
cally described in his excellent Book of Fishes; and *figure.*
for satisfaction of my own curiosity I have caused some
to be thus contrived out of the same Fishes.

Nor is onely the existency of this animal considerable, but many things delivered thereof, particularly its
poison and its generation. Concerning the first, according to the doctrine of the Ancients, men still affirm,
that it killeth at a distance, that it poisoneth by the
eye, and by priority of vision. Now that deleterious *Destructive.*
it may be at some distance, and destructive without
corporal contaction, what uncertainty soever there be
in the effect, there is no high improbabil;cy in the
relation. For if Plagues or pestilential Atoms have

been conveyed in the Air from different Regions, if men at a distance have infected each other, if the shadows of some trees be noxious, if *Torpedoes* deliver their opium at a distance, and stupifie beyond themselves; we cannot reasonably deny, that (beside our gross and restrained poisons requiring contiguity unto their actions) there may proceed from subtiller seeds, more agile emanations, which contemn those Laws, and invade at distance unexpected.

Effluxion of corporeal species.

That this venenation shooteth from the eye, and that this way a Basilisk may empoison, although thus much be not agreed upon by Authors, some imputing it unto the breath, others unto the bite, it is not a thing impossible. For eyes receive offensive impressions from their objects, and may have influences destructive to each other. For the visible species of things strike not our senses immaterially, but streaming in corporal raies, do carry with them the qualities of the object from whence they flow, and the medium through which they pass. Thus through a green or red Glass all things we behold appear of the same colours; thus sore eyes affect those which are sound, and themselves also by reflection, as will happen to an inflamed eye that beholds it self long in a Glass; thus is fascination made out, and thus also it is not impossible, what is affirmed of this animal, the visible rayes of their eyes carrying forth the subtilest portion of their poison, which received by the eye of man or beast, infecteth first the brain, and is from thence communicated unto the heart.

How the Basilisk kills at distance.

But lastly, That this destruction should be the effect of the first beholder, or depend upon priority of aspection, is a point not easily to be granted, and very hardly to be made out upon the principles of *Aristotle*,

Alhazen, *Vitello*, and others, who hold that sight is made by Reception, and not by extramission; by receiving the raies of the object into the eye, and not by sending any out. For hereby although he behold a man first, the Basilisk should rather be destroyed, in regard he first receiveth the rayes of his Antipathy, and venomous emissions which objectively move his sense; but how powerful soever his own poison be, it invadeth not the sense of man, in regard he beholdeth him not. And therefore this conceit was probably begot by such as held the opinion of sight by extramission; as did *Pythagoras*, *Plato*, *Empedocles*, *Hipparchus*, *Galen*, *Macrobius*, *Proclus*, *Simplicius*, with most of the Ancients, and is the postulate of *Euclide* in his Opticks, but now sufficiently convicted from observations of the Dark Chamber.

The generation of the Cocks egg.

As for the generation of the Basilisk, that it proceedeth from a Cocks egg hatched under a Toad or Serpent, it is a conceit as monstrous as the brood it self. For if we should grant that Cocks growing old, and unable for emission, amass within themselves some seminal matter, which may after conglobate into the form of an egg, yet will this substance be unfruitful. As wanting one principle of generation, and a commixture of both sexes, which is required unto production, as may be observed in the eggs of Hens not trodden; and as we have made trial in some which are termed Cocks eggs. It is not indeed impossible that from the sperm of a Cock, Hen, or other Animal, being once in putrescence, either from incubation or otherwise, some generation may ensue, not univocal and of the same species, but some imperfect or monstrous production, even as in the body of man from putrid humours, and peculiar ways of corruption, there have succeeded

Ovum Centeninum, or the last egg which is a very little one.

strange and unseconded shapes of worms; whereof
we have beheld some our selves, and read of others
in medical observations. And so may strange and
venomous Serpents be several ways engendered; but
that this generation should be regular, and alway
produce a Basilisk, is beyond our affirmation, and we
have good reason to doubt.

Again, It is unreasonable to ascribe the equivocacy
of this form unto the hatching of a Toad, or imagine
that diversifies the production, For Incubation alters
not the species, nor if we observe it, so much as concurs
either to the sex or colour: as appears in the eggs of
Ducks or Partridges hatched under a Hen, there being
required unto their exclusion only a gentle and continued heat: and that not particular or confined unto
the species or parent. So have I known the seed of
Silk-worms hatched on the bodies of women: and *Pliny*
reports that *Livia* the wife of *Augustus* hatched an
egg in her bosome. Nor is only an animal heat required hereto, but an elemental and artificial warmth
will suffice: for as *Diodorus* delivereth, the Ægyptians
were wont to hatch their eggs in Ovens, and many
eye-witnesses confirm that practice unto this day.
And therefore this generation of the Basilisk, seems
like that of *Castor* and *Helena*; he that can credit the
one, may easily believe the other: that is, that these
two were hatched out of the egg which *Jupiter* in the
form of a Swan, begat on his Mistress *Leda*.

The occasion of this conceit might be an Ægyptian
tradition concerning the Bird *Ibis*: which after became
transferred unto Cocks. For an opinion it was of that
Nation, that the *Ibis* feeding upon Serpents, that
venomous food so inquinated their oval conceptions, or
eggs within their bodies, that they sometimes came

forth in Serpentine shapes, and therefore they always brake their eggs, nor would they endure the Bird to sit upon them. But how causeless their fear was herein, the daily incubation of Ducks, Pea-hens, and many other testifie, and the Stork might have informed them; which Bird they honoured and cherished, to destroy their Serpents.

That which much promoted it, was a misapprehension of holy Scripture upon the Latine translation in *Esa.* 51, *Ova aspidum ruperunt et telas Arenearum texuerunt, qui comedent de ovis eorum morietur, et quod confotum est, erumpet in Regulum.* From whence notwithstanding, beside the generation of Serpents from eggs, there can be nothing concluded; and what kind of Serpents are meant, not easie to be determined, for Translations are here very different: *Tremellius* rendering the Asp Hæmorrhous, and the Regulus or Basilisk a Viper, and our translation for the Asp sets down a Cockatrice in the Text, and an Adder in the margin.

Another place of *Esay* doth also seem to countenance it, Chap. 14. *Ne læteris Philistæa quoniam diminuta est virga percussoris tui, de radice enim colubri egredietur Regulus, et semen ejus absorbens volucrem,* which ours somewhat favourably rendereth: *Out of the Serpents Root shall come forth a Cockatrice, and his fruit shall be a fiery flying Serpent.* But *Tremellius, è radice Serpentis prodit Hæmorrhous, et fructus illius præster volans*; wherein the words are different, but the sense is still the same; for therein are figuratively intended *Uzziah* and *Ezechias*; for though the Philistines had escaped the minor Serpent *Uzziah*, yet from his stock a fiercer Snake should arise, that would more terribly sting them, and that was *Ezeckias*.

But the greatest promotion it hath received from a

misunderstanding of the Hieroglyphical intention. For being conceived to be the Lord and King of Serpents, to aw all others, nor to be destroyed by any; the Ægyptians hereby implied Eternity, and the awful power of the supreme Deitie: and therefore described a crowned Asp or Basilisk upon the heads of their gods. As may be observed in the Bembine Table, and other Ægyptian Monuments.

CHAPTER VIII

Of the Wolf.

SUCH a Story as the Basilisk is that of the Wolf concerning priority of vision, that a man becomes hoarse or dumb, if a Wolf have the advantage first to eye him. And this is a plain language affirmed by *Plyny*: *In Italia ut creditur, Luporum visus est noxius, vocemque homini, quem prius contemplatur adimere;* so is it made out what is delivered by *Theocritus*, and after him by *Virgil*:

——*Vox quoque Mœrim*
Jam fugit ipsa, Lupi Mœrim videre priores.

Thus is the Proverb to be understood, when during the discourse, if the party or subject interveneth, and there ensueth a sudden silence, it is usually said, *Lupus est in fabula.* Which conceit being already convicted, not only by *Scaliger*, *Riolanus*, and others; but daily confutable almost every where out of *England*, we shall not further refute.

The ground or occasional original hereof, was probably the amazement and sudden silence the unexpected appearance of Wolves do often put upon Travellers;

not by a supposed vapour, or venomous emanation, but a vehement fear which naturally produceth obmutescence; and sometimes irrecoverable silence. Thus Birds are silent in presence of an Hawk, and *Pliny* saith that Dogs are mute in the shadow of an Hiæna. But thus could not the mouths of worthy Martyrs be silenced, who being exposed not onely unto the eyes, but the merciless teeth of Wolves, gave loud expressions of their faith, and their holy clamours were heard as high as Heaven.

That which much promoted it beside the common Proverb, was an expression in *Theocritus*, a very ancient Poet, οὐ φθέγξη λύκον εἶδες *Edere non poteris vocem, Lycus est tibi visus*; which *Lycus* was Rival unto another, and suddenly appearing stopped the mouth of his Corrival: now *Lycus* signifying also a Wolf, occasioned this apprehension; men taking that appellatively, which was to be understood properly, and translating the genuine acception. Which is a fallacy of Æquivocation, and in some opinions begat the like conceit concerning *Romulus* and *Remus*, that they were fostered by a Wolf, the name of the Nurse being *Lupa*; and founded the fable of *Europa*, and her carriage over Sea by a Bull, because the Ship or Pilots name was *Taurus*. And thus have some been startled at the Proverb, *Bos in lingua*, confusedly apprehending how a man should be said to have an Oxe in his tongue, that would not speak his mind; which was no more then that a piece of money had silenced him: for by the Oxe was onely implied a piece of coin stamped with that figure, first currant with the *Athenians*, and after among the *Romans*.

CHAPTER IX

Of the Deer.

THE common Opinion concerning the long life
of Animals, is very ancient, especially of
Crows, Choughs and Deer; in moderate accounts exceeding the age of man, in some the days of
Nestor, and in others surmounting the years of *Arte-
phius* or *Methuselah*. From whence Antiquity hath
raised proverbial expressions, and the real conception
of their duration, hath been the Hyperbolical expression of many others. From all the rest we shall single
out the Deer, upon concession a long-lived Animal,
and in longævity by many conceived to attain unto
hundreds; wherein permitting every man his own
belief, we shall our selves crave liberty to doubt, and
our reasons are these ensuing.

The first is that of *Aristotle*, drawn from the increment and gestation of this Animal, that is, its sudden
arrivance unto growth and maturity, and the small
time of its remainder in the Womb. His words in
the translation of *Scaliger* are these, *De ejus vitæ longi-
tudine fabulantur; neque enim aut gestatio aut incremen-
tum hinnulorum ejusmodi sunt ut præstent argumentum
longævi animalis*; that is, Fables are raised concerning
the vivacity of Deer; for neither are their gestation
or increment, such as may afford an argument of long
life. And these, saith *Scaliger*, are good Mediums
conjunctively taken, that is, not one without the other.
For of Animals viviparous such as live long, go long
with young, and attain but slowly to their maturity
and stature. So the Horse that liveth above thirty,
arriveth unto his stature about six years, and remaineth

above ten moneths in the womb: so the Camel that
liveth unto fifty, goeth with young no less then ten
moneths, and ceaseth not to grow before seven; and
so the Elephant that liveth an hundred, beareth its
young above a year, and arriveth unto perfection at
twenty. On the contrary, the Sheep and Goat, which
live but eight or ten years, go but five moneths, and
attain to their perfection at two years; and the like
proportion is observable in Cats, Hares, and Conies.
And so the Deer that endureth the womb but eight
moneths, and is compleat at six years, from the course
of Nature, we cannot expect to live an hundred; nor
in any proportional allowance much more then thirty.
As having already passed two general motions observable in all animations, that is, its beginning and
encrease; and having but two more to run thorow,
that is, its state and declination; which are propor-
tionally set out by Nature in every kind: and naturally
proceeding admit of inference from each other.

The other ground that brings its long life into
question, is the immoderate salacity, and almost un-
parallel'd excess of venery, which every *September* may
be observed in this Animal: and is supposed to shorten
the lives of Cocks, Partridges, and Sparrows. Certainly
a confessed and undeniable enemy unto longævity, and
that not only as a sign in the complexional desire and
impetuosity, but also as a cause in the frequent act, or
iterated performance thereof. For though we consent
not with that Philosopher, who thinks a spermatical
emission unto the weight of one drachm, is æquivalent
unto the effusion of sixty ounces of bloud; yet considering the exolution and languor ensuing that act in
some, the extenuation and marcour in others, and the
visible acceleration it maketh of age in most: we cannot

but think it much abridgeth our days. Although we also concede that this exclusion is natural, that Nature it self will find a way hereto without either act or object: And although it be placed among the six Non-naturals, that is, such as neither naturally constitutive, nor meerly destructive, do preserve or destroy according unto circumstance: yet do we sensibly observe an impotency or total privation thereof, prolongeth life: and they live longest in every kind that exercise it not at all. And this is true not only in Eunuchs by Nature, but Spadoes by Art: for castrated Animals in every species are longer lived then they which retain their virilities. For the generation of bodies is not meerly effected as some conceive, of souls, that is, by Irradiation, or answerably unto the propagation of light, without its proper diminution: but therein a transmission is made materially from some parts, with the Idea of every one: and the propagation of one, is in a strict acception, some minoration of another. And therefore also that axiom in Philosophy, that the generation of one thing, is the corruption of another: although it be substantially true concerning the form and matter, is also dispositively verified in the efficient or producer.

Eunuchs and gelded creatures generally longer lived.

From the parts of generation.

As for more sensible arguments, and such as relate unto experiment: from these we have also reason to doubt its age, and presumed vivacity: for where long life is natural, the marks of age are late: and when they appear, the journey unto death cannot be long. Now the age of Deer (as *Aristotle* not long ago observed) is best conjectured, by view of the horns and teeth. From the horns there is a particular and annual account unto six years: they arising first plain, and so successively branching: after which the judg-

ment of their years by particular marks becomes
uncertain. But when they grow old, they grow less
branched, and first do lose their ἀμυντῆρες, or *propug-*
nacula; that is, their brow-antlers, or lowest furcations
next the head, which *Aristotle* saith the young ones
use in fight: and the old as needless, have them not at
all. The same may be also collected from the loss of
their Teeth, whereof in old age they have few or none
before in either jaw. Now these are infallible marks of
age, and when they appear, we must confess a declination: which notwithstanding (as men inform us in
England, where observations may well be made), will
happen between twenty and thirty. As for the bone,
or rather induration of the Roots of the arterial vein
and great artery, which is thought to be found only in
the heart of an old Deer, and therefore becomes more
precious in its Rarity; it is often found in Deer much
under thirty, and we have known some affirm they
have found it in one of half that age. And therefore
in that account of *Pliny,* of a Deer with a Collar about
his neck, put on by *Alexander* the Great, and taken
alive an hundred years after, with other relations of this
nature, we much suspect imposture or mistake. And
if we grant their verity, they are but single relations,
and very rare contingencies in individuals, not affording a regular deduction upon the species. For though
Ulysses his Dog lived unto twenty, and the *Athenian*
Mule unto fourscore, yet do we not measure their days
by those years, or usually say, they live thus long.
Nor can the three hundred years of *John* of times, or *Psalm 90.*
Nestor, overthrow the assertion of *Moses,* or afford a
reasonable encouragement beyond his septuagenary
determination.

The ground and authority of this conceit was first

Hierogliphical, the *Ægyptians* expressing longævity by this Animal; but upon what uncertainties, and also convincible falsities they often erected such Emblems, we have elsewhere delivered. And if that were true

which *Aristotle* delivers of his time, and *Pliny* was not afraid to take up long after, the *Ægyptians* could make but weak observations herein; for though it be said that *Æneas* feasted his followers with Venison, yet *Aristotle* affirms that neither Deer nor Boar were to be found in *Africa*. And how far they miscounted the lives and duration of Animals, is evident from their conceit of the Crow, which they presume to live five hundred years; and from the lives of Hawks, which (as *Ælian* delivereth) the *Ægyptians* do reckon no less then at seven hundred.

The second which led the conceit unto the *Grecians*, and probably descended from the Egyptians was Poetical; and that was a passage of *Hesiod*, thus rendered by *Ausonius*.

> *Ter binos deciesque novem super exit in annos,*
> *Justa senescentum quos implet vita virorum.*
> *Hos novies superat vivendo gorrula cornix,*
> *Et quater egreditur cornicis sæcula cervus,*
> *Alipidem cervum ter vincit corvus.──*

> To ninety six the life of man ascendeth,
> Nine times as long that of the Chough extendeth,
> Four times beyond the life of Deer doth go,
> And thrice is that surpassed by the Crow.

So that according to this account, allowing ninety six for the age of Man, the life of a Deer amounts unto three thousand four hundred fifty six. A conceit so hard to be made out, that many have deserted the common and literal construction. So *Theon* in *Aratus* would have the number of nine not taken strictly, but for many years. In other opinions the compute so far exceedeth the truth, that they have thought it more probable to take the word *Genea*, that is, a generation consisting of many years, but for one year, or a single revolution of the Sun; which is the remarkable measure of time, and within the compass whereof we receive our perfection in the womb. So that by this construction, the years of a Deer should be but thirty six, as is discoursed at large in that Tract of *Plutarch*, concerning the cessation of Oracles; and whereto in his discourse of the Crow, *Aldrovandus* also inclineth. Others not able to make it out, have rejected the whole account, as may be observed from the words of *Pliny, Hesiodus qui primus aliquid de longævitate vitæ prodidit, fabulose (reor) multa de hominum ævo referens, cornici novem nostras attribuit ætates, quadruplum ejus cervis, id triplicatum corvis, et reliqua fabulosius de Phœnice et nymphis*. And this how slender soever, was probably the strongest ground Antiquity had for this longævity of Animals; that made *Theophrastus* expostulate with Nature concerning the long life of Crows; τετρακό-ρωνος. that begat that Epithete of Deer in *Oppianus*, and that expression of *Juvenal*,

——Longa et cervina senectus.

The third ground was Philosophical, and founded upon a probable Reason in Nature, that is, the defect of a Gall, which part (in the opinion of *Aristotle* and *Pliny*) this Animal wanted, and was conceived a cause and reason of their long life: according (say they) as it happeneth unto some few men, who have not this part at all. But this assertion is first defective in the verity concerning the Animal alledged: for though it be true, a Deer hath no Gall in the Liver like many other Animals, yet hath it that part in the Guts, as is discoverable by taste and colour: and therefore *Pliny* doth well correct himself, when having affirmed before it had no Gall, he after saith, some hold it to be in the guts; and that for their bitterness, dogs will refuse to eat them. The assertion is also deficient in the verity of the Induction or connumeration of other Animals conjoined herewith, as having also no Gall; that is, as *Pliny* accounteth, *Equi, Muli,* etc. Horses, Mules, Asses, Deer, Goats, Boars, Camels, Dolphins, have no Gall. In Dolphins and Porpoces I confess I could find no Gall. But concerning Horses, what truth there is herein we have declared before; as for Goats we find not them without it; what Gall the Camel hath, *Aristotle* declareth: that Hogs also have it, we can affirm; and that not in any obscure place, but in the Liver, even as it is seated in man.

That therefore the Deer is no short-lived Animal, we will acknowledge: that comparatively, and in some sense long-lived we will concede; and thus much we shall grant if we commonly account its days by thirty six or forty: for thereby it will exceed all other cornigerous Animals. But that it attaineth unto hundreds, or the years delivered by Authors, since we have no authentick experience for it, since we have reason and common experience against it, since the grounds are false and fabulous which do establish it: we know no ground to assent.

Concerning Deer there also passeth another opinion, that the Males thereof do yearly lose their pizzel. For men observing the decidence of their horns, do fall upon the like conceit of this part, that it annually rotteth away, and successively reneweth again. Now the ground hereof was surely the observation of this

part in Deer after immoderate venery, and about the
end of their Rut, which sometimes becomes so relaxed
and pendulous, it cannot be quite retracted : and being
often beset with flies, it is conceived to rot, and at last
to fall from the body. But herein experience will
contradict us : for Deer which either die or are killed
at that time, or any other, are always found to have
that part entire. And reason will also correct us : for
spermatical parts, or such as are framed from the
seminal principles of parents, although homogeneous
or similary, will not admit a Regeneration, much less
will they receive an integral restauration, which being
organical and instrumental members, consist of many
of those. Now this part, or Animal of *Plato*, containeth not only sanguineous and reparable particles :
but is made up of veins, nerves, arteries, and in some
Animals, of bones : whose reparation is beyond its own
fertility, and a fruit not to be expected from the
fructifying part it self. Which faculty were it communicated unto Animals, whose originals are double,
as well as unto Plants, whose seed is within themselves :
we might abate the Art of *Taliacotius*, and the new
in-arching of Noses. And therefore the fancies of
Poets have been so modest, as not to set down such
renovations, even from the powers of their deities : for
the mutilated shoulder of *Pelops* was pieced out with
Ivory, and that the limbs of *Hippolitus* were set
together, not regenerated by *Æsculapius*, is the utmost
assertion of Poetry.

CHAPTER X

Of the King-fisher.

THAT a King-fisher hanged by the bill, sheweth in what quarter the wind is by an occult and secret propriety, converting the breast to that point of the Horizon from whence the wind doth blow, is a received opinion, and very strange; introducing natural Weather-cocks, and extending Magnetical positions as far as Animal Natures. A conceit supported chiefly by present practice, yet not made out by Reason or Experience.

Unto Reason it seemeth very repugnant, that a carcass or body disanimated, should be so affected with every wind, as to carry a conformable respect and *Whence it is,* constant habitude thereto. For although in sundry *that some* *creatures* Animals we deny not a kind of natural Meteorology or *presage the* innate presention both of wind and weather, yet that *weather.* proceeding from sense receiving impressions from the first mutation of the air, they cannot in reason retain that apprehension after death, as being affections which depend on life, and depart upon disanimation. And therefore with more favourable Reason may we draw the same effect or sympathie upon the Hedg-hog, whose presention of winds is so exact, that it stoppeth the North or Southern hole of its nest, according to the prenotion of these winds ensuing; which some men observing, have been able to make predictions which way the wind would turn, and been esteemed hereby wise men in point of weather. Now this proceeding from sense in the creature alive, it were not reasonable to hang up an Hedg-hogs head, and to expect a conformable motion unto its living conversion. And though in sundry Plants their vertues do live after death, and we know that Scammony, Rhubarb and Senna will purge without any vital assistance; yet in Animals and sensible creatures, many actions are mixt, and depend upon their living form, as well as that of mistion; and though they wholly seem to retain unto the body, depart upon disunion. Thus Glow-worms alive, project a lustre in the dark, which fulgour notwithstanding ceaseth after death; and thus the Torpedo which being alive stupifies at a distance, applied after death, produceth no such effect; which had they retained in places where they abound, they might have supplied Opium, and served as frontals in Phrensies.

As for experiment, we cannot make it out by any we have attempted; for if a single King-fisher be hanged up with untwisted silk in an open room, and where the air is free, it observes not a constant respect unto the mouth of the wind, but variously converting, doth seldom breast it right. If two be suspended in the same room, they will not regularly conform their breasts, but oft-times respect the opposite points of Heaven. And if we conceive that for exact exploration, they should be suspended where the air is quiet and unmoved, that clear of impediments, they may more freely convert upon their natural verticity; we have also made this way of inquisition, suspending them in large and capacious glasses closely stopped; wherein nevertheless we observed a casual station, and that they rested irregularly upon conversion. Wheresoever they rested, remaining inconverted, and possessing one point of the Compass, whilst the wind perhaps had passed the two and thirty.

PRINTED IN GREAT BRITAIN BY
OLIVER AND BOYD, EDINBURGH